SHAW'S NEW HISTORY

OF

ENGLISH LITERATURE;

TOGETHER WITH

A HISTORY OF

ENGLISH LITERATURE IN AMERICA,

BY TRUMAN J. BACKUS, LL.D.

FORMERLY PROFESSOR OF ENGLISH LITERATURE IN VASSAR COLLEGE,
NOW PRESIDENT OF PACKER COLLEGIATE INSTITUTE.

REVISED EDITION.

SHELDON AND COMPANY,

NEW YORK AND CHICAGO.

SHAW'S SERIES ON ENGLISH AND AMERICAN LITERATURE.

SHAW'S NEW HISTORY OF ENGLISH AND AMERICAN LITERATURE. Revised Edition.

SHAW'S CHOICE SPECIMENS OF ENGLISH LITERATURE

CHOICE SPECIMENS OF AMERICAN LITERATURE. By Prof B. N. Martin, D.D, LL.D.

SMITH & McDOUGAL, ELECTROTYPERS,
82 Beekman St., N. Y.

CONTENTS

PART I.

CHAPTER XIX.

CHAPTER XX.

CHAPTER XXI.

CHAPTER XXII.

CHAPTER XXIII.

CHAPTER XXIV.

CHAPTER XXV.

CHAPTER XXVI.

CHAPTER XXVII.

CHAPTER XXVIII.

PART II.

ENGLISH LITERATURE IN AMERICA.

TO THE FIRST EDITION.

THOMAS B. SHAW'S *Outlines of English Literature*, rewritten by William Smith, LL.D., and published as *A Complete Manual of English Literature*, has been held in high esteem by American teachers during the last ten years. While its merits have been recognized, its defects, too, have been discovered. The work was intended by its American publishers to be used in colleges only, but, owing to the want of a more suitable text-book, it has come into extensive use in high-schools and academies. In order to meet the criticisms of teachers who have introduced it into these schools, a thorough revision of the Manual has been made.

In the revision I have attempted,—

(1). To improve the logical arrangement;
(2). To correct the lack of unity in several chapters;
(3). To simplify the style.

Mr. Shaw sought "to render the work as little dry—as readable, in short—as is consistent with accuracy and comprehensiveness"; but his abounding use of relative constructions and his involved sentences defeated his purpose to some extent; for they defied the patience of many students. In endeavoring to present the topics in a clearer style, it has been necessary for me to rewrite many of the chapters.

As compared with the Manual, the peculiarities of this volume are,—

(*a*). A fuller discussion of the " Old-English " and " Middle-English " literatures ;

(*b*). An assignment of prominent positions to the most famous writers ;

(*c*). A free use of short and striking quotations from the works of the keenest English and American critics—in some cases inserted in the text, in others given as footnotes, and in others placed at the head of a chapter, for the purpose of inciting the student to a more curious and appreciative reading of an author ;

(*d*). A collection of references to the best collateral readings upon the topics considered ;

(*e*). The use of a few simple diagrams, intended to aid the student in remembering important classifications of authors ;

(*f*). The omission of authors who have not contributed to the historical development of our literature.

It will be observed that several essays in this volume are printed in a conspicuous manner. A reason must be given for this innovation upon the usual typography of text-books. Among teachers of English literature, there is a growing conviction that much time is wasted in the class-room by attempting to learn about too many authors. Such an attempt is dissipating to the mind of the student, and is most unsatisfactory to the teacher. Wherever the students can have access to a good library, it will be found to be the most profitable use of the time generally allotted to this subject to have them study brief biographies of the few authors who have wielded potent influence over our thought and our language, to have them read the best criticisms upon these authors, and the best passages from their works. With this plan in view, the essays on Chaucer, Spenser, Shakespeare, Bacon, Milton, Dryden, Pope, Swift, Addison, Johnson, Goldsmith, Burns, Scott, and Byron, have been printed in the most attractive manner; references have been furnished to judicious criticisms of their works, and to choice specimens of their writings. This peculiarity of the book has not been allowed to disturb the orderly presentation of a general outline of the history of our literature.

Following Mr. Shaw's plan, I have refrained from discussing the lives and works of English authors who are now living.

Throughout the volume references are made to Professor Shaw's Choice Specimens of English and Professor B. N. Martin's Choice Specimens of American Literature. The black-faced figures (1) refer to the sections in these books.

TRUMAN J. BACKUS.

VASSAR COLLEGE, }
  August 29, 1874. }

PREFACE

TO THE SECOND EDITION.

IT has given me pleasure to comply with the request of fellow-teachers by enlarging this History of English Literature so that it includes discussion of the lives and writings of eminent English men of letters who have died since my former revision of Shaw's Manual of English Literature was made.

The generosity of the publishers in giving the book new type has made it possible for me to make changes throughout the text. I have used my opportunity by introducing heavy-faced side-headings, by inserting much new matter, by giving summaries at the close of chapters, and by desirable rearrangements. The amendments are intended to promote the adaptation of the book to the uses of the class-room—a quality for which it has received much kindly commendation.

The sketch of English Literature in America, new with this edition, is presented in compliance with a general demand from teachers. Difficulties attend any treatment of the subject, on account of the lack of perspective. Within brief limits I have endeavored to give something more than a catalogue of names and dates; in short, to direct the student's attention to all characteristic literary expressions of the American national genius. Many worthy names have been omitted or slightly touched, because their fame belongs to the history of special periods rather than to the main outline of literary growth. This is the less to be regretted, inasmuch as the excellent cyclopedia of the brothers Duyckinck, generally found in school libraries, will give ready aid to more extended study. While my plan of selection and classification may clash in some particulars with the preferences of my fellow-teachers, I hope that they will find it consistent in itself and sufficiently comprehensive.

In the revision of this work, my recent assistants in the Department of English Literature at Vassar College have placed me under obligation for most valuable help in matters demanding careful and scholarly research.

T. J. B.

THE PACKER COLLEGIATE INSTITUTE,
  Brooklyn, N. Y., April, 1884.

ENGLISH LITERATURE.

CHAPTER I.

INTRODUCTORY.

IN their literary inheritance, the readers of the English language are the richest people that the sun shines on. Their novelists paint the finest portraits of human character, their historians know the secrets of entrancing description and of philosophical narration, their critics have acumen, their philosophers probe far into the philosophy of mind, their poets sing the sweetest songs. But before beginning a discussion of the lives and the works of the great men who have contributed to the riches of our literature, it is well for us to remind ourselves of the long centuries of ignorance that passed over England before her nationality and her language were developed.

The most ancient inhabitants of the British Islands were of that Celtic race which once occupied a large portion of Western Europe. They were savages; they neglected agriculture, they had no cities, they had no laws, and by tattooing and staining their bodies they gave infallible proof of their barbarism.

55 B. C.] The first important intercourse between the primitive Britons and any foreign nation resulted from the invasion of the country by the Romans under Julius Cæsar. The resistance of the Britons, though obstinate and ferocious, was overpowered by the Roman

armies in the first century of the Christian era. The central
and southern portion of the country became a Roman province, and was subject to foreign domination for more than
three centuries. According to their custom, the invaders
strove to introduce their civilization among the barbarous
subjects. The Celts who yielded became enervated; those
who were unsubdued inhabited mountainous regions inac-
cessible to the Roman arms, and frequently descended from
the rugged fastnesses of Wales and Scotland, carrying terror
to the more civilized provinces. The withdrawal of the
Roman troops at the beginning of the fifth century, left the
Celts who had submitted to the yoke in a desperate position.
Swarms of northern Celts came upon them, to reclaim the
territory, and swept away every trace of civilization. Many
ancient legends tell of the vengeance wreaked upon the
Celts who had bowed to the Roman invader.

Traces of the Celtic element in the English language are
found only in the names of places, and in the titles of a
few familiar objects. In the vocabulary of one hundred
and four thousand words given in Webster's Unabridged
Dictionary, it would be difficult to find one hundred derived
directly from the Celtic. That most of the words to which
the lexicographer assigns a Celtic origin were not inherited from the old Britons is proved by the fact that they
are not to be found in the Anglo-Saxon. They were trans-
planted from the Celtic into some Romance tongue and
thence were grafted into modern English. The aboriginal
speech of Britain has bequeathed to us less than any other
language with which our Anglo-Saxon race has been associated. Nor did the Romans who held dominion over Britain contribute many words to our speech. The multitude
of our Latin derivatives were brought to our language in
a later century. A few geographical words in this Brito-
Roman period were indelibly stamped upon the face of the
country. They have survived invasions and revolutions,

and stand amid the modern names as venerable monuments of a mysterious age. Thus the termination *don*, as in "London," is the Celtic word "*dun*," a rock or natural fortress; the termination *caster* or *chester* is a memorial of the Roman occupation, indicating the spot of a *castrum* or fortified camp; and the last syllable of Lin*coln* indicates a Roman *colonia*.

The Teutonic Invasion. The foundations of the laws and language of the peoples who speak Modern English were laid between the middle of the fifth and the middle of the sixth century. Piratical adventurers, crossing the North Sea from the bleak shores of Jutland, Schleswig, Holstein and the coasts of the Baltic, gradually established themselves in those parts of Britain which the Romans had occupied. The mountainous districts of Wales and Scotland successfully resisted their invasion. The level and more easily accessible portion of Scotland was gradually subdued by them, and their language was established there as well as in South Britain. Possessing a physical organization less powerful than that of the Teutonic invaders, and, perhaps, having an inferior moral constitution, the degenerate Celts gradually disappeared from the presence of the superior race. The absorption or destruction of this nation was in accordance with what seems to be an inevitable law regulating the result of close contact between two unequal nationalities. That law is operating in our own land to-day, as it forces the North American Indians to the certain issue of their conflict with the same Anglo-Saxon race.

The English nation, then, had Teutonic parentage. The language spoken by the Saxon invaders was akin to the modern Dutch; and, like the people who spoke it, was of strong vitality. For a long time the colonization of Britain was carried on by detached Teutonic tribes. After two centuries of struggle they grouped themselves into several

827.] independent governments, known in history as the
Heptarchy, or Seven Kingdoms. In 827 these were
all made subject to Wessex (the country of the West Sax-
ns) and there was at last the prospect of a rapid and
gorous national development. But the union of the
Anglo-Saxon tribes was hardly effected before the Danes
invaded the country in large numbers, gained sovereignty
over much of the territory, and endeavored to subjugate
the Saxons as thoroughly as the Saxons had subjugated
the Celts. By the heroism and wisdom of the illustrious
Alfred, this threatening catastrophe was averted. The two
fierce races, nearly allied in origin, were amalgamated in a
union which did not materially change the language or institutions of the country. Still, in certain localities, as in
the north and east of England, and along the coast of
Scotland where the Danish colonies were established, evident marks of the Scandinavian occupation are found in the
idioms of the peasantry, and in the names of families and
places.

1066.]   The Effect of the Norman Conquest. Towards the
close of the eleventh century, William the Conqueror, by his victory in the battle of Hastings, brought
Englishmen under Norman rule. The most important
changes resulting from this conquest were the establishment in England of the feudal tenure of land, the introduction of the chivalric spirit, and the separation of society
into two great classes, a foreign nobility and a discontented
people. England was made the property of unfriendly foreigners; the Saxon thane, the friend and companion of his
humbler fellows, was superseded by the arrogant and op-
pressing Norman baron.

The Normans who settled in England were a mixed race.
Early in the tenth century piratical Scandinavians made
conquests of territory in the north of France, ultimately

wrested from the degenerate sons of Charlemagne the whole
of the province which has since borne the name of Nor-
mandy, held the conquered people in subjection by means
of the feudal system, and, with slight modifications, adopted
the French tongue. The gradual blending of these two
races produced the Norman nationality. Its culture was
expressed in literature, in the delicacy of ornament, in
architecture, in oratory, and was far superior to that of any
other European nation in the Middle Ages. Its refinement
was equaled by its valor. When this cultivated people invaded and conquered England, they found their subjects
illiterate, without social culture, given to coarse dissipation,
and determined to treat the victors with unyielding hatred.
That hatred was reciprocated. For two centuries the Norman swayed the tyrant's sceptre, the Saxon yielded unwilling homage. Nor was there any disposition to blend interests and sympathies until the Norman, exiled from Nor-
mandy, came to consider himself an Englishman, not a
foreigner in possession of English soil.

Their Influence upon the Language. But it is in the
effects of the Norman Conquest upon the English language
that we are interested. The speech which the Norman
invaders brought to England was one of two closely related
dialects of the Romance languages, and was known as the
Langue d'Oil in distinction from the other which was called
the *Langue d'Oc.* These names were derived from their
differing words for *yes.* The line of demarcation between
them nearly coincided with the Loire. They were both
results of the decomposition of the mediæval Latin. That
ancient language, in the process of its decay, lost nearly all
its inflections; the relations of words were expressed by the
more frequent use of prepositions.

After the Conquest, the Norman *trouvères,* poets who wrote
in the *Langue d'Oil,* and the poets of the sister dialect, the

troubadours, were held in high esteem by the Court in Eng-land. They furnished literature for the readers, and so wielded potent influence over English thought and lan-guage. They displaced the English Gleeman, crowding him into the society of the humblest people.

The Norman Conquest was not such as a civilized nation makes of a nation of barbarians. The subjugated people were not exterminated, nor were they diminished by con-siderable numbers, nor were they driven from their country. They remained upon their native soil. The change which the Conquest brought to them was merely a change in the administration of the government. They were left in pos-session of traditional customs and speech. With few excep-tions their conversation was with each other, almost never with the foreigner. Their Anglo-Saxon tongue remained, modified only by the abandonment of a few individual words, and by the adoption of other individual words from the speech of the conquerors.

The extent and rapidity of such modifications depended upon the numbers and social condition of the immigrants. These immigrants were the royal family, the nobility, the churchmen and the army. There was no mass of common people whose station would compel them to mingle with the despised Saxons. The royal family used the Nor-man speech, and continued to exert every influence in its favor until the fourteenth century. There was little attempt on the part of king or of court to understand the language of the subjects; the nobles, under the system of feudalism, needed not to talk with those whom they oppressed; the churchmen were satisfied with their ecclesi-astical benefices without understanding the confessions of humble worshipers; and the military forces, trained to consider themselves as men placed on guard against the discontented and dangerous Englishmen, did not seek com-panionship with them. These circumstances were unfavorable to changes in the form and structure of the English language. The mutual repulsion of the two races continued for a century; for another century the languages remained distinct ; in the third century after the Conquest all classes of people were united by their common interest in the foreign wars of England.

Blending of the Norman and the Saxon Speech. In the fourteenth century the languages began to coalesce rapidly, and the English language and the English nationality were evolved from the social confusion which attended the first centuries of the Norman occupation. The language remained Germanic in its grammatical character, but it received such large accessions of French words as to change its sound when spoken, and its appearance on the page According to Hallam, the change was brought about,—1st, by contracting or otherwise modifying the pronunciation and orthography of words; 2d, by omitting many inflections, especially of the noun, and consequently making more use of articles and auxiliaries ; and 3d, by the introduction of French derivatives.

In the first chapter of *Ivanhoe*, Walter Scott has given an illustration of the peculiar significance of the names of animals as applied by Saxons and Normans, and has shown that our language, as we speak it to-day, indicates the servitude of the Saxons.   He introduces Gurth, a Saxon swineherd, and Wamba, a jester.

"'Why, how call you those grunting brutes running about on their four legs?' demanded Wamba.

" 'Swine, fool, swine,' said the herd; 'every fool knows that.'

" ' And swine is good Saxon,' said the jester; 'but how call you the sow when she is flayed and drawn and quartered, and hung up by the heels like a traitor ?'

" ' Pork,' answered the swineherd.

"'I am very glad every fool knows that, too.' said Wamba, 'and pork, I think, is good Norman-French; and so when the brute lives, and is in charge of a Saxon slave, she goes by her Saxon name; but becomes a Norman, and is called pork, when she is carried to the castle-hall to feast among the nobles; what dost thou think of this, friend Gurth, ha?'

" ' It is but too true doctrine, friend Wamba, however it got into a fool's pate!'

" ' Now I can tell you more,' said Wamba, in the same tone; 'there is old Alderman Ox continues to hold his Saxon epithet while he is under the charge of serfs and bondsmen such as thou, but becomes Beef, a fiery French gallant, when he arrives before the worshipful jaws that are destined to consume him. Mynheer Calf, too, becomes Monsieur de Veau in the like manner; he is Saxon when he requires tendance, and takes a Norman name when he becomes matter of enjoyment.

The fusion of the Norman and Saxon languages was not effected until the fourteenth century. From that time until the present, our English speech has been extending its vocabulary, casting off local and dialectic peculiarities, abandoning old inflections, and more thoroughly blending its component elements. But despite the influence of language upon national character and the destructive processes of time, the English people have preserved two distinct types of character. The Norman's adherence to the laws of caste and his conservatism are still displayed by the aristocracy of England; while the democratic spirit of the old Saxon is seen in the open-hearted hospitality of the English commoner, and in his resolute ambition to obtain the fullest rights of citizenship for all.

In this chapter we have considered:—

1. *The Ancient Inhabitants of Britain.*
2. *The Teutonic Invasion.*
3. *The Normans and their Invasion.*
4. *Norman Influence upon the English Language.*
5. *The Blending of the Norman and the Saxon Speech.*

A CHART OF THE ENGLISH LITERATURE

DISCUSSED IN THIS VOLUME.

OLD ENGLISH LITERATURE.

- **POETRY.**
  - BEOWULF.
  - CAEDMON'S PARAPHRASE OF THE PSALMS.
- **PROSE WRITERS.**
  - KING ALFRED.
  - THE SAXON CHRONICLE.
  - THE VENERABLE BEDE.

MIDDLE ENGLISH LITERATURE.

- **POETS.**
  - LAYAMON.
  - ORM, or ORMIN.
  - GEOFFREY CHAUCER.
  - WILLIAM LANGLANDE.
  - JOHN GOWER.
  - THOMAS OCCLEVE.
  - JOHN LYDGATE.
  - JAMES I. OF SCOTLAND.
  - THE OLD BALLAD WRITERS.
- **PROSE WRITERS.**
  - SIR JOHN MANDEVILLE.
  - GEOFFREY CHAUCER.
  - JOHN WYCLIFFE.
  - WILLIAM CAXTON.
  - THE WRITERS OF THE PASTON LETTERS.

MODERN ENGLISH LITERATURE.

- **POETS.**
  - Of the first half of the 16th Century.
    - JOHN SKELTON.
    - HENRY HOWARD, Earl of Surrey
    - SIR THOMAS WYATT.
  - THE NON-DRAMATIC ELIZABETHAN POETS.
  - THE ELIZABETHAN DRAMATISTS.
  - THE METAPHYSICAL POETS.
  - JOHN MILTON.
  - SAMUEL BUTLER.
  - JOHN DRYDEN.
  - THE CORRUPT DRAMATISTS.
  - THE ARTIFICIAL POETS OF THE 18TH CENTURY.
  - THE FIRST ROMANTIC POETS.
  - WALTER SCOTT.
  - BYRON, MOORE, SHELLEY, KEATS, CAMPBELL, HUNT, AND LANDOR.
  - THE LAKE SCHOOL.
- **PROSE WRITERS.**
  - Of the first half of the 16th Century.
    - SIR THOMAS MORE.
    - LORD BERNERS.
    - ROGER ASCHAM.
    - WILLIAM TYNDALE.
  - OF THE ELIZABETHAN AGE.
  - THEOLOGICAL WRITERS OF THE CIVIL WAR AND THE COMMONWEALTH.
  - THE LITERATURE OF THE RESTORATION.
  - THE PHILOSOPHERS AND THEOLOGIANS OF LOCKE'S TIME.
  - PROSE WRITERS OF THE FIRST HALF OF THE 18TH CENTURY.
  - THE FIRST GREAT NOVELISTS.
  - THE FIRST GREAT HISTORIANS.
  - ETHICAL, POLITICAL, AND THEOLOGICAL WRITERS OF THE LATTER HALF OF THE 18TH CENTURY.
  - THE LITERARY IMPOSTORS OF THE 18TH CENTURY.
  - THE MODERN NOVELISTS.
  - THE MODERN HISTORIANS AND ESSAYISTS.

CHAPTER II.

ENGLISH LITERATURE BEFORE THE NORMAN CONQUEST.

FOR more than fourteen centuries the thoughts and feelings of the English people have found expression in the language which we now speak. The rude dialects that were brought to Britain by our forefathers, though differing in many particulars, were like the modern English in all essential respects. This venerable language has undergone many changes and modifications, has been affected by strong foreign influences, has stripped itself of many of its inflections, has acquired a vast vocabulary, has passed from youth to maturity. Between its youth and its maturity there has been wonderful growth, but the identity remains. The modern English is the Anglo-Saxon developed.

It is customary to use the terms "Anglo-Saxon," "Semi-Saxon," and "English," to designate three periods in the history of our language; but as the use of the first two of these terms might tempt us to think that we are considering a foreign language and literature, when we are considering merely the old fashions of our own speech, we shall do well to avoid the temptation by adopting the following division:

1. **The Old English,** from the dawn of the language until 1154.
2. **The Middle English,** from 1154 until about 1500.
3. **The Modern English,** from about 1500 to the present time.

It cannot be incorrect to apply the term "English" to even the first of these periods, for the renowned King Alfred, writing in the ninth century, uses that very term in describing his language.* The old English was highly inflected in its grammar, and had few words adopted from foreign languages. The middle English is the name we give to that period of transition in which the speech of

---

* Ælfred Kyning wæs wealhstod thisse bec, and hie of boclædene on *Englisc* wende. "Ælfred King was commentator of this book, and it from book-language into English turned."

the Normans was exerting its influence upon our language. During this period the more complicated forms of grammatical structure were abandoned, and the vocabulary was largely increased.

In the modern English, aside from the addition of new words, the changes have been slight. The printing-press has stereotyped the language.

OLD ENGLISH POETRY.

The Poem, Beowulf. No other spoken language of modern Europe has a literature as ancient as the English. Its earliest extant writing is an epic poem of more than three thousand lines, entitled " Beowulf." The scene of its action indicates that it was composed by Saxons who lived before the invasion of England, though a few eminent scholars give the poem an English birthplace in the county of Durham.

In their primitive home, when the banqueting-hall (the "mead-bench ") was filled, the *gleeman* stirred the courage of his listeners by the recital of the superhuman deeds of mighty Beowulf. As the story runs, King Hrothgar and his chosen subjects were wont to sit in his great hall listening to music, and drinking for their pleasure; but their pleasure was disturbed by their fear of Grendel, a grim and terrible giant, who dwelt in the neighboring marshes of Jutland. This monster would come into the palace at times to see " how the doughty Danes found themselves after their beer-carouse." On the occasion of his first visit he slew thirty sleeping men. For twelve years he was the terror of the land. At last the pitiful story came to the ears of Beowulf, a viking who was noted for his victories over the giants of the deep. He resolved to go to the relief of Hrothgar. Entering the haunted hall, he promised to fight the monster. When the mists of the night arose, Grendel came, and commenced a ferocious assault upon a sleeping man. Beowulf faced him, fought him valiantly, and wounded him so that he died. Then there was great rejoicing. But the joy was soon dispelled, for the mother of the monster came to seek revenge. Beowulf pursued her into deep, dark waters, where he was seized and dragged to the bottom of her cave; but he was able to let her soul out of its bone-house ("ban-hus ").

A description of this poem is comparatively uninstructive and valueless without an illustration of its quaint thought and its

terse expression. We will look at a short extract from the condensed and modernized version found in *Morley's English Writers.* [*]

"Ther came from the moor under the misty hills, Grendel
stalking: the wicked spoiler meant in the lofty hall to snare one
of mankind. He strode under the clouds until he saw the wine-
house, golden hall of men. Came then faring to the house the joy-
less man, he rushed straight on the door, fast with fire-hardened
bands, struck with his hands, dragged open the hall's mouth:
quickly then trod the fiend on the stained floor, went wroth of
mood, and from his eyes stood forth a loathsome light, likest to
flame. He saw in the house many war-men sleeping all together,
then was his mood laughter. Hope of a sweet glut had arisen in
him. But it was not for him after that night to eat more of mankind. The wretched wight seized quickly a sleeping warrior, slit
him unawares, bit his bone-locker, drank his blood, in morsels
swallowed him : soon had he all eaten, feet and fingers. Nearer
forth he stept, laid hands upon the doughty-minded warrior at his
rest, but Beowulf reached forth a hand and hung upon his arm.
Soon as the evil-doer felt that there was not in mid-earth a stronger
hand-grip, he became fearful in heart. Not for that could he
escape the sooner, though his mind was bent on flight. He would
flee into his den, seek the pack of devils; his trial there was such
as in his life-days he had never before found. The hall thundered,
the ale of all the Danes and earls was spilt. Angry, fierce were the
strong fighters, the hall was full of the din. It was great wonder
that the wine-hall stood above the war-like beasts, that the fair
earth-home fell not to the ground. But within and without it was
fast with iron bands cunningly forged. Over the North Danes
stood dire fear, on every one of those who heard the gruesome
whoop. The friend of earls held fast the deadly guest, would not
leave him while living. Then drew a warrior of Beowulf an old
sword of his father's for help of his lord. The sons of strife sought
then to hew on every side, they knew not that no war-blade would
cut into the wicked scather; but Beowulf had forsworn every
edge. Hygelac's proud kinsman had the foe of God in hand. The
fell wretch bore pain, a deadly wound gaped on his shoulder, the
sinews sprang asunder, the bone-locker burst, to Beowulf was war-
strength given. Grendel fled away death-sick, to seek a sad dwelling under the fen shelters; his life's end was come."

When Hrothgar died, the hero of the poem ascended the throne;
and after an adventurous reign of fifty-years, he died from wounds
received in slaying a terrible fire-fiend.

This, the most ancient and the most interesting of the old English poems, is full of the superstitions of heathen times, and yet

* Vol. I., p. 251, *seq.*

it presents a character instinct with chivalry and generosity. It is the picture of "an age brave, generous, right-principled.' Many strange but forcible compound words, many highly imaginative metaphors, and *five* similes are found in this venerable poem. It is supposed to be allegorical, the monster representing a poisonous exhalation from the marshes. If the supposition be a correct one, this literary relic shows the predilection of our ancestors for allegorical expression.

Although the action of this heroic story was not later than the beginning of the seventh century, the only MS. which has preserved the narrative for us was written not earlier than the close of the tenth century. This most valuable of English MSS., now kept in the British Museum, was probably the work of a monk. It was written in Danish characters. The writing is continuous, resembling our manuscript of prose. There is no rhyming, for rhyme was an adornment uncommon in English poetry until after the Norman Conquest. But in this, and in all other Old English (Anglo-Saxon) poems, a rude alliteration is found, which is explained in our discussion of "The Vision of Piers Plowman.'

Caedmon's Paraphrase of the Scriptures.

The next poem demanding our attention is free from the pagan sentiments of Beowulf. It was written about two centuries after the Angles and Saxons began their invasion of England, and by that time they had been won to the Christian faith. A monk named

Died 680.] **Caedmon** (Kăd′mon), was the first Englishman who has left us poetry inspired by the beauties of Christian sentiment. He was the author of a Metrical Paraphrase of the Scriptures. Connected with his work, we have one of the most interesting legends found in English literature. He was a servant at a monastery in Northumbria, where Hilda, a lady of royal blood, was Abbess.* Sitting, one evening, with a company of rustics, who were whiling away the time by singing and by recitation, his

---

* Above the small and land-locked harbor of Whitby rises and juts out towards the sea the dark cliff where Hild's monastery stood, looking out over the German Ocean. It is a wild, wind-swept upland, and the sea beats furiously beneath, and standing there one feels that it is a fitting birth-place for the poetry of the sea-ruling nation. Nor is the verse of the first poet without the stormy note of the scenery among which it was written.—*Stopford Brooke.*

ignorance compelled him to be silent when it was his turn to help on the entertainment. Bemoaning his stupidity, "he left the house of festivity, went out to the stables of the beasts, whose custody on that night was intrusted to him;" and there in his restless sleep a strange figure appeared to him and bade him sing. "I cannot sing," said Caedmon; "I have come out hither from the feast because I could not sing." Then he who spoke to him said, "But you have to sing to me." "What must I sing?" asked Caedmon; and the voice replied, "Sing the origin of creatures." At once an inspiration came to the ignorant peasant, and the words of his song lingered in his memory when he awoke. The people of the neighboring monastery pronounced his new endowment a miracle, called him a favored child of heaven, made him a member of their order, and ever treated him with deference.

Such is the legend. The marvelous story may have been told for the purpose of winning the reverent esteem of the people for Caedmon's teachings. But without the story he would have been eminent among men. His work continued to be the most popular expression of religious feeling, and won for him the deep reverence of five centuries of Englishmen.

It has been supposed that this great religious poet of the Anglo-Saxons suggested to Milton the subject of his renowned epic. That Milton must have read Caedmon with great interest seems probable, in view of the fact that the MS. of Caedmon, discovered in 1654, was first published in 1655, and that it discussed the Fall of Man, the very subject upon which Milton's imagination was at work. Both describe wicked angels, their expulsion from heaven, their descent into hell, and the creation of the world. In Satan's soliloquy in Hell we find a passage (others might be cited), in which the great English epic poet of the seventeenth century has thoughts closely resembling those that were written by the monk of the seventh century.

These poems of the Old English period, one produced while our ancestors were yet in paganism, the other after they had accepted Christianity, are the only extended works in verse which have been preserved. The shorter poems are not numerous. Fragments of verse and two or three unbroken passages are found amid the prose of the Saxon Chronicle. They are always spirited, but serious. They are the utterances of a people who, though unaccustomed to give vent to their feelings, yet, when excited by some great occasion, expressed themselves with earnest solemnity. They never show us the sparkle of lyric verse,—the national character was not adapted to its production.

OLD ENGLISH PROSE.

B. 849.]   **King Alfred's Literary Influence.** The name of King
D. 901.]   Alfred stands pre-eminent among the writers of prose in
Old English. No sooner had he delivered his people from their Danish enemies, than he set at work to free them from their bondage to ignorance. From various quarters, he invited men of learning to his court. He insisted upon the better education of the clergy. What he could do, he did, to restore the literary work that had been destroyed when the Danes burned English monasteries. In order to diffuse knowledge, he had standard writings on religion, morals, geography, and history, translated into the language of the people. He not only gave patronage to learning; he also gave his earnest personal efforts in contributing to the national literature. At a time of life when the task must have been irksome enough, he applied himself to a careful course of training in order to prepare himself for the work of a writer. By these means his patriotic desires were gratified; and, while he succeeded in increasing the intelligence of his country, he won for himself a lofty place among royal authors.

King Alfred's chief works were translations of Bede's *Ecclesiastical History*, the *Ancient History of Orosius*, and Boethius *On the Consolations Afforded by Philosophy*. But he was something more than a mere translator. The new matter introduced by way of comment or illustration, entitles him to be called an original author. His writings are pronounced " the purest specimens of Anglo-Saxon prose."

The patronage and the example of the great king must have induced the writing of many works in the native language. Time has spared us very few of them. One grand monument of prose literature, the **Saxon Chronicle,** still remains. It exists in seven separate forms, each named from the monastery in which it was completed. The usual unauthentic account of this work is that it was originally composed at the suggestion of King Alfred, and, beginning with the arrival of Julius Cæsar in Britain, was brought down to the year 891; and that from that time it was continued as a contemporary record until the accession of Henry II., in 1154. This chronicle is exceedingly interesting, as it is the first ever written in Teutonic prose, and is also most valuable, since it furnishes trustworthy statements concerning the early history of the English people.

At the beginning, the work is crude, meagre in its details, and altogether devoid of the qualities we expect to find in an elaborate historical narration; but as the record draws towards its close, the chroniclers occasionally rise into sustained descriptions, display vigor of style and a sober eloquence. "Putting aside the Hebrew annals, there is not anywhere known a series of early vernacular histories comparable to the Saxon Chronicles." Their close marks the close of the old language as well as of the old literature; for before the chronicler had thrown down his pen, he had begun to confuse his grammar and to corrupt his vocabulary.

Latin Authorship in England. The literature thus far referred to was written for the amusement or instruction of comparatively ignorant people; much of it was intended for recital to those who could not read. But there were monks in England who were studying and writing in Latin, then the only language of the republic of learning. During the first five or six centuries of England's history, her most highly cultivated men were contrib-uting to the well-stocked literature of Rome, and were withholding the fruits of their mental toil from the literature of their own nation.

One of these Latin authors, the **Venerable Bede,** by his record of the early history of England, has bequeathed to us **B. 673.]** most valuable information. He was placed in the **D. 735.]** Wearmouth Monastery when seven years of age. The rest of his biography is contained in the following brief passage, translated from one of his works : *

"Spending all the remaining time of my life in that monastery, I wholly applied myself to the study of Scripture, and amidst the observance of regular discipline, and the daily care of singing in the

* Bede, like Caedmon, was a Northumbrian. The extinction of Northumbrian literature marks the invasion by the Danes.

church, I always took delight in learning, teaching and writing. In the nineteenth year of my age I received deacon's orders; in the thirtieth, those of the priesthood, * * * from which time till the fifty-ninth year of my age I have made it my business, for the use of me and mine, to compile out of the works of the venerable fathers, and to interpret and explain, according to their meaning, these following pieces."

The enumeration itself is startlingly voluminous. " His writings form almost an encyclopædia of the knowledge of his day." Many of them were prepared as text-books for the hundreds of students who sought his teaching, and they included treatises on mathematics, on astronomy, on grammar, on rhetoric, on dialectics, on meteorology, on music and on medicine.* But it is by one work that he has made the English nation a lasting debtor to his fame: for his *Ecclesiastical History of the English* was a history of England, and was for centuries the only source of knowledge in matters relating to the nation's early career. Written for the purpose of preserving among the Angles and Saxons the memory of their conversion to the Christian faith, it told them, also, the story of their political life. In careful and successful research, in arrangement of materials, and in felicity of style, he rises far above all Gothic historians of that age. Green's *Short History of the English People*, gives the following version of the story of Bede's last hours, which were spent in finishing his Translation of the Gospel of John:

" ' There is still a chapter wanting,' said the scribe, as the morning drew on, 'and it is hard for thee to question thyself any longer.' 'It is easily done,' said Bede; 'take thy pen and write quickly.' Amid tears and farewells the day wore on to eventide. ' There is yet one sentence unwritten, dear Master,' said the boy. ' Write it quickly,' bade the dying man. ' It is finished now,' said the little scribe, at last. ' You speak truth,' said the master; 'all is finished now.' Placed upon the pavement, his head supported in his scholar's arms, his face turned to the spot where he was wont to pray, Bede chanted the solemn ' Glory to God.' As his voice reached the close of his song, he passed quietly away."

In the old English literature, the idea of duty and the claims of religion are everywhere recognized. They appear in the paganism of Beowulf, they are piously chanted in the verses of Caedmon, they are displayed in the achievements of King Alfred, they give

* See the *Development of English Literature*, O. E. Period, Brother Azarias.

sanctity to the life and works of the Venerable Bede. The serious tone of that first age has sounded through the later ages of English thought. The English Literature "has for its most distinctive mark the religious sense of duty. It represents a people striving through successive generations to find out the right and do it, to root out the wrong, and labor ever onward for the love of God." *

* Morley's *First Sketch of English Literature*, p. 1.

NOTE.—For extended reading upon the topics discussed in this chapter, the student is referred to Wright's *Biographia Britannica Literaria*, Morley's *English Writers*, Guest's *History of English Rhythms*, Conybeare's *Illustrations of Anglo Saxon Poetry*, Thorpe's edition of *Caedmon*, Craik's *English Literature and Language*, and Taine's *English Literature*.

In this chapter we have considered:

1. A general division of the English Language.

2. The Poem, Beowulf.

3. Caedmon's Paraphrase of the Scriptures.

4. King Alfred's Literary Influence.

5. The Saxon Chronicle.

6. The Venerable Bede.

CHAPTER III.

FROM THE CONQUEST TO GEOFFREY CHAUCER.

FOR more than a century after the Norman Conquest, English Literature was inert. That conquest, so fatal to the native aristocracy, seemed at first to have swept away in common ruin the laws, language, and arts of the English people, and to have blotted out England from the muster-roll of the nations. A foreign king and aristocracy, an alien language and literature, ruled in the land; the old speech was no longer heard in the halls of the great: native genius no longer strove to utter itself in the native tongue and the voice of the English nation seemed stilled forever. But it was not the stillness of death; in a few generations signs of returning life began to show themselves; and the English nation emerged from the fiery trial, with its equipment of language, laws and literature, materially altered indeed, and perhaps improved, but still bearing the ineffaceable Teutonic stamp. The national life was not annihilated in the Battle of Hastings; it was only suspended for a time.

Changes in the English Language. In the old English, as in other Teutonic languages, there was a tendency to shake off complicated inflections. This tendency existed before the Norman Conquest. That great political revolution gave it additional impulse. The vernacular speech was driven from literature for a time, and found its refuge in the cottages of ignorant people. No longer fixed by use in literature, it fell into disorder; the processes of change were thereby accelerated, and when, at the middle of the twelfth century, this speech rose to the surface once more, it had traveled far along its destined course. Still it was the old tongue. In the words of Max Müller, "not a single drop of foreign blood has entered into the organic system of the English language. The Grammar, the blood and soul of the language, is as pure and unmixed in the English spoken in the British Isles as it was when spoken on the shores of the German Ocean by the Angles, Saxons, and Jutes of the continent." *

This, the Middle English Stage, was a revolutionary period of the language. There was a general breaking up of the old grammatical system; uncertainty, confusion, and fluctuation prevailed. The Northern, the Midland, and the Southern dialects, each with certain peculiar inflectional forms, and each represented by literary works of some note, struggled for the mastery. The influx of French words too, though trifling at first, had already begun; and for the next three centuries the process went on with increasing rapidity.

The interest of the writings which form the subject of this chapter is almost exclusively philological and historical. Their literary merits are small; but they supply the means of tracing the course of the language through its many varying forms, and, occasionally, they throw a powerful light on the feelings and aspirations, the political and social condition of the people. We shall give them but a passing glance.

Layamon's Brut. If we except a few fragments of verse,—The *Hymn of St. Godric*, the Ely *Song of King Canute, the Here Prophecy*, none of them exceeding eight lines in length—the first to break the long silence was Layamon, author of the *Brut*. He was a priest, at Ernley, in Worcestershire, and seems to have been a gentle, pious, patriotic man, a lover of tradition. His work, written early in the thirteenth century, is a chronicle of Britain, and is mainly a translation from the French of the *Brut d'Angleterre;* but Layamon has introduced so much new matter into his work, and has made it so conversational in style, that it is more than double the length of the original. It is a free narration in verse of Celtic traditions which had been preserved in France and in parts of England. The story makes Brutus, a son of the Trojan Aeneas, the founder of the line of British Monarchs. The style of the work bears witness to Norman influence, but not to so great an extent as might have been expected from the translator of a French original. The fact that it was written for the common people of a rural district was favorable to the use of simple English, and makes it a valuable illustra-

* " Lectures on the Science of Language," 1st series, p. 81, Amer. Edition.

tion of the state of our language at that time. Written nearly one hundred and fifty years after the Norman Conquest, it is, nevertheless, a specimen of almost pure Saxon. The old text in its more than thirty thousand lines has not fifty words taken from the French. The foreign influence, however, appears in the occasional use of rhymes. Layamon's work was preserved in two manuscripts of the thirteenth century, which illustrate the progress of the language in ridding itself of Anglo-Saxon terminations.

The Ormulum, another monument of our old literature, is supposed to have been written in the thirteenth century. One of its editors describes it as "a series of homilies in an imperfect state, composed in metre, without alliteration, and, except in very few cases, without rhyme: the subject of the homilies being supplied by those portions of the New Testament which were read in the daily services of the church." The author himself says, "If any one wants to know why I have done this deed, why I have turned into English the Gospel's holy teaching; I have done it in order that all young Christian folks may depend upon that only, that they with their whole might follow aright the Gospel's holy teaching in thought, in word, in deed." The text reads more easily than Layamon's Brut, and that fact, together with many peculiarities of structure, indicates that the work is more recent. At the time of its writing, the conflict of languages and dialects in England was going on, and the people made sad work in their attempts to pronounce each other's speech. To save his verses from abuse or mispronunciation, Orm, or Ormin, adopted an ingenious use of consonants as a key to the sounds of vowels. After every short vowel the consonant was doubled, and the reader, of whatever speech he might be, was left with no excuse for marring the sound of the verse. A single couplet will illustrate:

> " Thiss boc iss nemmned Orrmulum,
> Forrthi that Orrm itt wrohhte."

(This book is called Ormulum, because Orm wrought it.)

Poetical Romances. In that age literary thought demanded the narration of romance in song. The taste was native to the French; and English writers, in considerable numbers, sought their laurels in this kind of composition. The stories, originally written in the French, full of love and adventure, were full of the spirit of chivalry. Professional minstrels, knights, and even kings had vied in their composition. These romances group themselves about great names, some having Alexander, some Charlemagne, as their central figure; but one cluster, the Arthurian, is of genuine native growth, and possesses the highest interest of all. Translations and imitations of these French romances slowly came into popular favor with the English people, and aided in the fusion of the languages.

Ballads. But the patriotic spirit of the common people was not fully satisfied in imitating foreign poesy. Many spirited political songs of English origin, and ballads full of characteristic English satire were written. One of these ballads, *The Owl and the Nightingale*, in giving an amusing account of a competition in song between the two birds, furnishes perhaps the finest specimen of the popular literature of the thirteenth century, and is especially interesting as the earliest narrative and imaginative English poem not copied from some foreign model.

Writings in the English tongue do not represent the entire intellectual wealth of the nation during this Anglo-Norman period, indeed they form but a small portion. For almost three centuries after the Conquest, French continued to be the language of polite literature, and Latin the language of theology, philosophy, science and history. Many Englishmen were writing in these departments; but they were contributors to a foreign, not to their national literature.

That national literature has now reached the eve of its first great expansion. It has been in existence for a thousand years, but has as yet produced no work of pre-eminent merit, no name that is entitled to rank among intellects of the highest order. Energy of thought and expression, natural sweetness and simple pathos, are not wanting; but there is still a complete absence of artistic form, literary skill, and the higher qualities of workmanship. Nothing appears to portend the magnificent outburst that is at hand; but the student of history can discern forces, political, social, and spiritual, at work beneath the smooth surface, destined within a few years to produce momentous results. The national life and thought of England are now passing through a quickening process; a brilliant page in her history is about to open, on which will appear many bright names, but none brighter than that of GEOFFREY CHAUCER, the first man who speaks to the hearts of all classes of the English people.

In this chapter we have considered:—

1. The Middle English.

2. Layamon's Brut.

3. The Ormulum.

4. Poetical Romances, and Ballads.

CHAPTER IV.

GEOFFREY CHAUCER.

" I consider Chaucer as a genial day in an English spring."—*Thomas Warton.*

" I take increasing delight in Chaucer. * * * How exquisitely tender he is, yet how perfectly free he is from the least touch of sickly melancholy or morbid drooping."—*S T. Coleridge.*

" Here was a healthy and hearty man, so genuine that he need not ask whether he were genuine or no, so sincere as to quite forget his own sincerity, so truly pious that he could be happy in the best world that God chose to make, so human that he loved even the foibles of his kind."

" There is no touch of cynicism in all he wrote."—*J. R. Lowell.*

THE fourteenth century is the most important epoch in the intellectual history of Europe. It is the point of contact between two widely-differing eras in the social, religious, and political annals of our race. Feudalism and chivalry had fulfilled their mission and were yielding to the pressure of ideas that foreshadowed the Revival of Letters and the Protestant Reformation. Of this great social transition from the old order to the new, the personal career and the works of Chaucer, the first great English poet, " the Father of English Poetry," furnish us with the most exact type and expression; for, like all men of the highest order of genius, he at once followed and directed the intellectual tendencies of his age, and was himself the " abstract and brief chronicle" of the spirit of his time. In the age in which he lived he was fortunate; the magnificent court of Edward III. had carried the splendor of chivalry to the height of its development; the victories of Sluys, of Crécy, and Poitiers, by exciting the national pride, tended to fuse into one vigorous nationality the two elements which formed the English people and the English language. The literature, too, abundant in quantity, if not remarkable for originality of form, was rapidly taking a purely English tone; rhyming chronicles and legendary romances were composed in the vernacular. This tendency to make the English a literary language is indicated by the following quotation from the *Testament of Love:* "Let clerks indite in Latin, and the Frenchmen in their French also indite their quaint terms, for it is kindly to their mouths; and let us show our fantasies in such words as we learned of our Mother's tongue." From the Norman Conquest until the time of Chaucer, the Latin had been used in England by those who wrote for the learned; the French was the language of fashionable literature, and the English was written only for the ignorant. Meantime the native tongue had developed until Chaucer, the greatest literary genius which the nation had produced, saw in that tongue the best material for his literary art. He addressed all classes of readers, not in the vulgar speech of the populace, but in refined English as it was spoken at the Court. He was the first author who used the " King's English; " and his success compelled all other writers in England to abandon the Latin and the French.

His Personal Appearance. An ancient and probably authentic portrait of Chaucer, attributed to his contemporary and fellow-poet, Occleve, as well as a curious and beautiful miniature, introduced, according to the fashion of those times, into one of the most valuable manuscript copies of his works, give the poet a pleasing and meditative countenance, and indicate that he was somewhat corpulent. In the prologue to *The Rime of Sir Thopas*, the host of the Tabard, himself represented as a " large man," and a " faire burgess," calls upon Chaucer in his turn to contribute a

story to the amusement of the pilgrims, and rallies him on
his corpulency, as well as on his studious and abstracted air:

> " What man art thou ?" quod he;
> " Thou lokest as thou woldest fynde an hare;
> For ever on the ground I se the stare.
> Approche nere, and loke merrily.
> Now ware you, sires, and let this man have spece.
> He in the wast is schape as well as I;
> He semeth elvisch by his countenance,
> For unto no wight doth he daliaunce.

B. 1340.] **Chaucer's Social and Political Career.** The
D. 1400.] date of Chaucer's birth is uncertain. There are
reasons for fixing it at 1328, but better ones in
favor of 1340. He is supposed to have been a child of
wealth. His surname, the French *Chaussier*, points to a
Continental origin, which at that time was almost a sure
sign of aristocratic rank. He was " armed a knight," he
held lucrative and responsible positions, he married one of
the Queen's maids of honor. These facts indicate that he
belonged to the higher classes of English society. But
whatever his social position may have been, his spirit was
tolerant and generous; he took broad views of life, and,
having the soul of a poet, he loved nature and humanity.

In the *Testament of Love*, Chaucer speaks of London as
his birth-place. In his *Court of Love* he speaks of himself
under the name and character of " Philogenet—*of Cambridge*, Clerk ;" but this hardly proves that he was educated
at Cambridge. Indeed there is no positive proof that he was
a student at either of the great universities. He was taken
prisoner by the French in 1359, and being ransomed, according to the custom of those times, was enabled to return to
England in 1360.

He next appears, in 1367, as one of the " valets of the
king's chamber," and writs are addressed to him as " *dilectus
valettus noster.*" His official career was active and even
distinguished; during a long period, he enjoyed various

profitable offices, having been for twelve years comptroller of the customs and subsidy of wools, skins, and tanned hides in the port of London; and he seems also to have been occasionally employed in diplomatic negotiations. Thus he was, in 1373, associated with two citizens of Genoa in a commission to Italy. On this occasion he is supposed to have made the acquaintance of Petrarch, then the most illustrious man of letters in Europe. Partly in consequence of his wife's attachment to the wife of John of Gaunt, and partly, perhaps, from sharing in some of the political and religious opinions of that powerful prince, Chaucer was identified with the household and with the party of the Duke of Lancaster. His *Complaynte of the Black Knight,* his *Dream,* and his *Boke of the Duchesse* were suggested to him, the first by the courtship of the duke and the duchess Blanche, the second by their marriage, and the third by her death in 1369. In the *Dream,* allusions to Chaucer's own courtship and marriage may be found. One of the most interesting particulars of his life was his election as representative for Kent in the Parliament of 1386. In the political turmoil of that year he lost all his offices.

In 1387, however, he was appointed to the office of clerk of the king's works, which he held for about two years. There is reason to believe that, though his pecuniary circumstances must have been, during a great part of his life, in proportion to the position he occupied in the state and in society, his last days were more or less clouded by financial embarrassment. His death took place at Westminster on the 25th of October, 1400.

His Literary Career. The literary and intellectual career of Chaucer divides itself into two periods, closely corresponding to the two great social and political tendencies which meet in the fourteenth century. His earlier productions bear the stamp of the Chivalric, his later and more original creations, of the Italian literature. It is more than probable that the poet's visits to Italy, then the fountain of new literary life, brought him into contact with the works and the men by whose example the change in the taste of Europe was brought about. The religious element, too, enters largely into the character of his writings. It is diffi cult to ascertain how far the poet sympathized with the bold doctrines of Wycliffe, who, like himself, was favored and protected by John of Gaunt, fourth son of Edward III. Many satirical passages in his poems indicate that in hos- tility to the monastic orders and in contempt for corrupt men in the church, he heartily sympathized with Wycliffe; but he probably did not accept the theological opinions of the man who was then considered the arch-heretic.

Chief among Chaucer's poems reflecting Romance influ- ences are the *Romaunt of the Rose*,* the *Court of Love*,* the *Assembly of Fowls*,* the *Cuckow and the Nightingale*, the *Flower and the Leaf*, *Chaucer's Dream*, the *Boke of the Duchesse*, and the *House of Fame*. Italian influences are most apparent in the *Legende of Goode Women*, *Troilus and Creseide*, *Anelyda and Arcyte*, and above all,the best of the *Canterbury Tales*.

Poems of the Chivalric Type. The *Romaunt of the Rose* is a translation of the famous allegory, *Le Roman de la Rose*, the most highly-prized specimen of the early French litera- ture. The original is of inordinate length, containing twenty-two thousand verses, even in the unfinished state in which it was left. According to the almost universal prac- tice of the old Romance poets, the story is put into the form of a dream or vision. Chaucer's translation is but a third as long as the original. The portions omitted either never were translated by the English poet, on account of his

* Chaucer's authorship of these poems has been called in question, mainly be cause of verbal peculiarities. But who else could have produced them in that age

dislike to their immoral and irreligious tone, or were omitted by the copyist from the early English manuscripts. The translation gives proof of Chaucer's remarkable ear for metrical harmony, and also of his picturesque imagination; for though in many places he follows the original with scrupulous fidelity, he not infrequently adds vigorous touches of his own. The most remarkable illustration of this is the description of the character of a true gentleman, not a hint of which can be found in the original.*

The *Court of Love*, a typical poem of the age, is written in the name of " Philogenet of Cambridge, clerk " (or student), who is directed by Mercury to appear at the Court of Venus. He gives a description of the Castle of Love, where Admetus and Alcestis preside as king and queen. Philogenet is conducted to the Temple, sees Venus and Cupid, and hears the oath of allegiance to the twenty commandments of Love administered to the faithful. The hero is then presented to the Lady Rosial, with whom, in strict accordance with Provençal poetical custom, he has become enamoured in a dream. The most curious part of the poem is the celebration of the grand festival of Love, on May-day, when a parody of the Catholic matin service for Trinity Sunday is chanted by various birds in honor of the God of Love.

In the *Assembly of Fowls* we have a debate carried on before the Parliament of Birds.

The *Cuckow and the Nightingale*, though of no great length, is one of the most charming among this class of Chaucer's productions: it describes a controversy between the two birds. To the poets and allegorists of the Middle Ages, the Cuckoo was the emblem of profligate celibacy, while the Nightingle was the type of constant and virtuous conjugal love. In this poem we meet with a striking example of that exquisite sensibility to the sweetness of external

* Lines 2187-2274.

nature, and especially to the song of birds, which was possessed by Chaucer in a pre-eminent degree.*

The *Flower and the Leaf* is an allegory, probably written to celebrate the marriage of Philippa, John of Gaunt's daughter, with John, king of Portugal. A lady, unable to sleep, wanders out into a forest, on a spring morning, and seating herself in a delightful arbor, listens to the alternate songs of the goldfinch and the nightingale. Her reverie is suddenly interrupted by the approach of a band of ladies clothed in white, and garlanded with laurel and woodbine. They join their queen in singing a roundelay, and are in their turn interrupted by the sound of trumpets and by the appearance of nine armed knights, followed by a splendid train of cavaliers and ladies. These joust for an hour, and then advancing to the first company, each knight leads a lady to a laurel, to which they make an obeisance. Another troop of ladies approaches, habited in green, and doing reverence to a tuft of flowers, while the leader sings a pastoral song, in honor of the daisy. The sports are broken off, first by the heat of the sun, which withers all the flowers, and afterwards by a violent storm, in which the knights and the ladies in green are pitifully drenched; while the company in white shelter themselves under the laurel. Then follows the explanation of the allegory: the white queen and her party represent Chastity; the knights, the Nine Worthies; the cavaliers crowned with laurel, the Knights of the Round Table, the Peers of Charlemagne, and the Knights of the Garter. The Queen and ladies in green represent Flora and the followers of sloth and idleness. In general, the flower typifies vain pleasure; the leaf, virtue and industry; the former being "a thing fading with every blast," while the latter "abides with the root, notwithstanding the frosts and winter storms." The poem is written in the seven-line stanza, and contains many curious and beautiful passages.

* See the inimitable passage from line 65 to line 85.

Poems of the Italian Type. For its extraordinary union of brilliant description with learning and humor, the *House of Fame* is sufficient of itself to establish Chaucer's reputation. Under the popular form of a dream, it gives a picture of the Temple of Glory, crowded with aspirants for immortal renown, and adorned with statues of great poets and historians. The description of this temple is the most interesting part of the poem. Its architectural details are carefully set forth, and its beauties are charmingly described. In richness of fancy it far surpasses Pope's imitation, the *Temple of Fame*. When the poet leaves the temple, he is, in his dream, borne away by an eagle to a house sixty miles in length, built of twigs and blown about in the wind. This is the House of Rumor, thronged with pilgrims, pardoners, sailors, and other retailers of wonderful reports.

> " And eke this hous hath of entrees
> As fell of leves as ben on trees,
> In somer whan they grene ben,
> And on the rove men may yet seer
> A thousand holes, and wel moo
> To leten wel the soune oute goo."

The *Legende of Goode Women* was one of Chaucer's latest compositions. Its apologies for what had been written in his earlier years, and its mention of many of his previous works, clearly prove that it was produced after much of his busy life was spent. The avowed purpose of the poem is to make a retraction of his unfavorable descriptions of the character of women; and for this purpose he undertakes to give a poetical sketch of nineteen ladies, whose lives of chastity and worthiness redeem the sex from his former reproaches. The work was left incomplete. The nine sketches given are closely translated from Ovid, but the coloring of the stories is Catholic and mediæval. Dido, Cleopatra and Medea are regarded as the martyrs of Saint Venus and Saint Cupid. Many striking descriptions are introduced by Chaucer. The Prologue is by far the finest portion of the poem. Here, and everywhere in Chaucer, **the rhythm is** perfect when the verses are properly read.

Chaucer's age placed his *Troilus and Creseide* **nearest to the** *Canterbury Tales.* The material for this poem **was** drawn from Boccaccio. The story was common, and ex-tremely popular in the Middle Ages, and even later. Shakespeare himself has dramatized it. In many passages Chaucer adhered closely to the text of Boccaccio; but in the conduct of the story, in the development of ideal characters, and in a delicate appreciation of moral senti-ment, he was far superior to his Italian contemporary. The poem is written in the musical Italian stanza of seven lines.

The Canterbury Tales. Chaucer's greatest and most original work is the *Canterbury Tales* **(13).*** It is in this that he has poured forth in inexhaustible abundance his stores of wit, humor, pathos, and knowledge of humanity it is this which will place him, till the remotest posterity, in the first rank among poets and character-painters. The magical power of the poet evokes our ancestors from the fourteenth century, and causes them to pass before our vision "in their habit, as they lived," acting and speaking in a manner invariably true to nature.

Its Plan. The plan of the *Canterbury Tales,* though very simple, is masterly. It enables the poet to make the repre-sentatives of various classes of society tell a series of tales, extremely beautiful when regarded as compositions and judged on their independent merits, but deriving an infi-nitely higher interest from the way in which they harmonize with their respective narrators. It also gives him opportunity to display his genius for descriptions of nature. After giving a brief, picturesque description of spring, the poet informs us that, being about to make a pilgrimage from London to the shrine of Thomas à Becket in the cathedral of Canterbury,

*The heavy-faced figures throughout this work refer to selections from Shaw's Choice Specimens of English Literature.

he passes the night previous to his departure at the Tabard Inn in Southwark. While at the "hostelrie" he meets many pilgrims bound to the same destination :—

> " In Southwerk at the Tabard as I lay,
> Redy to wenden on my pilgrimage
> To Canterbury with ful devout corage,
> At night was come into that hostelrie
> Wel nyne and twenty in a companye *
> Of sondry folk, by aventure y-falle
> In felawschipe, and pilgryms were thei alle,
> That toward Canterbury wolden ryde."

This goodly company, assembled in a manner so natural in those times of pilgrimages and of difficult and dangerous roads, agree to travel in a body; and at supper Harry Bailey, the host of the Tabard, a jolly and sociable fellow, proposes to accompany the party as a guide, and suggests that they may much enliven the tedium of their journey by relating stories as they ride. He is accepted by the whole society as a judge or moderator, by whose decisions every one is to abide. The plan of the work, had Chaucer completed it, would have comprised the adventures on the journey, the arrival at Canterbury, a description, in all probability, of the splendid religious ceremonies and the visits to the numerous shrines and relics in the cathedral, the return to London, the farewell supper at the Tabard, and the separation of the pleasant company. The jovial guide proposes that each pilgrim shall relate two tales on the journey out, and two more on the way home ; and that, on the return of the party to London, he who shall be adjudged to have related the best and most amusing story, shall sup at the common cost. Such is the general plan of the poem, and its development is natural. Some of the stories suggest others, just as would happen in real life, under the same circumstances. In the inimitable description of manners, persons, dress, and all the equipage, with which the poet has

* In his subsequent enumeration (see next page) Chaucer counts thirty persons.

introduced them, we behold a vast and minute portrait gallery of the social England of the fourteenth century. The pilgrims are from all classes of society :—(1) A Knight; (2) A Squire; (3) A Yeoman; (4) A Prioress, a lady of rank, superior of a nunnery; (5, 6, 7, 8) A Nun and three Priests, in attendance upon this lady; (9) A Monk, represented as handsomely dressed and equipped, and passionately fond of hunting and good cheer; (10) A Friar, or Mendicant Monk; (11) A Merchant; (12) A Clerk, or Student of the University of Oxford; (13) A Serjeant of the Law; (14) A Franklin, or rich country gentleman; (15, 16, 17, 18, 19) Five wealthy burgesses, or tradesmen,—a Haberdasher, or dealer in silk and cloth, a Carpenter, a Weaver, a Dyer, and a Tapisser, or maker of carpets and hangings; (20) A Cook, or rather the keeper of a cook-shop; (21) A Shipman, the master of a trading vessel; (22) A Doctor of Physic; (23) A Wife of Bath, a rich cloth-manufacturer; (24) A Parson, or secular parish priest; (25) A Ploughman, the brother of the preceding personage; (26) A Miller; (27) A Manciple, or steward of a college or religious house; (28) A Reeve; (29) A Sompnour, or Sumner, an officer whose duty was to summon delinquents to appear in the ecclesiastical courts; (30) A Pardoner, or vendor of Indulgences from Rome. To these thirty persons, must be added Chaucer himself, and the Host of the Tabard, making in all thirty-two.

The Plan Not Executed. If each of these pilgrims had related two tales on the journey to Canterbury, and two on the return, the work would have contained one hundred and twenty-eight stories, exclusive of the subordinate incidents and conversations; but the pilgrims do not arrive at their destination, and there are many evidences of confusion in the tales which Chaucer has given us, leading to the conclusion that the materials were not only incomplete, but also were left in a confused state by the poet. In no instance does he seem to have invented the intrigues of his stories He freely borrowed them, either from the *fabliaux* of the Provençal poets, the legends of the mediæval chroniclers, from the storehouse of the *Gesta Romanorum,* or from the early Italian writers. The stories that we possess are twenty-five in number,—three of which, the Cook's, the Squire's, and Chaucer's first, are "left half told," and one, *Gamelyn,** is either entirely spurious or written by the poet for a different purpose. Eleven of the pilgrims are left silent. A Canon and his Yeoman unexpectedly join the cavalcade during the journey, but it is uncertain whether this episode, which was probably an afterthought of the poet, takes place on the journey to or from Canterbury. The Canon, who is represented as an Alchemist, half swindler and half dupe, is driven away from the company by shame at his attendant's indiscreet disclosures; and the Yeoman, remaining with the pilgrims, relates a most amusing story of the villainous artifices of the charlatans who pretended to possess the Great Arcanum. The stories narrated by the pilgrims are admirably introduced by what the author calls "prologues," consisting of remarks and criticisms on the preceding tale, and of incidents of the journey.

The tales are all in verse, with the exception of two, that of the Parson, and Chaucer's second narrative. Those in verse exhibit an endless variety of metrical forms used with consummate ease and dexterity; indeed, no English poet is more exquisitely melodious than Chaucer.

Two Classes of Tales. The Tales themselves may be roughly divided into the two great classes of pathetic and humorous. We are filled with delight and admiration, whether we study their wonderful painting of character, the conciseness and vividness of their descriptions, the loftiness

---

* The Cook's Tale of *Gamelyn,* if really written by Chaucer, was a close copy of one of the ballad stories common among the people, and was perhaps intended to be related on the journey home.

of their sentiment and the intensity of their pathos, or revel
in the richness of their humor and the surpassingly droll,
yet perfectly natural extravagance of their comic scenes.
The finest of the pathetic stories are, the *Knight's Tale*—
the longest of them all, in which is related the adventure
of Palamon and Arcite; the *Squire's Tale*, a wild, half-
Oriental story of love, chivalry, and enchantment; the
Man of Law's Tale, the beautiful and pathetic story of Constance ; the *Prioress's Tale*, the charming legend of " litel
Hew of Lincoln," the child who was murdered for singing
his hymn to the Virgin ; and, above all, the *Clerk of
Oxford's Tale*, perhaps the most beautiful pathetic narration
in the whole range of literature. This, the story of Griselda,
the model and heroine of wifely patience and obedience, is
the tenderest of all the serious narratives, as the *Knight's
Tale* is the masterpiece among the descriptions of love and
chivalric magnificence.

The *Knight's Tale* is freely borrowed from the *Theseida*
of Boccaccio. Though the action and personages of this
noble story are assigned to classical antiquity, the sentiments, manners, and feelings of the persons introduced are
those of chivalric Europe; the " Two Noble Kinsmen,"
Palamon and Arcite, being types of the knightly character.

The *Squire's Tale* bears evident marks of Oriental origin ;
but whether it be a legend derived from Eastern literature,
or received by Chaucer after having filtered through a
Romance version, is now uncertain. It is equal to the preceding story in splendor and variety of incident and in
word-painting, but far inferior in depth of pathos and
elevation of sentiment; yet it was by the *Squire's Tale* that
Milton characterized Chaucer in that passage of the *Pense-
roso* where he evokes recollections of the great poet :—

> " Or call up him that left half told
> The story of Cambuscan bold,
> Of Cambal, and of Algarsife,
> And who had Canace to wife

That owned the virtuous ring and glass;
And of the wondrous horse of brass
On which the Tartar king did ride.

The *Man of Law's Tale* is taken with little variation from
Gower's voluminous poem, " *Confessio Amantis*," the incidents of Gower's narrative being in their turn traceable to a
multitude of romances.

The most pathetic of Chaucer's stories, that of Patient
Griselda, narrated by the Clerk of Oxford, is traceable to
Petrarch's Latin translation of the last tale in Boccaccio's
Decameron.

The finest of Chaucer's humorous stories are those of
the Miller, the Reeve, and the Sompnour. Among these it
is difficult to give the palm for drollery, acute painting
of human nature, and exquisite ingenuity of incident. It
is much to be regretted that the comic stories turn upon
events of a kind which the refinement of modern manners
renders it impossible to analyze; but it should be remembered that society in Chaucer's day, though perhaps not less
moral in reality, was far more outspoken and simple, and
permitted and enjoyed allusions which are proscribed by our
sense of decency.

Two of these tales, as has been stated, are written in prose.
These deviations from what seems to have been the original
plan, are very naturally made. When Chaucer is applied
to by the Host, he commences a rambling, puerile romance
of chivalry, entitled the *Rime of Sir Thopas*, which promises
to be an interminable story of knight-errant adventures,
combats with giants, dragons, and enchanters, and is written
in the exact style and metre of the Trouvère narrative
poems—the only instance of this versification in the *Canterbury Tales.* He goes on gallantly "in the style his books of
chivalry had taught him," like Don Quixote, "imitating, as
near as he could, their very phrase ;" but he is suddenly
interrupted, with many expressions of comic disgust, by the
merry host:—

> " ' No mor of this, for Goddes dignite ! '
> Quod our Hoste, ' for thou makest me
> So wery of thy verray lewednesse,
> That, al so wisly God my soule blesse,
> Myn eeres aken for thy drafty speche.
> Now such a rym the devel I byteche !
> This may wel be rym dogerel,' quod he."

Chaucer took this ingenious method of ridiculing and
aricaturing the Romance poetry, which had reached the
lowest point of the commonplace. Then, with great good
nature and a readiness which marks the man of the world,
he offers to tell "a litel thing in prose;" and commences
the long allegorical tale of *Melibeus and his wife Prudence*,
in which, though the matter is often tiresome enough, he
appears pre-eminent among the prose writers of his day.

The other prose tale is narrated by the Parson. He is represented as a simple and narrow-minded though pious and
large-hearted pastor, who characteristically refuses to indulge
the company with what can minister only to vain pleasure,
and proposes something that may tend to edification, "mo-
ralite and vertuous matiere"; and so he commences a long
and very curious sermon on the seven deadly sins, their causes
and remedies. His discourse is an interesting specimen of
the theological literature of the day. It is divided and subdivided with all the painful minuteness of scholastic divinity;
but it breathes throughout a noble spirit of piety, and in
many passages attains great dignity of expression.

Besides these two Canterbury Tales, Chaucer wrote in
prose a translation of Boethius's *De Consolatione*, an imitation of that work, under the title of *The Testament of Love*,
and an incomplete astrological work, *On the Astrolabe*, addressed to his son Lewis.

The general plan of the *Canterbury Tales* is believed to
have been taken from the Decameron of Boccaccio, though
the English poet's conception and method are superior to
that of the Italian, whose ten accomplished young gentlemen and ladies assemble in their luxurious villa to escape
from the terrible plague which is devastating Florence.

Chaucer easily read. The difficulty of reading and understanding Chaucer has been much exaggerated. The principal facts that the student should keep in mind are, that the many French words in his writings had not been so modified, by changes in their orthography and pronunciation, as to become Anglicized, and are therefore to be read with their French accent; secondly, that the final e which terminates many English words is to be pronounced as a separate syllable, where the word following does not begin with a vowel or with the letter h; and, finally, that the past termination of the verb, ed, is almost invariably to be made a separate syllable.* Some curious traces of the old Anglo-Saxon grammar are still retained, as the inflections of the personal and possessive pronouns, together with a few details of the Teutonic formation of the verb.

* The following metrical division of the first twelve verses of *The Prologue* gives illustration of these peculiarities of accent and pronunciation :

" Whan that | April | le with | his schow | res swoot | e,
  The drought | of Marche | hath per | ced | to | the root | e,
  And ba | thud eve | ry veyne | in suich | licour
  Of which | vertue | engen | dred is | the flour ;
  Whan Ze | phyrus | eek with | his swe | te breeth
  Enspi | rud hath | in eve | ry holte | and heeth
  The ten | dre crop | pes and | the yon | ge sonne
  Hath in | the Ram | his hal | fe cours | i-ronne.
  And sma | le fow | les ma | ken me | lodie
  That sle | pen al | the night | with o | pen yhe,
  So prik | eth hem | nature | in here | corages ;—
  Thanne lon | gen folk to gon | on pil | grimages," &c.

In these verses the French accent must be given to the words *licour, vertue, nature, corages,* in order to meet the requirements of the rhythm. When Chaucer uses them they had not become Anglicized in pronunciation. *Aprille, swete, yonge, halfe, smale,* have the final e pronounced as a separate syllable, for the words succeeding them do not begin with vowels nor with the letter h ; but in *Marche, veyne, holte, nature,* the final e is silent.

NOTE.—The student will find special pleasure in studying the annotations to the *Prologue* and the *Knight's Tale,* as edited by Dr. Richard Morris, in the Clarendon Press Series, Professor Carpenter's *Literature of the XIVth Century,* James Russell Lowell's essay on Chaucer, and an essay in the Westminster Review, published in July, 1866.

Many attempts have been made to reduce Chaucer's writings to modern English, in order to introduce him to popular favor; but, to be thoroughly enjoyed, his writings must be read in their original diction. Distinguished poets have tried their skill in interpreting him, but with indifferent success. Wordsworth has adhered with tolerable fidelity to the language, and consequently to the spirit, of the original. His *Cuckoo and Nightingale*, *Prioress's Tale*, and *Troilus and Cresida*, retain much of Chaucer; but the less sympathetic minds of Dryden and Pope, in attempting to improve his expression, have impaired his sentiment.

In this chapter we have considered :--

1. Chaucer's personal appearance.

2. His social and political career.

3. His literary career.

4. His Romantic poetry.

5. His poems of the Italian type.

6. The Canterbury Tales.

7. Their incomplete execution.

8. The two classes of tales.

9. The ease with which Chaucer may be read.

CHAPTER V.

THE CONTEMPORARIES OF CHAUCER

RARE intellectual power is never monopolized by one man of a generation; it is held and displayed by a group of men. In literature a "bright particular star" does not shine forth unattended. Other stars accompany it, and shed a steady, though less brilliant, lustre over the literary firmament. Throughout the epochs of English as well as of classical literature, we find the great names grouped into distinct constellations around stars whose surpassing radiance, by attracting the gaze exclusively to themselves, often makes us insensible to the real splendor of their humble companions.

The Vision of Piers Ploughman. No writings—not even those of Chaucer himself—so faithfully reflect the popular feeling during the great social and religious movements of the fourteenth century, as the bitterly satirical poem, *The Vision of Piers Ploughman.* (11.) The deep-seated discontent of the Commons with the course of affairs in Church and State found a voice in this vigorous allegory.

Among the imitations called forth by the popularity of the *Vision* are, the *Creed of Piers Ploughman*, and the *Complaint of Piers Ploughman*. They bear resemblance to the form and spirit of their model, but in style and execution they are of much lower order. Allusions in the *Vision* to the treaty of Bretigny, made in 1360, and to the great tempest of 1362, seem to fix the later year, or thereabouts, as the time of its composition; and tradition assigns its authorship to WILLIAM * LANGLANDE, who is otherwise unknown. Two facts are clear from the work itself,—that the writer was a Churchman, and that he sympathized heartily with the rising

* The author of this work is referred to as Robert, as William, and sometimes as John Langlonde. He calls himself " William."

spirit of the laboring classes. In this work Piers Ploughman (or Peter the Ploughman) is an allegorical personage. The Latin title more exactly conveys the nature of the *Vision;* it is *Visio Willielmi de Pietro Ploughman*—a vision seen by the author, who is here called William, concerning Peter, a ploughman, who is the personification of the peasantry of England. The dreamer, exhausted by his long wanderings, goes to sleep on the Malvern Hills, and soon becomes aware of a goodly company gathered before him in a field :—

> " A fair feeld ful of folk
> Fond I there bitwene.
> Of alle manere of men,
> The meene and the riche,
> Werchynge and wandrynge."

He is somewhat puzzled at first to understand what all this may mean, when a lady, descending from a castle, announces herself as Holy Church, expounds to him the meaning of the scene that lies before him, and after leaving the key of the mystery with him, departs. The poet describes the various incidents that take place in this typical assembly, each of which shadows forth in simple allegory some move in the great game played by king, ecclesiastic, and noble. The work contains nearly fifteen thousand verses, arranged in twenty sections, so little connected with one another as to appear almost separate poems. Its prevalent tone is one of spirited satire, aimed against abuses and vices in general, but specially against the corruptions of the Church.

The *Creed of Piers Ploughman* is supposed to have been written twenty-three years later than the *Vision*. Though an imitation of the earlier work, it differs from it in many important respects. In it Piers Ploughman is no longer an allegorical character, but a real son of the soil. The author, an ardent disciple of Wycliffe, attacks the doctrines as well as the discipline of the Church, and refrains from political satire. The *Complaint of Piers Ploughman* is a mere fragment.

These three works are without regularity in the length of the lines, and without rhyme. They attempt to revive the use of alliteration, which was a distinctive feature of poetry in England previous to the introduction of rhymes by the Normans. This alliteration consists in such an arrangement and selection of the

words, that at least two of the most important words in the first
line of a couplet, and at least one word in the second line, begin
with the same letter. The opening verses of the *Vision* are given in
illustration:

> " In a *s*omer *s*eson
> Whan *s*ofte was the *s*onne,
> I *sh*oop * me into *sh*roudes,‡
> As I a *sh*eep † weere.

> " In *h*abite as an *h*eremite,
> Un*h*oly of workes,
> *W*ente *w*ide in this world
> *W*ondres to here."

The quaintness of this metrical device and the character of the
allegory indicate that the author was attempting to gain whatever
advantage there might be in a return to the ancient English style
of poetry. This poem attained great popularity when it was first
printed and was effective in advancing the principles of the Reformation.

B. 1325?] **John Gower.** But the name most closely linked
D. 1408.] with Chaucer's is that of John Gower. During the
greater part of their lives there was an intimate
friendship between these two men. In their writings they gave
each other fond praises. Chaucer dedicated *Troilus and Creseide*
to " Moral Gower; " and the first edition of the *Confessio Amantis*
(12) compliments Chaucer highly.

Gower's life was not so public, nor so full of vicissitudes, as his
friend's. He was a man of wealth, and passed his years quietly in
literary work. He seems to have enjoyed a dignified self-satisfaction in his compositions. His learning was extensive, and he was
somewhat pedantic in its display. As the French was still the
language of educated people in England, he used the alien tongue
in the *Speculum Meditantis*, a work no longer to be found. When
he undertook to describe the diseased condition of English society,
he did not adopt his native speech, but, in the *Vox Clamantis*, gave
utterance to his feelings in Latin verse. When Chaucer had shown
the capabilities of English, Gower, in his blind old age, wrote the

---

* Shaped.   † Clothes.   ‡ Shepherd.

Confessio Amantis in that tongue. This work, though not his ablest, is by far the most interesting to us. It was undertaken at the request of Richard II., to whom, the poet says,

> " Belongeth my legeaunce,
> With all mine heartes obeisaunce."

The first edition contains the celebrated passage in which Venus represents Chaucer as her disciple and poet, and expresses a wish that in his " later age" he shall "sette an end to all his werke by writing the Testament of Love." A second edition differs from the first merely in the omission of this compliment, and in the introduction of a new prologue, which ignores the memory of Richard, and dedicates the work with "entire affection" to Henry IV.

The poem consists of eight books, in addition to the Prologue; one on each of the seven deadly sins, and another on the subject of philosophy generally. It is a collection of stories, strung together on a plan much inferior to Chaucer's. This poem has a certain charm for congenial minds; but its excellences, such as they are, are balanced by many defects. It is tedious, overlaid with pedantry to a wearisome extent, and utterly without Chaucer's humor, passion, and love of nature. The author, while deploring the state of society in his time, and the offences of men in high place, is yet a stout supporter of the old order of things. His popularity with the cultivated classes continued for many generations. James of Scotland, in the fifteenth century, describes him and Chaucer as

> " Superlative as poetis laureate,
> In moralitie and eloquence ornate;"

and Shakespeare, in the sixteenth century, not only borrows from him the materials of "Pericles," but also brings him upon the stage as chorus to that play.

PROSE LITERATURE IN THE TIME OF CHAUCER.

The most meritorious writer of English prose in Chaucer's time was Chaucer himself; but his rare power in this department has been eclipsed by his transcendent genius as a poet. Of those writers whose fame depends on prose works alone, the chief are Mandeville and Wycliffe.

Sir John Mandeville (1300–1372), who is sometimes erroneously called the father of English prose, published his well-known volume of travels in 1356. Mr. Hallam calls this our earliest English book. It professes to be an authentic account of what the author saw on his travels through the most distant countries of the East, and was intended to be a guide for those who made pilgrimages to Jerusalem. A collection of marvelous tales which he has recorded, are worthy only of being classed with the adventures of Baron Munchausen. The style, however, is straightforward and unadorned, and may still be read with little difficulty. The work was exceedingly popular in its time, for it gave accounts of strange peoples and countries about which Englishmen had never heard.

In his Prologue, Mandeville recognizes the confusion of the language of literature, and says that he has " put this boke out of Latyn into Frensche, and translated it again into Englyssche, that every man of my nation may understand it."

B. 1324.] **John Wycliffe.** No name of the time will be longer
D. 1384.] remembered than that of John Wycliffe, who first gave a complete copy of the Scriptures to the English people in the English tongue. This remarkable man, of almost equally great importance in the literary and in the political history of his nation, studied at Oxford, and rose to considerable academical and ecclesiastical preferments. His life was marked by many vicissitudes. After having been alternately supported and abandoned by men of great influence, he closed his life peacefully at his Lutterworth parsonage. It was here, after his enemies had driven him from his chair at Oxford, that he commenced his great translation, which is said to have been finished about the year 1380. The influence exerted by this work upon our language cannot be overrated. Translated, as it was, from the Latin Vulgate, it makes the Latin the principal source of our theological vocabulary.

---

* A priest named Hereford assisted Wycliffe, and is believed to have been the translator of the work as far as Baruch, in the Apocrypha. The remainder of the work is attributed to Wycliffe.

Wycliffe was the first eminent scholar who used the English tongue in attacking the ecclesiastical system. He was the forerunner of the Reformation. His sermons and polemical writings must be studied by those who would form a just notion of the highest intellectual power exerted at that time.

In this chapter we have considered:-

The contemporaries of Chaucer:
1. *Langlande and his vision.*
2. *John Gower.*
3. *Sir John Mandeville.*
4. *John Wycliffe.*

CHAPTER VI.

FROM CHAUCER TO SPENSER.

THE first great manifestation of English intellectual power terminated with the death of Chaucer. A period of decay followed, in which there was no display of literary genius. For more than a hundred and fifty years not a man of eminent intellect appeared. But the invention of printing and the revival of learning remind us that, though singularly deficient in great men, the time was by no means barren in results. The spiritual activities of the nation were gathering themselves for another marvelous outburst.

Three disciples of Chaucer, **Occleve, Lydgate,** and **James I.** of Scotland, have made their names worthy of mention as writers of verse in the first half of the fifteenth century.

In the finest passage of his best attempt at poetical composition, Occleve bewails the death of his master, Chaucer,* and, but for the simple earnestness of that lament, there would be nothing in his literary work to command our esteem.

B. 1370 ?]
D. 1460 ?] John Lydgate's writings were in high repute in his own century. He furnished poetical compositions for entertainments given by companies of merchants for May-day and Christmas festivals, for the pageants provided by the corporation of the City of London, and for the masks before the

---

* "But wel away! so is mine hertè wo
That the honor of English tongue is dede,
Of which I wont was have counsel and réde.

O mayster dere and fadir reverent,
My mayster Chaucer, floure of eloquence,
Mirrour of fructuous endendement,
O universal fadir in sciènce,
Alas that thou thine excellent prudence
In thy bed mortel mighteste not bequethe!
What eyled Death? Alas! why would he sle thee!

king. Two hundred and fifty-one of these productions attributed to the prolific versifier, indicate in what esteem he was held by his own generation. For nearly fifty years this monk was the most popular English poet. His best known productions are the *Story of Thebes*, the *Destruction of Troy*, and the *Fall of Princes*. The first, a translation from Statius, a Latin poet of the first century, is given as an additional Canterbury Tale, told by Lydgate, who represents himself as having met Chaucer's pilgrims at an inn in Canterbury, and as having been allowed to return to London in their company. The *Fall of Princes* is a translation from Boccaccio, and contains the famous reference to his " maister Chaucer," " the lode-sterre of our language." The *Destruction of Troy*, a translation from a Latin prose romance, is a poem of interest, as it portrays many features of the social life of the fifteenth century.

But the most brilliant poet of the fifteenth century is James I. (1394–1436) of Scotland. In 1405, when but eleven years old, he was captured on his way from Scotland to France, and was taken to the English court. Henry IV. and his successors detained him as a prisoner for nineteen years. Happy results for himself and for his nation followed from this captivity. Adversity developed those sterling qualities of character which made him the most eminent king of the Stuart line; and the loneliness of his earlier years prompted him to seek and gain that literary culture which has made his name famous in the world of letters. In the last year of his imprisonment he wrote his best work, the *King's Quair* (a quire, or book) (**18**), a poetical record of incidents in his life, and especially of his winning his queen, Jane Beaufort, granddaughter of John of Gaunt. From the window of his prison he caught a glimpse of

" The fairest or the freschest young floure,"

as she walked with her attendants " under the Toure." The poem contains nearly fourteen hundred lines, describing his hopes and despairs, the sudden appearance of the beautiful vision of peerless loveliness, and the happy ending of his courtship. No poem of equal merit was produced in the long interval between Chaucer and Spenser. It is distinguished by tenderness of expression, and by a manly delicacy of feeling. This poet's adoption of the Chaucerian stanza ha⸱ ⸱en to that stanza the name of *rhyme royal.*

Besides these three, not a respectable versifier appeared in England during the fifteenth century; and these three are professed disciples of Chaucer. His influence over them is shown in the very stanza in which they wrote.

William Caxton. To William Caxton (1412-1491), England owes her early participation in the benefits arising from the art of printing—the greatest invention of modern times. This invention, which was nothing more than the use of movable types in place of the old engraved wooden blocks, is now generally believed to have been made by John Gutenburg, of Mentz. He conceived the plan about 1438, but on account of poverty was unable to put it into execution until twelve years afterwards, when he met with John Fust, a wealthy merchant, by whose assistance he brought out in 1455 the first printed book, the Latin Bible long known as the Mazarin. The art was introduced into England by

Caxton. His printing-press was set up at Westminster,
1474.] and its first work, the *Game of the Chesse*, appeared in 1474.

From that time until his death in 1491, Caxton labored assiduously at his vocation, giving to the world sixty-four books. The majority of his publications were in English, consisting partly of translations and partly of original works. Many of these translations are from the printer's own pen. To other books he added prefaces of his own composition, so that he is fairly entitled to a place, though not a very high one, among English authors (26).

THE PASTON LETTERS, the earliest collection of the kind in the language, form a regular series, extending from 1424 until 1509, and are so numerous that they filled five volumes on their first publication. By far the greatest number are written either by or to members of the Paston family. The collection is of great historical importance, not only from the light it throws upon some of the dark passages of English history, but also from the valuable illustrations it supplies of the domestic manners and modes of thought and action that prevailed in the fifteenth century. The inner life of the period is laid open before us; its character and spirit are revealed to us through the very thoughts and words of men then living.

The early part of the sixteenth century was marked by some

improvements in our literature, although it produced no poet of special merit. The *Pastime of Pleasure*, by STEPHEN HAWES, a favorite of Henry VII., is a dull allegorical poem; and ALEXANDER BARCLAY's *Ship of Fools* is merely a translation of the once celebrated satire of Sebastian Brandt. These works, though of little value in themselves, attest the marked progress that versification was making towards grace and harmony; and in this respect they indicate an approach to the manner of Spenser and Shakespeare.

John Skelton (1460–1529) was the most prolific versifier of this period. He represents the spirit of revolt then prevalent against ecclesiastical arrogance and authority. (**21**) Skelton was himself a member of the clerical profession. We have the testimony of Erasmus, then a resident in England, to his eminence as a scholar and man of letters. His bitter tongue, however, is said to have drawn down upon him the wrath of Cardinal Wolsey, from which he was obliged to take refuge in the Sanctuary at Westminster, where he died in 1529. His Latin poems evince much classical elegance. His serious efforts in English are exceedingly heavy and tedious; but his satiric writings, coarse and vulgar as they are, show so much force and spirit that they still retain some degree of popularity. The peculiar doggerel measure in which his satiric works are composed, and his use of the familiar speech of the people, have attracted to him a degree of attention to which his intrinsic merits by no means entitle him. He has perfectly described and exemplified the character of his " breathless rhymes " in the following passage :—

> " For though my rime be **ragged**,
> Tattered and jagged,
> Rudely raine-beaten,
> Rusty and moth-eaten,
> If ye take wel therewith,
> It hath in it some pith."

His principal attacks upon Wolsey are found in the *Booke of Colin Clout*, *Why come ye not to Court?* and the *Bouge of Court* (*i. e.*, *Bouche à Court*, diet allowed at court). Notwithstanding the admiration that is often expressed for this writer, his satirical compositions hardly rise above the dignity of lampoons. " His learning," in the opinion of Mr. Marsh, "certainly did little for the improvement of his English style; and we may say of his diction in general, that all that is not vulgar is pedantic." Throughout his writings he seems to delight in alluding to the laurel, or degree in verse, conferred upon him at Oxford.

The Early Scotch Poets. During the latter part of the fifteenth and the first years of the sixteenth century, **Blind Harry, Robert Henryson, Gawin Douglas,** and **William Dunbar** * flourished. It is to Scotland and to these men that we look for the best English poetry during the time when the poets of England were in a state of torpor. They were the successors of James I. of Scotland, and the only men in the two generations before Surrey, whose song is worthy of mention.

Poetry in the first half of the Sixteenth Century. The poems of Wyatt and Surrey, though inferior to Skelton's works in force and vivacity, are superior in grace and elegance. They give the earliest indications of the dawn of the brightest day that English literature has seen. Although unequal in merit, they possess so much in common, and there is such marked similarity in their manner, that their names are closely associated.† The higher place is invariably assigned to the younger, **Henry Howard,** Earl of Surrey (1517–1547), whose early, unmerited death on the scaffold, has deepened the romantic interest that surrounds his name (**23, 24**). His contributions to poetry are not very extensive, but are of considerable importance, as well from their excellence as from the new metrical form and style in which many of them are written

---

* Mr. Craik says that "this admirable master, alike of serious and of comic song, may justly be styled the Chaucer of Scotland, whether we look to the wide range of his genius, or to his eminence in every style over all the poets of his country who preceded and all who for ages came after him. Burns is certainly the only name among the Scottish poets that can yet be placed on the same line with that of Dunbar; and even the inspired ploughman, though the equal of Dunbar in comic power, and his superior in depth of passion, is not to be compared with the older poet either in strength or in general fertility of imagination."

† "Henry, Earl of Surrey, and Sir Thomas Wyat, between whom I finde very little difference, I repute them for the two chief lanternes of light to all others that have since employed their pennes upon English Poesie; their conceits were loftie, their stiles stately, their conveyance cleanly, their termes proper, their metres sweete and well proportioned."—*Puttenham,* 1589.

To Surrey we owe two great literary innovations—the introduction of the sonnet, and the use of polished blank verse—
and he was the first to write in that involved style, which so
strikingly distinguishes the language of Shakespeare from that
of Chaucer. A version of the second and fourth books of the
Æneid, in what Milton called "English heroic verse without
rhyme," numerous sonnets on many subjects, chiefly amatory;
a satire on the citizens of London, together with paraphrases of
Ecclesiastes and some of the Psalms, constitute the main portion
of his writings. The fanciful theories of some later editors have
attached an undue significance to his connection with "the fair
Geraldine," in whose honor many of his best sonnets were written.

Sir Thomas Wyatt (1503–1542), though fourteen years older than
his friend, is generally regarded as his poetical disciple; but he is
undoubtedly a poet of a much lower type (22). He, too, composed many songs and sonnets on the one inexhaustible topic—
love. His satires and his metrical versions of the Penitential
Psalms supply an additional point of resemblance between himself
and Surrey. In both, the highly beneficent influences of an acquaintance with Italian literature are manifest; influences which
affected the entire structure and spirit of English poetry for more
than a century, imparting to it a smoothness and melody unknown
before, without impairing in the slightest degree its native strength
and manliness of tone. Their collected works were first published
ten years after Surrey's death.

English Ballads. The stirring English ballads belong to the
close of the fifteenth century. Their language is simple, their
verse rude, their thoughts rugged; they are full of sympathy for
the outlaw, yet they have a charm for those who delight in the
expressions of simple-hearted human nature. They were composed,
nearly all of them, in this comparatively barren period of English
literature, between the time of Chaucer and the time of Spenser.
Anarchy in the state, tyranny, and the constant warfare waged
along the Scottish Border, were among the causes which stirred the
rude poets to a recital of their loves and hatreds. Tradition
saved these compositions for us. They were not gathered into a
volume until the latter part of the eighteenth century, when
Bishop Percy brought them together, thinking that they might fur-

nish material for missing chapters in the history of our language. As we read his *Reliques of Ancient English Poetry*, the old minstrels place us under a spell, and, for the time, make us forgetful of the fascination of the modern poets. We are transported back to the days of rude life in England. We sup, and watch, and fight, and love with the brave, lawless yeomen. Strive as they may, our poets of a nobler civilization cannot produce companion-pieces to the *Ancient Ballad of Chevy Chase*, or to *Adam Bell, Clym of the Clough, and William of Cloudesley*. "Young Lochinvar" and "Sheridan's Ride" are spirited, but they do not approach the old ballads in graphic terseness, in poetic simplicity, in fiery fervor, in tenderness of pathos. The reproduction of such poetry is prevented by the civilization of this age. Law, not lawlessness, is honored now. Personal prowess, reckless daring, are dangerous to society in this day; they gave protection to little bands in the English wood; they received the grateful applause of men who lived amid the perils of the Scottish Border. It was the hardihood of this age that produced the old ballads. Many of them appear in two forms: the early genuine verses in their original rudeness, and a later edition, in which some versifier has endeavored to smooth and polish their crudities. These attempts at improvement invariably dissipate the energy of the original. To appreciate the spirit of these poems, they should be read in the earlier forms. For example, the familiar *Ballad of Chevy Chase* is an attempt at improving an old ballad; yet the old song (**32**) is superior in vigor, in vivacity, and is far more inspiring to the fancy. A few stanzas may illustrate its energy :

> " The Persè owt* of Northombarlande,†
> And a vowe to God mayd he,
> That he wolde hunte in the mountayns
> Off chyviat within‡ dayes thre,
> In the mauger § of doughti Doglas,
> And all that ever with him be.

> " The fattiste hartes in all cheviat
> He sayd he wold kill and cary them away;
> ' Be my feth,' sayd the doughti Doglas agayn,
> I wyll let ‖ that hontyng yf that I may.'

* Came out.	† The land north of the Humber.	‡ During.
§ In spite of.	‖ Hinder.	

> " Then the Persè owt of Banborowe cam,
>   With him a myghtye meany,*
>   With fifteen hundrith archares bold;
>   The wear chosen out of shyars † thre."

There follows a description of the foray, beginning on a Monday
morning, of the scattering of the huntsmen, of the gathering and
dressing of the deer, of the alert watchers, of the oncoming of
Douglas and his men, of the brave parley before the fight, of the
onset, of the bloody death of the two leaders, and of the unyielding
struggle until the sun went down with the battle not yet over.
The woe of bereaved women is touchingly depicted; and then the
poem closes as boldly and as bluntly as it began. It was of this
ballad that Sir Philip Sidney said, "I never heard the old song of
Percy and Douglas, that I found not my heart more moved than
with a trumpet."

The minstrelsy of the border counties has greater energy than
that of the southern provinces of England.

B. 1480.]   Prose-writers in the first half of the Sixteenth
D. 1535.] Century. Sir Thomas More stands pre-eminent
                among the English prose-writers of his time. He was
a man of profound scholarship, of earnest piety, and of irrepressible
good-humor. When he was yet in his youth it was said of him,
" There is but one wit in England, and that is young Thomas
More." The progressive scholars of the day applauded him when
he appeared, against desperate opposition, as a champion for
the introduction of the study of Greek into the universities of
England. The eminent Erasmus was his devoted and admiring
friend. He gained one position after another as a servant of the
state, until he reached the bench of the Lord Chancellor. But
when he ventured to thwart the purposes of Henry VIII. by refusing
to acknowledge the validity of that monarch's marriage to Anne
Boleyn, neither the eminence of his position nor his former intimacy
with the king could save him from a cruel death. Disaster did not
disturb his serene good-humor.‡ Disgrace, imprisonment, and

---

* A strong company.   † Shires.

‡ " On the eve of the fatal blow he moved his beard carefully from the block.
Pity that should be cut,' he was heard to mutter with a touch of the old, sad
irony, ' that has never committed treason.' "

threatening danger were brightened by his genial wit; and even as he climbed the scaffold to bow beneath the headsman's axe, he gayly said, "I pray you see me safe up; and for my coming down let me shift for myself."

Sir Thomas More's fame as a writer rests upon two works. The one most remarkable, on account of its literary style, is his *Life of Edward V.*, a work pronounced by Mr. Hallam "the first example of good English language—pure and perspicuous, well chosen, without vulgarisms or pedantry." But his best known work, the *Utopia*, written in Latin, is known to most modern readers through Burnet's translation. The work is full of fancy and invention. It is a romantic description of the ideal state of a republic on an island, where the laws and social and political usages are in strict accordance with philosophical perfection. Many of its suggestions are far in advance of the author's time. Every house has its spacious garden; every citizen understands agriculture, and is expert at some trade; six hours of work, no more no less, is allowed. There are no taverns in that happy land; and change of fashion, frivolity, cruelty, and wars are unknown. Utopia, the name of the republic, signifies "No land" (*ov' τοπος*). More's other works are not numerous. They are controversial, and are expressions of his ardent attachment to the Roman Catholic religion. Tradition assigns him a place among the most eminent of English orators.

Lord Berners's translation of Froissart's "Chronicle," published in 1523, should be mentioned among the best English prose writings of the early part of the sixteenth century.

The development of historical literature is by successive stages. Its earliest expression in the ancient as well as in the modern world, is legendary, and its form is poetical. The legends are succeeded by chronicles, and after ages of civilization the chronicles furnish the historian with the rude materials for his work. Thus, in the development of our historical literature, we have fabulous British legends, the chronicles of the monk and the *trouvère*, the systematically compiled narrative, and the philosophical treatise of the modern historian. In the pages of **Robert Fabyan** and of **Edward Hall** we find the first attempts made by English writers at a studied literary discussion of past events. Fabyan, an alderman and sheriff of London, gathers the mythical semi-mythical, and authentic events of English history, and re duces them to a regular narrative, called the *Concordance of Historyes.* Hall, a judge in the same city, under the title of the *Union of the Two Noble and Illustrate Families of York and Lancastre*, gives a history of England under these two royal families, and down to the year 1532. These writings, though totally devoid of any pretensions to history in the genuine sense of the word, are valuable, not only as storehouses of facts for modern narrators, but also as monuments of the language, and as examples of the popular sympathies of the time.

The *Toxophilus* of **Roger Ascham** (1515–1568), published in 1545, was written to revive decaying interest in the use of the bow, and is distinguished by quiet dignity of style and manliness of spirit. It is composed in the form of a dialogue between Philologus and Toxophilus. Eighteen years afterwards, when tutor to Queen Elizabeth, this same author brought out his more important work, *The Schoolmaster*, which is still valuable for the principles and rules of teaching therein expounded. For a learned man to write a scholarly book in the English language, at the middle of the sixteenth century, was a startling innovation, and therefore Ascham presents the following apology in the preface of his work:—

" As for the Latin or Greek tongue, everything is so excellently done in them that none can do better; in the English tongue, contrary, everything in a manner so meanly, both for the matter and handling, that no man can do worse. . . . . He that will write well in any tongue must follow the counsel of Aristotle, to speak as the common people do, to think as wise men do, as so should every man understand him, and the judgment of wise men allow him."

Tyndale's Version of the Scriptures. More than a century had passed since Wycliffe made his translation of the Bible. Meanwhile the language had so changed that Wycliffe's version was intelligible to but few English readers. There was great demand for a printed Bible. Englishmen wished to read the book for themselves. The nation was agitated upon religious subjects, and was on the verge of the Reformation. William Tyndale, burning with the desire to put the Word of God within the reach of the hum-

B. 1477?]
D. 1536.]

blest of his countrymen, set himself to the work of translating the
New Testament from the Greek. After many discouragements his
work was accomplished, and the first edition was printed at
Cologne and Worms in 1525. Its publication was hailed with
delight. Threats and severe penalties could not prevent men from
selling and buying it. The King of England frowned, the Church
pronounced its curses; but all in vain, for the people were determined to possess the book. Knowing that persecution and death
would stop his working, should he return to his own country,
Tyndale remained on the Continent. He was diligently translating
the Old Testament. *The Five Books of Moses* and *An English
Version of the Book of Job* were completed by him. At last he was
treacherously delivered to officers who were searching for him,
and, after eighteen months of imprisonment, he was tried at the
Castle of Vilvoord, near Brussels, was convicted of heresy, was
strangled and burned at the stake. In the agony of dying he gave
expression to the faith which had prompted his earnest efforts, as
he prayed, "O Lord, open the King of England's eyes!" All
critics accord praise to the literary excellence of Tyndale's work.
His language is pure and simple. His style is energetic. He has
done more than any other to establish our idioms and our diction.
All English translators of the Bible since his day have imitated
him closely. In his Lectures on the English Language, Professor
Marsh says,—

"Tyndale's translation of the New Testament is the most important philological monument of the first half of the sixteenth
century, perhaps I should say of the whole period between Chaucer
and Shakespeare, both as a historical relic, and as having more
than anything else contributed to shape and fix the sacred dialect,
and establish the form which the Bible must permanently assume
in an English dress."

1535.] **Miles Coverdale,** Bishop of Exeter, has the glory of
publishing the first *printed copy of the whole Bible.* It
lacks the simplicity and energy of Tyndale's version.

By this time the popular demand for the Scriptures, and the
impossibility of suppressing their publication, forced Henry VIII.
to name an authorized version. It appeared in 1537, bearing
the fictitious name of Thomas Matthews as its translator. John
Rogers, the "proto-martyr," who had been a co-worker with

Tyndale, was the real translator. In 1539, " The Great Bible " was issued, intended for use in the churches; and in the following year, without alteration, save that of a preface by Archbishop Cranmer, it appeared as the only authorized Scriptures of the English Church. From " Cranmer's Bible " were taken the passages of Scripture used in the English Prayer-Book.

King James's Version of the Scriptures. The common English version of the Scriptures, the most remarkable of Bible translations, was made by a company of forty-seven scholars who did their work at the request of King James I. The version was published in 1611.

In this chapter we have considered:—

1. *The Period from Chaucer to Spenser.*
2. *William Caxton and John Skelton.*
3. *The Early Scotch Poets.*
4. *Poetry in the first half of the Sixteenth Century.*
5. *English Ballads.*
6. *Prose-writers in the first half of the Sixteenth Century—Sir Thomas More.*
7. *The Development of Historical Literature.*
8. *Tyndale's Version of the Scriptures.*
9. *Miles Coverdale.*
10. *King James's Version of the Scriptures.*

CHAPTER VII.

THE NON-DRAMATIC ELIZABETHAN POETS.

"THE ELIZABETHAN AGE" is marked by features which give it peculiar distinction in the history of the literary world. The language had just reached its thorough development. Thought was rejoicing in a recent and sudden emancipation. The writers were men of originality and of high intellectual culture, who found the ancient and foreign literatures filled with materials and imagery which had not yet had time to become commonplace for English readers. They united freshness and dignity in their poetry and in their prose. The art of printing, just made available, enabled them to address the people. The literary activity begun in the reign of Elizabeth was carried on through the reign of James I.

But the progress of this age was not in literature alone. There was an awakening of the people to general social improvement. Life was recognized as worth enjoying, and its enjoyment was found in a new way of living. Comforts were invented and used.*

* Holinshed, writing at the beginning of Elizabeth's reign, says: "There are old men yet dwelling in the village where I remain which have noted three things to be marvellously altered in England within their sound remembrance. One is the multitudes of chimneys lately erected; whereas in their young days, there were not above two or three, if so many, in the most uplandish towns of the realm (the religious houses and manor places of their lords always excepted, and peradventure some great personage); but each made his fire against a reredosse in the hall, where he dined and dressed his meat. The second is the great amendment of lodging; for said they, 'our fathers and we ourselves have lain full oft upon straw pallets, covered only with a sheet, under coverlets made of dogswaine, and a good round log under their heads instead of a bolster.' . . . . As for servants, if they had any sheet *above* them it was well, for seldom had they any under their bodies to keep them from the pricking straws that ran oft through the canvass and rased their hardened hides. The third thing they tell us of is the exchange of treene platters (so called, I suppose, from tree or wood) into pewter, and wooden spoons into silver or tin. For so common were all sorts of treene vessels in old time, that a man should hardly find four pieces of pewter (of which one was peradventure a salt) in a good farmer's house."

Houses were built upon improved plans. There was wonderful improvement in the use of materials. In this startling age the national mind was interested in questions of state. For the first time the average Englishman was using his brain. Society was active, thoughtful, aspiring; and its influence upon those who had genius for letters was stimulating. The writers who shine in the literary splendor of the Elizabethan age were the natural product of the newly awakened, thoughtful English nation of that day.

The first name that gains a lasting distinction is that of **Thomas Sackville,** Lord Buckhurst, (1536–1608), who won lasting fame as the author of the first English tragedy. He planned a work entitled *A Mirror for Magistrates.* It was to narrate in verse a series of tragic stories drawn from the history of England. These narratives were to serve as lessons of virtue, and as warnings to future kings and statesmen. Other, and dreary poets carried out the details of Sackville's ingenious ·plan. In 1559 the first edition of the work appeared. Other editions followed, each succeeding one containing new contributions of verse, until the sixth edition, published in 1571, was of enormous bulk. Although the work was admired in its own day, it has not sufficient poetical merit to attract the attention of the modern reader. Sackville himself wrote the *Induction* (the introduction) and the *Complaint of Henry, Duke of Buckingham;* and by these parts he saved the work from utter stupidity. These poetic passages were written in his early life, and they are all that he has contributed to literature. They fill but a small place on the printed page, yet they are so far superior to what was written by the contemporaneous poets of his early life, that we may appropriately style him herald of the splendors of the Elizabethan Literature. After his early manhood all his years were crowded with the cares of state.

Sir Philip Sidney (1554–1586) exerted a potent influence over the spirit of his age. The qualities of his character commanded the loving respect of all men. His tastes were scholarly, his love for virtue was intense, he was magnanimous, he had heroic traits, and after living nobly he died a hero. His definition of gentlemanliness—" high erected thoughts seated in a heart of courtesy "— might be pronounced the fitting description of his manliness. In his own time and until the present day he has been regarded as the model English gentleman. The charm of his life has led to an over-estimate of the worth of his writings. His contributions to our literature consist of a small collection of sonnets called *Astrophel and Stella* (**44**); a prose romance entitled *The Countess of Pembroke's Arcadia*; and *A Defence of Poesy* (**55.**) The sonnets have a languid elegance. The Arcadia, full of the spirit of chivalry, though it would be tedious to the devoted reader of Scott or Dickens, was popular in the days of Shakespeare, and was the most charming of books to the people of leisure and fashion in the first half of the seventeenth century. Sidney's *Defence of Poesy* is the work on which his fame in literature now rests. It is an attempt to set forth the worth of the poet, and was written in opposition to the doctrine of the radical Puritans of that day, who, in their fanatical zeal, denounced whatever contributed to a taste for the beautiful.

———————

EDMUND SPENSER.

"Our sage and serious Spenser."—*Milton.*

"Milton has acknowledged to me that Spenser was his original."—*Dryden.*

"There is something in Spenser that pleases one as strongly in one's old age as it did in one's youth."—*Pope.*

"Do you love Spenser? I love him in my heart of hearts."—*Southey.*

"The poetry of Spenser is remarkable for brilliant imagination, fertile invention, and flowing rhythm; yet with all these recommendations, it is cold and tedious."—*Chateaubriand.*

"Spenser seems to me a most genuine poet, and to be justly placed after Shakespeare and Milton, and above all other English poets."—*Mackintosh.*

"We must not fear to assert, with the best judges of this and former ages, that Spenser is still the third name in the poetical literature of our country, and that he has not been surpassed, except by Dante, in any other."—*Hallam.*

"Among the numerous poets belonging exclusively to Elizabeth's reign, Spenser stands without a class and without a rival. . . . . There are few eminent poets in the language who have not been essentially indebted to him."—*Campbell.*

"One unpardonable fault, the fault of tediousness, pervades the whole of the *Faerie Queene.* We become sick of cardinal virtues and deadly sins, and long for the society of plain men and women. Of the persons who read the first canto, not one in ten reaches the end of the first book, and not one in a hundred perseveres to the end of the poem."—*Macaulay.*

"But some people will say that all this (the *Faerie Queene*) may be very fine, but they cannot understand it on account of the allegory. They are afraid of the allegory, as if they thought it would bite them; they look at it as a child looks at a dragon, and think it will strangle them in its shining folds. This is very idle. If they do not meddle with the allegory, the allegory will not meddle with them. Without minding it at all, the whole is as plain as a pike-staff."—*Hazlitt.*

T HE only non-dramatic poet of the Elizabethan age who
could rank by the side of the best poets of this century was the illustrious Edmund Spenser. After
B. 1553.] the long and dreary interval of nearly two
D. 1599.] centuries, he appeared as the worthy successor
to Chaucer. He was born in London about 1553. During
his youth he lived in humble circumstances. He was educated at the University of Cambridge. After acquiring
much genuine culture at the university, he began his brilliant and unhappy career as a man of letters. Two years
were spent in the north of England, where he wrote the
Shepherd's Calendar, finding in its composition some solace
for his grief and disappointment as a lover.* At Cambridge
he had formed an intimate friendship with Gabriel Harvey,
a man of learning and of considerable literary reputation.
This friend summoned Spenser from the north of England
to London, and introduced him to Sir Philip Sidney. Sidney welcomed the poet to his house, treated him with the
utmost kindness, and cheered him on in his literary ambition. At Sidney's mansion Spenser revised his Shepherd's
Calendar, and, under the title of the *Poet's Year,* dedicated

---

* "Early in Spenser's life he had worshipped a fair Rosalind, whose faithless trifling with him and eventual preference of a rival are recorded in the *Shepherd's Calendar.* E. K. (supposed to be Edward Kirke) tells us that 'the name being well ordered will betray the *very name* of Spenser's love,' whence it has been conjectured that she was a lass of the name of *Rosa Lynde.* . . . He remained some twelve or fourteen years without thoughts of marriage. But in the years 1592–3 he fell in with an Elizabeth (her surname is lost), towards whom his heart turned; and after a courtship set forth in his *Amoretti* or sonnets, he married her in 1594. His wife was of lowly origin. 'She was certes but a country lasse,' but beautiful—'so sweet, so lovely, and so mild as she.' Her eyes were 'sapphires blue,' her hair of 'rippling gold.'"—*Clarendon Press Series—The Faery Queene,* p. 8

it to "Maister Philip Sidney, worthy of all titles, both of chivalry and poesy." He was anxious to win the patronage of some great person who would enable him to devote his life to literary pursuits. In our day, such an ambition would be considered unmanly and servile; but it must be remembered that before Shakespeare no man had been able to earn his bread by literary work. Whoever had love for letters, if he were a poor man, must either quench that love or secure the patronage of wealth. Spenser's object was well-nigh accomplished when Sidney became his friend. Sidney presented him to Dudley, Earl of Leicester, the favorite of Elizabeth, and Dudley brought him under the notice of the Queen. To her Spenser paid his literary homage, gaining her applause, and receiving an appointment in Ireland in 1580.

His residence in Ireland. Six years afterwards, a grant of about three thousand acres of confiscated lands, not far from Cork, was given to him. Kilcolman Castle was his residence; and there, surrounded by the charms of wonderfully beautiful scenery, but far removed from the society of men of letters, and bitterly hated by the Irish peasantry, he composed the most important of his poetical works. In 1591 a pension of fifty pounds a year was decreed to him by the Queen. Occasional visits from English gentlemen and infrequent journeys to England relieved the monotony of his secluded life. In 1598 Tyrone's Rebellion broke out in the southern part of Ireland. English residents could look for no mercy from the insurgents. Spenser was specially disliked by them. His castle was attacked and burned, and his infant child perished in the flames. Overwhelmed by his misfortune and his grief, the poet hastened to London, where he died in January, 1599. There was great pomp at his funeral. "Poets attended upon his hearse, and mournful elegies, with the pens that wrote them, were thrown into his tomb." He was buried in Westminster Abbey, near the tomb of Chaucer. The years of his life were almost coincident with the years of the reign of the great Queen.*

His literary purpose. Spenser's avowed aim was to write in the spirit of Chaucer and Piers Ploughman, rather than after the spiritless versifiers of the fifteenth century. His first fame was gained by the publication of the *Shepherd's Calendar*. This work is a series of pastorals, divided into twelve parts, a part for each month, in which, as in Virgil's Bucolics, the imaginary interlocutors discuss questions of morality and of state. By depicting English scenery, and by selecting English names for his rustics, he endeavored to give a national air to these eclogues. They abound in fine descriptions of nature. Towards their close he anticipates the greater glory that will be found in his later writing. The work was thought by his contemporaries to mark an epoch in literature. In language and in sentiment it was more rustic than pastoral poetry had been.

The Faery Queene, (38–42) Spenser's greatest work, is the latest and most brilliant poetical expression of the sentiments of chivalry. Whatever charms may be in allegory, in graphic narration, in splendid description, are found in this extended, though incomplete poem. The original plan proposed twelve books of moral adventures, each book recounting the exploit of a knight and the triumph of a virtue. The hero of the entire poem was Prince Arthur, the

* " Short curling hair, a full moustache, close-clipped beard, heavy eyebrows, and under them thoughtful brown eyes, whose upper eyelids weigh them dreamily down ; a long and straight nose, strongly developed, answering to a long and somewhat spare face, with a well-formed, sensible-looking forehead ; a mouth almost obscured by the moustache, but still showing rather full lips, denoting feeling, well set together, so that the warmth of feeling shall not run riot, with a touch of sadness in them. Such is the look of Spenser, as his portrait hands it down to us. A refined, thoughtful, warm-hearted, pure-souled Englishman."—*Clarendon Press Series—The Faery Queene*, p. 10.

legendary type of noble manhood, who was to be perfected in twelve *moral* virtues. The poet purposed, if this work succeeded, to write a second, in which the *political* virtues of the hero should be sung. But six of the first twelve books were published. Tradition asserts that the latter portion was completed and lost at sea; but it is probable that the design was never executed. That the work is incomplete need not be regretted; for the vigor, invention, and splendor found in the first three books decline in the fourth, fifth, and sixth. The reader has keen sympathy for the toiling patience which polished and decorated even the most obscure parts of the poem. This very fidelity to details probably prevented the completion of the work.

The Argument of the Poem. The hero, Prince Arthur, arriving at the court of the Faery Queene, in Fairy-Land, finds her holding a solemn festival during twelve days. At the court there is a beautiful lady, for whose hand twelve most distinguished knights are rivals; and in order to settle their pretensions these twelve heroes undertake twelve separate adventures, which furnish the materials for the action. The First Book relates the expedition of the Red-Cross Knight, who is the allegorical representative of *Holiness,* while his mistress Una represents true *Religion ;* and the action of the knight's exploit shadows forth the triumph of Holiness over the enchantments and deceptions of Heresy. The Second Book recounts the adventures of Sir Guyon, or *Temperance ;* the Third, those of Britomartis—a female champion—or *Chastity.* Each of these books is subdivided into twelve cantos; consequently the poem, even in the imperfect form under which we possess it, is extremely voluminous. The publication of these three books was long delayed on account of the unfavorable criticism of Harvey; but in 1589, Sir Walter Raleigh visited Spenser, heard the fragment of the poem, gave it enthusiastic applause, and persuaded the author to go with him to England in order that what was written might be given to the public without delay.*

The three books appeared in 1590, and were dedicated to Elizabeth. He returned to Ireland to prosecute his work, and in 1596 published the fourth, fifth, and sixth books, allegories of *Friendship, Justice*, and *Courtesy*.

The quality of his poetry. There are no blazing passages of passion in Spenser's writing. " He has auroral lights in profusion, but no lightning." † We may smile or we may be saddened in reading him, but we neither laugh nor weep. The power of his genius is displayed in an unequaled richness of description. He describes *to the eye*. To the airy conceptions of allegory he gives the distinctness of real objects.

Those who would read him with the intensest delight ‡ must not try to interpret the allegory. They must yield themselves to the magic of his imagination. Though tiresome to many a reader, he is the most enchanting of poets to one who is endowed with a lively fancy. He is justly called " the poet's poet."

* " When we conceive Spenser reciting his compositions to Raleigh in a scene so beautifully appropriate, the mind casts pleasing retrospect over that influence which the enterprise of the discoverer of Virginia and the genius of the author of the *Faery Queene* have respectively produced in the fortune and language of England. The fancy might easily be pardoned for a momentary superstition that the genius of their country hovered, unseen, over their meeting, casting her first look of regard on the poet that was destined to inspire her future Milton, and the other on her maritime hero, who paved the way for colonizing distant regions of the earth, where the language of England was to be spoken, and the poetry of Spenser to be admired."—*Thomas Campbell.*

† Whipple.

‡ " ' Much depends,' says Charles Lamb, ' upon *when* and *where* you read a book. In the five or six impatient minutes before the dinner is quite ready, who would think of taking up the *Faery Queene* for a stop-gap?' Select rather a June morning, when the brilliant white clouds are sailing slowly through a blue sky, a grassy bank under a tree, looking down a long valley with broken hills in the distance; let mind and body both be at ease, and both be disposed to dream, but not to sleep, and when the influences of nature have had their due effect, open, if you please, at the middle of the Legend of Sir Guyon."—*Professor F. J. Child.*

No poetry can be more uniformly and exquisitely musical than Spenser's. The richness of the sound, the sweetness of the rhythm, would surfeit the ear and make the verse enervate, were he not a master who modulates the sound, and paints the pictures for the fancy. The stanza he used, named after him the *Spenserian*, consists of nine lines, and is formed by adding an Alexandrine to Chaucer's stanza of eight lines. It demands a frequent recurrence of the same rhymes—four of one ending, three of another, and two of a third—and in supplying this demand throughout the poem, Spenser was obliged to do violence to the orthography and accentuation of the language, to use many archaic and provincial words, and even, in some cases, to invent the word that should furnish his verse with the needed rhyme. His vocabulary was considered pedantic by his contemporaries. His peculiarities have affected the language less than those of any other great writer.

Whenever Spenser was not playing the part of a courtier he manifested a retiring spirit. He was imaginative rather than observant. Still he has sympathy with the spirit of his nation. Throughout his works there are allusions to her greatness and warm applause for her championship of justice and progress, and there is a breathing of the purest loyalty for the nation's queen.

Among the more important of his minor poetical works are *Mother Hubberd's Tale*, a satire, written in his youth, upon the hypocrisy of certain classes of the clergy, and upon the heartlessness of the life at court; *Daphnaida* and *Astrophel*, elegies on the deaths of Lady Howard and Sir Philip Sidney; and above all his *Epithalamium*, written in celebration of his own marriage to the "fair Elizabeth," the chastest and most beautiful marriage-hymn to be found in the whole range of literature. The ardor of his love transfused it with a rapture not found elsewhere in his verse. Hallam says of it,—"It is a strain redolent of a bridegroom's

joy, and of a poet's fancy. The English language seems to
expand itself with a copiousness unknown before, while he
pours forth the varied imagery of this splendid little poem."

Spenser has left one work which displays his energy and
skill as a writer of prose. It is *A View of the State of Ireland*, setting forth his estimate of the character and condition of the Irish people, and recommending a severe and
cruel policy to the English government.*

Spenser's Contemporaries. Samuel Daniel (1562–1619), who
is said to have succeeded Spenser as Poet Laureate, enjoyed among
his contemporaries a respect merited by his talents and by his character. His life was quiet and studious. He wrote many lyrics, a
few dramatic compositions, a poem on the contest between the
houses of York and Lancaster (46), and a *History of England from
the Conquest to the Reign of Richard II.* His language is pure,
limpid, and free from the affectation of archaism, which is found
in Spenser's writing.

Michael Drayton (1553–1631) was an industrious poet; also
much admired by his contemporaries. His longest and most celebrated work, entitled *Polyolbion* (48), is a poetical ramble over
England and Wales, and is unique in literature. In thirty ponderous cantos, containing fifteen thousand monotonous Alexandrine
couplets, he enthusiastically, but with painful accuracy, describes
the rivers, mountains, and forests of his country, giving also detailed accounts of local legends and antiquities. Many poetic passages are found in the work. Among his other writings are *The
Barons' Wars*, a poem describing the principal events of the unhappy
reign of Edward II., *England's Heroical Epistles*, letters supposed
to have been written by illustrious Englishmen to the objects of
their love, and the exquisite *Nymphidia* (47), in which everything

---

* The following generally accessible works contain specially interesting discussions of the life and writings of Spenser :

Whipple's *Literature of the Age of Elizabeth*, The Introduction to the Clarendon
Press edition of the *Faery Queene*, the Memoir in Professor Child's Edition of
Spenser's works, Hallam's *Literature of Europe*, Taine's *English Literature*, Black-
wood's Magazine for November, 1833, Campbell's Specimens of English Poetry
Hazlitt's Lectures on the English Poets, Lectures II. and III.

that is delicate, quaint, and fantastic in fairy mythology is accumu lated, and touched with consummate felicity.

Giles and Phineas Fletcher. The success of Spenser led many aspirants to seek poetical fame in allegorical composition. Two brothers, Giles (1588–1623) and Phineas Fletcher (1584–1650), cousins of Beaumont's colleague, were the only imitators who had enough of Spenser's spirit to copy him with any success. The first published a poem entitled *Christ's Victory and Triumph* (53); the second, under the title of *The Purple Island,* wrote an allegorical description of the human body and mind. But allegorical anatomy, however skilfully managed, is not attractive to the reader. When the veins and arteries of the body are described as brooks and rivers of blood, poetical fancy cannot redeem verse from the ludi-crous misuse.

English Satire. The origin of English poetical satire is gener ally assigned to this age. Many passages, indeed, of social and personal invective are found in earlier writers; Chaucer's pictures of the monastic orders abound in open and implied censure; both the spirit and matter of Langlande's work are satirical; but it neither of these authors is satire an essential characteristic; a cer tain infusion of it was inevitable to the task they undertook, but it was far from being a primary condition. Skelton was too ribald, too full of mere venom and spite against individuals, to be ranked as anything more than a mere lampooner; and Surrey and Wyatt pointed out the way to this kind of composition without following it themselves. The first English writer who distinctly calls him-self a satirist is **Joseph Hall** (1574–1656) (118); and the general opinion of later critics has acquiesced in his assertion. In 1597, fresh from Cambridge, he published three books of *biting satires,* and two years afterwards, three more of *toothless satires.* To the collective work he gave the name of *Virgidemarium,* or a har-vest of rods (51). These poems seem to fulfill all the conditions of satire; with great energy and some humor, they attack the pre-vailing follies and affectations of both literature and social life. Though the numbers are often harsh and the meaning obscure, they possess enough of the spirit of Juvenal to make them still readable. In later life Hall won greater distinction by his sermons; and as a champion of episcopacy he ventured to grapple with Milton him-self.

The number of minor poets produced indicates the unparalleled literary activity of the Elizabethan age. As many as two hundred have been reckoned who gave evidence of skill in constructing verse.

It is, besides, a special distinction of the same age that it produced translations of unusual excellence. The finest of them, the *Iliad* and *Odyssey* of **George Chapman** (1557–1634), appeared early in the seventeenth century. They have won the enthusiastic admiration of several generations of poets, from Waller to Keats. "The earnestness and passion," says Charles Lamb, "which he has put into every part of these poems would be incredible to a reader of more modern translations."

But the grandest phenomenon of the epoch of Elizabeth is the Drama, and to it we shall now address ourselves.

In this chapter we have considered:—

1. The Non-Dramatic Poets of the Elizabethan Age,— Thomas Sackville and Sir Philip Sidney.

2. Edmund Spenser.

3. His Residence in Ireland.

4. His Literary Purpose.

5. The "Faery Queene."

6. The Argument of the Poem.

7. The Quality of the Poetry.

8. Spenser's Contemporaries,—Samuel Daniel, Michael Drayton, Giles and Phineas Fletcher, Joseph Hall, and George Chapman.

CHAPTER VIII.

THE DAWN OF THE DRAMA.

SPAIN and England alone, among modern civilized nations possess a theatrical literature independent in its origin characteristic in its form, and reflecting faithfully the moral, social and intellectual features of the people among whom it arose.

The Miracle Plays and Mysteries. The dawning of the English dramatic literature can be traced to a period not far removed from the Norman Conquest; for the custom of dramatizing the lives of the saints and striking episodes of Bible History, existed as early as the twelfth century. To these the names of Miracle Plays and Mysteries were respectively given. The earliest "Miracle" on record is the *Play of St. Catherine*, which was represented at Dunstable about 1119, written in French, and was in all **1119.**] probability a rude picture of the miracles and martyrdom of that saint. These performances were an expedient employed by the clergy for giving religious instruction to the people, and for extending and strengthening the influence of the Church. At first the plays were composed and acted by monks; the cathedral was transformed for the nonce into a theatre, the stage was a graduated platform in three divisions—representing Heaven, Earth, and Hell—rising one over the other, and the costumes were furnished from the vestry of the church. The simple faith of the dramatists and of their audience, saw no impropriety in representing the most supernatural beings, the persons of the Trinity, angels, devils, saints, and martyrs. It was absolutely necessary that some comic element should be introduced to enliven the graver scenes; and this was supplied by representing the wicked personages of the drama as placed in ludicrous situations; thus the Devil generally played the part of the clown or jester, and was exhibited in a light half terrific and half farcical. The modern puppet-play of Punch is a tradition handed down from these ancient miracles, in which the Evil One was alternately the conqueror and the victim of the human Buffoon, Jester, or Vice, as he was called. The morality of the time did not prevent the use of vulgar or of profane language.

Some idea of these religious dramas may be formed from their titles. The *Creation of the World*, the *Fall of Man*, the story of *Cain and Abel*, the *Crucifixion of Our Lord*, the *Massacre of the Innocents*, *The Play of the Blessed Sacrament*, the *Deluge*, are in the list, besides an infinite multitude of subjects taken from the lives and miracles of the saints. The plays are generally written in mixed prose and verse; and, though abounding in absurdities, they contain passages of simple and natural pathos, and scenes of genuine, if not very delicate humor. In the *Deluge*, a comic scene is produced by the refusal of Noah's wife to enter the Ark, and by the beating which terminates her resistance and scolding; while, on the other hand, a Mystery entitled the *Sacrifice of Isaac* contains a pathetic dialogue between Abraham and his son. The oldest manuscript of a Miracle play in English is that of the *Harrowing of Hell*, i. e., the Conquering of Hell by Christ, believed to have been written about 1350.

The Miracle play is not quite extinct even yet; in the retired valleys of Catholic Switzerland, in the Tyrol, and in some seldom visited districts of Germany, the peasants still annually perform dramatic spectacles representing episodes in the life of Christ.*

The Moralities. These plays, once the only form of dramatic representation, continued to be popular from the eleventh to the end of the fourteenth century, when they were supplanted by the Moralities. The subjects of these new dramas, instead of being purely religious, were moral, as their name implies; and their ethical lessons were conveyed by action of an allegorical kind. Instead of their Deity and his angels, the saints, the patriarchs, and the characters of the Old and New Testament, the persons who figure in the Moralities are, Every-Man, a general type or expression of humanity; Lusty Juventus, who represents the follies and weaknesses of youth; Good Counsel, Repentance, Gluttony, Pride,

* See description of the play at Oberammergau in *Harper's Monthly*, Vol. XLII. p. 174.

Avarice, and the like. The same necessity existed as before for the introduction of comic scenes. The Devil was therefore retained, and his hard blows and scoldings with the Vice, furnished many " a fit of mirth." * The oldest English Morality now extant is *The Castle of Perseverance*, which was written about 1450. It is a dramatic allegory of human life, representing the many conflicting influences that surround man in his way through the world. Another, called *Lusty Juventus*, contains a vivid and humorous picture of the extravagance and debauchery of a young heir, surrounded by the Virtues and the Vices, and ends with a demonstration of the inevitable misery which follows a departure from the path of virtue and religion.

The Interludes. Springing from the Moralities, and bearing some general resemblance to them, though exhibiting a nearer approach to the regular drama, are the Interludes, a class of compositions in dialogue, much shorter in extent and more merry and farcical. They were generally played in the intervals of a festival, and were exceedingly fashionable about the time when the great controversy was raging between the Catholic Church and the reformed religion in England. The most noted author of these grotesque and merry pieces was **John Heywood,** a man of learning and accomplishments, who seems to have performed the duties of entertainer at the court of Henry VIII. His *Four P's* is a good specimen of this phase of the drama. It turns upon a dispute between a Peddler, a Pardoner, a Palmer and a Poticary, in which each tries to tell the greatest lie. They tax their powers, until at last, by chance, the Palmer says that he never saw a woman out of temper; whereupon the others declare his lie the greatest that can be told, and acknowledge him the victor.

* "As for the Vice, he commonly acted the part of a broad, rampant jester and buffoon, full of mad pranks and mischief-making, liberally dashed with a sort of tumultuous, swaggering fun. He was arrayed in fantastic garb, with something of drollery in his appearance, so as to aid the comic effect of his action, and armed with a dagger of lath, perhaps as symbolical that his use of weapons was but to the end of provoking its own defeat. Therewithal he was vastly given to cracking ribald and saucy jokes with and upon the devil, and treating him in a style of coarse familiarity and mockery; and a part of his ordinary business was to bestride the Devil, and beat him till he roared, and the audience roared with him; the scene ending with his being carried off to Hell on the Devil's back."—*Hudson* · *Shakespeare's Life, Art and Characters,* Vol. I., p. 78.

town-halls, court-yards of inns, cock-pits, and noblemen's dining halls; and the parts were taken by amateurs. Soon, however, companies of actors, singers, and tumblers, calling themselves the servants of some nobleman whose livery they wore, were formed, and wandered about the country, performing wherever they could find an audience. Protected by the livery of their master against the severe laws which branded strollers as vagabonds, they sought the patronage of the civil authorities. Records of the municipal bodies and the household registers of illustrious families abound in entries of permissions granted to such strolling companies, and of moneys given to them. The most interesting of these entries is found in the municipal records of Stratford-upon-Avon, from which we learn that the players visited that place for the first time in 1569. Their performance was probably given under the patronage of Shakespeare's father, who was high-bailiff of the town in that year.

But in the year 1575, under the powerful patronage of the Earl

1575.]
of Leicester, James Burbadge built the first English theatre. The venture proved so successful, that twelve theatres were soon furnishing entertainment to the citizens of London. Of these the most celebrated was "The Globe." It was so named because its sign bore the effigy of Atlas supporting the globe, with the motto, "*Totus Mundus agit Histrionem*," and was situated in Southwark, near London Bridge. The majority of the London theatres were on the southern or Surrey bank of the Thames, in order to be out of the jurisdiction of the city, whose officers and magistrates, being under the influence of the severe doctrines of Puritanism, carried on a constant war against the players and the play-houses. Some of these theatres were cock-pits (the name of "the pit" still suggesting that fact); some were arenas for bull-baiting and bear-baiting; and, compared with the magnificent theatres of the present day, all were poor and squalid, retaining in their form and arrangements many traces of the old model—the inn-yard. Most of the theatres were entirely uncovered,* excepting over the stage, where a thatched roof protected the actors from the weather. The spectators were exposed to sunshine and to storm. The boxes, or "rooms," as they were

---

* Shakespeare's company owned the Blackfriars Theatre and the Globe. During the winter the company played in the former, which was the smaller and entirely roofed over; but during the summer they used the Globe.

when styled, were arranged nearly as in the present day; but the musicians, instead of being placed in the orchestra, were in a lofty gallery over the stage.

The Early Theatres. The most remarkable peculiarities of the early English theatres were the total absence of painted or movable scenery, and the necessity that the parts for women should be performed by men or boys, actresses being as yet unknown. A few screens of cloth or tapestry gave the actors the opportunity of making their exits and entrances; a placard, bearing the name of Rome, Athens, London, or Florence, as the case might be, indicated to the audience the scene of the action. Certain typical articles of furniture were used. A bed on the stage suggested a bedroom; a table covered with tankards, a tavern; a gilded chair surmounted by a canopy, and called "a state," a palace; an altar, a church; and the like. A permanent wooden structure like a scaffold, erected at the back of the stage, represented objects according to the requirements of the piece, such as the wall of a castle or besieged city, the outside of a house, or a position enabling one of the actors to overhear others without being seen himself.

Although thus scantily equipped in some respects, in costumery the early stage was lavish and splendid. "The Prologue" appeared in a long, flaming, velvet robe, made after the pattern of the Middle Ages, and all the other actors were attired in the richest dress of their own day. Its picturesqueness, instead of marring, heightened the effect. But the use of contemporary costume in plays whose action was supposed to take place in Greece, Rome, or Persia, naturally led to amazing absurdities, such as arming the assassins of Cæsar with Spanish rapiers, or furnishing Carthaginian senators with watches. Anachronisms, however, were not offensive to the uncritical spectators of those times. Certain attributes were associated with supernatural personages. A "roobe for to goo invisibell" is one of the items in an old list of properties; and in all probability the spectral armor of the Ghost in *Hamlet* was to be found in the wardrobe of the ancient theatres. The curtain is supposed to have opened perpendicularly in the middle; and besides this principal curtain, there seem to have been others occasionally drawn so as to divide the stage into several apartments.

The foregoing statements concerning the early theatre show how meagre were the material aids on which the dramatist could rely. That very poverty of the theatre was among the conditions of the excellence of the Elizabethan dramatist. He could not depend upon the painter of scenes for any interpretation of the play, and therefore he was constrained to make his thought vigorous and his language vivid.

The performance began early in the afternoon, and was announced by flourishes of a trumpet. The prologue was generally declaimed by its author, who was dressed in antique costume. Black drapery hung around the stage, was the symbol of a tragedy; and rushes strewn on the stage, enabled the best patrons of the company to sit upon the floor. Dancing and singing took place between the acts; and, as a rule, a comic ballad, sung by a clown with accompaniment of tabor and pipe and farcical dancing, closed the entertainment.

The social position of an actor and playwright, even at the end of the sixteenth century, was not enviable. He was still regarded by many as scarcely a shade removed above the " rogues and vagabonds " of former generations; but this drawback seems to have been fully compensated for by extraordinary profits. That these were unusually great is proved, not only by historical evidence, such as the frequent allusions made by the preachers and moralists of the day to the pride, luxury, and magnificence in dress of the successful performers, but also by the rapidity with which many of them, as Shakespeare, Burbadge, and Alleyn, amassed considerable fortunes.

Notwithstanding the social discredit that attached to the actor's profession, the drama reached such popularity, and the employment was so lucrative, that it soon became the common resort of literary genius in search of employment. Indeed, nothing is more remarkable than the marvelously rapid growth of this department of our literature. It passed from infancy to maturity in a single generation. Twenty years after the appearance of the first rude tragedy, the theatre entered upon the most glorious period of its history,—a period without parallel in the literature of any country. This was mainly the work of a small band of poets, whose careers all began about the same time.

Shakespeare's Early Contemporaries. They were most of them men of liberal education, but of dissolute lives. One or two of them left rural homes to seek their fortunes in London, and were lured into the new profession by the prospect of swift gain. They all possessed abilities of a high order. William Shakespeare is the giant of the group, and beside him the others dwindle into comparative insignificance. These men, George Chapman, John Lyly, George Peele, Robert Greene, Christopher Marlowe, and Thomas Kyd, are often spoken of as the predecessors of Shakespeare; but as none of them preceded him by more than a year or two, and as all were fellow-workers with him for a time, it seems proper to style them the contemporaries of his early literary life.

The careers of these men in their general outlines were the same. They attached themselves as dramatic actors and poets to one of the numerous companies, and after a short apprenticeship passed in rewriting and rearranging plays, they gradually rose to original works, written either alone or in partnership with a brother playwright. As there was no dramatic copyright at this time, the playwrights had the strongest motive for taking every precaution that their pieces should *not* be printed, publication instantly annihilating their monopoly, and allowing rival companies to profit by their labors; and this is the reason why so few of the dramas of the period, in spite of their unequaled merit and their great popularity, were given to the press during the lives of their authors. It also explains the singularly careless execution of such copies as were printed, these having been published in many cases surreptitiously, and contrary to the wishes and interests of the author. Only the briefest mention can be made of the subordinate members of this remarkable group of writers.

John Lyly (1553-1601?), educated at Oxford, a man of classical culture, composed plays for the court, and pageants. His writings exhibit genius, though strongly tinctured with a peculiar affectation, with which he infected the language of elegant conversation, and even of literature, till it fell under the ridicule of Shakespeare. This pedantic, superfine use of language is known as *Euphuism.*[*] The name was taken from the title of one of Lyly's works,

---

[*] "To this day every man who has anything of the coxcomb in his brain, who desires a dress for his thought more splendid than his thought, slides unconsciously into Euphuism."—*E. P. Whipple.*

"Euphues; the Anatomy of Wit." Without drinking from this fountain of affectation, one can know its flavor from the language of Sir Piercie Shafton, in Scott's novel, "The Monastery."

George Peele (1552–1598 ?), like Lyly, had received a liberal education at Oxford. He was one of Shakespeare's fellow-actors and fellow-shareholders in the Blackfriars Theatre. His earliest work, *The Arraynement of Paris*, was printed anonymously in 1584. His most celebrated dramatic works were *David and Bethsabe*, and *Absolon*, in which there are great richness and beauty of language, and indications of a high order of pathetic and elevated emotion. His *Edward I.* is supposed to be our first historical play.

Thomas Kyd, the "sporting Kyd," of Ben Jonson, was possibly the author of the famous play called *Jeronimo*, to which, in consequence of the many recastings it received, so many authors have been ascribed. The *Spanish Tragedy*, which is a continuation of *Jeronimo*, was undoubtedly his.

Robert Greene (1560–1592) was a Cambridge man, and the author of a multitude of tracts and pamphlets on miscellaneous subjects. Sometimes they were tales, often translated or expanded from the Italian novelists; sometimes amusing exposures of the various arts of *cony-catching*, i. e., cheating and swindling, practised at that time in London, and in which, it is to be feared, Greene was personally not unversed; sometimes moral confessions, like the *Groatsworth of Wit*, or *Never too Late*, purporting to be a warning to others against the consequences of unbridled passions. In this group of dramatists his place is next below Marlowe.

But by far the most powerful genius among them was **Christopher Marlowe** (1564–1593). On leaving the University of Cambridge he joined a troop of actors, among whom he was remarkable for vice and debauchery. His career was as short as it was disgraceful : he was stabbed in the head with his own dagger, which he had drawn in a quarrel with an antagonist, and he died of this wound at the age of thirty. His works are not numerous ; but they are strongly distinguished from those of preceding and contemporary dramatists by an air of astonishing energy and elevation—an elevation, it is true, which is sometimes exaggerated, and an energy which occasionally degenerates into extravagance. He established the use of blank verse in the English drama. His first work was the tragedy of *Tamburlaine the Great*. The declamation in this piece, though sometimes bombastic, led Ben Jonson to speak of

"Marlowe's mighty line." But in spite of the bombast, the piece contains many passages of great power and beauty. Marlowe's best work is the drama of *Faustus* (71), founded upon the same popular legend which Goethe adopted as the groundwork of his tragedy ; and though the German poet's work is on the whole vastly superior, there is certainly no passage in the tragedy of Goethe in which terror, despair, and remorse are painted with so powerful a hand as in the great closing scene of Marlowe's piece. The tragedy of the *Jew of Malta*, though inferior to *Faustus*, is characterized by similar merits and defects. The hero, Barabas, is the type of the Jew as he appeared to the rude and bigoted imaginations of the fifteenth century—a monster half-terrific, half-ridiculous, impossibly rich, inconceivably bloodthirsty, cunning, and revengeful, the bugbear of an age of ignorance and persecution. The intense expression of his rage, however, his triumph and his despair, give occasion for many noble bursts of Marlowe's powerful declamation. The tragedy of *Edward II.* (70), which was the last of this great poet's works, shows that in some departments of his art, and particularly that of moving terror and pity, he might, had he lived, have become no insignificant rival of Shakespeare himself.

Marlowe is honorably known in other departments of poetry also. His charming poem, *The Passionate Shepherd*, had the rare distinction of being quoted by Shakespeare, and of being answered in "The Nymph's Reply," by Sir Walter Raleigh.

The merits of GEORGE CHAPMAN (1557–1634) as a translator have entirely eclipsed his dramatic fame.

Richard Grant White's admirable "Account of the Rise and Progress of the English Drama to the time of Shakespeare," and Rev. H. N. Hudson's "Historical Sketch of the Origin and Growth of the Drama in England," are the finest discussions to be found by the student upon the topic treated of in this chapter.

In this chapter we have considered :—

1. The Mysteries and Miracle Plays.
2. The Moralities.
3. The Interludes.
4. The Pageants.
5. The First Regular Tragedy and Comedy.
6. The Early Theatres.
7. The Social Position of Actor and Playwright.
8. Shakespeare's Early Contemporaries.

5

CHAPTER IX.

WILLIAM SHAKESPEARE.

"I loved the man and do honor to his memory, on this side idolatry, as much as any. He was indeed honest and of an open and free nature."—*Ben Jonson.*

"Sweetest Shakespeare, Fancy's child."—*Milton.*

"But Shakespeare's magic could not copied be,
    Within that circle none durst walk but he."—*Dryden.*

"I hold a perfect comedy to be the perfection of human composition; and firmly believe that fifty Iliads and Aeneids could be written sooner than such a character as Falstaff's."—*Horace Walpole.*

"I am always happy to meet persons who perceive the transcendent superiority of Shakespeare over all other writers."—*R. W. Emerson.*

"I cannot account for Shakespeare's low estimate of his own writings, except from the sublimity, the super-humanity of his genius."—*Wordsworth.*

"Shakespeare is of no age. He speaks a language which thrills in our blood in spite of the separation of two hundred years. His thoughts, passions, feelings, strains of fancy, all are of this day as they were of his own; and his genius may be contemporary with the mind of every generation for a thousand years to come."—*Prof. Wilson.*

"More full of wisdom and ridicule and sagacity than all the moralists and satirists that ever existed, Shakespeare is more mild, airy and inventive, and more pathetic and fantastic, than all the poets of all regions and ages of the world, and has all those elements so happily mixed up in him, and bears his high faculties so temperately, that the most severe reader cannot complain of him for want of strength or of reason, nor the most sensitive, for defect of ornament or ingenuity."—*Lord Jeffrey.*

"The name of Shakespeare is the greatest in our literature—it is the greatest in all literature. No man ever came near him in the creative powers of the mind; no man ever had such strength at once, and such variety of imagination. Coleridge has most felicitously applied to him a Greek epithet, given before to I know not whom, certainly none so deserving of it,—μυριόνους, the *thousand-souled* Shakespeare."—*Hallam.*

" I think most readers of Shakespeare sometimes find themselves thrown into exalted mental conditions like those produced by music. Then they may drop the book to pass at once into the region of thoughts without words."— *O. W. Holmes.*

" Whatever other learning he wanted, he was master of two books unknown to many profound readers, though books which the last conflagration alone can destroy, —I mean the Book of Nature and that of Man."—*Edward Young.*

THE authentic biography of the most famous writer in English literature is very brief. The following facts can be positively stated about **William Shakespeare**: John and Mary Shakespeare were his parents. He was christened in the little town of Stratford-on-Avon, in Warwickshire, England, the 26th day of April, 1564. He was married when eighteen years old. Three years after his marriage he went from Stratford to London. He was an actor, and one of the proprietors of the Globe Theatre, in 1589. Ben Jonson was his intimate acquaintance. His last years were spent in his native place, where he was one of the influential citizens. He was once a plaintiff in a suit-at-law. He died on the 23d day of April, 1616.

1564.]

Tradition says that he was a man of fine form and features, that he was sometimes too convivial, that he was beloved by nearly all who knew him, that he had the personal acquaintance of Elizabeth and James I. His father, John Shakespeare, probably a glover, had married Mary Arderne, whose family had figured in the courtly and warlike annals of preceding reigns.

That John Shakespeare had been in flourishing circumstances is proved by his having long been one of the Aldermen of Stratford, and by his having served in the office of Bailiff or Mayor in 1569. Mary Arderne had brought her husband a small property. This acquisition seems to have tempted him to engage, without experience, in agricultural pursuits, which ended disastrously in his being obliged at different times to mortgage and sell, not only his farm, but even one of the houses in Stratford of which he had been owner. He at last retained nothing save that small, but now venerable dwelling, consecrated to all future ages by being the spot where the greatest of poets was born. His distresses appear to have become severe in 1579; and he was unable to extricate himself from his embarrassments, until his son had gained a position of competence, and even of affluence.

That William Shakespeare could have derived even the most elementary instruction from his parents seems impossible; for neither of them could write—an accomplishment, however, which, it should be remarked, was comparatively rare in Elizabeth's reign. But there existed at that time, and there exists at the present day, in the borough of Stratford, an endowed "free grammar-school;" and it is inconceivable that John Shakespeare Alderman and Past Bailiff as he was, should have neglected the opportunity for educating his son. This opportunity, together with the extensive though irregular reading of which his works give evidence, and the vague tradition that he had been "in his youth a schoolmaster in the country," make it probable that the poet had more training than some of his admirers would give him credit for. It has been reasonably inferred that during his early years he must have been a student in the office of a lawyer; for throughout his works he shows extraordinary knowledge of the technical language of the law.*

The most familiar of the legends concerning him represents his youth as wild and irregular, and tells of a deer-stealing expedition in company with riotous young fellows, to Sir Thomas Lucy's park at Charlcote, near Stratford. According to the story, Shakespeare was seized, brought before the indignant justice of the peace, and flogged. For this indignity he revenged himself by writing a satiric ballad and attaching it to the gates of Charlcote.† Then the wrath

* See *Atlantic Monthly*, Vol. IV., p. 84.

† For a discussion of this legend, and for a stanza of the ballad, see *White's Memoirs of Shakespeare*, p. xxxvi., seq.

of the Knight blazed so high that Shakespeare sought refuge in London, where he earned his livelihood by holding horses at the doors of the theatres, until his wit attracted the notice of the actors and gained him a position where by degrees he became a celebrated actor and author. We must discredit one part of the legend, inasmuch as boats—not horses—furnished conveyance across the Thames from the city to the theatres. But even though the story about the deer-stealing may have a foundation of truth, Shakespeare's departure from Stratford and his entrance into theatrical life in London may be explained in a different and less improbable manner. He was then twenty-two years of age. He had been married three years to Anne Hathaway, a young woman seven years his senior.* His three children had been born. It was necessary to provide means for the support of his family, and that, too, without delay; for his father's wealth was nearly gone.

His Career as a Dramatist. London was the resort for such a needy adventurer as he in search of fortune ; and the theatrical profession, with its ready reward for the successful actor, was the most advantageous calling for him. His native taste for the drama must have been attracted to that calling before this time, for troops of actors had made frequent visits to Stratford; moreover the greatest tragic actor of the day, Richard Burbadge, was a Warwickshire man, and Thomas Greene, a distinguished member of the troop of the Royal Theatre, then the first theatre in Lon-

* There are several facts which seem to indicate that the married life of the poet was not brightened by love. Bitter allusions to marriages like his own occur in his works ; during the long period of his residence in London, his wife did not live with him; and in his will he leaves her only his " second-best bed with furniture." The significance of the slighting bequest is diminished by the fact that, as his property was chiefly in land, her legal right to one-third gave her a large estate. But, on the other hand, several most tenderly loving passages in his poems seem unintelligible unless interpreted as addressed to her. For a discussion of the respective sides of this question see *White's Memoirs of Shakespeare*, p. xlix., seq., and *Hudson's Life of Shakespeare*, p. 19, seq.

don, was a native of Stratford.   And so, as the companies
of actors were always ready to enlist men of talent, it
happened that when Shakespeare arrived in London he
naturally entered the service of one of those companies.
Like other young men of that time, he made himself useful
to his company both as an actor and as a re-writer of dramatic pieces; and his early professional career probably
differed in no respect from that of Marlowe and others, save
in the industry and success with which he pursued it, and
in the prudence with which he accumulated wealth.   By
adapting old plays to the demands of his theatre he acquired
that masterly knowledge of stage-effect, and discovered the
dramatic genius, which enabled him to write the grandest
dramas in the literature of the world.   His theatrical career
continued from 1586 until 1611 (?), a period of twenty-five
years, including his youth and the dignity and glory of his
manhood.

The dramatic company to which Shakespeare belonged
was the most respectable and the most prosperous of that
time.   By carefully avoiding political allusions and by gaining the patronage of influential men, it secured unusual
freedom from the interference of the authorities of the city.
In this company Shakespeare reached a high position.   To
his good sense, prudence, and knowledge of the world its
success may have been due; for no sooner had he retired
from the theatre than repeated causes of complaint arose,
and severe penalties were inflicted by the authorities upon
his former comrades.

Shakespeare quickly rose to such importance in his profession as to call down upon him the attacks of disappointed
rivals; for, in 1592, Greene makes bitter allusion to his
name, accuses him of plagiarism, and plainly shows that
envy dictated the attack.   The scurrilous pamphlet containing this accusation was published after Greene's death,
and evidently provoked criticism by its meanness.   Chettle,

its editor, promptly published an apology, in which he says of Shakespeare,—"I am as sorry as if the originall fault had beene my fault, because myself have seene his demeanor no less civill than he exclent in the quality he professes : besides, divers of worship have reported his uprightnes of dealing which argues his honesty, and his facetious [felicitous] grace in writing that approves his art."

That he was acquainted with his art is clear from the inimitable "directions to the players" put into the mouth of Hamlet, which, in incredibly few words, contain its whole system. There is a tradition that tells of his acting the Ghost in his tragedy of *Hamlet* (81), the graceful and touching character of Adam, the faithful old servant, in his *As You Like It* (72), the deeply pathetic impersonation of grief and despair in the popular tragedy of *Hieronymo*, and the sensible citizen, Old Knowell, in Ben Jonson's *Every Man In His Humor*. John Davies, in *The Scourge of Folly*, ascribes to him some excellence in the performance of kingly characters. But the first masterly actor of the great tragic characters, Richard III., Hamlet, Othello, and the others, was Shakespeare's comrade, Richard Burbadge.

Shakespeare's reputation grew apace. Six years after his arrival in London, he had won his way to the foremost rank of literary men. He was already wielding influence. Riches were flowing into his hands. The gifted and the noble applauded him, and sought his society. The young Earl of Southampton is said to have expressed his admiration for the worth and the genius of the poet by making him the princely gift of a thousand pounds. Through succeeding years his prosperity continued. In 1597, at the age of thirty-three, he purchased "New Place," the finest house in Stratford, making it a home for his family, and a refuge for his parents.* In 1602 he purchased one hundred and seven

* It was Shakespeare's ambition to gain the rank and title of "gentleman ;" and, therefore, at about the time when he bought New Place he solicited a coat of

acres of land, and at about the same time he invested four hundred and forty pounds in the tithes of Stratford. In 1611 (?) he sold his interest in the Globe Theatre, left London, and withdrew to the quietude of his home. There five years were spent in a leisure that must have been a strange contrast to the busy, thronging cares that had attended his professional life. An active interest in the welfare of his town, an occasional visit to London, generous entertainment of his friends, and the composition of one or two of his grandest dramas, seem to have **1616.**] occupied these years of retirement. He died on the 23d of April, 1616, probably on the anniversary of his birthday, having just completed his fifty-second year. There is a tradition that he rose from a sick-bed to entertain Ben Jonson and Drayton, and that he brought on a relapse by "drinking too hard." He was buried in the parish church of Stratford. In the wall, above his grave, a monument is erected, containing his bust.* This bust and the coarse engraving by Droeshout, prefixed to the first folio edition of his works published in 1623, are the most trustworthy of his portraits. In eulogistic verses Ben Jonson vouches for the faithfulness of Droeshout's picture.

But few relics of Shakespeare still remain. The house of New Place has long been destroyed; but the garden in which it stood, and, in another street, the house where the poet was born, are preserved. His will, which was made a month before his death, testifies to his kind and affectionate

---

arms for his father. His own defamed profession would have been an obstacle in the way of his securing the honor; but he succeeded in obtaining it for his father, and so gained it for himself by inheritance. He was the last to bear the family title; for his only son, Hamnet, died when eleven years of age.

* The pavement over his grave bears the following startling inscription:

'' Good friend, for Iesvs sake forbeare,
To digg the dvst encloased heare:
Bleste be ye man yt spares thes stones,
And cvrst be he yt moves my bones."

disposition. To each of his old comrades and "fellows" he leaves some token of regard, generally "twenty-six shillings and eight pence apiece, to buy them rings." The three autographs attached to this document, and one or two more, are the only specimens of his writing that have been preserved.*

Early Non-Dramatic Poems. Shakespeare's first original poems were not dramatic. He was the creator of a peculiar species of narrative composition, which achieved an immediate and immense popularity. *Venus and Adonis*, which, in his dedication to Lord Southampton, he calls "the first heir of his invention," was published in 1593. It is probable that this poem—exhibiting all the luxuriant sweetness, the voluptuous tenderness, of a youthful genius—was conceived, if not composed, at Stratford. It was re-issued in five several editions between the years 1593 and 1602 ; while the *Rape of Lucrece*, during nearly the same time, appeared in three. When he abandoned the adaptation of old plays for original dramatic composition, it is quite impossible to ascertain ; for some of the works which bear the strongest impress of his genius were undoubtedly based upon earlier productions. As examples of this may be mentioned *Hamlet* (81, 82), *Henry V.*, and *King John* (77).

Classification of His Plays. There are internal evidences which distinguish his earlier and his later plays, but nothing from which a chronological list could be made. To obtain such a list, many acute investigators have exercised their ingenuity, and have found startling discrepancies in their results. No reliance can be placed upon the order of the

---

* " The manner in which the name is spelled in the old records varies almost to the extreme capacity of various letters to produce a sound approximating to that of the name as we pronounce it. . . . But Shakespeare himself, and his careful friend Ben Jonson, when they printed the name, spelled it *Shake-speare*, the hyphen being often used; and in this form it is found in almost every book of their time in which it appeared."—*White's Memoirs of William Shakespeare*, p. iv., note

pieces given in the first edition—the folio published in 1623 by Heminge and Condell, Shakespeare's friends. The most superficial examination is sufficient to prove that, in spite of the assurances of the editors as to its having been based upon the "papers" of their colleague, this publication must be regarded as little better than a hasty speculation, entered into for the sake of profit and without much regard to the literary reputation of the great poet. And though the system of grouping plays as Tragedies, Comedies, and Histories, has at all events the advantage of clearness, and is that upon which most editions of the dramas are based, it also is open to objection. Some of the pieces indeed (such as *Othello, King Lear, Hamlet*), are distinctly tragedies, and others (*As You Like It* [72] or *Twelfth Night*) are as decidedly comedies; but many more might, from their tone and incidents, be ranged under either head. Indeed, in all the tragic and comic elements are more or less intermixed, and it is this blending of the two in the same piece which constitutes the distinguishing trait of the English drama in the Shakespearean age, and gives it superiority over the national drama of every other country.

For us, the most useful mode of classification is based upon the *sources* from which Shakespeare drew the materials for his dramas. Those sources are *historical* and *fictitious*. The historical plays depict events of recent reigns in England. Holinshed's Chronicles furnished much of the material for them, beginning with *King John* (77), and ending with *Henry VIII.* (79, 80). They are grand panoramas of national glory or national distress. *Richard II., Richard III.* (78), the two unequaled dramas on the reign of *Henry IV.* and that chant of patriotic triumph, *Henry V.,* illustrate his power in representing epochs in the history of his nation. Shakespeare, though not the inventor, was the most prolific author, of such historical dramas.

In addition to the plays founded on authentic facts of

history, he wrote many which had a semi-historical character, and drew their stories from the legends of various
countries; thus *Hamlet* was taken from a Danish chronicler;
Macbeth, *Lear* and *Cymbeline* refer to more or less fabulous
legends of Scottish and British history; while *Coriolanus*,
Julius Cæsar and *Antony and Cleopatra* are derived from
ancient Roman annals.

Nineteen of his dramas are based upon *fiction*. Of these
a large majority can be traced to the Italian novelists and
their imitators, who supplied the light literature of the sixteenth century. The short tales of those writers were most
singularly adapted to furnish an appropriate groundwork
for the poet's delineations of humor or pathos. They depended for their popularity upon amusing and surprising
incidents.

From the classification given on the next page it will be
seen that many of these plays were based upon preceding dramatic works. A few of the more ancient pieces themselves
are preserved, exhibiting different degrees of imperfection
and barbarism. In one or two cases we have more than one
edition of the same play in its different stages towards complete perfection under the hand of Shakespeare. *Hamlet*
is the most notable instance. Some of these thirty-seven
plays show evident marks of an inferior hand. The three
parts of *Henry VI.* were in all probability older dramas,
retouched here and there with Shakespeare's inimitable
strokes of nature and poetic fancy. So, too, the last of the
English historical plays, *Henry VIII.*, bears distinct traces
of having been in part composed by a different author; in
the diction, the turn of thought, and in the peculiar structure of the verse, there are indications that in its composition Shakespeare was associated with another poet. Such
literary partnership was in vogue in that age.

On reading Shakespeare's historical dramas, the first impression is of the amazing apprehension and ready delinea-

A Classification of Shakespeare's Plays, the Probable Dates of their Composition,
and the Sources whence the Materials were Derived,

I.—HISTORICAL.

PLAYS.	PROBABLE DATE OF COMPOSITION.	SOURCES FROM WHICH MATERIALS WERE DERIVED.
HENRY VI., Part I... ...... " " " II......... " " " III.........}	1590–91	Old play, entitled *The Contention between the Famous Houses of York and Lancaster;* and the *True Tragedy of Richard, Duke of York.*
RICHARD II.............	1594–5	Holinshed's Chronicles
" III. (78).............	1593	The Chronicles of Hall and of Holinshed.
KING JOHN (77)............	1596	An older play.
HENRY IV., Part I.......... " " " II.........}	1596 1597	An older play, entitled *The Famous Victories of King Henry V.*
HENRY V..................	1599	
HENRY VIII (79, 80)........	1613	The Chronicles of Hall and of Holinshed, and Fox's *Book of Martyrs.*

II.—SEMI-HISTORICAL, OR LEGENDARY.

TITUS ANDRONICUS..........	1587–9	Probably an older play.
HAMLET (81, 82).............	1600	The Chronicle of Saxo-Grammaticus and an older play.
KING LEAR.................	1605	Holinshed and older plays.
MACBETH (84, 85)...........	1605	Holinshed's Chronicles of Scotland.
JULIUS CÆSAR (83)..........	1606–8	
ANTONY AND CLEOPATRA.....	1606–8	North's Translation of Plutarch's Lives.
CORIOLANUS.....	1609–11	
CYMBELINE	1609–11	Boccaccio and Holinshed.

III.—FICTITIOUS.

LOVE'S LABOUR 'S LOST	1588–9	Unknown ; probably of French origin.
COMEDY OF ERRORS........ ...	1589	The *Menæchmi* of Plautus.
TWO GENTLEMEN OF VERONA ..	1589–90	Unknown.
A MIDSUMMER NIGHT'S DREAM (75, 76, 87)	1594	
THE MERCHANT OF VENICE (74)	1594	*Il Pecorone,* an Italian tale.
ROMEO AND JULIET	1596	Paynter's *Palace of Pleasure.*
MUCH ADO ABOUT NOTHING....	1598–9	An Italian novel.
TWELFTH-NIGHT.............	1599	An Italian novel, by Bandello.
AS YOU LIKE IT (72, 73).....	1599	Lodge's *Rosalynde.*
THE TAMING OF THE SHREW...	1601	An older play.
PERICLES......................	1602	Gower's *Confessio Amantis,* and *The Patterne of Painfull Adventures.*
MERRY WIVES OF WINDSOR..-	1603	Unknown.
MEASURE FOR MEASURE	1603–4	Cinthio's *Hecatomithi.*
ALL'S WELL THAT ENDS WELL.	1604	Paynter's *Palace of Pleasure,* translated from Boccaccio.
TIMON OF ATHENS.............	1605–7	Plutarch, Lucian, and *The Palace of Pleasure.*
TROILUS AND CRESSIDA........	1606–8	Chaucer and Caxton's *Recuyell of the Historyes of Troy.*
OTHELLO	1609–11	Cinthio's *Hecatomithi.*
THE WINTER'S TALE....	1611	Greene's *Pandosto; The Triumph of Time.*
THE TEMPEST (86)............	1611	Unknown.

* According to Richard Grant White.

tion of the peculiarities of the age and country which the poet reproduces. He gave reality to every character in the play. From the most prominent down to the most obscure, each one has a distinct individuality,—true at the same time to that individuality, to his nation, and to the universal man. There may be, here and there, anachronisms, but they never affect the truthfulness of the poet's representation of human nature.

His Comprehension of Nature. Even the influence of climate is not forgotten in his creations. Take the characters of Ophelia and Juliet as types of the woman of the North and the woman of the South. Both are in love. As you read through the pages in which Ophelia lives, you find yourself communing with a woman whose sincerity and constancy and depth of soul, you recognize and admire. She speaks few words and they are very quietly spoken. When she discovers that her love is reciprocated, though she is chary of her words, you detect her delight. Then her trials come. Her lover is separated from her. Her cruel fortune is patiently borne until her reason is dethroned. Then, even in her insanity, her nature is true to its clime. Still there is reserve. Her grief finds little utterance in words, but sings itself to rest in snatches of song. Her emotional nature is under control. Her anxiety, her joy, her grief, are alike subdued by the reserve that is natural to the Northern temperament.

Juliet stands in striking contrast. No calm exterior hides her impulsive spirit. Her love comes suddenly to its full expression. Her womanliness appears in emotions that are profound, though easily moved; in a constancy of love, though that love would seem to expend itself in demonstration. Her womanliness is as pure as Ophelia's. She is simply true to the impulsive nature of the Southerner.

His Delineation of Character. His *mode* of delineating

passion is unique. Others fall more or less into the error of making their personages mere embodiments of moral qualities,—of ambition, of avarice, of hypocrisy. They accumulate in their creations only kindred characteristics. Shakespeare never forgets the infinite complexity of human nature. As Macaulay justly observes, the primary characteristic of Shylock is revengefulness; but a closer insight discloses a thousand other qualities, whose mutual play and varying intensity go to compose the complex being that Shakespeare has drawn in the terrible Jew. Othello is no mere impersonation of jealousy, nor Macbeth of ambition, nor Falstaff of selfish gayety, nor Timon of misanthropy, nor Imogen of wifely love: in each of these personages, the more closely we analyze them, the deeper and more multiform will appear the springs of action which make up their personality. To this wonderful power of conceiving complex character may be attributed another distinguishing peculiarity of our poet, namely, the total absence from his works of any tendency to egotism. From his dramas we learn nothing whatever of his own sympathies and tendencies. He is absolutely impersonal, or rather he is all persons in turn, for no poet ever possessed to a like degree the power of successively identifying himself with a multitude of the most diverse individualities, and of identifying himself so completely that we cannot detect a trace of preference. Shakespeare, when he has once thrown off such a character as Othello, never recurs to it again. Othello disappears from the stage as completely as a real Othello would disappear from the world, and leaves behind him no similar personage. He has given us other pictures of jealous men,— Leontes, Ford, Posthumus; but how differently is the passion manifested in each of these! In the characters of women, too, what a wonderful range, what inexhaustible variety!* In no class of his impersonations are the depth,

* " It would be very gratifying, no doubt, perhaps very instructive also, to be let into the domestic life and character of the poet's mother. That both her nature and

the delicacy, and the extent of Shakespeare's creative power more visible than in his women; and this is all the more wonderful when we remember that in drawing these varied types of character, he knew that they would be intrusted in representation to boys or young men—English women not appearing on the stage before 1661, long after the age which witnessed such creations as Ophelia, Lady Macbeth, Rosalind, and Juliet. The author must have felt what he so powerfully expressed in the language of his own Cleopatra:

> " The quick comedians
> Extemporary shall stage us : Antony
> Shall be brought drunken forth, and I shall see
> Some squeaking Cleopatra *boy* my greatness."

These Shakespearean characters—men or women—do not appear as pictures on the page of a book. We come to know them, not from descriptions of them, but by actual inter- course with them. They live. They talk in our presence; —some of them rude, grotesque, eccentric ; some of them grand and energetic ; some of them in the various phases of insanity; but all of them *real.* This is Shakespeare's miraculous power, that he makes realities out of that which others make into pictures or dreams. We have been in the Roman Senate and have seen Julius Cæsar bleed away his life. King Lear is not a man about whom we have simply read. He is a man whom we have seen, whose folly has disgusted us, whose rage has startled us, whose despair has stirred the depths of our pity.

In the expression of strong emotion, as well as in the delineation of character, Shakespeare is superior to all other

---

her discipline entered largely into his composition, and had much to do in making him what he was, can hardly be questioned. Whatsoever of woman's beauty and sweet- ness and wisdom was expressed in her life and manners could not but be caught and repeated in his susceptive and fertile mind. He must have grown familiar with the noblest parts of womanhood somewhere ; and I can scarce conceive how he should have learned them so well, but that the light and glory of them beamed upon him from his mother."—*Hudson's Life of Shakespeare,* p. 14.

poets. He never produces the effect he desires by violent rhetoric, or by unnatural combinations of qualities. He instructs and interests us by exhibiting passions and feelings as we see them in the world. He draws illustrations from simple and familiar objects. Sometimes his natural fond- ness for making subtile distinctions, sometimes his passion for punning, does violence to our notions of good taste; but it must be borne in mind that such mannerism was the literary vice of his day. These defects disappear in the mo- ments of his earnestness.

His Plots Borrowed. In no instance has Shakespeare taken the trouble of inventing a plot for himself. Appro- priating without hesitation materials already prepared, he directed all his energies to that department in which he shines unrivaled,—the portrayal of human nature and human passion. We are not, however, to infer that the poet necessarily consulted the tales and dramas in the original tongues. A careful examination of his works seems to prove that he has rarely made use of any ancient or foreign literature not then existing in English transla- tions; a fact which lends some corroboration to the well- known statement of Ben Jonson that he had "small Latin and less Greek."

His Metaphorical Style. His style is often criticised for its obscurity. It is the profundity of his thinking and the reach of his imagination which make him subject to that criticism. He often thinks in metaphors; and we have to discern the figure clearly, before we can apprehend his thought. The same quality of style will be noticed in Bacon; for he, too, does his severest thinking in boldest metaphors. This habit is characteristic of the poetic mind. It is simply the power of condensing much thought into brief expression. It is because he has that power pre- eminently, that Shakespeare is quoted more frequently than any other English writer.

His Influence in the History of our Language. It is noticeable that he left no impress upon the political life of his nation. But upon the spirit of social sympathy, upon the spirit of historical inquiry, and, most of all, upon the history of his language, his influence was powerful and has been lasting. To him, more than to any other man since Chaucer, the English language is indebted. **1611.**] The common version of the Bible, made in 1611, and the writings of Shakespeare, have been the conservators of English speech. The general reading of two books that are models of simplicity, of sincerity in expression, and of discrimination in the choice of words, has given to the millions of the English speaking race a rich and constant vocabulary. It was nearly three centuries ago that Shakespeare wrote, yet we read him to-day to find that, while he made the language of his predecessors obsolete, his vocabulary * has withstood the assaults of time, and is still fresh and vigorous.

Of his plays, fifteen were printed during his lifetime, probably without his sanction. He was careless of the fate of his works, leaving them to the mercy of speculating publishers. This indifference to the preservation of his most famous writing, his early abandonment of the stage, and some allusions in his sonnets, give much reason for thinking that he was not well pleased with his calling. The first edition of his plays, a folio edited by his former comrades, Heminge and Condell, appeared in 1623. A second edition followed in 1632, and a third in 1662. Another folio in 1685 supplied the demands of his English readers, until Nicholas Rowe published the first critical edition in 1709.

---

* " An examination of the vocabulary of Shakespeare will show that out of the fifteen thousand words which compose it, not more than five or six hundred have gone out of currency or changed their meaning, and of these, some no doubt are misprints, some borrowed from obscure provincial sources, and some, words for which there is no other authority, and which probably never were recognized as English."—*Marsh's Lectures on the English Language*, p. 264.

His Sonnets. The sonnets of Shakespeare (88) possess a peculiar interest, not only from their intrinsic beauty, but also from the fact that they contain allusions to the personal feelings of their author,—allusions which point to some deep disappointment in love and friendship. They were first printed in 1609, though, from references found in contemporary writings, it is clear that many of them had been composed previously. They are one hundred and fifty-four in number. Some of them are evidently addressed to a man, while others are as plainly intended for a woman. Through all of them there flows a current of sadness, discontent, and wounded affection, which bears every mark of being the expression of a real sentiment. No clew, however, has as yet been discovered by which we may hope to trace the persons to whom these poems are addressed, or the painful events to which they allude. Had his dramatic works been unwritten, these sonnets, together with his early amatory poems, would have given him rank among the most brilliant poets of his age; but the superior glory of his dramas overshadows the minor works.

Shakespeare's writings are often censured on account of their obscenity. With but one or two exceptions his plays, as they are placed upon the modern stage, are much expurgated. The apology for this defect is plain and satisfactory. He was writing at a time when, in every circle of society, there was license in language. What is to us shockingly obscene in many of his passages, was no transgression of propriety in his day. In this very particular he is remarkably pure in comparison with his contemporary dramatists. That he could not have been grossly indelicate is evident to all who appreciate the tenderness with which he guards purity in his impersonations.

The works which he has left show such stores of knowledge, such powers of discrimination, such resources of wit, such pathos, such exhaustlessness of language, such scope of imagination, as can be found in no other English poet. Moreover, he seems to have been a symmetrical *man*. The fact that, working in a defamed profession, he commanded respect ; the fact that, being the most eminent of poets, he was at the same time successful in practical affairs; and the fact that, out of the resources of his mind, he has drawn every phase of humanity, indicate his own completeness and balance of character.

In the large library of volumes which discuss the life and the literature of Shakespeare, the following works and brief papers will be of special interest to the student who is beginning to form an opinion of the dramatist :—The first volume of White's edition of Shakespeare, Hudson's *Shakespeare's Life, Art, and Characters*, Whipple's essay on *The Literature of the Age of Elizabeth*, Taine's *English Literature*, Vol. I., p. 296, seq., Reed's *British Poets*, Vol. I., Lecture V., De Quincey's Works, Vol. II., Coleridge's Works, Vol. IV., Giles's *Human Life in Shakespeare* J. R. Lowell's essay *Among My Books.* Separate plays of Shakespeare edited by H. N. Hudson, or those edited by W. J. Rolfe should be used by the student.

In this chapter we have considered:—

William Shakespeare.

1. *His Career as a Dramatist.*

2. *His Early Non-Dramatic Poems.*

3. *Classification of His Plays.*

4. *His Comprehension of Nature.*

5. *His Delineation of Character.*

6. *The Origin of His Plots.*

7. *His Metaphorical Style.*

8. *His Influence in the History of our Language.*

9. *His Sonnets.*

CHAPTER X.

THE SHAKESPEAREAN DRAMATISTS.

THE age of Elizabeth and James I. produced a galaxy of great dramatic poets. In the general style of their writings they bear a strong resemblance to Shakespeare; and, indeed, many of the peculiar merits of their great prototype may be discovered in his contemporaries. Intensity of pathos hardly less touching than that of Shakespeare, may be found in the dramas of Ford; gallant animation and dignity in the dialogues of Beaumont and Fletcher; deep emotion in the sombre scenes of Webster; noble moral elevation in the graceful plays of Massinger; but in Shakespeare, and only in Shakespeare, do we see the union of the most opposite qualities of the poet, the observer, and the philosopher.

BEN JONSON.

"He did a little too much Romanize our tongue."—*John Dryden.*

"Jonson possessed all the learning that was wanting to Shakespeare, and wanted all the genius which the other possessed."—*David Hume.*

> "Then Jonson came, instructed from the school,
> To please in method, and invent by rule;
> His studious patience and laborious art
> By regular approach essay'd the heart."—*Samuel Johnson.*

"Many were the wit-combats betwixt him [Shakespeare] and Ben Jonson; which two I behold like a Spanish great galleon and an English man-of-war; Master Jonson, like the former, was built far higher in learning; solid, but slow in his performances. Shakespeare, with the English man-of-war, lesser in bulk but lighter in sailing, could turn with all tides, tack about, and take advantage of all winds by the quickness of his wit and invention."—*Thomas Fuller*, 1662.

"I was yesterday invited to a solemn supper by Ben Jonson, where there was good company, excellent cheer, choice wines, and jovial welcome. One thing intervened which almost spoilt the relish for the rest—that Ben began to engross all the discourse; to vapour extremely of himself: and by vilifying others to magnify his own name. T. Ca. [Thomas Carew] buzzed me in the ear, that Ben had barrelled up a great deal of knowledge, yet it seems he had not read the ethics, which, amongst other precepts of morality, forbid self-commendations, declaring it to be an ill-favored solecism in good manners."—*James Howell*, 1636.

B. 1573.]
D. 1637.] The name which stands next to that of Shakespeare in this list is that of **Ben Jonson, (89, 90)**. Although compelled by his step-father to follow the trade of a bricklayer, he succeeded in making himself one of the most learned men of the age.* After a short service as a soldier in the Low Countries, where he distinguished himself by his courage in the field, he began his theatrical career at about twenty years of age, when we find him attached as an actor to one of the minor theatres, called the Curtain. His success as a performer is said to have been very small; probably on account of his unattractiveness of person. Having killed a fellow-actor in a duel, while still a young man, he was (to use his own words) "brought near the gallows." While in prison awaiting his trial, he was converted to the Roman Catholic faith; but twelve years afterwards he returned to the Protestant Church.

Jonson, like Shakespeare, probably began his dramatic work by recasting old plays. His first original piece, the comedy *Every Man in His Humor*, is assigned to the year 1596. As first represented it was a failure, and Shakespeare, then at the height of his popularity, is said to have interested himself in behalf of the young aspirant, suggesting changes in the play, securing its acceptance by the managers of the Globe, and himself taking a prominent part, when, two years later, it was brought out with triumphant success. Thus, probably, was laid the foundation of that sincere and enduring attachment between the two poets, which is commemorated by many pleasant anecdotes of their genial social intercourse, as well as by that enthusiastic eulogy in which Jonson has honored the genius of his friend. Jonson's literary reputation was established by this

---

* The story is told of Jonson that his fondness for study tempted him to carry books in his pocket while working at his trade, in order that he might improve leisure moments by refreshing his memory upon his favorite passages in classical authors, and that one day, while working on the scaffolding of a building at Lincoln's Inn, a lawyer heard him recite a passage of Homer with surprising appreciation, was attracted to him, and, upon discovering his thirst for learning, gave him opportunities for renewing his studies at the University of Cambridge.

fortunate reproduction of his comedy. Henceforward, for more than a quarter of a century, though the success of individual plays may have fluctuated, he held rank as the most prominent figure in the literary society of the day.

Jonson's prosperity and intellectual power reached their culmination between 1603 and 1616. In the former year *The Fall of Sejanus*, a tragedy, appeared, followed in rapid succession by some of his finest works,—*Volpone*, *Epicene*, *The Alchymist*, and *Catiline*. He was frequently employed by the Court in arranging those splendid and fantastic entertainments called *masques*, in which he exhibited his stores of invention and all the resources of his profound and elegant scholarship. In 1616 he received the office of Laureate, with an annual pension of one hundred marks; and though writing little between 1616 and 1625, his fortunes suffered no material abatement until the death of James I., in 1625. Disappointment, poverty, ill-health, and too great fondness for sack combined their forces to break down the veteran. Many of his later plays were unsuccessful; and in one of them, *The New Inn*, acted in 1630, he complains bitterly of the hostility and bad taste of his audience. He died in 1637, and was buried in an upright posture in the Poet's Corner of Westminster Abbey. Above his grave a plain stone bears the laconic inscription, "O RARE BEN JOHNSON."*

Jonson's Dramatic Works. His dramatic works are of various degrees of merit, ranging from an excellence unsurpassed by any contemporary except Shakespeare, to the lowest point of laborious mediocrity. He seems to have won his high place among the writers of the Elizabethan era, not so much by virtue of creative imagination, or by any strictly poetic faculties, as by weight and breadth of understanding, quickness of fancy, power of analysis, and preternatural keenness of observation. Thorough and extensive study strengthened these native qualities, but could not supply the deficiencies. His tragedies, *The Fall of Sejanus* and *Catiline's Conspiracy*, display the riches of a profound and learned intellect. They reproduce the details of Roman manners, religion and senti-

---

* In that inscription his name is spelled "Johnson." The common spelling is "Jonson."

ment, with minute fidelity, and contain passages of wonderful force. But as wholes, they are stiff and lifeless, lacking that spirit of *reality* through which Shakespeare could "transform a series of incidents into a succession of events." It is mechanical, not vital energy with which Jonson has endowed his creations. Nor is it strange that there was this difference between these two dramatists. Shakespeare disregarded the traditional laws of dramatic poetry and wrote with unfettered hand. Free from restraint, his English nature expressed itself in a drama that was true to the spirit of his age and his nation. His plays, therefore, have what we call *reality*. Jonson, as we have said, was a profound classical scholar. He was an enraptured admirer of the great works of the classic drama. The laws by which Greek dramatists had attained their success were to him the essential laws of a true drama; and as a student of dramatic art and a dramatist, he must obey those laws. By so much as he violated them, he was false to his profession. As a proof of his earnestness in holding this opinion, read his prologue to *Every Man in His Humor*. In his attempt to be loyal to his culture he placed himself under a bondage which made it impossible for him to give characters a native freedom. Bound to observe the unities of time, place, and action,* he could not portray life naturally.

But worse than the defects springing from Jonson's servitude to classical laws is his singular want of what is called *humanity*. His humor is never genial, his fun never infectious; his point of view is always that of the satirist. He takes his materials, both for intrigue and for character, from odious sources. For instance, the action of two of his finest plays, *Volpone* and *The Alchymist*, turns entirely upon a series of ingenious cheats and rascalities, all the persons being either scoundrels or their dupes.

Nevertheless, Jonson's knowledge is so vast, the force and vigor of his expression so unbounded, the tone of his morality so high and manly, that his plays retain a high place in literature.

---

* Three rules were carefully observed in the composition of a Grecian Drama: 1. That there should be a distinct plot with one main action, to which all the minor parts of the play should contribute. 2. That the incidents of the play should naturally come within one day. 3. That the entire action should naturally occur in one place. These three rules are known as the Unity of Action, the Unity of Time and the Unity of Place, or as " the dramatic unities."

His faults were the typical faults of the conceited man; his virtues were his own. Egotistical to the last degree, self-willed and overbearing, he was yet frank, generous, and social in temper, and truly upright and earnest in purpose. At the famous "wit-combats" of the Mermaid Tavern he was the self-constituted auto-crat. He scrupled not to lay down the laws of the drama to Shakespeare himself. In *Every Man Out of His Humor*, and in *Cynthia's Revels*, he proclaimed his mission as a dramatic reformer; and he satirized "the ragged follies of the time" with such savage acrimony as provoked a storm of recrimination from his lampooned contemporaries. Decker and Marston were his chief opponents in the literary war that ensued. They accused him of plagiarism, they mocked his bombast, they questioned his learning. *The Poetaster*, *The Tale of a Tub*, and many passages in Jonson's other plays, attest the vigor with which he bore his part. Yet the same egotism which rendered him insensible to Shakespeare's influence guarded him against servile imitation, and made him, next to Shakespeare, the most original dramatist of the era; and the intrepid self-confidence which would guide, not follow, popular taste, kept his works pure from the gross immorality which stains the brightest pages of Beaumont and Fletcher. Doubtless his resolute self-assertion aided him in winning recognition for the admirable qualities of his heart and head. There is reason to be-lieve that his social position was superior to Shakespeare's; and in an age when play-writing was hardly considered "a creditable employ," Clarendon affirms that "his conversation was very good, and with men of the best note."

It is remarkable that while Jonson in his plays is distinguished for that hardness and dryness which we have endeavored to point out, the same poet, in another field, should be remarkable for elegance and refinement of invention and style. In the thirty-five *Masques* and *Court Entertainments*, which he composed for the amusement of the king and the great nobles, as well as in the charming fragment of a pastoral drama entitled the *Sad Shepherd*, Jonson appears quite another man. Everything that the richest and most delicate invention could supply, aided by extensive, choice and recondite reading, is lavished upon these courtly com-pliments. Their gracefulness almost makes us forget their adula-tion and servility. Among the most beautiful of these masques we

may mention *Paris Anniversary*, the *Masque of Oberon*, and the *Masque of Queens*. Besides his dramatic works, Jonson left writings in both prose and verse. The former portion, called *Discoveries*, contains many valuable notes on books and men—those on Shakespeare and Bacon being the most interesting.

As a literary man Jonson stands alone. All critics say it; he says it. In pedantry he was as distinguished as he was for scholarship. His diction was as rotund as his figure. While you read his writings some one is continually telling you that the thoughts and the words are weighty and wonderful, and that one is Ben Jonson. He was his own ideal. He was a genuine Englishman. Shakespeare was a cosmopolitan. Jonson was to Shakespeare what England is to the world. While we may smile at some of Jonson's traits, we admire the resoluteness of purpose that lies behind his self-confidence; we admire his lofty theory of virtue, though his own vices are not concealed; we admire the learning which supports his pedantry we admire the bravery that comes to the rescue of his boasting.

BEAUMONT AND FLETCHER.

Superior to Ben Jonson in variety and animation, though not equal to him in solidity of knowledge, were **Francis Beaumont** (1586–1616) and **John Fletcher** (1576–1625) (**91, 92**), by birth and by education of a higher social status than their fellow-dramatists; Beaumont being the son of a judge, and Fletcher the son of a bishop (**91**). Concerning the details of their lives and characters we possess but vague and scanty information.

Their Literary Partnership. There seems to be reason for ascribing to Beaumont more of the sublime and tragic genius, to Fletcher most of gayety and comic humor. Fletcher was the more prolific and versatile writer, and the volatile creativeness of his fancy may have been restrained and directed by the sounder judgment of his friend.* But so blended is their glory that neither biography nor

---

* "There was a wonderful similarity between Mr. Francis Beaumont and Mr. John Fletcher, which caused the clearness of friendship between them. I have heard Dr. John Earle, since Bishop of Sarum, say, who knew them, that his (Beaumont's) business was to correct the superflowings of Mr. Fletcher's wit. They lived together on the Bankside, not far from the playhouse; both bachelors, had one bench of the house between them, which they did so admire, the same cloathes, cloaks, etc., between them."—*Aubrey.* 1697.

criticism has been able to separate their names. Their respective
plays cannot be indicated with certainty, their tastes cannot be dis
tinguished, their talents cannot be discriminated. Charles Lamb
praises the "noble practice" of the time when eminent authors
shared each other's labors and each other's fame. It must have
been remembrance of the marvelous literary partnership existing between Beaumont and Fletcher that prompted his praise. A thought
beyond them would have reminded him of the feuds of the Elizabethan authors, of the criminations, recriminations, and scandals
of that time. Human nature had its selfishness and its jealousies
then, and the great dramatists had their share of the weaknesses
of human nature. Greene hated Marlowe, and was jealous of
Shakespeare ; Marlowe was indignant at Nash ; Chapman shot
poisoned arrows at Ben Jonson, and Jonson applied his cudgels to
the backs of Decker and Marston. No niche in the temple of
        literary fame is large enough to receive two men, save that
1606?] in which Beaumont and Fletcher appear. Their part-
        nership was formed when Beaumont was twenty and
Fletcher thirty years of age, and was continued for ten years.

Their Dramatic Works. Their works afford constant evidence
of the influence and inspiration of Shakespeare ; and several of their
plays, in which the graceful, humorous, and romantic elements pre-
dominate, are by no means unworthy of comparison with such
comedies as *Much Ado About Nothing, As You Like It,* and *Measure
for Measure.* But in the delineation of sustained passion they are
immeasurably inferior to their master. The range of their character-painting is comparatively limited, and their pathos is tender
rather than deep. Their numerous portraits of valiant soldiers may
be pronounced unequaled, and they are skilled in depicting noble
and magnanimous feeling. It is in their pieces of mixed sentiment,
containing comic matter intermingled with romantic and elevated
incidents, that their powers are best displayed. Of this class, no
better examples can be selected than the comedies of the *Elder
Brother, Rule a Wife and Have a Wife, Beggars' Bush,* and the
Spanish Curate. In the more farcical intrigues and characters,
such as are to be found in the *Little French Lawyer,* the *Woman-
Hater,* the *Scornful Lady,* the eccentricity is laughably extravagant;
and the authors seem to enjoy the amusement of heaping up

absurdity upon absurdity out of the very exuberance of their humorous conceits. Some of their pieces furnish stores of antiquarian and literary material; for example, the *Beggars' Bush* contains abundant illustrations of the slang dialect; and the *Knight of the Burning Pestle* is a storehouse of ancient English ballad poetry. They occasionally attempt some good-humored banter of Shakespeare. In the play just mentioned, the droll, pathetic speech on the installation of Clause as King of the Gypsies is a parody of Cranmer's speech in the last scene of *Henry VIII.*

The pastoral drama of *The Faithful Shepherdess* was written by Fletcher alone. Its exquisitely delicate sentiments are too often soiled by passages of loose and vicious thinking. Ben Jonson's best poetry, *The Sad Shepherd,* and Milton's *Comus,* were inspired by this poem.

Philip Massinger (1584–1640) spent two years in the University of Oxford. His works prove that he had an intimate knowledge of the classical writers of antiquity. In 1604 he began his theatrical life, and continuing it until his death, found it an uninterrupted succession of struggles, disappointments, and distress. Unlike Beaumont and Fletcher, who were servile in their deference to the Court, he was an outspoken critic of the government, and an advocate of republican principles. According to the practice of the time, he frequently wrote in partnership with other playwrights— the names of Decker, Field, Rowley, and Middleton being often found in conjunction with his. We have the titles of thirty-seven plays, either entirely or partly of his composition. Only eighteen of them are extant. "Eleven of them in manuscript were in possession of a Mr. Warburton, whose cook, desirous of saving what she considered better paper, used them in the kindling of fires and the basting of turkeys, and would doubtless have treated the manuscript of the *Faery Queene* and the *Novum Organum* in the same way, had Providence seen fit to commit them to her master's custody."* The best known are *The Virgin Martyr* (**93**), *The Fatal Dowry, The Duke of Milan, The Bondman, The City Madam,* and *The New Way to Pay Old Debts.* The last named is occasionally put upon the modern stage, and contains the famous character of Sir Giles Overreach.

* Whipple's *Literature of the Age of Elizabeth.*

This writer has the power of delineating the sorrows of pure and lofty minds exposed to unmerited suffering. Massinger had no aptitude for pleasantries; but a desire to please the mixed audiences of those days tempted him to introduce stupid buffoonery and loathsome indecency into his plays. His style and versification are singularly sweet and noble. No writer of that day is so free from archaisms and obscurities; and perhaps there is none in whom more constantly appear the force, harmony and elevation of which the English language is susceptible. Dignity, tenderness and grace, are the qualities in which he excels. At the close of a life of poverty he died in obscurity, and in the notice of his death the parish register names him "Philip Massinger a stranger."

To John Ford (1586–1639?) the passion of unhappy love has furnished almost exclusively the subject-matter of his plays. He was a lawyer, who found time to use a poetic pen while carrying on the work of his profession. He began his dramatic career by working with Decker. One of their productions was the touching tragedy of the *Witch of Edmonton*, in which popular superstitions are skilfully combined with a pathetic story of love and treachery. The works attributed to him are not numerous. He wrote the tragedies of the *Brother and Sister*, the *Broken Heart* (beyond all comparison his most powerful work), a graceful historical drama on the subject of *Perkin Warbeck*, and the following romantic or tragic-comic pieces: the *Lover's Melancholy* (**94**), *Love's Sacrifice*, *Fancies Chaste and Noble*, and the *Lady's Trial*. His personal character, if we may judge from slight allusions found in contemporary writings, was sombre and retiring; and in his works pensive tenderness and pathos are carried to a higher pitch than in any other dramatist.

John Webster is perhaps the most original genius among the Shakespearean dramatists of the second order. But one fact in his biography is known,—he belonged to the Merchant Tailors' Company. His writing has something of that dark, bitter, and woful expression which thrills us in the work of Dante. The number of his known works is very small; the most celebrated among them is the tragedy of the *Duchess of Malfy* (**95**); but others are not inferior to that strange piece in intensity of feeling and savage grimness of treatment. Besides the above, we have *The Devil's Law Case; Guise; or the Massacre of France*, in which the St. Bartholomew massacre is, of course, the main action; the *White Devil*, and *Appius and Virginia*. We thus see that he worked by preference on themes which offered a field for the portrayal of the darker passions and of the moral tortures of their victims. As Charles Lamb says, "To move a horror skilfully, to touch a soul to the quick, to lay upon fear as much as it can bear, to wean and weary a life till it is ready to drop, and then step in with mortal instruments to take its last forfeit; this only a Webster can do."

As we pass on to the lower grades of dramatic talent, we are almost bewildered by the number and variety of its manifestations. Two writers, however, should have notice : **Thomas Decker** usually appears as a fellow-laborer with other dramatists, yet in the few pieces attributed to his unassisted pen, he shows great elegance of language and deep tenderness of sentiment. **Thomas Heywood** exhibits a graceful fancy, and one of his plays, *A Woman Killed with Kindness*, is among the most touching of the period.

The Close of the Dramatic Era. The dramatic era of Elizabeth and James closes with **James Shirley** (1596–1666), whose comedies, though in many respects bearing the same general character as the works of his great predecessors, still seem the earnest of a new period (**96**). He excels in the delineation of gay and fashionable society; and his dramas are more remarkable for ease, grace, and animation, than for portraiture of character. The glory of the English drama had almost departed; and its extinction was hastened by the breaking out of the Civil War in 1642 and by the enactments of Parliament in 1642, 1647 and 1648, which closed the theatres and suppressed the dramatic profession. From that date until the Restoration, all theatrical performances were illegal; but with the connivance of Cromwell, Davenant gave dramatic entertainments at Rutland House; and upon the great Protector's death in 1658, he ventured to re-open a public theatre in Drury Lane. With this event began an entirely new chapter in the history of the English stage.

The Elizabethan Drama is the most wonderful and majestic outburst of literary genius that any age has yet seen. It displays richness and fertility of imagination combined with the greatest vigor of familiar expression; an intimate union of the common and the refined; bold flights of fancy and scrupulous fidelity to actual reality. The great object of these dramatists being to produce intense impressions upon a miscellaneous audience, they sacrificed everything to strength and nature. Their writings reflect not only faithful images of human character and passion under every conceivable condition, not only the strongest as well as the most delicate coloring of fancy and imagination, but also the profoundest and simplest precepts derived from the practical experience of life.

For brief discussions of authors named in this chapter see Hazlitt's Works, Vol. III., Coleridge's Works, Vol. IV., Lamb's Works, Vol. IV., Hallam's *Literature of Europe*, Vol. III.

In this chapter we have considered:—

Shakespearean Dramatists.

1. Ben Jonson,—His Dramatic Works.

2. Beaumont and Fletcher,—Their Literary Partnership,—Their Dramatic Works.

3. Philip Massinger, John Ford, John Webster, Thomas Decker, and Thomas Heywood

4. The Close of the Dramatic Era.

5. The Elizabethan Drama.

CHAPTER XI.

THE PROSE LITERATURE OF THE ELIZABETHAN PERIOD.

THE object of the present chapter is to trace the nature and the results of that revolution in philosophy brought about by the writings of Bacon; and at the same time to give a general view of the prose literature of the Elizabethan era. As Bacon was the grandest thinker of that age who wrote in prose, he must be the principal figure of the chapter; and other authors of inferior merit must be but briefly mentioned.

Much of the peculiarly practical tendency of the political and philosophical literature of our own time can be traced to its beginning in the Elizabethan era, when, as a result of the Reformation, education first found many devotees among English laymen, and prose literature, for the first time, was generally used for other than ecclesiastical purposes. The clergy had no longer the monopoly of that learning and of those acquirements which, during preceding centuries, had given them the monopoly of power. Laymen were wielding the pen. It must be admitted that the prose of that era makes but a poor figure when compared with the splendor of the Elizabethan poetry.

In the humble department of historical chronicles, **John Stow**, before the end of the sixteenth century, published his *Summary of English Chronicles*, *Annals* and *A Survey of London ;* and **Raphael Holinshed,** who died in 1580, wrote the pages from which Shakespeare drew the material for some of his half-legendary, half-historical dramas, and for the majority of his purely historical plays.

Sir Walter Raleigh. One of the most extraordinary men of this era was Sir Walter Raleigh (1552–1618), whose romantic career belongs to the political rather than to the literary history of England **(45, 56)**. He was among the foremost courtiers of the

Queen; he was a bold navigator, exploring unknown regions of the globe; he was a brave soldier, winning laurels on the Continent and in Ireland. When James I. came to the throne, Raleigh's fortunes declined. He was unjustly charged with treason, was tried, and sentenced to the Tower, where he was imprisoned for thirteen years. During this weary imprisonment he devoted himself to literary and scientific work ;—some of the time experimenting in chemistry with the hope of discovering the philosopher's stone, and much of the time, with the help of friends, writing his *History of the World*. By that work he won his literary fame. Later histories have shown that what he supposed to be historical facts were merely fancies, and that many of his theories were groundless; still he holds and deserves the honor of being the pioneer in the department of dignified historical writing. After his long imprisonment he was sent to South America in quest of riches for the king. The expedition was unfortunate. One of Raleigh's exploits enraged the Spanish Court, and to appease the wrath of the Spaniards, Raleigh was seized upon his return to England, and was beheaded. A man of remarkable patience and resolution, and showing many signs of powerful intellect, Raleigh must have been one of the eminent literary men of his age, had his life been devoted to letters. He was the founder of that famous "Mermaid Club" in which Jonson, Fletcher, probably Shakespeare, and other wits of the day, gathered to enjoy each other's conversation; and was himself accounted one of the most charming members of that literary company. His resources of character were equal to his reputation, for in the most desperate circumstances he was thoroughly self-possessed. In his trial for treason, when the Attorney-General, hurling fierce invectives at him, said, "I want words to express thy viperous treasons," "True," said Raleigh, "for you have spoken the same thing half a dozen times over already; " and when he was brought to the block, taking the axe in his hand, he ran his fingers over its keen edge, smiling as he said, "This is a sharp medicine, but it will cure all diseases." It is to be regretted that he did not use his ever-present wit, his poetic talent and his ready pen, in making more varied and more valuable contributions to our literature.

Richard Hooker (1553–1600), a man of piety and vast learning, was the great champion of the principles of the Church of England against the encroachments of Puritan sentiments. He was for four years a Fellow of the University of Oxford, where he gained fame as a lecturer on Oriental literature. In 1585 his eloquence and learning obtained for him the eminent post of Master of the Temple of London. Here his colleague, Walter Travers, propounded doctrines of church government similar to those of Calvin, and therefore incompatible with Hooker's opinions. Hooker was the morning lecturer and Travers held forth in the afternoon. Thus, it was said, "the forenoon sermon spoke Canterbury, and the afternoon Geneva." The mildness and modesty of Hooker's character made controversy odious to him. He induced his ecclesiastical superior to remove him to the more congenial duties of a country parish, and there he devoted the remainder of his life to that work which has placed him among the most distinguished of Anglican divines, and among the best prose-writers of his age. The title of this work is *A Treatise on the Laws of Ecclesiastical Polity* (57), and its purpose is to investigate and define the principles which underlie the right of the Church to claim obedience from its members, and the duty of the members to render obedience to the Church. But while thus fortifying the organization of the English Church against the attacks of the Roman Catholics on the one hand and of the Puritans on the other, Hooker has built up his arguments upon those eternal truths which are the foundation of all law, all duty, and all rights, political as well as religious. *The Ecclesiastical Polity* is a work of profound and cogent reasoning. It gave new dignity to English prose literature. Its style is wholly free from pedantry, clear and vigorous. To Hooker belongs the glory of first fully developing the English language as a vehicle of refined and philosophic thought. The breadth and power of his mind are fitly expressed in the stately majesty of his periods.*

* One of the most famous sentences in our literature, found in the first book of *The Ecclesiastical Polity*, reads as follows: "Of law there can be no less acknowledged than that her seat is the bosom of God, her voice the harmony of the world: all things in heaven and earth do her homage; the very least as feeling her care, and the greatest as not exempted from her power; both angels and men, and creatures of what condition soever, though each in different sort and manner, yet all with uniform consent, admiring her as the mother of their peace and joy."

FRANCIS BACON.

" The wisest, brightest, meanest of mankind."—*Pope.*

" The great secretary of nature and all learning."—*Walton.*

" He had the sound, distinct, comprehensive knowledge of Aristotle, with all the beautiful lights, graces, and embellishments of Cicero."—*Addison.*

" He may be compared with those liberators of nations who have given laws by which they might govern themselves, and retained no homage but their gratitude."—*Hallam.*

" Who is there that upon hearing the name of Lord Bacon does not instantly recognize everything of genius the most profound, everything of literature the most extensive, everything of discovery the most penetrating, everything of observation of human life the most distinguishing and refined."—*Burke.*

" My conceit of his person was never increased towards him by his place or honors ; but I have and do reverence him for the greatness that was only proper to himself : in that he seemed to me ever, by his work, one of the greatest men and most worthy of admiration that had been in many ages. In his adversity I ever prayed God would give him strength ; for greatness he could not want."—*Ben Jonson.*

B. 1561.]   In his manhood **Francis Bacon** was extrava-
D. 1626.]   gant, fond of display, a servile courtier, while
everywhere a close observer, a keen critic, and a
profound thinker. His seemingly incongruous qualities,
if native to his character, had been fostered by the fortune
of his childhood and youth. He was the younger and
the favorite son of Sir Nicholas Bacon. His father, the
Lord-Keeper of the Great Seal of England, was one of the
statesmen who gave the reign of Elizabeth its glory. His
mother was a woman of stern integrity of character, trained
in the learning of that day. Under parental influences in
which were blended dignity, vigor, intelligence, refinement,
and practical shrewdness, in the elegance of an English nobleman's palace, amid the clustering associations of cultivated
society, there was every opportunity for the development of
extravagant tastes, of courtiership, of self-esteem, of observation, and of thoughtfulness. In boyhood his body was very

delicate, his mind was precocious. The great Queen, petting him, would call him her little Lord-Keeper. When thirteen years old he was sent to Cambridge. Life at the university roused a spirit courageous enough to attack the monstrous system of scholastic learning, and honest enough to tell the world that what they had been reverencing as a divine philosophy was, as they were beginning to suspect, false and effete. His observation discovered that in the system of instruction at the universities there was slavish deference to authority, that men did not dare to think beyond the thoughts of former generations, that progress was thereby impossible. In his fellow-students he saw men like "becalmed ships, that never move but by the wind of other men's breath, and have no oars of their own to steer withal."

At sixteen he went to live in France as an *attaché* of the English ambassador. There he saw new phases of the courtier's life, studied the national character, and confirmed his opinions of the need of improvement in the intellectual pursuits of men. He must have displayed some talent in business affairs, for he gained the confidence of the ambassador, and was intrusted by him with despatches to the Queen. During the two years spent upon the Continent he was observing and studious, and was interested in gathering material for his first literary work, *Of the State of Europe.*

In 1579 he was summoned to England on account of the death of his father. He was then nearly nineteen years old, without money, with only his ambition and his intellect to help him in winning his way to eminence. Living in that stirring age, schooled in the ways of the world, knowing the methodless life of the professed philosophers, a mind as observing, as positive as his, necessarily resolved upon a definite pursuit, and established for itself certain principles of action. If we can detect that purpose and those principles, we may be able to understand some of the mysterious contrasts of his life.

It is reasonable for us to believe that he had become convinced—

1st. That learning was not doing the sort of work it
should do for mankind.

2d. That whoever would inaugurate a reformation in
learning must be a person eminent in the public confidence.

3d. That no person could attain eminence and public
confidence who had not the sanction and patronage of the
Court.

4th. That scholarly attainments, without the courtier's
shrewdness, could not win the needed sanction and patronage.

Passages in his letters and the course he pursued, show
that these were his earnest convictions.

His Relations to Burleigh and to Essex. He promptly
began the study of the law, and in 1582 was called to the
bar. Those who condemn him say that he made servile and
persistent appeals for patronage. He did beg of his uncle
Burleigh, the Lord Treasurer, that some office, with light
duties, and yet with generous compensation, might be given
to him, in order that he might have the time and the means
for becoming " a pioneer in the deep mines of truth." In
one of his letters, he said that he had " vast contemplative
ends," and that he had " taken all knowledge for his province." These earnest declarations doubtless seemed to the
sturdy old uncle like the aspirations of a dreamer. He had
no faith in the practical shrewdness of his nephew, and
therefore pushed him away from the approaches to preferment. Failing in his repeated attempts to gain the favor of
Burleigh, Bacon sought and won the friendship of Essex,
his uncle's rival. Essex gave him large sums of money, and
tried, unsuccessfully, to secure his political advancement.
Bacon soon discovered that Essex was a dangerous friend,
because a reckless man. Their intimacy ceased. In a

few years Bacon, having been appointed Queen's counsel, was called upon to prosecute his old friend for acts of treason. The charges were proved, and the penalty of death was inflicted. For his part in the prosecution Bacon has been accused of ingratitude and of most malicious selfishness. It has been said that he might have saved his friend, or, at least, from very shame, might have refused to appear against him. But the truth seems to be that Bacon did all that he could do to prevent Essex from pursuing his mad follies; that in the trial he dealt as gently with him as he could ; and that when, by the Queen's command, he prepared the government's defence for its treatment of Essex, his expressions were so moderate as to call forth from the angry Queen the rebuking words, " I see old love is not easily forgotten." The charge that Bacon desperately sought the life of Essex, for the sake of ingratiating himself with Elizabeth, is altogether improbable.

His Political Success. He was now on the way to high political honors. In the House of Commons he was recognized as a masterly orator ; * in his profession he was renowned for brilliancy and learning. He was still seeking advancement, was using persistent and studied complaisance towards the Court. But surely he was not actuated merely by the infatuation of the politician. His early ambition for the reform of learning was still inspiring him. With all his eloquence he urged the government to aid the reforms which he had projected. The busy whirl of his public life

---

* " There happened in my time one noble speaker who was full of gravity in his speaking. His language, when he could spare or pass a jest, was nobly censorious. No man ever spoke more neatly, more pressly, more weightily, or suffered less emptiness, less idleness in what he uttered. No member of his speech but consisted of his own graces. His hearers could not cough or look aside from him without loss. He commanded where he spoke, and had his judges angry and pleased at his devotion. No man had their affections more in his power. The fear of every man that heard him was lost he should make an end."—*Ben Jonson, referring to Bacon.*

did not keep him away from the study of practical philosophy. His lament is pitiful as again and again he tells of the
limited time he has to give to his inquiries after the truths
of nature. These phases of his life indicate that the more
reasonable as well as the more generous view of his servility
to the Court shows him to have been seeking something
beyond political success.

The story is told that when Bacon was a little boy the
Queen asked him his age. He replied, "I am two years
younger than your Majesty's happy reign." That was an
answer for a native courtier, a devotee of royalty, to make.
When he was sixty years old, and was selected as the scapegoat to bear away the abuses of James's administration, he
bowed his head, submissively acknowledged his faults, and
received the punishment which a cowardly king permitted
to be inflicted upon him. That was an act for a devotee of
royalty to perform. From childhood, when he gave his
honest compliment to the Queen, until old age, when he
surrendered his office and some of his honor for the comfort
of the King, he showed to the English crown a loyalty, a
reverence, which seems to us like superstition. For this he
has been condemned by many an historian, and has been
lashed by the scourge of many a critic. When he is named
as the apostle of progress his revilers allege that he was the
blind advocate of kingcraft. That there is ground for such
statement cannot be denied. It covers nearly all the charges
that are made against his character; still it does not make
him a hypocrite. His reverence for a crown was inbred.
Nicholas Bacon, the Keeper of the Great Seal, had taught
his son to cherish a religious loyalty for the person who
might be sitting on the throne of England.

On the coronation of James I., in 1603, Bacon was
knighted, and at the same time was married to Alice Barn-
ham, the daughter of a London alderman. He was afterwards elected to more than one Parliament, and was ap-

pointed Solicitor-General, then Attorney-General, then Lord Keeper, with the title of Baron Verulam, and his titles were finally completed by those of Lord-Chancellor and Viscount St. Albans. In the discharge of his varied and great responsibilities the versatility and energy of his genius were well displayed. His loyalty to the Crown was hearty, his reward was the most humiliating punishment which a resentful public could heap upon the servant of a despised king. It was his deference to a weak and arrogant monarch, combined, it may have been, with unbridled personal ambition, which made Bacon a scapegoat for the acts of folly marking the reign of James I.

His Political Disgrace. His political disgrace occurred in 1621. He was convicted of corruption in office, was condemned to lose the chancellorship, to pay a fine of forty thousand pounds, to be imprisoned during the King's pleasure, to be ineligible to any office in the state, and was forbidden to sit in Parliament, or to come within twelve miles of the court. But a remission of these penalties was soon granted, and, in 1624, an annual pension of twelve hundred pounds was bestowed upon him for life.

The life of the fallen minister was prolonged for five years after his disgrace. In spite of his misfortunes and of his pecuniary embarrassments, those were his most fruitful years. He died in 1626. Riding in his carriage one spring day, when the snow was falling, it occurred to him that snow might serve as well as salt in preserving flesh. So stopping at a cabin by the roadside, he bought a fowl, for the purpose of trying the experiment. By the slight exposure he was chilled, and thrown into a sudden and fatal fever. To use the words of Lord Macaulay, "The great apostle of experimental philosophy was destined to be its martyr."

Bacon's Service to Science. In order to appreciate the

services which Bacon rendered to science, we must dismiss from our minds the common and erroneous idea that he was an inventor or discoverer in any specific branch of knowledge. He attempted, not to teach the results of investigation, but to show the method by which investigations should be made. We must also remind ourselves of that philosophy which Bacon wished to supplant. It had nothing in common with the practical science of modern times. It was the old Aristotelian philosophy robbed of its veneration for Nature and perverted by many unwarranted interpretations. We call it scholasticism. No one of his devotees was bold enough to step from the platform of authority. Aristotle, misrepresented, was respected as the dictator of all correct thinking. Verbal distinctions, not useful investigations, consumed the talents of the thoughtful; quibbles took the place of earnest questionings. Failure to advance was due to no want of retirement and meditation, to no distaste for argument and wrangling. The intellect was in thraldom; and reason was the vassal of a worthless faith. This scholastic period is generally spoken of as extending from the ninth to the close of the fifteenth century. It was the age of superstitions and of futile reasoning. Speculation was carried in every direction. Natural science, as well as psychology, was made the subject of vain imaginings. Like a huge breakwater this scholasticism skirted the sea of thought. For three centuries it had broken the wave of every advancing opinion. But as the fifteenth century drew to its close the sea gave indications of an approaching storm, the sky was overcast by portentous clouds, wave after wave came rolling shoreward from the ocean of free thought, and, at last, the surge of the Reformation burst with terrifying roar against that time-worn scholasticism, tumbling it out of the way. Then thought advanced.

The Aristotelian method of investigation, after it had been perverted by the schoolmen, was open to the charge

of infertility—of being essentially unprogressive. Its principal aim was the attainment of abstract truth; practical
utility was regarded as an end which, whether attained or
not, was beneath the dignity of the sage. The object of the
Inductive Method, as proclaimed by Bacon, was *fruit*,—
the improvement of the condition of mankind. He wished
man to become "the minister and interpreter of nature."
He would have the laws of nature understood, in order that
they might be observed intelligently by the sailor, the farmer,
the miner, by whomsoever might be a worker in the world.
From the knowledge of the laws of nature, industries would
be more effective, comforts would be multiplied, the condition of man would be ameliorated. Those laws he would
have discovered by means of a methodic, scientific observation of the phenomena of nature. He gave induction its
rightful place in philosophic method, he elaborated a plan
for the collation of facts, he dictated rules for the estimate
of their value. His system is contained in the series of
works to which he intended to give the general title of
Instauratio Magna, or The Great Institution of True
Philosophy. Its scope is magnificent, and that is what
displays the genius of the author.

The *Instauratio* was to consist of six parts, of which the
following is a short synopsis :

I. *Partitiones Scientiarum.* This work includes his
earlier treatise on *The Advancement of Learning*, and gives
a general summary and classification of human knowledge,
with indications of those branches in which science was
specially defective.

II. *Novum Organum.* This "new instrument" he describes as "the science of a better and more perfect use of
reason in the investigation of things, and of the true aids of
the understanding." It sets forth the methods to be adopted
in searching after truth, points out the principal sources of
error in former times, and suggests the means of avoiding

errors in the future. Of the nine sections into which this part of the work was divided, only the first was fully discussed.

III. *Historia Naturalis.* This part was designed to be a collection of well-observed facts and experiments in what we call Natural Philosophy and Natural History, and was to furnish the raw material to be used in the new method. Bacon's *Sylva Sylvarum* is a specimen of the work he would have done in this division of his *Instauratio.* His *History of the Winds,* of *Life and Death,* are also contributions to this division.

IV. *Scala Intellectus,* the ladder of the mind. This fourth part was to give rules for the gradual ascent of the mind from particular instances or phenomena to principles more and more abstract.

V. *Prodromi.* Prophecies, or anticipations of truths "hereafter to be verified," were to have furnished the material for this part.

VI. *Philosophia Secunda.* This was intended to be the record of practical results springing from the application of the new method.

But a small portion of the magnificent plan was executed. The founder himself presented no claims to the rank of a discoverer. His genius as a philosopher is displayed only in the comprehensiveness of his scheme. His greatness as a man appears in the incisiveness and discrimination of his thinking, in his brave declaration of the cause of fruitlessness in former philosophy, and in the sublime conviction which prompted him to urge the improved method of investigation, and to foretell what the future would bring. His keen thinking made him the intelligent critic of errors that had been ; his imagination made him the glowing prophet of the glory that was to be.

His admirers overstate his work in the study of Nature. They find him the first to expose the childish wisdom of his predecessors, the first to announce the new era, the first to point out the direction in which discovery must move. The succeeding progress was in accordance with his prophecy; and therefore the modern reader is misled into calling Bacon the Father of Modern Philosophy. As Craik says, "The mistake is the same as if it were to be said that Aristotle was the father of poetry."

Twenty centuries had elapsed after Aristotle had shown his method of searching after truth, before Bacon undertook to introduce a new method. Aristotle made thought active; Bacon aimed to make it useful. Aristotle made logic the fundamental science, and considered metaphysics of greater importance than physics. His theory, imperfectly carried into practice, produced twenty centuries of fruitlessness; two centuries and a half of the practical investigations which were advocated by Bacon, have revolutionized the literary, the commercial, the political, the scientific world. The ancients had a philosophy of words; Bacon called for a philosophy of works. His glory is founded upon a union of speculative power with practical utility, which were never so combined before. He neglected nothing as too small, despised nothing as too low, by which our happiness could be augmented; in him, above all, were combined boldness and prudence, the intensest enthusiasm, and the plainest common sense.

It is probable that Bacon generally wrote the first sketch of his works in English, but afterwards caused them to be translated into Latin, which was in his time the language of science, and even of diplomacy. He is reported to have employed the services of many young men of learning as secretaries and translators; among these the most remark-able is Hobbes, afterwards so celebrated as the author of the *Leviathan*. The style in which the Latin books of the *Instau-ratio* were given to the world, though certainly not a model of classical purity, is weighty, vigorous, and picturesque.

His English Writings. Bacon's writings in English are
numerous. The most important among them is the volume
of *Essays, or Counsels Civil and Moral* (58, 61), of which
the first edition, containing ten essays, was published in
1597. The number gradually increased to fifty-eight, many
of the later ones giving expression to the author's profoundest thought and richest fancy. These short papers discuss
various subjects, from grave questions of morals down to the
most trifling accomplishments. As specimens of intellectual
activity, of original thinking and aptness of illustration,
they surpass any other writing of equal extent in our literature. "Few books are more quoted. . . . . It would be
somewhat derogatory to a man of the slightest claim to
polite letters were he unacquainted with the *Essays* of
Bacon." * They illustrate the author's comprehensiveness
of mind and his wonderful power of condensing thought.
In his style there is the same quality which is applauded in
Shakespeare—a combination of the intellectual and imaginative, the closest reasoning in the boldest metaphor. Many
of Bacon's essays—as the inimitable one on *Studies*—are
absolutely oppressive from the power of thought compressed
into the smallest possible compass. It is through his brief
Essays that Bacon is most widely influential. "Coming
home," as he says himself, "to men's business and bosoms,"
they gained, even in his own time, an extensive popularity,
which they still retain.

In his *Wisdom of the Ancients,* he endeavored to explain
the political and moral truths concealed in the mythology
of classical ages, and exhibited an ingenuity which Macaulay calls morbid. His unfinished romance, the *New
Atlantis,* was intended to set forth the fulfilment of his
dreams of a philosophical millennium. He also wrote a
History of Henry VII., and a vast number of state-papers,
judicial decisions, and other professional writings. All

* Hallam.

these are marked by a vigorous and ornate style, and are among the finest specimens of the prose literature of that age. His writing on religious themes, though invariably condensed into short passages, is full of profound and reverent thought. He gave many striking interpretations of scripture, made versions of some of the Psalms, and, as Taine says, wrote several prayers which are among the finest known.

For more extended reading on this topic consult Macaulay's essay on Bacon, Whipple's essays in *The Literature of the Age of Elizabeth*, Lewes's *Biographical History of Philosophy*, Hallam's *Literature of Europe*, *The Baconian Philosophy*, by Tyler, Fischer's *Bacon and His Times*, Spedding's *Francis Bacon and His Times* G. H. Lewes's *Aristotle*, and Mill's *Logic*.

In this chapter we have considered:—

The Prose Literature of the Elizabethan Period

1. John Stow and Raphael Holinshed.

2. Sir Walter Raleigh.

3. Richard Hooker.

4. Francis Bacon.

    a. His Relations to Burleigh and Essex.

    b. His Political Success.

    c. His Political Disgrace.

    d. His Service to Science.

    e. His English Writings.

THE ELIZABETHAN LITERATURE,
As discussed in the five preceding chapters.

POETS.

NON-DRAMATIC.
- THOMAS SACKVILLE,
- SIR PHILIP SIDNEY,
- EDMUND SPENSER,
- WALTER RALEIGH.

[The Dawn of the Drama.]

DRAMATIC.
- JOHN LYLY,
- GEORGE PEELE,
- THOMAS KYD,
- ROBERT GREENE,
- CHRISTOPHER MARLOWE,
- WILLIAM SHAKESPEARE,
- BEN JONSON,
- BEAUMONT AND FLETCHER,
- PHILIP MASSINGER,
- JOHN FORD,
- JOHN WEBSTER.

PROSE WRITERS.
- WALTER RALEIGH, *the Historian.*
- RICHARD HOOKER, *the Churchman.*
- FRANCIS BACON, *the Philosopher.*

CHAPTER XII.

THE SO-CALLED METAPHYSICAL POETS.

ALTHOUGH the literature of the seventeenth century indicates no marvelous outburst of creative power, it has yet left deep and enduring traces upon English thought and upon the English language. The influences of the time produced a style of writing in which intellect and fancy played a greater part than imagination or passion. Samuel Johnson styled the poets of that century the metaphysical school; that tendency to intellectual subtilty which appears in the prose and verse of the Elizabethan writers, and occasionally extends its contagion to Shakespeare himself, became with them a controlling principle. As a natural consequence, they allowed ingenuity to gain undue predominance over feeling; and in their search for odd, recondite, and striking illustrations they were guilty of frequent and flagrant violations of sense. Towards the close of the period Milton is a grand and solitary representative of poets of the first order. He owed little to his contemporaries. They were chiefly instrumental in developing the artificial manner which characterizes the classical writers of the early part of the eighteenth century.

John Donne (1573–1631) was declared by Dryden to be the greatest of English wits. He was a representative of the highest type of the extravagances of his age (**50**). His ideal of poetical composition was fulfilled by clothing every thought in a series of analogies, always remote, often repulsive and inappropriate. His versification is singularly harsh and tuneless, and the crudeness of his expression is in unpleasant contrast with the ingenuity of his thinking. In his own day his reputation was very high. "Rare Ben" pronounced him "the first poet of the world in some things," but declared that "for not being understood he would perish." This prophecy was confirmed by public opinion in the eighteenth century, but has been somewhat modified by the criticism of our day, which discovers much genuine poetical sentiment beneath his faults of taste. His writings certainly give evidence of rich, profound, and varied learning.

Donne's early manhood was passed in company with the famous wits of the Mermaid Tavern. The chief productions of his youthful muse were his *Satires*, the *Metempsychosis*, and a series of amatory poems. When forty-two years old, he was ordained as a priest in the Church of England. He soon became a famous preacher, and was appointed Dean of St. Paul's.

Favoring circumstances rather than substantial desert give **Edmund Waller** (1605–1687) his prominent position in the literary and political history of his time. From his youth his associations were with that polished society which could at once appreciate and develop his varied talents. Versatility, brilliant wit, graceful and fascinating manners, and an underlying fund of time-serving shrewdness gained him political distinction, and made him a social idol. But his character was timid and selfish; and his principles were modified by every change that affected his own interests. Unfortunately for him he was a relative of Cromwell and a member of the Long Parliament. Although constrained by policy to avow the republican principles of the Puritans, he was at heart a royalist, and lost no opportunity of secretly abetting the Stuart cause. His consummate adroitness long averted the consequences of this double-dealing; but in 1643 he was convicted of a plot for restoring the authority of Charles I. Severe penalties were inflicted upon him, and he bowed to them in abject submission. The Restoration renewed his prosperity, and he promptly panegyrized Charles II. with the same fervor which had marked his encomiums of the Protector. He died shortly after the accession of James II., having, with characteristic sagacity, foretold the ruinous issue of that monarch's policy.

Most of Waller's poems are the verses of love (107), addressed to Lady Dorothy Sidney, whom he long wooed under the name of Sacharissa. Playfulness of fancy, uniform elegance of expression and melody, which are the chief merits of his verse, can scarcely atone for its lack of enthusiasm. Two eulogies of Cromwell, one composed during the Commonwealth, the other after the Protector's death, contain passages of dignity and power. He was less felicitous in a poem on Divine Love, and in his longer work, *The Battle of the Summer Islands*, which describes in a half-serious, half-comic strain an attack upon two stranded whales in the Bermudas.

Both Dryden and Pope have acknowledged their obligations to Waller's influence as the "Maker and model of melodious verse."

Abraham Cowley (1618–1667) was the popular English poet of his time (**110**). He was "an author by profession, the oldest of those who in England deserve the name."[*] He affords a remarkable instance of intellectual precocity; when a mere child he had a passionate admiration for the *Faery Queene*, and his first poems were published when he was only fifteen years of age. After a residence of seven years at Cambridge, whence he was ejected on account of his being a royalist, he studied at Oxford until that town was occupied by the Parliamentary forces. He then joined Queen Henrietta, the wife of Charles I., who was residing in France; and

1660.] he remained upon the Continent for years, exerting all his energies in behalf of the House of Stuart. When the Restoration was accomplished and his fidelity and self-sacrifice were forgotten by Charles II., Cowley resolved "to retire to some of the American plantations and forsake the world forever;" but he abandoned this purpose and settled in rural life at Chertsey on the Thames. He received a lease of lands belonging to the Crown, and from it he derived a moderate revenue, which secured him against actual want.

Cowley was highly esteemed as a scholar, a poet, and an essayist. Extensive and well-digested reading, sound sense and genial feeling, joined to a pure and natural expression, render his prose works very entertaining. As a poet he exhibits the bad qualities of the metaphysical school in their most attractive form. He has not poetic passion; he seems to be ever on the alert for striking analogies, and when he finds one he shows the electric spark of wit, rather than the fervent glow of genius. This fantastic play of the intellect displaces the natural outpouring of feeling, even in the collection of his amatory verses called *The Mistress*. The *Anacreontics* exhibit his poetical powers to better advantage; their tone is joyous and spirited, and they abound in images of natural and poetic beauty. He planned and began a work of great pretensions, en-

* Taine, Vol. I., p. 146.

titled the *Davideis.* It was intended to celebrate the sufferings and glories of the King of Israel; but it was left unfinished and is now utterly neglected. His talents were lyric, rather than epic, and he was therefore not qualified to develop so grand a theme in a masterly way.

Donne, the founder of "the Metaphysical School," and his two disciples, Waller and Cowley, were the most prominent literary figures and the most influential and popular writers in the generation immediately after the Elizabethan period. Davenant and Denham held secondary, but important positions.

Sir William Davenant (1605–1668) derives his chief claim upon posterity from his connection with the revival of the drama at the termination of the Puritan rule. He succeeded Ben Jonson in the office of Poet Laureate, and during the reign of Charles I. was manager of the Court Theatre. An energetic and useful partisan of the Cavaliers, his share in the intrigues of the Civil War had nearly brought him to the scaffold; but his life was saved by the intercession of an influential Puritan whom tradition asserts to have been John Milton. After the Restoration, Davenant flourished under royal favor, continuing to write dramas and to superintend their performance, until his death. The French drama, in its most artificial and frivolous type, was the ideal of Charles II. and of his court. French influence revolutionized the English stage. Actresses, young, beautiful, and skillful, took the places filled by the boys of the Elizabethan era.* In every respect the mechanical adjuncts of the drama were improved. It is easy to see in Davenant's own plays and in those which he remodeled, how completely the taste for splendor of scenery, music, dancing and costumery, had displaced the passion of the earlier public for faithful picturing of life and nature. He was an ardent worshiper of the genius of Shakespeare and of Shakespeare's great contemporaries; yet conformity to the degraded standard of the age obliged him, in attempting to revive their works, to transform their spirit so entirely that every intelligent reader must regard the change with disgust. Davenant's most popular dramas were, *The Siege of Rhodes, The Law Against Lovers, The Cruel Brother* and *Albovine.*

---

* The first English actress appeared on the stage in the play of Othello, in the reign of Charles II., 1661.

Sir John Denham (1615–1668) was indifferent to learning in his youth, and throughout his life was addicted to the vice of gambling. No one had expected anything from him that would be worthy of a place in literature; but at twenty-six years of age he published a tragedy, *The Sophy*, which won the applause of the public. Two years later, his poem called *Cooper's Hill* appeared **(109)**. That poem established his fame. It contains passages of fine description, and suggests many beautiful thoughts concerning the landscape near Windsor. Denham's language is pure and perspicuous, and is free from the fantastic metaphors abounding in the writings of his contemporaries. Dryden is thought to have been influenced by the regularity and vigor of Denham's verse.

In this age of artificial poets there were many who were interested in the religious agitations of the Puritan and the Cavalier. We can mention but four of them. **George Wither** (1588–1667) was in sympathy with the political and religious sentiments of Oliver Cromwell. He was a prolific writer in both prose and verse. The modern critics have given him more praise than former generations considered his due. His prose attracts little attention. His pastoral poetry **(97)** has much melody and beauty of sentiment. His *Hymns and Songs of the Church*, and his *Hallelujah*, display his religious thought in worthy form. The whimsical conceits of the poetry of his day are occasionally found in his pages, but his style is generally simple, and expressive of natural and earnest feeling. *Abuses Stript and Whipt* was the title of his most famous satire, published in 1613. For that satire he was imprisoned.

Francis Quarles (1592–1644) was an ardent royalist. He exhibits many points of intellectual likeness to Wither, to whom, however, he is inferior in poetical sentiment. His most popular work was a collection of *Divine Emblems* **(98)**, whose moral and religious precepts are inculcated in short poems of almost laughable quaintness, and illustrated by equally grotesque engravings.

George Herbert (1583–1632) and **Richard Crashaw** (died 1650) exemplify the exaltation of religious sentiment; and both are worthy of admiration, not only as Christian poets, but as good and pious priests. Herbert's poems are principally short religious lyrics combining pious aspirations with frequent and beautiful pictures of nature (**99**). He decorates the altar with the sweetest and most fragrant flowers of fancy and of wit. Although not entirely devoid of that perverted ingenuity which deformed Quarles and Wither, his most successful efforts almost attain the perfection of devotional poetry,—a calm yet ardent glow, a well-governed fervor which seems peculiarly to belong to the Church of which he was a minister. His collection of sacred lyrics is entitled, *The Temple; or Sacred Poems and Private Ejaculations.*

Crashaw was reared in the Anglican Church; but during the Puritan troubles he embraced the Romish faith and became canon of the Cathedral at Loretto. That he possessed an exquisite fancy, great talent for producing melody of verse, and that magnetic power over the reader which springs from deep earnestness, no one can deny (**100**). The most favorable specimens of his poetry are the *Steps to the Temple,* and the beautiful description entitled *Music's Duel.*

In the social life of the first half of this seventeenth century the gallant and frivolous Cavalier stands in contrast with the stern, serious Puritan. In its literature, romantic love and airy elegance appear beside the reverent sentiments of religious poetry. The best representatives of the gayer poets are **Robert Herrick** (1591-1674) (**101**), **Sir John Suckling** (1609–1641) (**102**), **Sir Richard Lovelace** (1618–1658) (**103**), and **Thomas Carew** (1589–1639) (**104**). Herrick, after beginning his life in the brilliant literary society of the town and the theatre, took orders; but he continued to exhibit in his writings the voluptuous spirit of his youth. His poems were published under the names of *Hesperides* and *Noble Numbers.* They are all lyric, and the former are principally songs concerning love and wine; the latter are upon sacred subjects. In him we find the strangest mixture of sensual coarseness with exquisite refinement; yet in fancy, in spirit, in musical rhythm, he is never deficient.

Suckling and Lovelace are representative Cavalier poets; both suffered in the royal cause; both exemplify the spirit of loyalty to the king, and of gallantry to the ladies. Suckling's best production is the exquisite *Ballad Upon a Wedding,* in which, assuming the character of a rustic, he describes a fashionable marriage. Lovelace is more serious and earnest than Suckling; his lyrics breathe devoted loyalty rather than the passionate, half-jesting love-fancies of his rival. Such are the beautiful lines to *Althea*, composed while the author was in prison.

Carew's lyrics have all the grace, vivacity and elegance which should characterize such works.

In this chapter we have considered:—

The So-Called Metaphysical Poets.

1. John Donne.

2. Edmund Waller.

3. Abraham Cowley.

4. Sir William Davenant.

5. Sir John Denham.

6. George Wither, Francis Quarles, George Herbert, and Richard Crashaw.

7. Robert Herrick, Sir John Suckling, Sir Richard Lovelace, and Thomas Carew.

CHAPTER XIII.

THEOLOGICAL WRITERS OF THE CIVIL WAR AND THE COMMONWEALTH.

THE Civil War of the seventeenth century was a religious as well as a political contest; and the prose literature of that time, therefore, exhibits a strong religious character. The Church of England made her most brilliant display of theological eloquence; and in the ranks of the dissenters many remarkable men appeared, hardly inferior to the churchmen in learning and genius, and their equals in sincerity and enthusiasm.

William Chillingworth (1602–1644), an eminent defender of Protestantism against the Church of Rome, was converted to the Roman Catholic religion while studying at Oxford, and went to the Jesuits' College at Douay. After an absence of but two months he returned to Oxford, renounced his new faith, and published his work, entitled *The Religion of the Protestants a Safe Way to Salvation* (**113**). "His chief excellence," says Mr. Hallam, "is the close reasoning which avoids every dangerous admission, and yields to no ambiguousness of language. In later times his book obtained a high reputation; he was called the immortal Chillingworth; he was the favorite of all the moderate and the latitudinarian writers, of Tillotson, Locke, and Warburton."

The writings of **Sir Thomas Browne** (1605–1682), though miscellaneous, belong to this department (**114**). He was an exceedingly learned man, and passed the greater part of his life in practising physic in the ancient city of Norwich. Among the most popular of his works are the treatise on *Hydriotaphia, or Urn-Burial*, and essays on *Vulgar Errors*, or *Pseudodoxia Epidemica*. But the book which affords the most satisfactory insight into his character is the

Religio Medici, a species of confession of faith which gives a minute account of his own religious and philosophical opinions. These writings are the frank outpourings of a most eccentric and original mind. They show varied and recondite reading; and their facts and suggestions are blended by a strong and fervent imagination. At every step some extraordinary theory is illustrated by unexpected analogies, and the style is bristling with quaint Latinisms, which in another writer would be pedantic, but in Browne seem the natural garb of thought. All this makes him one of the most fascinating of authors; and he frequently rises to a sombre and touching eloquence.

Thomas Fuller (1608–1661) has in some respects an intellectual resemblance to Browne. Educated at Cambridge, he entered the Church, and was a famous orator in the pulpit. At the outbreak of the Civil War he incurred the displeasure of both factions by his studied moderation; but was for a time attached as chaplain to the Royalist army. During his campaigning Fuller industriously collected the materials for his most popular work, a *History of the Worthies of England*. This, more than his *Church History of Britain*, has made his name known to posterity. His *Sermons* exhibit peculiarities of style which make him one of the remarkable writers of his age (**115**). His writings are amusing, not only from the multitude of curious details, but also from the quaint yet frequently profound reflections suggested by these details. The *Worthies* contains biographical notices of eminent Englishmen, with descriptions of the botany, scenery, antiquities, and other matters of interest connected with their shires. It is an invaluable treasury of racy and interesting anecdotes. Of whatever subject Fuller treats, he places it in so many novel lights that the attention of the reader is constantly stimulated. One source of his picturesqueness is his frequent use of antithesis; not a bare opposition of words, but the juxtaposition of apparently discordant ideas, from whose sudden contact there flashes forth the spark of wit. But the spark is always warmed by a glow of sympathy and tenderness; for there is no gloom in Fuller's thought. The genial flash of his fancy brightens the gravest topics.

Jeremy Taylor (1613–1667) was the greatest theological writer of the English Church at this period. He was a thoroughly educated man, and from his early years was conspicuous on account of his talents and his learning. He entered the service of the Church, and is said, by his youthful eloquence, to have attracted the notice of Archbishop Laud, who made him one of his chaplains, and procured him a fellowship in All Souls' College, Oxford. During the Civil War he stood high in the favor of the Cavaliers and the Court. After the downfall of the king, Taylor taught a school, for a time, in Wales, and continued to take an active part in religious controversies. His opinions were of course obnoxious to the dominant party, and on several occasions subjected him to imprisonment. At the Restoration he was made a bishop, and during the short time that he held the office he exhibited the brightest qualities that can adorn the episcopal dignity.

Taylor's writings (**116**) deal with sacred thoughts. To be reverent towards his subject, he did not find it necessary to curb his fancy, or to quench his rhetorical fervor. Jeffrey called him "the most Shakespearean of our great divines;" but it would be more appropriate to compare him to Spenser. He has the same pictorial fancy, the same harmony of arrangement as Spenser. Together with Spenser's sweetness he has somewhat of the languor of Spenser's style. His study of ancient authors seems to have infected him with their Oriental and imaginative mode of thought. In his scholarly writing there may be an occasional indication of pedantry; in his religious life there is no cant, no hypocrisy. He was nearer abreast the truth than any former religious man of letters had been. In argument, in exhortation, he writes with the freedom and exuberance of his honest, happy soul. This man, with the genial style springing from his happy nature, is a most interesting character among polemical writers. His geniality did not prevent his being firm in his convictions. Living in an age when convictions had to be maintained against assaults, even Jeremy Taylor was compelled to enter the arena with other thinkers. His polemical writings are unique. They are free from personal abuse; they are as broad in spirit as they are lofty in style. They are thoroughly benevolent. His style is unfit for the close reason-

ing of the polemic. His fancy will beguile him from the direct line of an argument.

The best known of Taylor's controversial writings is the treatise *On the Liberty of Prophesying.* That work gives him the glory of being the one who put forth the " first famous plea for tolerance in religion, on a comprehensive basis and on deep-seated foundations." * Although intended by Taylor to secure indulgence for the persecuted Episcopal preachers, it is, of course, equally applicable to the teachers of all forms of religion. *A Justification of Authorized and Set Forms of Liturgie* was an elaborate defence of the noble ritual of the Anglican Church. Among his works of a disciplinary and practical tendency may be mentioned *The Life of Christ, or the Great Exemplar,* in which the scattered details of the Evangelists and the Fathers are co-ordinated in a continuous narrative. Still more popular than these are the two admirable treatises, *On the Rule and Exercises of Holy Living,* and *On the Rule and Exercise of Holy Dying,* which mutually correspond to and complete each other. The least admirable of Taylor's productions is the *Ductor Dubitantium,* a treatise on questions of casuistry. His *Sermons* are very numerous, and are among the most eloquent, learned, and powerful in the whole range of Christian literature. As in his character, so in his writings, Taylor is the ideal of an Anglican pastor ; in both he exemplifies the union of intellectual vigor and originality with practical simplicity and fervor.

Richard Baxter. Many men eminent for learning, piety, and zeal, appeared in the ranks of the Nonconformists at this time; but if we omit Milton and Bunyan, who are reserved for subsequent chapters, the only writer claiming a distinct notice is Richard Baxter. He was the consistent and able defender of the right of religious liberty; and in the evil days of James II. was exposed to the virulence and brutality of the infamous Jeffreys. With the exception of *The Saint's Everlasting Rest* and *A Call to the Unconverted,* his works are little known at the present day. Amid danger and persecution, and in spite of the feebleness of his body, he toiled with his busy pen until he had contributed to the polemical and religious literature of his lan-

* Hallam, Vol. II., p. 425.

guage the astounding number of one hundred and sixty-eight publications.*

* In the *Narrative of His Own Life and Times*, Baxter says: " I wrote them in the crowd of all my other employments, which would allow me no great leisure for polishing or exactness, or any ornament; so that I scarce ever wrote one sheet twice over, nor stayed to make any blots or interlinings, but was fain to let it go as it was first conceived ; and when my own desire was rather to stay upon one thing long than run over many, some sudden occasion or other extorted almost all my writings from me."

In this chapter we have considered :—

The Theological Writers of the Civil War and the Commonwealth.

    1. William Chillingworth.

    2. Thomas Fuller.

    3. Jeremy Taylor.

    4. Richard Baxter.

CHAPTER XIV.

JOHN MILTON.

> Thy soul was like a star and dwelt apart;
> Thou hadst a voice whose sound was like the sea—
> Pure as the naked heavens, majestic, free ;
> So didst thou travel on life's common way
> In cheerful godliness : and yet thy heart
> The lowliest duties on herself did lay."— *Wordsworth.*

"John Milton, the poet, the statesman, the philosopher, the glory of English literature, the champion and the martyr of English liberty."—*Macaulay.*

The old blind poet hath published a tedious poem on the Fall of Man. If its length be not considered as a merit, it hath no other."—*Waller.*

" The first place among our English poets is due to Milton."—*Addison.*

"There is no force in his reasonings, no eloquence in his style, and no taste in his compositions."—*Goldsmith.*

" It is certain that this author, when in a happy mood and employed on a noble subject, is the most wonderfully sublime of all poets in the language."—*Hume.*

> " Three poets in three distant ages born,
> Greece, Italy and England did adorn :
> The first in loftiness of thought surpassed ;
> The next in majesty; in both the last.
> The force of nature could no further go ;
> To make a third she joined the other two."—*Dryden.*

" Was there ever anything so delightful as the music of the Paradise Lost ? It is like that of a fine organ ; has the fullest and the deepest tones of majesty, with all the softness and elegance of the Dorian flute ; variety without end, and never equaled, unless, perhaps, by Virgil."—*Cowper.*

" After I have been reading the Paradise Lost I can take up no other poet with satisfaction. I seem to have left the music of Handel for the music of the street."— *Landor*

"Milton is as great a writer in prose as in verse. Prose conferred celebrity on him during his life, poetry after his death; but the renown of the prose-writer is lost in the glory of the poet."—*Chateaubriand*.

HISTORY furnishes no example of entire consecration to intellectual effort more illustrious than the life of John Milton. From childhood he seems to have **B. 1608.]** been conscious of superior powers; and through- **D. 1674.]** out his career circumstances combined to develop his peculiar genius. He was born December 9th, 1608, and was the son of a London scrivener, whose industry and ability had gained a considerable fortune. Contempo- raneous accounts prove the elder Milton to have been a man of forcible character, and—though a Puritan—a lover of art and literature. He was thus able and willing to foster the early indications of genius in his son, and gave to him the rare advantage of special preparation for a literary career.* A thorough training under his private tutor, Thomas Young, was supplemented by a few years at St. Paul's School in London. At the age of sixteen he was admitted to Christ's College, at Cambridge. His poetical tastes manifested themselves in an overweening fondness for the classics, and for poetical literature, and in an equally strong dislike to the dry scholastic sciences then in vogue at the university. His intellectual independence is said to have involved him in difficulty with the authorities of his college; but the disgrace must have been temporary, for he received both degrees at the usual intervals. To this period of his life many of his Latin poems are attributed ; and the *Hymn on the Nativity* (121) was produced as a college exercise. After leaving the university in 1632 he went to live at his father's country-seat at Horton, in Bucking-

* "My father destined me, while yet a child, to the study of polite literature, which I embraced with such avidity, that from the twelfth year of my age I hardly ever retired to my rest from my studies till midnight,—which was the first source of injury to my eyes, to the natural weakness of which were added frequent head- aches."

hamshire. There he passed five years in devotion to study, disciplining his mind with mathematics and the sciences, and storing his memory with the riches of classical litera-ture. There also he indulged his passionate fondness for music—a fondness to which the invariably melodious struc-ture of his verse and the majestic harmony of his prose style, bear constant testimony. The chief productions of this studious retirement were *L'Allegro, Il Penseroso, Comus,* the *Arcades,* and *Lycidas.*

In 1638 he determined to carry out a long-cherished plan for Continental travel. Furnished with influential intro-ductions, he visited the principal cities of France, Italy and Switzerland, and was everywhere received with respect and admiration.* He seems to have made acquaintance with men who were most illustrious for learning and genius; he visited Galileo, "then grown old, a prisoner in the Inqui-sition." At Paris he was entertained by Grotius; at Flor-ence he was received into the literary academies, and gained the praise of wits and scholars by some of his Latin poems and Italian sonnets. His plans for further travel were suddenly abandoned upon the news of the rupture between Charles I. and the Parliament; "for," he says, "I thought it base to be traveling for amusement abroad while my fellow-citizens were fighting for liberty at home." He had hardly been restrained from uttering his religious opinions within the walls of the Vatican; † he was now ready, at the

---

* "In the present day, when we examine the archives and visit the libraries of the Italian sovereigns, it is curious to observe how frequently, in the correspon-dence of the most eminent writers of that age, we find the name of this young Englishman mentioned."—*Lamartine.*

† "Whilst I was on my way back to Rome" (from Naples), he tells us, "some merchants informed me that the English Jesuits had formed a plot against me if I returned to Rome, because I had spoken too freely of religion: for it was a rule which I laid down to myself in those places, never to be the first to begin any conversation on religion, but, if any questions were put to me concerning my faith to declare it without any reserve or fear. I, nevertheless, returned to Rome. I took no steps to conceal either my person or my character, and for about the space of two months, I again openly defended, as I had done before the Reformed religion, in the very metropolis of Popery.

first occasion, to throw himself with ardor, into the conflict that was rending Church and State. While waiting to be called into active service, he conducted a private school in London, and spent some of his time in poetical contemplation. Before leaving Horton he had written to his friend Diodati, "I am meditating, by the help of heaven, an immortality of fame, but my Pegasus has not yet feathers enough to soar aloft in the fields of air;" and in a letter written to another friend just after his return from his travels, he said, "Some day I shall address a work to posterity which will perpetuate my name, at least in the land in which I was born." Intercourse with Continental scholars and authors stimulated his ambition, and formed his purpose. He had resolved to spend his strength on a poem of the highest order, either epic or dramatic—the Fall of Man may have already occurred to him as a topic. To this end he was pursuing his studies when the situation of affairs called forth his first pamphlet, in 1641. It was entitled, *Of Reformation*, and made a violent attack on the Episcopal Church. The storm of argument which it provoked, drove Milton to controversy; and for the following twenty years he was the most powerful and active champion of Republicanism against Monarchy. Among the most successful of his early prose writings was his *Apology for Smectymnuus.* * In 1644 he turned his attention to a question which was in no way related to the political agitation of the time, and wrote a series of elaborate and spirited *Works on Divorce.* An unfortunate incident in his domestic life had provoked these papers; for in 1643, after a brief courtship, he had married Mary Powell, the daughter of an Oxfordshire Royalist. Disgusted with one month's experience of the austere gloom of a Puritan household, the bride left her unsocial husband to

---

* Stephen Marshall, Edward Calamy, Thomas Young, Matthew Newcomen and W(uu)illiam Spurstow were joint writers of a Puritan polemic, which was named *Smectymnuus*, the word being composed of the initials of their five names.

his studies, and sought the merriment of her father's home.
When Milton wrote requesting her to return, she ignored
his letter; his messenger she treated ungraciously. Making
up his mind that his bride had forsaken him, he elaborated
his views on the question of divorce. The estrangement continued for two years, and then, learning that her husband
was about to illustrate his faith in his own doctrines by
marrying again, Mary Milton repented with all due humility.
So thoroughly was she forgiven that her husband's house
was opened as a refuge for her family when the Civil War
drove them into poverty and distress. In the meantime
Milton had written *Of Education,* and, in 1644, had addressed to Parliament the most masterly of his prose compositions, the *Areopagitica; a Speech for the Liberty of
Unlicensed Printing* (**139**).

His Services to the Government. In 1649 he was appointed Latin Secretary to the Council of State. The
elegance of his scholarship and the soundness of his judgment qualified him for the responsible position. His state-
papers show with what zeal and ability he discharged his
duties. While holding this office he undertook the last and
most important of his literary controversies. At the insti-
gation of Charles II., then an exile in France, Salmasius,
an eminent scholar and the picked champion of the royalists,
published an elaborate and powerful pamphlet in Latin,
maintaining the divine right of kings and invoking vengeance upon the regicides in England. The royalists declared the argument to be unanswerable; and, indeed, it
was too weighty to be disregarded. The Council, therefore,
commanded Milton to undertake a reply. Accordingly he
prepared his *Defensio Populi Anglicani.* In elegant Latinity
he proved himself the equal of his adversary; in vitupera-
tion and in weight of argument, he was adjudged the
superior, and he received public thanks for the victory won.

It is said that the death of Salmasius was hastened by the
mortification of his defeat.   But Milton's work in the preparation of his argument had hastened the loss of sight which
had menaced him for years.   Before 1654 he was totally
blind ; however, he continued to write many of the more
important state-papers until the year of the Restoration,
and was also occupied with a *History of England,* with a
body of divinity, and perhaps with his great poem.

Through tracts and letters, Milton had opposed to the
last the return of the monarchy.   The Restoration was the
signal for his distress and persecution.   A proclamation
was issued against him, and for a time his fate was uncertain ; but he lived in concealment until the passing of
the Act of Indemnity placed him in safety.*   From that
time until his death he lived in retirement, busily occupied
in the composition of *Paradise Lost,* and *Paradise*
1665.]   *Regained.*   The former of these works had been
his principal employment for about seven years.
The second epic and the tragedy of *Samson Agonistes* were
published in the year 1671.   On the 8th of November, 1674,
Milton died.   He was buried in Cripplegate Churchyard.
His first wife died leaving him three daughters ; his second
Katharine Woodcock, died in 1658, after little more than
a year's marriage ; but the third, Elizabeth Minshull, whom
he espoused in 1664, survived him for more than half a
century.

Three Periods of his Literary Career.   Milton's literary
career divides itself into three great periods,—that of his
youth, that of his manhood, and that of his old age.   The
first may be roughly stated as extending from 1623 to 1640 ;

---

* "He [Charles II.] offered to reinstate Milton in his office of government advocate, if he would devote his talents to the cause of monarchy.   His wife entreated
him to comply with this proposal. 'You are a woman,' replied Milton, 'and your
thoughts dwell on the domestic interests of our house ; I think only of posterity,
and I will die consistently with my character.' "—*Lamartine.*

the second from 1640 to 1660, the date of the Restoration, and the third from the Restoration to the poet's death in 1674. During the first of these he produced most of his minor poetical works; during the second he was chiefly occupied with his prose controversies; and in the third we see him slowly elaborating the *Paradise Lost* (**126–134**), the *Paradise Regained* (**135**), and the *Samson Agonistes* (**136**).

The First Period. Those qualities which distinguish Milton from all other poets appear in his earliest productions,—in the poetical exercises written at school and at college. The *Hymn on the Nativity*, composed at the age of twenty-one, is a fit prelude to the *Paradise Lost*. With a peculiar grandeur and dignity of thought he combines an exquisite, though somewhat austere harmony and grace. The least elaborate of his efforts are characterized by a solemn, stately melody of versification that satisfies the ear like the sound of a mighty organ. Apart from the energy of rhythm, his youthful poems are mostly tranquil, tender, or playful in tone.

The *Masque of Comus* (**122**) was written in 1634, to be performed at Ludlow Castle before the Earl of Bridgewater. The Earl's daughter and two sons had lost their way while walking in the woods; and out of this simple incident Milton wrote the most beautiful pastoral drama that has yet been produced. The characters are few, the dramatic action is exceedingly simple, the eloquence is pure and musical, and the songs are exquisitely melodious. In this poem are suggestions of Fletcher's *Faithful Shepherdess*, and of the *Masques* and the *Sad Shepherd* of Jonson; but in elevation of thought, in purity, if not in delineation of natural beauty, Milton has far surpassed both Jonson and Fletcher.

Lycidas, an elegy (**123**), was a tribute to the memory of Milton's friend and fellow-student, Edward King, who was lost at sea in a voyage to Ireland. In its form, as well as in the irregular and ever-varying music of its verse, may be traced the influence of Milton's study of Spenser and the Italian classics. This poem was fiercely condemned by Samuel Johnson. He declared that "no man could have fancied that he read *Lycidas* with pleasure had he not known its author." But few who read the poem will accept such criticism. For force of imagination and ex-haustless beauty of imagery it answers to a true poetic sensibility.

The two descriptive poems, *L'Allegro* (124) and *Il Pense-roso* (125), are perhaps the best known and best appreciated of all Milton's works. They are of nearly the same length, and are perfect counterparts. *L'Allegro* describes scenery and various occupations and amusements as viewed in the light of a joyous and vivacious nature; *Il Penseroso* dwells upon the aspect presented by similar objects to a person of serious, thoughtful and studious character. The tone of each is admirably sustained; the personality of the poet appears in the calm cheerfulness of the one, as well as in the tranquil meditativeness of the other. His joy is with-out frivolity; his pensive thoughtfulness is without gloom. But no analysis can do justice to the bold yet delicate lines in which these complementary pictures present various aspects of nature—beautiful, sublime, smiling or terrible. They are inexhaustibly suggestive to the thoughtful reader; and they have been justly pronounced, not so much poems as stores of imagery, from which volumes of picturesque description might be drawn. Written in the seclusion of his home at Horton, they are fancies about mirth and melancholy; they are poems of theory, not of observation. They show us how a man who knew neither mirth nor melancholy would per-sonify them. They are intellectual studies of emotion, not its irrepressible utterances.

Milton's Latin and Italian poems belong principally to his youth; many of the former were college exercises. He has had no rival among the modern writers of Latin verse. The felicity with which he has reproduced the diction of classical antiquity is equaled only by the perfection with which he has sustained the style of antique thought.

Shakespeare, Spenser, Sidney, and inferior poets had written sonnets, some of a high degree of beauty, but it was reserved for Milton to transplant into his native country the Italian sonnet in its highest form. He has seldom chosen the subject of Love; religion, patriotism, and domestic affection are his favorite themes; and most of them are ennobled by that sublime gravity which was characteristic of his mind. Among his sonnets the following are worthy of special admiration: I. *To the Nightingale;* VI. and VII., containing noble anticipations of his poetical glory; XVI., a recapitulation of Cromwell's victories XVIII., *On the Massacre of the Protestants in Piedmont* **(138)**; XIX. and XXII., on his own blindness **(137)**.

The Second Period. The second period of Milton's literary life was filled with political and religious controversy and in the voluminous prose works which were its results, we see the ardor of his convictions, the lofty integrity of his character, and the force of his genius. They are crowded with erudition, fused into a glowing mass by the fervor of enthusiasm. Whether in Latin or in English, their style is remarkable for a weighty and ornate magnificence, cumbrous and pedantic in other hands, but in his, a fit armor for breadth and power of thought. Milton seems to think in Latin. The length and involution of his sentences, their solemn and stately march, his preference for words of Latin origin—all contribute to make him one of the most Latinic of English authors. This quality, while it attests his learning, has combined with the fact that many of his subjects possessed only a temporary interest, to exclude his prose treatises from their true place among

English classics. They are becoming every day better known to the general reader.*

The *Areopagitica,* addressed to the English Parliament in defence of the liberty of the press, is an oration after the antique models, and is the sublimest plea that any age or country has produced for the great principle of freedom of thought and opinion. Its almost superhuman eloquence is rivaled by a passage in the pamphlet *Against Prelaty,* in which Milton confutes the calumnies of his foes by a glorious epitome of his studies, projects, and literary aspirations. The tractate, *Of Education,* embodies a beautiful but Utopian scheme for bringing modern educational training into conformity with ancient ideas. Others of his finest prose treatises are the *Iconoclastes,* the *Defensio Populi Anglicani, Defensio Secunda,* and *A Ready and Easy Way to Establish a Free Commonwealth.*

The Third Period. There is no spectacle in the history of literature more touching and sublime than Milton blind, poor, persecuted, and alone, "fallen upon evil days and evil tongues, in darkness and with dangers compassed round," retiring into obscurity to compose those immortal epics, *Paradise Lost* and *Paradise Regained.* The **Paradise Lost (126)** was originally composed in ten books, which were afterwards so divided as to make twelve. Its composition, though the work was probably meditated long before,† occupied about seven years, from 1658 to 1665;

---

* " It is to be regretted that the prose writings of Milton should in our time be so little read. As compositions, they deserve the attention of every man who wishes to become acquainted with the full power of the English language. They abound with passages compared with which the finest declamations of Burke sink into insignificance. They are a perfect field of cloth of gold. The style is stiff with gorgeous embroidery."—*Macaulay.*

† According to Voltaire, " Milton, as he was traveling in Italy, in his youth, saw at Florence a comedy called *Adamo.* The subject of the play was the Fall of Man; the actors, God, the Angels, Adam, Eve, the Serpent, Death, and the seven Mortal

and it was first published in 1667. Its subject is the grand‹ est that ever entered into the heart of man to conceive. The entire action moves among celestial and infernal per‹ sonages and scenes ; and the poet does not hesitate to usher us into the awful presence of Deity itself.

Argument of the Poem. In *Book I.*, after the proposition of the subject,—the Fall of Man,—and a sublime invocation, the council of Satan and the infernal angels is described. Their determination to oppose the designs of God in the creation of the Earth and the innocence of our first parents are then stated, and the book closes with a description of the erection of Pandemonium, the palace of Satan. *Book II.* records the debates of the evil spirits, the consent of Satan to undertake the enterprise of temptation, his journey to the Gates of Hell, which he finds guarded by Sin and Death. *Book III.* transports us to Heaven, where, after a dialogue between God the Father and God the Son, the latter offers himself as a propitiation for the foreseen disobedience of Adam. In the latter portion of this canto, Satan meets Uriel, the angel of the Sun, and inquires the road to the new-created Earth, where, disguised as an angel of light, he descends. *Book IV.* brings Satan to the sight of Paradise, and contains the picture of the innocence and happiness of Adam and Eve. The angels set a guard over Eden, and Satan is arrested while endeavoring to tempt Eve in a dream. He is allowed to escape. In *Book V.* Eve relates her dream to Adam, who comforts her ; and they, after their morning prayer, proceed to their daily employment. They are visited by the angel Raphael, sent to warn them ; and he relates to Adam the story of the revolt

---

Sins. That topic, so improper for a drama, was handled in a manner entirely coi. formable to the extravagance of the design. The scene opens with a chorus o. angels, and a cherub thus speaks for the rest: *Let the rainbow be the fiddlestick of the heavens ! Let the planets be the notes of our music ! Let time beat carefully the measure, etc.* Thus the play begins, and every scene rises above the last in pro‹ fusion of impertinence. Milton pierced through the absurdity of that performance to the hidden majesty of the subject: which, being altogether unfit for the stage, yet might be, for the genius of Milton, and his only, the foundation of an epic poem. He took from that ridiculous trifle the first hint of the noblest work which human imagination has ever attempted, and which he executed more than twenty years after."

of Satan and the disobedient angels. In *Book VI.* the narrative of Raphael is continued. *Book VII.* is devoted to the account of the creation of the world, given by Raphael, at Adam's request. In *Book VIII.* Adam describes to the angel his own state and recollections, his meeting with Eve, and their union. The action of *Book IX.* is the temptation, first of Eve, and then, through her, of Adam. *Book X.* contains the judgment and sentence of Adam and Eve. Satan, triumphant, returns to Pandemonium, but not before Sin and Death construct a causeway through Chaos to Earth. Satan recounts his success, but he and all his angels are transformed into serpents. Adam and Eve bewail their fault, and determine to implore pardon. *Book XI.* relates the acceptance of Adam's repentance by the Almighty, who, however, commands that he be expelled from Paradise. The angel Michael is sent to reveal to Adam the consequences of his transgression. Eve laments her exile from Eden, and Michael shows Adam in a vision the destiny of man before the Flood. *Book XII.* continues the prophetic picture shown to Adam by Michael of the fate of the human race from the Flood. Adam is comforted by the account of the redemption of man, and by the destinies of the Church. The poem terminates with the wandering forth of our first parents from Paradise.

No synopsis can satisfy the reader or assist him materially in comprehending the poem. Nothing but an acquaintance with the work itself would suffice.

The peculiar form of blank verse in which *Paradise Lost* and *Paradise Regained* are written, was first adapted to epic poetry by Milton. He has gifted it with a distinctive tone and rhythm, solemn, dignified and sonorous, yet of musical and ever-varying cadence, and as delicately responsive to the sentiments it embodies as the harmonies of the Homeric hexameter. Where it suited his purpose, he closely followed the severe condensation of the Scriptural narrative; but where his subject required him to give freedom to his thought, he showed that no poet ever surpassed him in fertility of conception, that no poet ever saw the splendors of a more glorious vision. In alluding to the blending of simple Scriptural story with imagination in *Paradise Lost*, Lamartine pronounces the poem "the dream of a Puritan who has fallen asleep over the first pages of his Bible." The description of the fallen angels, the splendor of Heaven, the horrors of hell, the loveliness of Paradise, as exhibited in the poem, pass the bounds of earthly experience and give us scenes of superhuman beauty or horror, that are pre-sented to the eye with a vividness rivaling that of the memory itself. Milton's Satan (127) is no caricature of the demon of vulgar superstition; he is not less than archangel, though archangel ruined; he is invested, by the poet, with the most lofty and terrible attributes of the divinities of classical mythology. Milton is pre-eminently the poet of the learned; for however imposing his pictures may be even to the most uncultivated mind, it is only to a reader who is familiar with classical and Biblical literature that he dis-plays his full powers.

Dryden and many later critics have criticised the subject of this epic poem, inasmuch as it makes Adam but the nominal hero, while Satan is the real one. The inferior nature of man, as compared with the powers by which he is surrounded, reduces him, apparently, to a secondary part in the action of the poem.*

After Milton's retirement from public life he was sought out by scholarly foreigners, who were curious to see him on account of the fame of his learning; and he received loving and admiring attention from many of his own countrymen. Among them was Thomas Ellwood, a Friend,

* It seems probable that Milton had some difficulty in finding a publisher for his epic; but in 1667 he effected a sale of the copyright to Samuel Symons. By the terms of the sale, Milton was to receive five pounds on signing the agreement, five pounds more on the sale of a first edition of thirteen hundred copies, and five pounds for each of the two following editions when they should be exhausted. He lived to receive the second payment. In 1680 his widow sold to the publisher all of her "right, title, and interest" in the work for eight pounds; so that the author and his heirs received but eighteen pounds for the grandest poem of our literature.

who frequently read Latin books to the blind poet. One day Milton handed him a manuscript, and asked him to read it with care. Upon returning it, Ellwood said, " Thou hast said much here of Paradise Lost, but what has thou to say to Paradise Found?" This question suggested to Milton the writing of **Paradise Regained**. By general con sent the second epic is placed far below the first in point of interest and variety; still it displays the same solemn grandeur, the same lofty imagination, the same vast learning. Christ's Temptation in the Wilderness is the theme, and the narrative of that incident, as recorded in the fourth chapter of St. Matthew's gospel, is closely followed. This poem is said to have been preferred to the grander epic in the esteem of the poet himself.

The noble and pathetic tragedy of **Samson Agonistes (136)** belongs to the closing period of Milton's literary career. It is constructed according to the strictest rules of the Greek drama. In the character of the hero, his blind. ness, his sufferings, and his resignation to the will of God, Milton has given a most touching representation of his old age.* So closely has Milton copied all the details of the ancient dramas, that there is no exaggeration in saying that a modern reader will obtain a more exact impression of what a Greek tragedy was, from the study of *Samson Agonistes*, than from the most faithful translation of Sophocles or Euripides.

---

* " They charge me "—thus he wrote to one of his friends, a foreigner—" they charge me with poverty because I have never desired to become rich dishonestly ; they accuse me of blindness because I have lost my eyes in the service of liberty ; they tax me with cowardice, and while I had the use of my eyes and my sword I never feared the boldest among them ; finally, I am upbraided with deformity, while no one was more handsome in the age of beauty. I do not even complain of my want of sight ; in the night with which I am surrounded, the light of the divine presence shines with a more brilliant lustre. God looks down upon me with tenderness and compassion, because I can now see none but himself. Misfortune should protect me from insult, and render me sacred ; not because I am deprived of the light of heaven, but because I am under the shadow of the divine wings, which have enveloped me with this darkness."

His Solitariness. The last years of Milton's life, in which darkness nestled him under her wing, are a reminder of the fact that the world from which he was thus shut out had not then, nor has since had, nor will ever have, a distinct view of him. Milton's soul was the soul of a recluse. He was in, but not of, the seventeenth century. In moral and in intellectual power he was a giant, beside whom his contemporaries were pigmies. The beauty and dignity of his life were such as might be looked for in a man chosen from some lofty and bracing epoch of history; and we are surprised at finding him in that sickly age, breathing the miasma that brought disease to other men. He was miraculously kept from the religious fever that made some men insane, and from the taint of the moral plague that made others loathsome. This exemption makes his life somewhat a mystery, and the effect of the mystery is heightened by the purity and elevation of his thought, and by the glittering magnificence of his style.

Although we know much about Milton, we do not know him. We do not hope to commune closely with him. He seems to us a little more than human. When we have read the loftiest praises of him we feel that the critic has failed of reaching the elevation which a just criticism of Milton should attain. The rhetoric, the enthusiasm of Macaulay, do not cast as clear a light as we could wish for, in viewing " the genius and virtues of John Milton, the poet, the statesman, the philosopher, the glory of English literature, the champion and the martyr of English liberty." There is a grandeur in the man that cannot be fitly described by the flushed fancy and the lavish strength of the rhetorician's grandest periods. There is something about him that crowds our capacity for admiring, and yet forbids the familiar acquaintance that would give us rapturous love for him. Our ideal of him is less satisfactory than our ideal of any other of the great men in our literature; and the cause

8

of his eluding us is found in the fact that he was a recluse Wordsworth truly said of him,

" Thy soul was like a star and dwelt apart."

The mystery that is about him, the haughtiness that some critics detect in him, the grandeur that evades analysis, and the strange reverence felt by all who study him, are trace- able to an awe-inspiring peculiarity that may be described as the loneliness of Milton. The companionships of other historic characters help the student; but Milton seems to have been without intimacies: the social temptations to which they yielded or over which they were victorious, the constancy or inconstancy of their friendships, the influence that they exerted over those who loved them, give us an idea of what our attitude would have been towards them, had we been of their company. But where shall we find the men who had intimate friendship with Milton. His loneliness was recognized and respected. His fellow-students at the uni- versity detected something peculiarly unlike themselves in him, and named him "The Lady of the College." The gentlewoman who came to his house to be his wife soon found that she could not intrude upon his solitude. Amid the excitement of the Civil War he seems to have been companionless ; and when the victory had brought joy to all other men of his political party he was found in the seclusion of his quiet study, and was summoned to the public service of the state. During the years of the Com- monwealth two men rise superior to all other Englishmen,— the man of action, Cromwell; and the man of thought, Milton. Although mutually dependent, they were not intimate companions, for Milton stood in intellectual isola- tion. When the days of blindness and poverty and threaten- ings came to him and he was in his hiding-place, he was not withdrawn further than he had ever been from the world. His whole career was separate from the intimate acquaintance of men. His religious opinions would have been acceptable to neither party. Although he was a Puritan in politics, his theology would have been criminal heresy to the Puritans. In forming his political opinions he was not influenced by the same motives which swayed the men of his party; they beheaded Charles I. because he was the leader of a hated church; Milton justified the regicide because the unconstitutional exercise of regal power is insulting to nationality. It is this lack of affinity between Milton and other men, this want of contact between him and the world, this independence in political, poetical, and religious thinking—this loneliness of the man—that gives a peculiar dignity to his character, that overawes our love, and forbids our thorough knowledge of him.

The student is referred to Masson's *Life of Milton,*—Dr. Johnson's *Life of Milton,*—De Quincey's *Life of Milton,*—Hallam's *History of Literature*, Vol. IV.,—Macaulay's Essay on Milton,—Lamartine's *Celebrated Characters,*—Channing's Essay on Milton,—Reed's *Lectures on the British Poets*, Vol. I.,—Hazlitt's *Lectures on the English Poets,*—Lowell's Essay on Milton and Shakespeare, *North American Review*, April, 1868,—the article on Milton in the Encyclopedia Britannica,—Campbell's *Specimens of the British Poets,*—Taine's *English Literature,*—Landor's Works,—Masson's *Essays on the English Poets,*—and Addison's criticisms on Paradise Lost in *The Spectator*, Nos. 267, 273, 279, 285, 291, 297, 303, 309, 315, 321, 327, 333, 339, 345, 351, 359, 363, 369.

In this chapter we have considered:—

John Milton.

    1. His Services to the Government.

    2. Three Periods of His Literary Career.

    3. The Argument of Paradise Lost.

    4. Milton's Solitariness.

CHAPTER XV.

THE LITERATURE OF THE RESTORATION.

FOR worthlessness of character and for the shamefulness of his public life, Charles II., the prince to whom the crown of the Stuarts was restored, stands without a rival in the line of **1660.]** English kings. During the time of the Commonwealth he had found refuge on the Continent. His good-nature and his rank had won him hosts of friends; but as he was wanting in dignity of character, his friendships were not with the good. When he ascended the throne he inaugurated a reign of debauchery and shame. The dissipated companions of his exile, and foreign adventurers who had fastened themselves upon him, were the favorites of his Court. His ambition was to ensure these worthless courtiers a good time. The gambler, the drunkard, and the libertine, found him ever ready to give them the royal smile and to join them in their criminal pleasures. Patriotism made no successful appeal to him. Decency fled from his presence. His halls of state were lavishly furnished, the doors were thrown open, and the rollicking king welcomed his subjects to his presence, where they could hear the profanity, could see the drunkenness and could suspect the baser infamies of the highest circle of English life. Under Cromwell's government severe restraints had been thrown about the people. Public amusements had been forbidden. Many innocent pleasures had been denounced. And now the Court laughed loudest at the unreasonable severity of the Puritans, and went to the farthest reach in a reckless pursuit of pleasure. The effect of such a revolution at court was immediate and fearful. The nation plunged madly into excesses.

Popular literature in any generation is but the reflection of that generation's thought, and so we must expect to find that the applauded writers of the time of Charles II. are men who laugh at seriousness and apologize for vice. The drama of the time, as it appeared most directly to popular attention, was indecent; but whatever writings came from other than Puritan pens were tainted with the disease of the Court.

Samuel Butler. The most illustrious literary representative of the party of the Cavaliers is Samuel Butler (1612–1680). When more than fifty years of age, after witnessing the success and the failure of the Puritans, he wrote a satire upon their follies in which he subjected them to a ridicule so keen that his work still holds an eminent place in our literature of satire. His early life was passed in obscurity. He was of lowly parentage. Lack of funds cut short his stay at the University of Cambridge; still he was there long enough to acquire some of the learning displayed in his works. For several years he was clerk in the office of a country justice, and afterwards became a secretary in the service of the Countess of Kent. In these positions he found opportunities for study and for intercourse with scholarly and accomplished men. Next we find him a tutor in the family of Sir Samuel Luke, a wealthy gentleman of Bedfordshire, who, as a violent republican member of Parliament, and as one of Cromwell's satraps, took an active part in the agitations of the Commonwealth. In the person of this dignitary Butler probably saw the most radical type of Puritan character.

The Restoration brought Butler no special reward for his loyalty. He became secretary to Lord Carbury, and for some time acted as steward of Ludlow Castle; but this situation was neither permanent nor lucrative.

1662.] **Hudibras.** It was in 1662 that he published the first part of *Hudibras;* and the second part followed in 1664. The poem soon became the popular book of the day; for its wit and ingenuity won the praise of the critics, while its tone and subject flattered the vindictive triumph of the royalists. Charles II. carried it about in his pocket, and was constantly quoting and admiring it; but all efforts to secure patronage for its author, either from the king or his favorites, proved fruitless. A fatality combined with the usual ingratitude of the Court to leave the great wit in his poverty and obscurity. Two years after the appearance of the third part of his famous work he died in 1680, at a miserable lodging in London; and the expenses of his modest burial were defrayed by a friend.

Hudibras is a burlesque satire upon the Puritan party, and especially upon its two dominant sects,—Presbyterians and Independents. It describes the adventures of a fanatical justice of the peace and his clerk, who sally forth, in knight-errant style, to enforce the violent and oppressive enactments of the Rump Parliament against the popular amusements. Sir Hudibras, the hero,—in all probability a caricature of Sir Samuel Luke, Butler's whilom employer—represents the Presbyterians. He is depicted as, in mind, character, person and bearing, a grotesque compound of pedantry, ugliness, hypocrisy and cowardice; his clerk, Ralph, is sketched with equal unction as the type of the sour, wrong-headed, but more enthusiastic Independents. The doughty pair having set out on their crusade, first encounter a crowd of ragamuffins who are leading a bear to be "baited," and refuse to disperse at the knight's command. A furious mock-heroic battle ensues, in which Hudibras is finally victorious. He puts the chief delinquents in the parish stocks; but their comrades soon return to the charge, set them free, and imprison the knight and squire. They are in turn liberated by a rich widow, to whom the knight is paying court. Hudibras afterwards visits the lady; and her servants, in the disguise of devils, give him a sound beating. He consults a lawyer and an astrologer, to obtain revenge and satisfaction; and at that point the narration breaks off, incomplete.

Evidently the fundamental idea of this poem was suggested by the *Don Quixote* of Cervantes; but its spirit and the style of its development are entirely original. Cervantes makes his hero laughable, without impairing our respect for his noble and heroic character; Butler invests his personages with the utmost degree of odium that is compatible with the sentiment of the ludicrous. As his object was exclusively satirical, he could not and did not consider any of the noble qualities of the fanatics whom he attacked. *Hudibras* is the best burlesque in the English language. "The same amount of learning, wit, shrewdness, ingenious and deep thought, felicitous illustration and irresistible drollery has never [elsewhere] been comprised in the same limits."

Butler's style is at once concise and suggestive; many of his expressions have the terse strength of proverbs, and at the same time open boundless vistas of comic association. His language is easy, conversational, careless; familiar and even vulgar words are found side by side with the pedantic terms of art and learning; the short octosyllabic verse moves with unflagging vivacity; and the constant recurrence of fantastic rhymes tickles the fancy. Yet, although no English author was ever more witty than Butler, he is utterly destitute of genial humor; his analysis of character is pitilessly keen and clear; but he shows no power in sustaining the interest of a story. Hence he neither enlists our sympathy nor attracts that curiosity which is gratified by a well-developed intrigue. "If inexhaustible wit could give perpetual pleasure," says Johnson, "no eye could ever leave half-read the work of Butler; . . . . . however, astonishment soon becomes a toilsome pleasure, and the paucity of events fatigues the attention and makes the perusal of the book tedious."

Among Butler's miscellaneous writings which were published after his death, the most entertaining are a series of prose sketches. Many of his posthumous poems are caustic and undiscriminating satires upon the physical investigators of his day. He is particularly severe upon the Royal Society, which he ridicules in his *Elephant in the Moon.*

John Bunyan (1628–1688.) In this age of debauchery, John Bunyan, the master of religious allegory, appeared. He came from the lowest grade of social life, grew up to manhood with an education so meagre that he barely knew how to read and write, and yet he produced a work which places him foremost among the writers of his class. What Shakespeare is to English dramatists, what Milton is to English epic poets, that John Bunyan is to writers of English allegory. In this department of our literature none approach him.

He was the son of a poor Bedfordshire tinker, and followed his father's trade until his eighteenth year. He then served for a few months in the Parliamentary army. Returning to his native village, Elstow, he married "one as poor as himself." He says that "they had neither dish nor spoon betwixt them." Until this time Bunyan's course of life had been the ordinary one of a poor, uneducated village lad, stained with the vice of profanity, and

too much given to rough sports. Doubtless his follies had often
been denounced as heinous sins by the earnest Puritans of his
acquaintance. His young wife was a devout woman, and she
sought his reformation. By inducing him to read two religious
books bequeathed to her by a dying father, and by leading him to
the church of which she was a member, she succeeded in awaken.
ing his anxiety concerning the future life. Once aroused, his sensitive and imaginative soul could not rest. For about two years his
mind was in a state of intense gloom, tormented with fears for
his eternal welfare, and perplexed with the theological quandaries
of the day. Finally, by what he always deemed a special exercise
of divine mercy, his soul found peace. He united with the Baptist
church of Bedford, and, yielding to the wishes of his fellow-
members, he availed himself of his journeyings as a tinker to
exercise the vocation of a preacher. The fervent piety and rude
eloquence of his discourses gradually gained him wide reputation,
and he became a leading man among the Baptists. As such he was
exposed to rigorous persecution; for Dissenters were regarded by
the government of Charles II. as in sympathy with republican
doctrines. In 1660, having been arrested and convicted as a
"common upholder of conventicles," he was shut up in Bedford
jail. There he remained for twelve years, steadfastly refusing to
purchase freedom by a sacrifice of his faith. The weary years were
spent in working for the support of his family and in writing
religious books. His patient and cheerful piety so won the con
fidence of his keepers that, during the last two years of his confinement, he was often allowed to leave the prison. In 1671 he was
chosen preacher of the Baptist congregation in Bedford. A year
later, when liberated by the royal proclamation of religious toleration, he entered upon his pastoral labors with energy, and prosecuted them to the end of his life. The fame of his sufferings, his
genius as a writer, his power as a speaker, gave him unbounded
influence among the Baptists; while the beauty of his character
and the catholic liberality of his views secured him universal
esteem. His ministrations extended over the whole region between
Bedford and London, and involved occasional visits to the metropolis itself. It was in London that his death occurred, in 1688,
having been hastened by the exposure and fatigue of a journey
which he had undertaken for the benevolent purpose of reconciling
a father and son.

Bunyan's works are numerous, and entirely of a religious character. Only three among them demand our special notice.—the
religious autobiography entitled *Grace Abounding to the Chief of
Sinners,* and the two religious allegories, *Pilgrim's Progress* and
the *Holy War.* The first gives a candid account of Bunyan's own
conversion, portraying in detail the struggles of a human soul
striving to burst its bonds of sin and worldliness. It contains passages of sublime simplicity and pathos. The picture has interest
for the philosopher of mind as well as for the religious devotee;
though it is evident that both its lights and shades have been
exaggerated by the enthusiasm of Bunyan's character. He was a
dreamer; and from his childhood, as he tells us in this book, he
had been haunted by fearful visions of the lake of fire.

**The Pilgrim's Progress from this World to that which Is
to Come (155)** narrates the experience of a Christian in going from
a life of sin to everlasting bliss. Christian, dwelling in the City of
Destruction, is incited by an agonizing consciousness of his lost
estate to journey towards the New Jerusalem. All the adventures
of his travels, the scenes through which he passes, the friends and
fellow-pilgrims whom he finds upon the road, typify the joys and
trials of a religious life. Bunyan's imaginary persons excite all the
interest and sympathy which belong to human beings. The doctrine of salvation by grace is the burden of his thought and the
moral of his story; he writes for sinners perishing in an abyss whence
he has been snatched. This makes him direct, fervent, pathetic.
Occasionally, too, a vein of rich humor, outcropping in argument
or description, indicates the genial healthfulness of his mind, and
draws him into closer sympathy with his readers.

> " Ingenious dreamer! in whose well-told tale
> Sweet fiction and sweet truth alike prevail;
> Whose humorous vein, strong sense, and simple style
> May teach the gayest, make the gravest smile;
> Witty and well employed, and like thy Lord
> Speaking in parables his slighted word."— *Cowper.*

He had read but few books; the Bible and Fox's *Book of Martyrs*
comprised his entire library during the twelve years of his imprisonment. He is said to have known the former almost by heart.
That his mind was saturated with its spirit is indicated by the
mode of his thinking, by the character of his imagery, by the very

form of his expression. His style is nervous, plain, idiomatic; it derives strength and terseness from its large proportion of Saxon words; is often picturesque and poetical, sometimes ungrammatical; but it is always that language of the common people which attains its highest vigor and purity in the English Bible. Macaulay says that "the style is delightful to every reader, and invaluable as a study to every person who wishes to obtain a quick command over the English language. The vocabulary is the vocabulary of the common people. There is not an expression, if we except a few technical terms of theology, which would puzzle the rudest peasant. We have observed several pages which do not contain a single word of more than two syllables."

Pilgrim's Progress is in two parts. The first was written in Bedford jail, to " divert Bunyan's vacant seasons," and was **1678.]** published in 1678. Its popularity was most remarkable. After it had passed through eight editions, Bunyan incorporated with it the second part, in which the celestial pilgrimage is accomplished by Christian's wife and children whom he had left in the City of Destruction. From that day till this its popularity has continued; childhood and old age find delight in its story. Its translation may be found in every language which contains a religious literature.

The *Holy War* is an allegory typifying, in the siege and capture of the City of Mansoul, the strife between sin and religion in the human spirit. Diabolus and Immanuel are the leaders of the hostile armies. The narrative is far less interesting than the *Pilgrim's Progress*. Its style is less piquant and vivacious.

Izaak Walton. Few authors have secured a firmer hold upon the affection and sympathy of their readers than Izaak Walton (1593-1683). He was born in Stafford, and passed his early manhood in London, where he carried on the business of a linen-draper. At fifty years of age he retired from trade with a competence sufficient for his modest desires; and he lived to the great age of ninety in ease and tranquillity, enjoying the intimate friendship of many learned and accomplished men, and amusing himself with literature and rural pleasures. He produced the *Lives* of five distinguished contemporaries,—Donne, Wotton, Hooker, George Herbert, and Bishop Sanderson, the first, second, and last of whom he had known personally. These biographies stand alone in literature; they are written with such tender grace, with such an unaffected fervor of personal attachment and simple piety, that they will always be regarded as masterpieces. But Walton's best production is *The Compleat Angler* (**158**), a treatise on his favorite pastime of fishing. It is thrown into the form of dialogues —first carried on by a hunter, a falconer, and an angler, each of whom, in turn, extols the delights of his favorite sport, until the hunter is vanquished by the eloquence of the angler, and desires to become his disciple. The veteran then initiates him into the mysteries of the gentle craft, and as the two continue their discourse, technical precepts are interspersed with exquisite pictures of English river scenery, and racy descriptions of the fortunes of "angling days." Every page is spiced with the quaint thought of the philosopher of the rod; his sensibility to the beauties of Nature, and his cheerful piety find constant and happy expression; while the language of the book is as pure as its thoughts. An occasional touch of innocent, old-world pedantry only adds to its indefinable charm; and its popularity seems destined to endure as long as the language. A second part was added to the *Compleat Angler* by CHARLES COTTON, the poet, an adopted son of Walton.

Another writer of this epoch, whose interests were divided between literary pursuits and the never-cloying amusements of rural life, is **John Evelyn** (1620–1706). He was a gentleman of good family and considerable fortune, and merits distinction as one of the first Englishmen who practised the art of gardening and planting on scientific principles. To the timely publication of his *Sylva* (1664), a work on the management of forest trees, England is largely indebted for her present abundance of timber. *Terra*, his treatise on agriculture and gardening, appeared in 1675. Both books display much practical good sense, animated by a genuine love of Nature.

Evelyn's personal character was a model of purity and benevolence; his household and his friends seem to have formed a little oasis of virtuous refinement in the general depravity of their time. Through a *Diary* (**159**), which extends over the greater part of his life, he has given us valuable historical information concerning business and social customs, and a mournful description of the unparalleled corruption of Charles II.'s court.

N

Samuel Pepys (1632–1703). Pepys began life as a subordinate clerk in one of the government offices. By his punctuality, honesty and devotion to business, he rose to the important position of Secretary to the Admiralty. He was one of the few able and upright officials connected with the government during the reigns of Charles II. and James II. The accession of William and Mary deprived him of his position, and the last years of his life were passed in retirement.

The *Diary* (**160**), through which Pepys has immortalized himself and won the gratitude of posterity, was written in short-hand, and was first deciphered and published in 1825. It extends over the nine years from 1660 to 1669, and is the gossipy chronicle of a gay and profligate time. We have no other book which gives so life-like a picture of that extraordinary state of society which fell under the author's observation. Not only was Pepys by nature curious as a magpie, and somewhat convivial in his tastes withal; but his official duties brought him into contact with every class, from the king and his ministers down to the poor, half-starved sailors whose pay he distributed. Writing entirely for himself, he chronicles with ludicrous *naïveté* the successive details of his own rise in wealth and importance, all the minutiæ of his domestic affairs, and of the dress, manners, and social amusements of himself and his associates. King, statesmen, courtiers, players, live again in his pages, and Pepys's own character—an interesting compound of shrewdness, vanity, worldly wisdom and simplicity—infinitely enhances the piquancy of his revelations.

Edward Hyde, first Earl of Clarendon (1608–1674), was one of the most prominent figures in the Long Parliament and in the Age of the Restoration. He was educated for the profession of law; but at an early age he quitted the bar, and engaged in the more exciting struggles of political life. He sat in the Short Parliament of 1640, and was also a conspicuous orator in the Long Parliament, at first supporting the Opposition; but after a violent quarrel with the more radical champions of the national cause, he gradually transferred his support to the Royalists. Upon the outbreak of civil war he fled from London to join the king at York; and from that time forth was one of the most faithful and one of the most discreet adherents of the royal cause. In 1644 he was named a member of the Council appointed to advise and take charge of Prince Charles, whom he accompanied to Jersey, and whose exile and misfortunes he shared from the execution of Charles I. until the Restoration. After the throne of the Stuarts had been re-established, Hyde reaped the reward of his services. He was made Lord Chancellor of England, created first a Baron, afterwards, in 1661, Earl of Clarendon, and for several years exercised a pow-erful influence in the national counsels. However, his popularity, as well as his favor with the king, soon began to decline. The austerity of his morals was a constant rebuke to the profligate Court; his advice, generally in favor of prudence and economy, was distasteful to the king; while, like many other statesmen who have returned to power after long exile, he failed to accommodate himself to the advanced state of public opinion. The people looked with distrust upon his increasing wealth and power, and demanded his removal from office after he had used his influence for the sale of Dunkirk. Charles II. was all too ready to sacrifice his minister to the general clamor. Clarendon was impeached for high treason. He went into exile, and passed the rest of his life in France, occupied in completing his *History.*

Clarendon's principal work is the *History of the Great Rebellion* **(156**), as he, a Royalist, designated the history of the Civil War. It comprises a detailed account of the struggle, generally in the form of political memoirs, together with a narrative of the cir-cumstances which brought about the Restoration. As much of the material was derived from the author's personal experience, the work is of high value; while the dignity and animation of the style, in spite of occasional carelessness and obscurity, will ever give him rank among English classics. Impartial he is not; but his partiality is less frequent and less flagrant than could fairly have been anticipated. Genuine regard for the welfare of his country is as evident in his writings as in most of the acts of his life. He is skilled in the delineation of character. Natural pene-tration and great knowledge of the world combined to make him an acute observer of human nature; and we are indebted to his spirited pen for many a life-like portrait of his distinguished con-temporaries.

"The great Cavalier-prince of historical portrait painters out-lived the great Puritan-prince of epic poets but a few days. Born in the same year, Clarendon and Milton stood all their lives apart, towering in rival greatness above their fellows in the grand struggle of their century. The year of the Restoration, which brought splendor to the Cavalier, plunged the blind old Puritan in [into] bitter poverty. But a few years more, and the great Earl, too, was stricken down from his lofty place, and sent a homeless wanderer to a stranger's land. To both, their sternest discipline was their greatest gain ; for when the colors of hope and gladness had faded from the landscape of their lives, and nothing but a waste of splendorless days seemed to stretch in cheerless vista before them, they turned to the desk for solace, and found in the exercise of their literary skill, not peace alone, but fame. Milton wrote most of his great poem in blindness and disgrace; Clarendon completed his great history during a painful exile." *

Thomas Hobbes (1588–1679) was a metaphysician, some of whose works belong to this period of our literature. He was born at Malmesbury, was educated at Oxford, as a student at the university was devoted to Logic and Philosophy, and in his maturity was a man of wonderful mental activity. Upon leaving Oxford he traveled on the Continent as a tutor to the young Earl of Devonshire, and till the end of his long life retained an intimacy with the Earl's family. His patron secured him the acquaintance of the most distinguished men of the day—among them Bacon, Ben Jonson, and Lord Herbert. Subsequently Hobbes passed several years in France and in Italy, and enlivened his studious pursuits by association with the most illustrious of his contemporaries—with Galileo and with Descartes.

Hobbes's earliest literary work was a translation of Thucydides. The first hints of his philosophical system were conveyed in two political treatises, published in 1642 and in 1650, for the avowed purpose of quelling the spirit of republicanism in England. They were both incorporated into his most celebrated work, the *Leviathan ; or the Matter, Form, and Power of a Commonwealth, Ecclesiastical and Civil.* Therein he asserts that the primary motive of all human action is selfish interest ; that human nature is therefore essentially ferocious and corrupt, requiring the restraint of arbitrary power to bridle its passion. From these premises the expediency

* Collier.

of despotic rule is deduced. The *Behemoth*, a history of the Civil War, embracing the period between 1640 and 1660, was finished shortly before his death. The doctrines promulgated by Hobbes were odious to the religious people of his time, and were most welcome to the Court. His style is a model of its kind—clear, nervous, forcible, it conveys the exact meaning and produces the exact impression intended. He was a man whose reading was profound; in the various branches of science and literature which he cultivated, he displayed that vigor which belongs to the thoughtful reader of few books.

The most energetic assailant of Hobbes's conclusions in Philosophy was Dr. RALPH CUDWORTH (1617–1688), Regius Professor of Divinity at Cambridge, a vigorous writer and a candid polemic. So fairly did he put the arguments of the Atheists, that he brought down on himself—most unjustly indeed—the imputation of Atheism. His great work is the *True Intellectual System of the Universe.*

JOHN DRYDEN.

" Without either creative imagination or any power of pathos, he is in argument, in satire, and in declamatory magnificence, the greatest of our poets."—*G. L. Craik.*

"He was of a very easy, of a very pleasing access ; but somewhat sour, and, as it were, diffident in his advances to others."—*William Congreve.*

"My conversation is slow and dull, my humour saturnine and unreserved. In short, I am none of those who break jests in company, and make repartees."—*John Dryden.*

"What a sycophant to the public taste was Dryden ! Sinning against his feelings, lewd in his writings, though chaste in his conversation."—*William Cowper.*

" His plays, excepting a few scenes, are utterly disfigured by vice or folly or both. His translations appear too much the offspring of haste and hunger; even his fables are ill-chosen tales conveyed in an incorrect though spirited versification. Yet amidst this great number of loose productions, the refuse of our language, there are found some small pieces, his ' Ode to St. Cecilia,' the greater part of ' Absalom and Achitophel,' and a few more which discover so great genius, such richness of expression, such pomp and vanity of numbers, that they leave us equally full of regret and indignation on account of the inferiority, or rather, great absurdity of his other writings."—*David Hume.*

" I admire Dryden's talents and genius highly ; but his is not a poetical genius. The only qualities I can find in Dryden that are essentially poetical are a certain ardor and impetuosity of mind with an excellent ear. . . . . . There is not a single image from nature in the whole of his works."—*William Wordsworth.*

In the last year of the fourteenth century Chaucer died. Just three hundred years later **John Dryden** (1631–1700) dropped his pen, closed the bulky volume of his writings, and ended his eventful career. As poets they were utterly unlike. Chaucer's muse would not dwell in-doors, would roam the fields and the highways, addressing itself to the leaves, the flowers, the birds and the people; but the retirement and the conveniences of the library gave inspiration to the muse of Dryden. His pleasure was in an argument rather than in a landscape; there was for him more music in the rhythm of the epigram than in all the melodies of nature. During the Civil War and the Commonwealth the interests of his friends were identified with the Puritan cause. His association with the austere and unpoetical may account for his displaying few signs of literary precocity. At the age of twenty-nine he had written nothing but school-boy translations and odes, and an elegy on the death of Cromwell. Under a continuance of republican rule he might have used his abilities to achieve position in the state, without one thought of a poetical career. But the Restoration took place just as he was ready to enter active life; and the powerful relatives from whom he had expected preferment came into disgrace. It was necessary for him to begin the world on his own account, and he chose to begin it on the winning side. Taste to appreciate literary talent, and power to reward it, were both with the party of the royalists. Accordingly, Dryden abandoned his Puritan predilections, published an ode of fervent welcome to the returning king, and joined the crowd which struggled for place and distinction around the throne. The revival of the drama had just re-opened a lucrative field for the professional author, and Dryden found it expedient to devote himself principally to the stage. He worked with energy and tact, choosing the subjects suited to the taste of the time, and soliciting in laudatory prefaces the patronage of the powerful.

His Non-Dramatic Works. He had already attained much dramatic popularity, when, in 1667, his first narrative poem attracted general admiration. This was the *Annus Mirabilis*

(142), written to commemorate the terrible Plague
1666.] and Fire of London, and the War with the Dutch.

Its dignity of style and its harmonious verse merited praise; and the fact that it was filled with unfounded eulogy of the worthless king by no means detracted from the fame of its author. The subject of Dryden's next production was equally fortunate. In an elaborate prose *Essay on Dramatic Poetry*, he upheld the use of rhyme in tragedy, and ranged himself with those who were trying to engraft French dramatic rules upon the English stage. From this time the rise of his fortunes was rapid. In 1670 he was appointed Poet Laureate and Royal Historiographer. The King's Company of Players contracted with him to supply them with three dramas a year.* He associated with the favorites at Court. He enjoyed the patronage of the king; his income was respectable; the prestige of his honorable descent, his fine personal appearance and his brilliant talent, won him an Earl's daughter for a wife. He was the oracle of scholarly circles, and an admired member of fashionable society; while the versatile character of his mind, as well as regard for his own interests, led him to take an active share in public affairs. We owe some of the most powerful efforts of his genius to his participation in political intrigues. *Absalom and Achitophel* **(144)**, his first and best satire, appeared in 1681, when such intrigues were especially virulent. It was a political pamphlet, written in the interests of the king's party, attacking the policy of Chancellor Shaftesbury; and at the same time it gave Dryden an opportunity to revenge himself upon his personal foes and

---

* This engagement he did not long fulfill, for in 1694, he had produced but twenty-eight plays in thirty-two years. He was still employed by the company, his services evidently being considered too valuable to be relinquished on any terms.

literary rivals,—the Duke of Buckingham * and the poets
Settle and Shadwell. It is full of masterpieces of character-
painting, not always just, but always vigorous. The enthusiasm with which it was received, confirmed Dryden's
poetical supremacy. The attack upon Shaftesbury was
renewed, in a second satire entitled *The Medal*, and in the
following year his brilliant *MacFlecknoe†* brought discom-
fiture again to Settle and Shadwell.

In the same year the *Religio Laici* (147), was written in
defence of the Anglican Church against Deists, Papists, and
Presbyterians. It was probably the utterance of a man
already perplexed concerning religious questions which were
afterwards answered by him in a way altogether inconsistent
with the sentiments of this poem. In 1686 he forsook the
church which he had so powerfully defended, and entered
the Roman Catholic communion. The good faith of this
conversion has often been called in question; for it coincided
suspiciously with King James's proselyting measures. Many
circumstances, however, tend to prove its sincerity; he
patiently suffered deprivation and some persecution on
account of his new faith, he carefully trained his children
in the venerable church of Rome, he wrote his *Hind and
Panther* in sympathy with her reverses. The *Religio Laici*
and the *Hind and Panther* display Dryden's power in that
most difficult species of writing which masks abstract reasoning in poetical form. The arguments of each are clear.
The powerful march of the thought, the noble outbursts of
enthusiasm, the rhetoric, and the beauty of the abundant

* In this satire, names from the Old Testament indicate the leaders of the
Whigs, in Dryden's day. The Duke of Monmouth was Absalom; the Earl of
Shaftesbury Achitophel; and the Duke of Buckingham, Zimri (145). Dryden had a
special grudge against Buckingham for his share in the production of a popular
farce, *The Rehearsal*, in which Dryden's dramatic faults were mercilessly ridiculed.

† Flecknoe was a vain, busy scribbler for whom Dryden felt great contempt.
By assigning the name with a patronymic to Shadwell, that poet is represented as
the heir of Flecknoe's stupidity.

illustration, take the judgment by storm, and make us alternately converts to the one faith and to the other. *Religio Laici* is a direct expression of doctrinal views. The *Hind and Panther* is half-allegorical in form. Two animals are represented as engaging in an elaborate argument concerning the churches which they symbolize. The "milk-white hind" is the Roman Catholic, the panther the Established Church, while various minor sects take part in the discussion in the characters of the wolf, the bear, the fox, etc. The absurdity of this plan, half-excused by its novelty, is sometimes wholly forgotten in the scope it gives for picturesque imagery and witty descriptive touches.

Dryden's non-dramatic poems were generally written in the heroic couplet, a measure which he wielded with peculiar power. Its regular structure served his purpose alike in argument, description, narration, and declamation. The music of that rhythm, instead of weakening his thought, seemed to give it energy.

Dryden's Adversity. The Revolution of 1688, by which William and Mary were placed upon the throne of England, deprived Dryden of his Laureateship. The Protestant Court did not smile upon the Catholic poet. But poverty, advancing age, failing health, and the malice of exultant foes, proved powerless to impair his energy; and his last years were the most illustrious of his literary career. He continued to write for the stage until 1694; but after that year he busied himself chiefly with translation. His poetical versions of Juvenal, Persius and Virgil appeared in 1693; and the very last year of his life was made illustrious by his *Fables*, a series of renderings from Chaucer and Boccaccio (149).

For twelve years Dryden had lived in obscurity and neglect; yet when he died in 1700, evidence of the high esteem in which he was held was promptly given; for while his family was preparing to bury him in a style suited to humble circumstances, a large subscription was raised to give him whatever tribute there might be in an imposing funeral. His body was conveyed in state to Westminster Abbey, and was interred between the tombs of Chaucer and Cowley.

His Literary Development. Critics have justly said that Dryden, more than any other poet, would gain appreciation from a chronological survey of his writings. In range of thought, and in power of expression, he was a man of steady growth. This development is indicated by the departments of composition to which he successively devoted himself. His panegyrical poems and the dramas which pandered to the corrupt sentiments of his age, were produced in the years of his struggle for recognition; his best dramas, his thoughtful criticisms, his satires, polemics, translations, fables and odes,—in short, all those works exhibiting the higher qualities of his mind, were written in the dignified maturity of his manhood, or in his noble old age.

His Dramas. In his first plays he is the representative of the great revolution in taste which followed the Restoration, supplanting the noble romantic drama of the Elizabethan era by a travesty of French models. His comedies are degraded to the immoral public sentiment. There is in them no fine delineation of character, no flow of humor. They were popular because they were gross; and their author courted popularity as the means by which he could replenish his shrunken purse. Like all other productions of mercenary art, these dramas were soulless and mean.* In

---

* His [Dryden's] indelicacy was like the forced impudence of a bashful man."
—*Walter Scott.*

tragedy he strove towards superhuman ideals of heroic and amorous life, and succeeded in being incredibly bombastic and unnatural. He seems to have been conscious of his own defects, for he exercised much ingenuity in concealing them from the public. His comedies were enlivened by witty allusions and curious intrigue; his tragedies were sustained by picturesque situations and powerful declamation. Over all he threw the veil of graceful versification, easy, melodious, balancing grievous defects of sense by harmony of sound. His recognition of his own indebtedness to this help may have made him so long an advocate of the use of rhyme in tragedy. In his later years, an intimate acquaintance with the Shakespearean authors led Dryden to a juster idea of the province of the drama. He returned to the national use of blank verse, and developed considerable power in portraying violent passion and strongly-marked character. There is splendid imagery in many of his passages. In the preface of *All for Love*, the poet thus acknowledges the source of his inspiration: "In my style I have professed to imitate the divine Shakespeare. . . . . . I hope I may affirm, and without vanity, that by imitating him I have excelled myself."

Many beautiful *songs* are interspersed among the scenes of Dryden's dramas; but his most admired lyric is the *Ode on St. Cecilia's Day.** (150)*. It was written to be set to music, and celebrates the powers and triumphs of that art. In energy and in harmony it surpasses all other lyrics of our language.

---

* " Mr. St. John, afterwards Lord Bolingbroke, happening to pay a morning visit to Dryden, whom he always respected, found him in an unusual agitation of spirits, even to a trembling. On inquiring the cause—' I have been up all night, replied the old bard; ' my musical friends made me promise to write them an ode for the Feast of St. Cecilia; I have been so struck with the subject which occurred to me, that I could not leave it till I had completed it—here it is, finished at one sitting.—*Warton.*

Dryden's Translation of the Æneid. Dryden's version of
the *Æneid* is the most famous of his translations. The
translator had a spirit much unlike that of the old master,
and could not reproduce the spirit of the poem. The
majesty of Virgil's manner is always tempered by consummate grace; and Dryden, however endowed with majesty,
was deficient in elegance and grace. He was too free and
careless to give a faithful version of the most accurate of
poems. A similar lack of adaptability is noticed in his renderings of the *Fables* from Chaucer and Boccaccio; but their
flowing ease of expression, the frequent recurrence of beautiful lines and striking images, and their freedom from the
author's fault of occasional coarseness, make them most
welcome illustrations of his poetical power.

His Prose. Dryden's prose writings are numerous, and
must have weight in determining our estimate of his ability
and influence. They are in the forms of essays, prefaces,
or dedications prefixed to his various works. He was the
first enlightened critic who wrote in the English language;
but in criticism as in poetry he was a development. Macaulay acutely remarks, that no man influenced his age so
much as Dryden, because no man was so much influenced
by his age. *An Essay on Dramatic Poetry* was the earliest
statement of his critical system. Its general spirit is that
of servile conformity to popular opinion; but its reasoning,
albeit from false premises, is cogent. The style of his prose
writing was admirable; his English was lively, vigorous,
idiomatic, equally removed from mannerism and from carelessness.

Interesting discussions of Dryden's life and works may be found in Johnson's
Lives of the Poets, Macaulay's *Essays*, Wilson's *Essays* (*Blackwood's Magazine*,
Vol. LVII.), Reed's *British Poets*, Vol. I., Hazlitt's Works, Vol. IV., Part II., Sec.
IV., Hallam's *Literature of Europe*, Vol. IV., *North American Review*, July, 1868,
Taine's *English Literature*.

In this chapter we have considered:—

The Literature of the Restoration.

1. *Samuel Butler,—Hudibras.*
2. *John Bunyan,—Pilgrim's Progress from thi World to that which Is to Come.*
3. *Izaak Walton.*
4. *John Evelyn, and Samuel Pepys.*
5. *Edward Hyde.*
6. *Thomas Hobbes.*
7. *John Dryden.*
   a. *His Non-Dramatic Works.*
   b. *His Adversity.*
   c. *His Literary Development.*
   d. *His Translation of the Æneid.*
   e. *His Prose.*

CHAPTER XVI.

THE CORRUPT DRAMA

WHEN Dryden wrote for the stage, he degraded his talents as we have seen, to the service of an immoral public. That same corrupt society debauched a company of brilliant men, younger than Dryden, who devoted themselves exclusively to dramatic composition. In aim and in manner they are so unlike the great playwrights of the preceding century that they are often spoken of as the authors of "The New Drama." The aim of Shakespeare and his comrades had been to portray nature and natural passion. Recognizing the fact that nature is infinitely complex, they had introduced comic scenes and characters into their tragedies, as they admitted elevated feeling and language into their comedies.

The Style and Spirit of the New Drama. In the new drama that followed the Restoration, an exaggerated, bombastic tragedy, on the one hand, was counterbalanced, on the other, by the comedy of artificial life. Material was drawn not from nature, but from society. Declamation and pompous tirades displaced the old dialogue—a dialogue so varied, so natural, touching every key of human feeling. Wit usurped the province of humor; and the comic dramatists delineated, not character, but manners. They were apt in reflecting the spirit of their age; but they had no deep philosophic insight into human nature. Their works are a splendid revelation of the powers of the English language; yet few among them are capable of awakening a thrill of genuine sympathetic feeling. They do not deal with the springs of human passion and action; moreover there is an ingrained profligacy about them; and so, while they lack the one quality that would make them attractive, they display the spirit that makes them repulsive to the modern taste.

The works of Dryden may be regarded as the link connecting the older drama with the new.

The Comic Dramatists. **William Wycherley** (1640–1715) was the first of the comic dramatists who reproduced to the fullest extent the peculiar influences of his day. He received his education in the household of a French noble, and returned to England to become a brilliant figure in the society of London. His first comedy, *Love in a Wood*, was acted when he was thirty-two years old. *The Gentleman Dancing Master*, *The Country Wife*, and *The Plain Dealer* followed at irregular intervals, the last one appearing in 1677; and these four plays are the only results of his dramatic work. He soon after lost the favor of the Court through an unfortunate marriage, and the remainder of his life was melancholy and ignoble. At the age of sixty-five he made a vain attempt to regain public admiration by means of a collection of poetical miscellanies; but being stained with all the immorality of his youthful productions, and redeemed by none of their intellectual brilliancy, the book fell dead upon the market.

The small number of Wycherley's dramatic works, as well as the style of their composition, indicates that he was neither very original in conception, nor capable of producing anything, save by patient labor and careful revision. The leading ideas of his two best comedies are derived from Molière. But Wycherley, infected with the corruption of his age, modified the data of the great French dramatist, and so changed what was pure as to outrage moral sensibility. Setting aside this ingrained fault, Wycherley's plots and characters reveal much ingenuity and humorous power. His plays are admirably adapted for representation. Frequent sudden transitions of the intrigue fascinate the attention without fatiguing it, and give rise to striking "situations," which are always treated with masterly comic effect. The dialogue is easy, vivacious, amusing, and its touches of witty satire are frequent. *The Country Wife* is generally pronounced to be the best of his comedies.

In the esteem of his contemporaries **William Congreve** (1670 *-

---

* The inscription on his monument says that he was born in 1672.

1729) stood pre-eminent among the comic dramatists. He had the tastes of the man of fashion, with the talents of the man of letters; and his education at Trinity College, Dublin, gave him scholarship far superior to that of his rivals. Going to London to study law, his graces soon made him a favorite in fashionable circles. Between 1692 and 1700 he devoted the intervals of social dissipation to dramatic writing, and produced five plays,—*The Old Bachelor* (1693), *The Double Dealer* (1694), *Love for Love* (1695), *The Mourning Bride* (1697), and *The Way of the World* (1700). They were all received with favor by the public and by the critics. The brilliancy of the young author's talents won for him rich patronage. After the beginning of the eighteenth century he published only a volume of trifling miscellanies; but his reputation and prosperity continued to the end of his life. Successive ministers of the government vied with each other in granting him lucrative sinecures. He accumulated a large fortune, and commanded the society of wealth and of intellect. Dryden named him his successor in poetical supremacy, and Pope, in dedicating a translation of Homer, passed by powerful and illustrious patrons to recognize Congreve as the patriarch of letters. When he died, in 1729, he was honored with almost a national funeral.

Congreve's scenes are one incessant flash and sparkle of the finest repartee; and his wit, like all wit of the highest order, is invariably allied with shrewd sense and acute observation. He stands alone in his power of divesting this intellectual sword-play of every shade of formality. The conversations of his characters are accurate imitations of the conversation of fashionable life. His characters are artificial, modeled after the affected men and women of Congreve's society. Not one of his scenes is relieved by a breath of nature; indeed we have little intimation that he knew aught of either nature or simplicity. *Love for Love* is Congreve's masterpiece. Its characters are strikingly varied, and they relieve each other with unrelaxing spirit. Its intrigue, too, is effectively managed, and is better than that of any of his other comedies. His one tragedy, *The Mourning Bride*, written in solemn and pompous strain, though rapturously applauded when first given to the public, has now no power of pleasing. Its scenes of distress cannot touch the heart; its lofty tirades cannot stir the passions. What enchantment it has for the modern reader is found in the power and melody of its descriptive passages.

Another popular author of this school was **Sir John Vanbrugh** (Văn-broo) (1666–1726), a famous architect. His dramatic talent is exhibited in comedies,— *The Relapse, The Provoked Wife, Æsop, The Confederacy*, several adaptations from Molière, and *The Provoked Husband*, left incomplete at the author's death. His fund of invention enables him to surpass either Wycherley or Congreve in developing a character or an incident to its full capacity for comic effect. His personages have an incurable habit of getting into difficulties, and inexhaustible ingenuity in getting out. All are sketched from life—swaggering fops, booby squires, pert chambermaids, and intriguing dames—and sketched with such vivacity as would make amends for any fault, save that of pervading coarseness and obscenity. The reader finds himself in bad company ; for all the men are rascals, and none of the women are as good as they should be.

The comic drama of this generation found its last expression in the works of **George Farquhar** (1678–1707). He was an Irishman, who was dismissed from Trinity College, Dublin, at the age of eighteen, on account of some boyish irregularities. He then pursued the calling of an actor; but having accidentally inflicted a dangerous wound upon a comrade on the stage, he quitted his profession and entered the army. He soon entered the lists as a dramatist, and wrote his comedies in rapid succession. His literary career was crowded into ten years,—from 1698, when his first play was acted, until 1707, the date of his early death. His principal plays are *Love and a Bottle, The Constant Couple, The Inconstant, The Twin Rivals, The Recruiting Officer* and *The Beaux' Stratagem*. His heroes are in sympathy with himself,—happy, hot-blooded, rattling fellows, whose madcap pranks are prompted by the rashness of youth. They are much given to deceptions and wanton tricks, but betray none of the vicious coarseness of Wycherley's villains, nor any of the refined rascality of Vanbrugh's sharpers. *The Beaux' Stratagem* was the last of his comedies, and is also considered the best. It is an entertaining and ingenious portrayal of the adventures of two gentlemen who went into the country disguised as master and servant. Whole scenes are filled with a rich humor which recalls the spirit of the older drama. In several of the other plays there are passages worked up into brilliant comic effect.

"The one feature which above all others forces itself upon our notice in every work of the whole school, is the absolute shamelessness of every person portrayed, male or female. Not one of their leading characters is represented with the slightest conception that the grossest vices are things to be concealed; chastity is derided by the ladies as unblushingly as by the gentlemen, and vice is not only rampant but triumphant." *

Jeremy Collier. Such glaring shamelessness did not go unrebuked. A sturdy clergyman, Jeremy Collier (1650–1726), faced the scorn of play-goers, and presented himself as the champion of decency. He published *A Short View of the Immorality and Profaneness of the English Stage*, in which he defiantly attacked Wycherley, Congreve and Dryden. The pamphlet was written with fiery energy and with wit, and rallied the sympathies of all moral and thoughtful men in the nation. Dryden himself sincerely and gracefully acknowledged the justice of Collier's strictures.† A defence was undertaken by Wycherley, Congreve and Vanbrugh; but the assault had been so vigorous, and was pushed with such resoluteness, that victory remained with the assailant. The controversy resulted in giving a better tone to the drama and to lighter literature in general, and from that time there has been a gradual improvement which has given to the readers of English the purest modern literature. Collier was the author of *An Ecclesiastical History of Great Britain*, and an industrious writer in various lines of thought; but as his grandest triumph was won in his battle with the corrupt dramatists, his name is placed with theirs.

* C. D. Yonge.

† "I shall say less of Mr. Collier, because in many things he has taxed me justly; and I have pleaded guilty to all thoughts and expressions of mine which can be truly argued of obscenity, profaneness or immorality, and retract them. If he be my enemy, let him triumph; if he be my friend, as I have given him no personal occasion to be otherwise, he will be glad of my repentance."—*Dryden, Preface to Fables.*

The Tragic Dramatists. Among the exclusively tragic dramatists of this epoch the first place belongs to **Thomas Otway** (1651-1685), who died at the early age of thirty-four, after a life of wretchedness and irregularity. He received a regular education at Oxford, and very early entered the profession of an actor. During this part of his career he produced three tragedies,—*Alcibiades*, *Don Carlos*, and *Titus and Berenice*. After a brief service in the army he returned to the stage; and in the years from 1680 to his death he wrote four more tragedies,—*Caius Marius*, *The Orphan*, *The Soldier's Fortune*, and *Venice Preserved*. These works, with the exception of *The Orphan* and *Venice Preserved*, are now nearly forgotten; but the glory of Otway is so firmly established upon these two plays, that it will probably endure as long as the language itself. As a tragic dramatist, his most striking merit is his pathos. The distress in his poems reaches a pitch of terrible intensity. His style is vigorous and racy. In reading his best passages we may continually notice a flavor of Ford, Beaumont and other masters of the Elizabethan era.

Nathaniel Lee (1657?-1692), in spite of protracted attacks of insanity, was able to acquire a high reputation for dramatic genius. In all his plays there is a wild and exaggerated imagery, sometimes reminding the reader of Marlowe. He assisted Dryden in the composition of several of his pieces, and wrote eleven original tragedies.

Nicholas Rowe (1673-1718), like Congreve, furnishes a happy contrast to the wretched lives of many dramatists who were by no means his inferiors in talent. He was an admired member of the fashionable society of his day, and belonged to Pope's circle of wits and scholars. Secured against want by the possession of a fortune, he also held many lucrative offices and was made Poet Laureate as a reward for his literary work. Rowe was the first who undertook the critical editing of Shakespeare; and to this work he owes his celebrity as a literary man. His own dramatic works comprise seven tragedies, of which *Jane Shore*, *The Fair Penitent* and *Lady Jane Grey* are the most noteworthy.

From the time of Dryden until the end of the first quarter of the eighteenth century, English poetry exhibits a character equally remote from the splendid imagery of the Elizabethan era, and from the picturesque intensity of the modern school. Correctness and an affected regard for what was called "sense" were the qualities chiefly cultivated. The abuse of ingenuity which disfigures the poetry of Cowley, Donne and Quarles was avoided; but there was likewise a want of feeling. It is remarkable how many of the non-dramatic poets of this time were men of rank and fashion, whose literary efforts were simply the accomplishments of amateurs.

Consult Macaulay's Essay on *The Comic Dramatists of the Restoration*, *The Dramatic Works of Wycherley, Congreve, Vanbrugh and Farquhar*, edited by Leigh Hunt, Hallam's *Literature of Europe*, Vol. IV., Hazlitt's *Lectures on the English Comic Writers*, Lect. IV.

In this chapter we have considered:—

The Corrupt Drama.
  1. The Style and Spirit of the New Drama.
  2. The Comic Dramatists.
      a. William Wycherley.
      b. William Congreve.
      c. Sir John Vanbrugh.
      d. George Farquhar.
  3. Jeremy Collier.
  4. The Tragic Dramatists.
      a. Thomas Otway.
      b. Nathaniel Lee.
      c. Nicholas Rowe.
  5. Poetry after Dryden's Epoch.

CHAPTER XVII.

THE PHILOSOPHERS AND THEOLOGIANS OF LOCKE'S TIME.

JOHN LOCKE.

" The most elegant of prose writers."—*W. S. Landor.*

" All his contemporaries, and, what is better, all the known actions of his life, testify that no one was more sincerely and constantly attached to truth, virtue, and the cause of human liberty."—*Victor Cousin.*

" He gave the first example in the English language of writing on abstract subjects with a remarkable degree of simplicity and perspicuity."—*Thomas Reid.*

" We who find some things to censure in Locke, have perhaps learned how to censure them from himself; we have thrown off so many false notions and films of prejudice by his help that we are become capable of judging our master."—*Henry Hallam.*

" If Bacon first discovered the rules by which knowledge is improved, Locke has most contributed to make mankind at large observe them. . . . . . His writings have diffused throughout the civilized world the love of civil liberty; the spirit of toleration and charity in religious differences; the disposition to reject whatever is obscure, fantastic, or hypothetical in speculation; to reduce verbal disputes to their proper value; to abandon problems which admit of no solution; to distrust whatever cannot be clearly expressed; to render theory the simple expression of facts; and to prefer those studies which most directly contribute to human happiness."—*Sir James Mackintosh.*

" Few among the great names in philosophy have met with a harder measure of justice from the present generation than Locke, the unquestioned founder of the analytical philosophy of mind,"—*John Stuart Mill.*

THE English Revolution of 1688 secured constitutional freedom for the state, and gave a powerful impulse to practical progress in science and philosophy. The period displays the names of Newton and Locke, the former famous in physical, the other in intellectual science.

John Locke (1632–1704), son of an officer in the Puritan army, was reared in an atmosphere of political independence and devout enthusiasm. A tendency to metaphysical speculation seems native to the followers of Calvinistic theology; and, doubtless, the natural bent of Locke's mind was encouraged by his early associations. When he entered Oxford, at the age of nineteen, he had already developed a taste for psychological study, and a habit of independent thinking. Independent thinking was not encouraged in a university which " piqued itself on being behind the spirit of the age." Locke soon discovered Oxford to be the citadel of the outworn scholasticism of the Middle Ages. He became filled with disgust at the empty subtleties which sheltered themselves under the name of Aristotle. In after years he frequently regretted that his early manhood had been passed under such adverse influences. However, there can be no doubt that standing in constant antagonism to the conservative spirit of the university training was influential in forming his intellectual character. During the thirteen years which he spent at Oxford—first as bachelor, then as master— much of his time was devoted to preparation for the practice of medicine. He thus came into contact with the vigorous and progressive spirit which was transfusing physical science. Meanwhile his interest in metaphysics was stimulated by study of Bacon and Descartes, and by familiar discussions with his friends. Locke possessed fine conversational powers ; and his associates were chosen from among the brilliant and entertaining rather than from among the studious and profound. In its bearing upon the circumstances of his later life, and the tendency of his works, this fact is worthy of note. It indicates his remarkable union of the talents of the student with such tastes and practical abilities as make the man of the world.

Locke's Relation to Shaftesbury. In 1664 Locke assumed the secretaryship of a diplomatic mission, and remained on the Continent for a year. After his return to Oxford, he was for a time in doubt whether to continue in diplomatic service, or to begin the practice of medicine. The latter alternative seemed inexpedient on account of his delicate health. Conscientious motives prompted him also to reject a flattering offer of preferment in the Irish Church. At this juncture, a chance acquaintance with Lord

Ashley, afterwards Earl of Shaftesbury, determined his career. He recommended himself to this nobleman by a fortunate exercise of his medical skill, and confirmed his regard by charms of character and of conversation. Shaftesbury's own social qualities were of the most attractive order. Under the influence of mutual admiration and intellectual sympathy, a warm and enduring friendship arose between the two. Locke took up his residence in Shaftesbury's house, conducted the education, first of his son and afterwards of his grandson, and to a great degree became identified with his political fortunes. Enjoying the friendship and familiar converse of the talented statesmen who surrounded his patron, Locke's attention was naturally directed to theories of politics and government. He filled various offices during Shaftesbury's two seasons of political ascendency, and in 1679 assisted him and others in framing the constitution of the province of Carolina. When, in 1682, Shaftesbury fled to Holland under the accusation of high treason, Locke shared his exile and his disgrace. He bore his misfortunes with true philosophical fortitude, and chose to remain in Holland during the reign of James II. In the congenial society of many distinguished men who, like him, were exiles for conscience's sake, he devoted himself with renewed zest to philosophical study. His *Letter on Toleration* and an abstract of the *Essay on the Human Understanding* were both published before his return to England in 1689.

Under the rule of William and Mary, Locke's public career was active and useful. He was made a commissioner of appeals; and as a member of the Council of Trade rendered important assistance in the reformation of the coinage. In 1690, the full edition of his *Essay on the Human Understanding* attracted general attention (**161**). In fourteen years it passed through six editions—an unprecedented sale, considering the character of the work. In 1700 Locke's failing health compelled him to resign his official duties. He found a tranquil retreat in the home of his friend, Sir Francis Masham. The last years of his life were devoted to Scriptural study and devout contemplation, and in 1704 he died, at the ripe age of seventy-two.

Locke's Contribution to English Thought.
In order to form a just estimate of the power of Locke's mind and of the extent of

his influence, it is necessary to consider the age of which he was a part. He has been called the most illustrious of Bacon's apostles. The praise is not misplaced. Hobbes had already proclaimed psychology to be a science of observation, but he had been too intent on establishing such of its laws as might support his political views to make a comprehensive study of the whole. It was reserved for Locke to demonstrate the utility of the method of observation and experiment. Like his great master, Bacon, he sought *fruit;* his most abstract study evinced his union of the philosopher with the business man. In his great work, the *Essay on the Human Understanding*, he proposes to give a rational and clear account of the nature of the human mind, of the real character of human ideas, of the source whence they are derived, and of the manner in which they are presented to the consciousness. With unwearied patience he travels over the immense field of mental phenomena, describing, analyzing, classifying, with a practical sagacity which is equaled only by the purity of his desire for truth. His work is, as Mr. Hallam justly observes, " the first real chart of the coasts, wherein some may be laid down incorrectly, but the general relations of all are perceived." The obligation under which he has placed succeeding thinkers can scarcely be over-estimated. When we censure his superficial investigations and his narrow views, we forget that he was the pioneer of a new path. We complain of his language as careless and unphilosophical. The style of his expression was determined by the object of his writing. He hated the empty and illusive jargon of the schools; he tried to bring abstract knowledge within the range of the popular comprehension. The Essay was the first English work which attracted general attention to metaphysical speculation. When public curiosity was stimulated by the attacks which were made upon its liberal views, the public read it, understood it, thought about it. Now that the inquiry which it provoked has produced such grand results, it is of no slight significance that a great modern philosopher calls it " the richest contribution of well-observed and well-described facts which was ever bequeathed by a single individual, and the indisputable, though not always acknowledged, source of some of the most refined conclusions with respect to the intellectual phenomena which have been since brought to light by succeeding inquirers."

From the causes which we have already noted, Locke was less exposed than most thinkers to the dangers of visionary speculation. On the other hand, he frequently wrote upon subjects of interest to himself and his nation, and deserves credit for his freedom from passion and party prejudice. Witness the calm and impartial tone of his *Letter on Toleration*, composed while he himself was under the ban of his university and his government. The same qualities characterize his *Treatise on Civil Government*. This work inaugurated a new state of political sentiment in Europe. Undertaken in order to justify the principles of the English Revolution, it vindicates the justice of popular sovereignty. Locke's views are not always the most profound, nor his arguments always unimpeachable. Like the Essay, the value of the Treatise is now in great measure superseded by the investigation which it provoked. In a practical way, the essay on *Education* has been hardly less influential than the two preceding works. Locke himself had felt all the disadvantages of the prevailing method of instruction. He makes an impressive plea for a more liberal and practical system, both in the choice of the subject-matter to be taught, and in the mode of conveying instruction. Taken as a whole, his work is a monument of good sense and sincere benevolence. It did much to bring about that beneficial revolution which the last century has effected in the training of the young. Besides these works, there may be mentioned a treatise *On the Reasonableness of Christianity*, pervaded by a spirit of calm piety which decisively contradicts the statements of those bigots who have accused Locke of irreligious tendencies. After his death a small but admirable little work was published, entitled, *On the Conduct of the Understanding*. It is a manual of reflections upon those natural defects and evil habits of the mind which unfit it for the task of acquiring knowledge, and was designed to form a supplementary chapter to his greater work.*

Isaac Barrow (1630–1677) stands at the head of the theologians of his time. He was a man of profound attainments. At the University of Cambridge, his studies took a wide range. He began his preparation for the Church before the establishment

---

* For further discussions of this topic consult Lewes's *History of Philosophy* Vol. II., and Sir James Mackintosh in the *British Essayists*.

of the Commonwealth. After the ascendency of Puritan principles seemed to have destroyed his prospects for preferment, he transferred his attention to medicine and the natural sciences. Even after his return to theological studies, he devoted much time to the classics and mathematics. In both he attained distinguished proficiency. ' At the age of twenty-nine he was made professor of Greek in the University; and with this appointment he soon combined the professorship of Geometry in Gresham College. In 1663 he resigned both chairs, to accept the Lucasian professorship of mathematics. In this position, which he filled with ability for six years, he fostered and befriended the rising genius of Newton, and it was to Newton that he resigned his office in 1669. His Latin treatises on Optics, Mechanics, and Astronomy, established his rank among the best mathematicians of his age. Indeed, it is Barrow's misfortune that his scientific reputation is eclipsed by the superior splendor of his great successor. Had he not lived in Newton's time, and pursued nearly the same branches of investigation, he would have held a proud place among English scientists.

Previous to resigning his professorship, Barrow had taken holy orders, and had resolved to devote himself to theological pursuits. A brilliant and useful career opened at once before him. He was made one of the King's chaplains; his sermons soon became famous (**162**). In 1672 he was elected Master of Trinity College, the King remarking, as he confirmed the appointment, that he had given the place to the best scholar in England. In 1675 the list of his honors was augmented by the Vice-Chancellorship of the University of Cambridge; but he did not long survive this last distinction. His death occurred at the early age of forty-six, in the splendid maturity of his activity and his talents.

His Pulpit Eloquence. Contemporaneous accounts state that Barrow's appearance in the pulpit was far from imposing, and that the beginning of his discourses was always hampered by diffidence and embarrassment. They add, however, that when his enthusiasm was fairly awakened by his subject, the magnetic influence of his oratory was irresistible. The dignity and grandeur of his sermons have rarely been equaled. He attacks and vanquishes the most ponderous difficulties of Protestant theology with heroic ease. Many of his best sermons form series, devoted to the exhaustive explanation of particular departments of religious doctrine. For instance, one excellent series discusses the Lord's Prayer, which is anatomized, clause by clause. Another, consisting of eight discourses, treats of the government of the tongue; another, of the Decalogue; another, of the Sacraments. Each and all of these voluminous productions—for Barrow's sermons are seldom less than an hour and a half long—is instinct with fervent and devout purpose. The ideas are expanded with such mathematical breadth and exactness, that the expression sometimes becomes involved and laborious. But there is no empty writing; the language is always filled with thought. He is said to have been scrupulously attentive to the composition of his sermons, and to have subjected many to a third and fourth revision. His style is always pure and nervous, and sometimes vivacious; occasionally single passages attain a rich conciseness. He writes almost without imagery or illustration. The teeming fancy which made Jeremy Taylor's discourses such marvels of poetical beauty was in him displaced by the activity of reason. There is no English prose writer of that day whose works would be more invigorating to the mind or better adapted to the formation of a pure taste. Nor can there be a better proof that the most capable critics have agreed in this opinion, than the fact that Chatham recommended Barrow to his son as the finest model of eloquence, and that the accomplished Landor has not hesitated to place him above the greatest of the ancient thinkers.

John Tillotson (1630–1694), though his mental force was far inferior to that of Barrow, stands next him among the pulpit-orators of the time. While studying at Cambridge he made himself conspicuous by his decided Puritan sympathies; but in later life his views gradually assimilated themselves to those of the Anglican Church. He finally took holy orders, and in the reign of William and Mary rose to the dignity of Archbishop of Canterbury. The change of party seems to have wrought no effect upon him beyond an increase of candor and of indulgence for all shades of sincere opinion. He was renowned as a preacher; although his sermons fall far short of Barrow's in power and originality, they are quite as well adapted to command popularity. Good sense and earnestness are their most laudable characteristics; their piety is sincere without being very elevated, and their style is easy, perspicuous, and unaffected (**163**). Languor and tediousness sometimes mar their excellence of expression; the sentences are often singularly unmusical; and the evident effort to maintain a colloquial tone frequently introduces trivial images and illustrations. But Tillotson's sermons long preserved a wide reputation, not only as examples of practical piety, but as admirable specimens of composition. Dryden did not hesitate to own that his own prose style was formed after Tillotson's. "If I have any talent for English," he said, "it is owing to my having often read the writings of the Archbishop Tillotson."

Robert South (1633–1716), reputed the wittiest churchman of his time, was also the most bigoted of those clergymen who upheld the peculiar principles of the Stuart dynasty. He was an apostate from the Puritan party. Oxford had imbued him with the doctrines of passive obedience and the divine right of kings; and his resolute maintenance of these opinions combined with the qualities of his pulpit oratory to secure him great popularity during the reigns of Charles II. and James II.

By the animation of his manner, and by an amiable conformity to the prevailing sentiment of polite society, he charmed his courtly audiences. His sermons are easy and colloquial in tone, frequently enlivened by witty passages and pleasant anecdotes. The judgment of our day detects his lack of devout sincerity, and condemns his fulsome homage to the royal power no less than his intolerant denunciation of liberal principles. But it must be admitted that he is a master of racy, idiomatic English (**164**). He has surpassed his greater and worthier contemporaries in his admirable blending of ease and harmony of expression with masculine vigor of thought.

The Progress of Physical Science. There are few episodes in the history of human knowledge more surprising than the sudden and dazzling progress made in the physical sciences towards the end of the seventeenth century. This progress is visible in Germany, in Holland, and in France; but in none of these countries more than in England. It was just and natural that the vivifying effect produced by the writings and by the method of Bacon should be peculiarly powerful in that country which gave birth to the

great reformer of philosophy. There is no doubt that the development of free institutions and open discussion exercised a powerful
influence in facilitating research, in promoting a spirit of inquiry,
and in rendering possible the open expression of opinion. The
renowned Royal Society * played a prominent part in the great
movement, especially in the branches of physics and natural
history.

Sir Isaac Newton (1642–1727) was born at Woolsthorpe, in
Lincolnshire. From his earliest boyhood he showed taste and
aptitude for mechanical invention; and entering the University
of Cambridge in 1660, he made such rapid progress in mathematical studies that in nine years Barrow resigned in his favor
the Lucasian professorship. The greater part of Newton's life was
passed within the quiet walls of Trinity College. It was there
that he elaborated those admirable discoveries and demonstrations
in Mechanics, Astronomy, and Optics, which have placed his
name in the foremost rank of the benefactors of mankind. He sat
in more than one Parliament as member for his university; but he
appears to have been of too reserved and retiring a character to take
an active part in political discussion. He was appointed Warden
of the Mint in 1695, and promptly abandoned those researches in
which he stands almost alone among mankind, devoting all his
energy and attention to the public duties that had been committed
to his charge. In 1703 he was made president of the Royal Society,
and knighted two years afterwards by Queen Anne. He died in
1727. His character, whose only defect seems to have been a somewhat cold and suspicious temper, was the type of those virtues
which should distinguish the scholar, the philosopher, and the
patriot. His modesty was as great as his genius; and he invariably ascribed the attainment of his discoveries to patient attention
rather than to any unusual capacity of intellect. His English
writings are chiefly discourses upon the prophecies and chronology
of the Scriptures. They are composed in a manly, plain, and unaffected style, breathe an earnest spirit of piety, and indicate that
his opinions inclined towards the Unitarian theology. His glory,

* This society originated in the meetings of a few learned men at each other's
houses. It was incorporated in 1662, by Charles II.

however, rests upon his purely scientific works, the *Philosophiæ Naturalis Principia Mathematica;* and the invaluable treatise on *Optics,* of which latter science he may be said to have first laid the foundation (**169**).

Robert Boyle (1627–1691). " No Englishman of the seventeenth century, after Lord Bacon, raised himself to so high a reputation in experimental philosophy as Robert Boyle; it has even been re-marked that he was born in the year of Bacon's death, as the person destined by Nature to succeed him. . . . . His works occupy six large volumes in quarto. They may be divided into theological or metaphysical, and physical or experimental. The metaphysical treatises of Boyle, or rather those concerning Natural Theology, are very perspicuous, very free from system, and such as bespeak an independent lover of truth." His discussions of physics contain views that were new then, but now are commonly held ; he discovered the law concerning the elasticity of the air, and was the first to note that the science of chemistry pertains to the atomic constituents of bodies (**166**).

Thomas Burnet (1635–1715), Master of the Charter-house, was one of the most extraordinary writers of this period. He was author of the eloquent and poetic declamation, *The Sacred Theory of the Earth,* a work written in both Latin and English, and giving an hypothetical account of the causes which produced the various irregularities and undulations in the Earth's surface. His geo-logical and physical theories are fantastic in the extreme; but his pictures of the devastation caused by the unbridled powers of Nature are grand and magnificent, and give him a claim to be placed among the most eloquent and poetical of prose-writers of the seventeenth century.

This writer must not be confounded with GILBERT BURNET (1643-1715), a Scotchman, who was one of the most active poli-ticians and divines during the latter part of the seventeenth century (**168**). He held a middle place between the extreme Episcopal and Presbyterian parties ; and although a man of ardent and busy character, he was tolerant and candid. He was celebrated for his talents as an extempore preacher, and was the author of a very large number of theological and political writings. Among these his *History of the Reformation* is still considered one of the most valuable accounts of that important revolution. He also gave an account of the life and death of the witty and infamous Rochester, whose last moments he attended as a religious adviser, and whom his pious arguments recalled to repentance. He at one time enjoyed the favor of Charles II., but soon forfeited it, by the bold-ness of his remonstrances against the profligacy of the King, and by his defence of Lord William Russell. Burnet also published an *Exposition of the XXXIX Articles*. On falling into disgrace at Court he traveled on the Continent, and afterwards attached him-self closely to the service of William of Orange at the Hague. At the Revolution, Burnet accompanied the Deliverer on his expedition to England, took a very active part in controversy and political negotiation, and was raised to the Bishopric of Salisbury. In this office he gave a noble example of the zeal, tolerance, and humanity which should be the chief virtues of a Christian pastor. He died in 1715, leaving the MS. of his most important work, the *History of My Own Times*, which he directed to be published after the lapse of six years. This work is not inferior in value to Clarendon's, which represents the events of English history from a nearly oppo-site point of view. Burnet is minute, familiar, and gossipy, but lively and generally trustworthy. No one who desires to make acquaintance with a very critical and agitated period of English history can dispense with the materials he has accumulated.

In this chapter we have considered:—

The Philosophers and Theologians of Locke's Time.

1. John Locke,—His Relation to Shaftesbury,— His Contribution to English Thought.

2. Isaac Barrow,—His Pulpit Eloquence.

3. John Tillotson, Robert South.

4. The Progress of Physical Science.

5. Sir Isaac Newton, Robert Boyle, Thomas Bur-net, Gilbert Burnet.

ENGLISH LITERATURE, *from the Elizabethan to the Augustan Age, as discussed in the six preceding chapters*

THE SO-CALLED METAPHYSICAL POETS.
- JOHN DONNE,
- EDMUND WALLER,
- ABRAHAM COWLEY,
- SIR WILLIAM DAVENANT,
- SIR JOHN DENHAM,
- GEORGE WITHER,
- FRANCIS QUARLES,
- GEORGE HERBERT,
- RICHARD CRASHAW.

RELIGIOUS WRITERS OF THE CIVIL WAR AND THE COMMONWEALTH.
- WILLIAM CHILLINGWORTH,
- SIR THOMAS BROWNE,
- THOMAS FULLER,
- JEREMY TAYLOR.

JOHN MILTON.

THE LITERATURE OF THE RESTORATION.
- SAMUEL BUTLER,
- JOHN BUNYAN,
- IZAAK WALTON,
- JOHN EVELYN,
- SAMUEL PEPYS,
- EDWARD HYDE, Earl of Clarendon,
- THOMAS HOBBES.

JOHN DRYDEN.

THE CORRUPT DRAMA.
- WILLIAM WYCHERLEY,
- WILLIAM CONGREVE,
- SIR JOHN VANBRUGH,
- GEORGE FARQUHAR,
- [JEREMY COLLIER],
- NATHANIEL LEE,
- NICHOLAS ROWE.

THE PHILOSOPHERS AND THEOLOGIANS OF LOCKE'S TIME.
- JOHN LOCKE,
- ISAAC BARROW,
- JOHN TILLOTSON,
- ROBERT SOUTH,
- SIR ISAAC NEWTON,
- ROBERT BOYLE,
- THOMAS BURNET,
- GILBERT BURNET.

CHAPTER XVIII.

THE ARTIFICIAL POETS OF THE EIGHTEENTH CENTURY.

THE *Augustan Age* was the name given to the epoch of literature immediately succeeding the time of Dryden. It is generally spoken of as bounded by the reign of Queen Anne; but the best fruit of the writers of her reign ripened in the reign of George I. The vigor, harmony, and careless yet majestic regularity found in the powerful writers of the school of the Restoration were given a yet higher polish by the elegant writers of the first third of the eighteenth century. Three men—Pope, Swift, and Addison—stand in the front rank; and these three men, who make their generation famous in the history of English literature, were great as satirists. They expressed the critical spirit of the age. One of them was a poet; but his song, instead of breathing such love of nature or of man as other songs have, was filled with hatred and contempt; another was an eminent clergyman, but his zeal spent itself in violating rather than in teaching the gentle precepts of the gospel; the third, a man distinguished in the service of the state, was so genial, so gentle, so mirthful, that though he poked his fun at all sorts of English follies, he did it with such winning words and with such charming grace that satire lost its severity and was redeemed from its meanness.

ALEXANDER · POPE.

"He was about four feet six inches high, very humpbacked and deformed. He wore a black coat, and, according to the fashion of that time, had on a little sword. He had a large and very fine eye, and a long, handsome nose ; his mouth had those peculiar marks which are always found in the mouths of crooked persons, and the muscles which run across the cheek were so strongly marked that they seemed like small cords."—*Sir Joshua Reynolds.*

"King Alexander had great merit as a writer, and his title to the kingdom of wit was better founded than his enemies have pretended."—*Henry Fielding.*

"If Pope must yield to other poets in point of fertility of fancy, yet in point of propriety, closeness, and elegance of diction he can yield to none.'"—*Joseph Warton.*

"No poet's verse ever mounted higher than that wonderful flight with which the Dunciad concludes. In these astonishing lines Pope reaches, I think, to the very greatest height which his sublime art has attained, and shows himself the equal of all poets of all times."—*W. M. Thackeray.*

"At fifteen years of age I got acquainted with Mr. Walsh. He encouraged me much, and used to tell me that there was one way left of excelling ; for though we have several great poets, we never had any one great poet that was correct."—*Alexander Pope.*

"Pope's rhymes too often supply the defect of his reasons."—*Richard Whately.*

"There are no pictures of nature or of simple emotion in all his writings. He is the poet of town life and of high life and of literary life, and seems so much afraid of incurring ridicule by the display of feeling or unregulated fancy that it is not difficult to believe that he would have thought such ridicule well directed."—*Francis Jeffrey.*

"The most striking characteristics of his poetry are lucid arrangement of matter, closeness of argument, marvellous condensation of thought and expression, brilliancy of fancy ever supplying the aptest illustrations, and language elaborately finished almost beyond example."—*Alexander Dyce.*

"As truly as Shakespeare is the poet of man as God made him, dealing with great passions and innate motives, so truly is Pope the poet of society, the delineator of manners, the exposer of those motives which may be called acquired, whose spring is in institutions and habits of purely worldly origin."—*J. R. Lowell.*

Alexander Pope (1688–1744) stands far above all other poets of his time. He was born in London and was of a Catholic family. His father was a merchant who had acquired sufficient property to retire from business and to enjoy the leisure of his rural home near Windsor. The boy was dwarfish in body, and so deformed that his life was "that long disease." His mind was precocious. Before he was twelve years old, he had written an *Ode to Solitude*, displaying a thoughtfulness far beyond his years. In referring to his early literary attempts he says,

> " As yet a child, and all unknown to fame,
> I lisped in numbers, for the numbers came."

During his childhood he indulged that taste for study and poetical reading which became the passion of his life. He had special admiration for Dryden, and once obtained a glance at the revered poet seated in his easy chair at Will's Coffee House. At sixteen he composed his *Pastorals* and translated portions of Statius. From this time his activity was unremitting; and an uninterrupted succession of works, varied in their subjects and exquisite in their finish, placed him at the head of the poets of his age.

He was a man most peculiar in his appearance; so little that a high chair was needed for him at the table, so weak and sickly that he could not stand unless tied up in bandages, so sensitive to the cold that he was wrapped in flannels and furs, and had his feet encased in three pairs of stockings. He was in constant need of the attentions of a body-servant; he could not dress or undress himself. His deformity gave him the nickname of "The Interrogation Point." But this unfortunate man had a fine face and a glowing eye. In his dress he was fastidious, appearing in a court suit, decorated with a little sword. His manners, too, were elegant. Whether patient or impatient about it, he had to bear the constant reminder of his physical infirmities as he looked upon the stately figures of men who were his companions and his literary rivals. Rollicking Dick Steele was large and strong, Addison had the fatness ascribed to good-nature, Swift was compelled to exercise most vigorously in keeping down his flesh, Gay and Thomson were hale; these jolly men could spend their nights in choice revelries, laughing over the best of wit and humor, but "poor Pope" had no stomach, he must be quiet and thin and sick.

Pope's culture was not gained in the school-room. He was permitted to roam over the fields of learning wherever his fancy might lead him. The songs of stately writers had most charm for him, and so he studied Spenser, Waller and Dryden. They were men who believed that poetry consisted in elegant expression, rather than in the thought; they had detected and disclosed the arts of poetry. They had gained more success than others in the very walk where Pope must journey, if he would listen to the call of his muse, and he was true to the bent of his nature in seeking culture from them. Pope's father was a merchant, who had taste for literature as well as pride in the precocity of his son. He fondly watched the spark of genius in his boy, and gently fanned it into flame by assigning the subjects for his song, and by praising or censuring when the little poet had done his singing.

The Influence of His Intimate Friends. On account of his helplessness throughout his life, Pope, like a child, was specially subject to the influence of those who petted him. His mother, though ignorant, simple-hearted, and ruled by her doting love, influenced him in all things, even in his literary work. Until her death the poet was her child, her "deare." She could tell him more confidingly than another could, how wonderful he was. As he was more sensitive to ridicule than any other man ever was, he was also fonder of praise. He had a sickly craving for admiration ; and that doting mother, by satisfying his craving, helped him. She nursed the self-appreciation which cheered him in his work. Swift, too, gave him the praise he asked. The Dean of Dublin had but to say, " When you think of the world, give it one more lash at my request," and he could inspire the poet. The *Dunciad* is more defiant, sharper, more cruel than it could have been had Pope not found an applauding brother in Swift, a man who hated and detested everything and everybody except the few whom he loved. The wit, the eloquence, the elegance, the literary taste and the political sentiments of Bolingbroke made him the object of Pope's admiration. Bolingbroke's dazzling life blinded Pope to his faults. An intimate friendship between them brought the poet under powerful and pernicious influences. To have one's distinguishing weakness nourished as Pope's was by his mother, to be loved by the sturdiest, heartiest and most terrible of haters, and to receive the patronage and praises of the most dashing, the most attractive and the most worthless public man of the time, was enough to deform even a poet's soul.

Great Influence of His Age. Before considering Pope's literary work, we must remind ourselves of the peculiar influence exerted upon him by his age. Much that has been charged upon him belongs to the time in which he wrote. Was he narrow? was he shallow? was he conceited? The age was so. All of its writers caught its spirit, though it may be that Pope is its most striking representative. There was conceit in the air. It was the special weakness of Englishmen throughout the eighteenth century, and especially in the earlier part of it, to be satisfied with their work. The security of the government seemed to be established, wealth was accumulating, the influence of the nation abroad was increasing, and the moral tone of the literature was improving. Indeed, there was a peculiar complacency towards the literature; and there was reason in this complacency, for the age was the first one using the press to an extent that made it a far-reaching power among the people. Under these influences, political, social, and literary, the national conceit was stimulated. There was a conviction that the age had better *sense* than any one of its predeces

sors. In his essay on Dryden and Pope, Hazlitt calls attention to the expression of this sentiment in the poetry of the
time, and shows that Pope was subject to its influence.
Even the rhyming of his verse was unconsciously affected
by the watch-word, " sense." *

The Essay on Criticism (170), published in 1711, was the
first poem that fixed Pope's reputation and gave him a foretaste of the popularity which he was to enjoy during the
remainder of his life. It was a remarkable production for
a man of twenty years; yet much of the praise given to it
is extravagant. It has no claim to originality. It is merely
a collating of the principles of criticism stated by Horace,
by Shakespeare and by other poets and critics. Still in the

* " As a proof of the exclusive attention which it occupied in their minds, it is remarkable that in the *Essay on Criticism* (not a very long poem) there are no less
than half a score of successive couplets rhyming to the word *sense*. This appears
almost incredible without giving the instances, and no less so when they are given."

" But of the two, less dangerous is the offence
  To tire our patience than mislead our sense." (Lines 3, 4.)

" In search of wit these lose their common sense,
  And then turn critics in their own defence." (Lines 28, 29.)

" Pride, where wit fails, steps in to our defence,
  And fills up all the mighty void of sense." (Lines 209-10.)

" Some by old words to fame have made pretence,
  Ancients in phrase, mere moderns in their sense." (Lines 324-5.)

'Tis not enough no harshness gives offence,
  The sound must seem an echo to the sense." (Lines 364-5.)

" At every trifle scorn to take offence;
  That always shows great pride or little sense." (Lines 386-7.)

" Be silent always, when you doubt your sense,
  And speak, though sure, with seeming diffidence." (Lines 566-7.)

" Be niggards of advice on no pretence,
  For the worst avarice is that of sense." (Lines 578-9.)

" Strain out the last dull droppings of their sense,
  And rhyme with all the rage of impotence." (Lines 608-9.)

" Horace still charms with graceful negligence,
  And without method talks us into sense." (Lines 653-4.)

poem there are sparkling beauties, and there is music in its cadence answering to the severe demands of poetic art. It is dainty, but not insipid; it has fervor, without any sacrifice of dignity; though lacking originality, it is not lacking in excellence of judgment. Pope's general aim seems to have been to produce faultless verse; but in this poem his aim was not certain. Many an unfriendly critic has called attention to his faulty rhymes. Indeed, he gave himself license to do what he would have ridiculed in another. But whatever its defects may be, the *Essay on Criticism* has the excellence of concise and vigorous expression to such a degree that it has supplied our current literature with quotations in larger numbers than any other poem of equal length not written by Shakespeare or Milton.

The Rape of the Lock. A man of over-nice taste exhausts himself and wearies his readers by discussing profound themes. Had Pope confined his thoughts to the philosophy of criticism, or to the study of man, his charming poetical talent would have been undiscovered. The lighter argument, the fanciful narrative, the raillery of the drawing-room, display his sparkling talents. The Rape of the Lock (172), sketched in his early literary life, is the most sparkling of his works, a masterpiece, equally felicitous in its plan and in its execution. Addison pronounced it "a delicious little thing," and later critics agree in thinking that it is superior to any other mock-heroic composition. Lord Petre, a man of fashion at the court of Queen Anne, had cut a lock of hair from the head of Arabella Fermor, a beautiful young maid of honor, and by the act had given such offence that a quarrel had ensued between the two families. Pope's poem was an attempt to laugh the quarrelers into good nature. In this he was not successful, but he wrote with such grace and pleasantry that his fame was heightened. Addison was so delighted by the first sketch of the poem that he strongly advised Pope to refrain from attempting any amendment ; but Pope, fortunately for his glory, added supernatural characters to the story, with exquisite skill adapting sylphs and gnomes to the frivolous persons and events of the poem.

His Eclogues. In 1713 he published his pastoral eclogues entitled *Windsor Forest.* Their beauty of versification and neatness of diction do all they can to compensate for the absence of that deep feeling for Nature which the poetry of the eighteenth century did not possess. The plan of this work is principally borrowed from Denham's *Cooper's Hill.* In 1715 Pope published modernized versions of Chaucer, as if he were desirous in all things to imitate his master Dryden.

His Translation of Homer. At this time, too, Pope undertook the laborious enterprise of translating into English verse the Iliad and the Odyssey. He was disheartened when brought face to face with the vastness of his undertaking; but with practice came facility, and the whole of the Iliad was successfully given to the world by the year 1720. The work was published by subscription, and brought about seven thousand pounds to Pope. That money laid the foundation of the competence which he enjoyed with good sense and moderation. The Odyssey did not appear till five years later ; and of this he himself translated only twelve of the twenty-four books, employing for the remaining half the assistance of contemporary poets. Mechanically this translation is not unfaithful; but in reproducing the spirit of the original, the ballad-like version of Chapman is far superior. Bentley's criticism is, after all, the best and most comprehensive that has yet been made on this work: "It is a pretty poem, Mr. Pope, but you must not call it Homer." It seems unfortunate that Dryden and Pope had not exchanged parts in their selection of the two ancient epic writers as subjects of translation. Dryden, though perhaps incapable of reproducing the wonderful freshness and grandeur of Homer, still possessed more of the Homeric quality of fire and animation; while Pope, in whom grace and finish are the prevailing merits, would have far more successfully reproduced the dignity, the chastened majesty, of Virgil. In Dryden, a careless, self-assured dexterity is perceptible, not accompanied by much passion, nor by much depth of sentiment, but imposing from its conscious ease; in Pope, we find keener thought, more refined acuteness, and neatness of expression. Both are deficient in appreciation of external nature and of simple humanity.

Other compositions of Pope belonging to his early life, are the *Elegy on an Unfortunate Lady*, the *Epistle from Sappho to Phaon*, borrowed from the *Heröides* of Ovid, and the *Epistle of Eloïsa to Abelard*. During this part of his life Pope was living with his father and mother at Chiswick; but on the death of his father, he removed with his mother to a villa he had purchased at Twickenham, at a most beautiful spot on the banks of the Thames. There he passed the remainder of his life, in easy, if not in opulent circumstances; his taste for gardening, and his grotto and quincunxes, in which he delighted, amused his leisure. He lived in familiar intercourse with illustrious statesmen, orators, and men of letters of his day,—with Swift, Atterbury, Bolingbroke, Prior, Gay, and Arbuthnot. In 1725 he published an edition of Shakespeare, in six volumes. This work was severely and justly criticised by Theobald in his *Shakespeare Restored*, an offence deeply resented by the sensitive poet. We shall see by-and-by how savagely he revenged himself. During the three years following he was engaged with Swift, Arbuthnot, Gay, and others, in composing that famous collection of *Miscellanies* to which each of the friends contributed. The aim of the fellow-laborers was to satirize the abuses of learning and the extravagances of philosophy. It was entitled *Memoirs of Martinus Scrib lerus.* Pope's admirable satiric genius, however, seems to have deserted him instantly when he abandoned verse for prose. With the exception of Arbuthnot's burlesque *History of John Bull,* these Miscellanies are hardly worthy the fame of their authors.

The Dunciad. Pope's brilliant success, his popularity, the tinge of vanity and malignity in his disposition, and above all, the supercilious tone in which he speaks of other authors, raised around him a swarm of enemies, animated alike by envy and revenge. Determining, therefore, to in-flict upon these gnats and mosquitoes of the press a memo-rable castigation, he composed the satire of the *Dunciad,* the primary idea of which may have been suggested by Dryden's *MacFlecknoe.* It is incomparably the fiercest, most sweep-ing, and most powerful satire that exists in the whole range of English literature. In it he flays and dismembers and boils and roasts the scribblers whom he attacks. Most of them are so obscure that their names are now rescued from oblivion by being embalmed in Pope's satire, like rubbish preserved in the lava of a volcano; but in the latter part of the poem, and particularly in the portion added in the editions of 1742 and 1743, the poet has given a sketch of the gradual decline and corruption of taste and learning in Europe. The plot of the poem—the Iliad of the Dunces— is not very ingenious. Pope supposes that the throne of Dulness is left vacant by the death of Shadwell, and that the various aspirants to " that bad eminence" engage in a series of trials, like the Olympic Games of old, to determine who shall inherit it. In the original form of the poem, as it appeared in 1728 and 1729, the palm of pedantry and stupidity was given to Theobald, Pope's successful rival in editing Shakespeare. In the new edition of 1743, published just before the poet's death, Theobald was degraded from the throne, and the crown was given to the Poet Laureate, Colley Cibber, an actor, manager, and dramatic author of the time, who, whatever were his vices, certainly was in no sense an appropriate King of the Dunces. In this, as in many other instances, Pope's bitterness of enmity ran away with his judgment. The poem is an admirable—almost a fearful—example of genius applied to selfish ends.

In the four years extending from 1731 to 1735, Pope was engaged in the composition of his *Epistles*, addressed to Burlington, Cobham, Arbuthnot, Bathurst, and other distinguished men. These poems, half satirical and half familiar, were in their manner a reproduction of the charming epistles of Horace.

The Essay on Man, written in this period of his literary work, was published in four epistles addressed to Bolingbroke. The arguments of the poem are not convincing, nor are the conclusions just. It furnishes an illustration of the incompatibility between poetry and abstract reasoning; for close reasoning is generally found to injure the effect of verse, and the ornament of verse as generally detracts from the vigor of argument. The first epistle treats of man in his relation to the universe, the second in his relation to himself, the third in his relation to society, and the fourth deals with his ideas of happiness. Throughout the poem the neatness and conciseness of the language, the melody of the verse, and the beauty and fidelity of the illustrations prove that if the poet has not produced a perfect model of didactic poetry, it is simply for the reason that such an object is beyond the attainment of man (171).

Imitations of Horace, in which he adapted the topics of the Roman satirist to the persons and vices of his own day, were Pope's latest works.

On the 30th of May, 1744, this poet died. The last years of his life were very gloomy, for his health was feeble, and he was without the genial companionships in which he had found delight. Swift was sunk in idiocy. Atterbury and Gay were dead, and his mother too was gone.

Pope's Quarrel with Addison. Pope's quarrel with Addison has been explained in various ways, but a knowledge of their characters and a plain statement of a few facts are enough to show how impossible it was that the man of grand self-respect and the man of intense self-esteem should retain each other's confidence. When the young poet began his literary career, he paid deference to the name of the great Oxford scholar, sought his friendship, and won his favor. Whether Addison was jealous of Pope's increasing fame may be questioned, but it is certain that Pope was resentful towards Addison for his too frank criticisms of the *Essay on Criticism* and *The Rape of the Lock*. Their open unfriendliness was probably caused by Pope's spiteful assault on old John Dennis for his " Remarks on the Tragedy of Cato." Addison was suspected of making this assault, and in relieving himself of the suspicion, he quietly said that, had he answered the remarks, he would have done it as a gentleman should. Pope never forgave this rebuke. It was too severe to be forgotten. The attempts of friends, and even their own interchange of literary compliments, did not restore friendly relations. It was a most dignified quarrel on the part of Pope, when compared with the bitterness of his quarrels with others. The victims of the *Dunciad*, and Lady Mary Wortley Montagu, knew the cruelty of "The Wicked Wasp of Twickenham." Pope was a strange mixture of selfishness and generosity, malignity and tolerance; he was fond of indirect and cunning courses ; and his literary ambition showed itself sometimes in meannesses and jealousies.

Two Classes of Poets. Concerning his merits as a poet, the critics have had many and spirited encounters. They began to quarrel in Pope's day, and though they are not now as excited as they were then, they are quite as arrogant. This irrepressible conflict of opinion is due to the fact that there are two divisions of poetry, and two races of poets. There is the poetry that is natural, and the poetry that is artificial; the poetry that is spontaneous, bursting into blaze, giving fire and energy to the language which expresses the intense feeling of the poet, and the verse in which the emotions flicker and must be patiently fanned into flame. There is poetry having the power and dignity of passion, and poetry having the power and dignity of elegance. There are among the poets those who please by accuracy of details and those who charm by the massive grandeur of their thoughts.

What end does poetry serve? Jeffrey, the keenest of critics, Wordsworth and Coleridge, patient thinkers in the philosophy of poetry, teach that the end of poetry is to give pleasure. Their definitions turn against them when they propose to strike Pope's name from the list of poets. If there be two general divisions of taste among people of literary culture, there must be two general classes of poets. The array of critics who have praised Pope's verse, proves that no mean place can be assigned him among our poets. He must be ranked first among those whose power of pleasing is found in their conformity to the laws of rhythm, in the studied music of their song. He must not be named with Chaucer, Shakespeare and Milton, for he has not sublime thoughts, he has not broad and profound sympathies. Nature does not inspire him. Art in life and in literature commanded his highest esteem, and, therefore, he struck the chords that would please the elegant rather than the earnest. "He was the poet-laureate of polite life."

Pope's influence upon the poetry of his own and the suc-

ceeding generation was pernicious. A throng of writers,
in striving to imitate him, produced verse so thoroughly artificial that it was soulless and contemptible. The only thing
about it to remind one of poetry was its form. They were
satisfied with rhythm. They did not try to express thought.
They forgot the spirit of poetry in their devotion to its
mechanical properties.*

John Gay (1688–1732) was one of those easy, amiable, good-
natured men whose talents excite admiration without jealousy,
while their characters are the object of fondness rather than respect.
Pope describes him as

> " Of manners gentle, of affections mild,
>   In wit a man, simplicity a child."

He was apprenticed to a tradesman, but believing that he had
poetical talent, he exchanged his calling for a thriftless literary
career. He had the good fortune to secure the patronage of the
Duchess of Monmouth, and in her household he lived, " lapped in
cotton, and had his plate of chicken, and his saucer of cream, and
frisked, and barked, and wheezed, and grew fat, and so ended." †
The Shepherds' Week, in Six Pastorals, written to ridicule the pastorals of Ambrose Phillips, was full of humor and of rural description. His next publication, *Trivia, or the Art of Walking in the
Streets of London*, is interesting not only for its easy humor, but also
for the curious details it gives of the scenery, costume and manners
of the street at that time. Keen political allusions contributed
to the popularity of Gay's dramatic pieces. His most successful
venture in that line was *The Beggars' Opera*, the pioneer of English
operatic works. His *Fables* (**178**), written in easy verse and
abounding in good humor, still retain favor in collections of poetry
for the young. His songs and ballads are musical, touching, and
playful.

* The student is referred to the following interesting discussions of Pope and his
poetry :
  Johnson's *Lives of the Poets*,—DeQuincey's *Biographical Essays*,—Reed's *Lec-
tures on the British Poets*, Lect. IX.—Thackeray's *English Humorists*,—Taine's
English Literature,—Hazlitt's *Lectures on the English Poets*,—Elwin's *Life of Pope*,—
Lowell's *My Study Windows*.

  † Thackeray.

Matthew Prior (1664-1721) was a poet and diplomatist who played a prominent part on the stage of politics as well as on that of literature (**177**). He took part with Charles Montagu in the composition of the *Country Mouse and City Mouse*; a poem intended to ridicule Dryden's *Hind and Panther;* and as the sentiments of the satire were approved by the government, the door of public employment was soon opened to him. Though he had entered public life as a partisan of the Whigs, he deserted them for the Tories, on the occasion of the impeachment of Lord Somers. In 1715 he was ordered into custody by the Whigs, on a charge of high treason, and remained two years in confinement. But for his college fellowship, which he prudently retained throughout the period of his prosperity, he would have been reduced to poverty. His longer and more ambitious poems are *Alma*, a metaphysical discussion carried on in Hudibrastic verse, exhibiting a good deal of thought and learning disguised under an easy conversational garb, and the religious epic entitled *Solomon*, a poem somewhat in the same manner, and with the same defects, as the *Davideis* of Cowley. The ballad *Henry and Emma*, he founded on the ballad of *The Nutbrowne Maid*, but his work has not the charming simplicity of the old poem. His claim to poetic fame rests mainly upon his easy, animated love-songs.

Edward Young (1681-1765) began his career by the unsuccessful pursuit of fortune in the public service. He obtained his first literary reputation by a satire entitled the *Love of Fame, the Universal Passion*. When nearly fifty years of age, he abandoned his hopes of political preferment, and, entering the service of the church, was made chaplain to George II.

His place in the history of English literature is due to his poem *The Night Thoughts* (**180**). This work, consisting of nine nights of meditations, is in blank verse, and is made up of reflections on Life, Death, Immortality,—the most solemn subjects that can engage the attention of the Christian and the philosopher. The general tone of the work is sombre and gloomy, perhaps in some degree affectedly so. There are other faults. No connection exists among the nine parts; the expression is unnatural; there is lack of simplicity. "Short, vivid, and broken gleams of genius" are frequently seen. The march of his verse is generally majestic, though it has little of the melody of Milton. The epigrammatic nature of some of his most striking images is attested by the large number of expressions which have passed from his writings into the colloquial language of society; such as " procrastination is the thief of time," " all men think all men mortal but themselves."

The poetry of the Scottish Lowlands found an admirable representative at this time in **Allan Ramsay** (1686–1758), who was born in humble life, was first a wigmaker, and afterwards a bookseller in Edinburgh. He was of a happy, jovial, and contented humor, and rendered great services to the literature of his country by reviving the taste for the old Scottish poets, and by editing and imitating the songs and ballads current among the people. He was also the author of an original pastoral poem, *The Gentle Shepherd*, which grew out of two eclogues he had written, descriptive of the rural life and scenery of Scotland. The complete work consists of a series of dialogues in verse, written in the melodious and picturesque dialect of the country, and woven into a simple but interesting love-story.

In this chapter we have considered:—

The Artificial Poets of the Eighteenth Century.

1. Alexander Pope, — a. *The Influence of His Friends,*—b. *Great Influence of His Age,*— c. *The Essay on Criticism,*—d. *The Rape of the Lock,*—e. *His Eclogues,*—f. *His Translation of Homer,*—g. *The Dunciad,*—h. *The Essay on Man,*—i. *His Quarrel with Addison*

2. Two Classes of Poets.

3. John Gay.

4. Matthew Prior.

5. Edward Young.

6. Allan Ramsay.

CHAPTER XIX.

PROSE WRITERS OF THE FIRST HALF OF THE EIGHTEENTH CENTURY.

JOSEPH ADDISON.

"Give days and nights, sir, to the study of Addison, if you mean to be a good writer, or, what is more worth, an honest man."—*Samuel Johnson.*

"Addison was the best company in the world."—*Lady Mary Montagu.*

"He was not free with his superiors. He was rather mute in his society on some occasions; but when he began to be company he was full of vivacity, and went on in a noble stream of thought and language, so as to chain the attention of every one to him."—*Edward Young.*

"The great satirist who alone knew how to use ridicule without abusing it who without inflicting a wound effected a great social reform, and who reconciled wit and virtue after a long and disastrous separation, during which wit had been led astray by profligacy, and virtue by fanaticism."—*T. B. Macaulay.*

THE writers of prose who were contemporaneous with Pope, developed a new form of English literature, which has exerted a powerful and beneficial influence on the manners and culture of English readers. In the form of a periodical, a scanty supply of news was published, together with a short, lively essay on some moral or critical theme. The aim of the dissertations was to inculcate principles of virtue, good taste and politeness.

The most illustrious writer in this department of literature was **Joseph Addison** (1672–1719). He was the son of Lancelot Addison, a clergyman of some reputation for learning. In his early years he was sent to the Charter-house, a famous school in London, and there began his friendship for "Dick" Steele. At fifteen years of age he entered Queen's College, and two years later secured a scholarship at Magdalen College, where he distinguished himself by the style of his scholarship, and by his taste in Latin poetry.

His Early Writings. His first attempt in English verse (1693) was an *Address to Dryden*, by which the old poet's friendship was won. A eulogistic poem on William III. attracted the attention of the Court, and gained for the young author a pension of three hundred pounds. He at once began to travel in France and Italy, that he might cultivate his tastes; but he was soon deprived of his pension by the death of King William. He returned to London, where he lived in poverty, maintaining that dignified patience and quiet reserve which made his character so estimable. While Addison was living in obscurity, Marlborough won the memorable victory of Blenheim. The Lord Treasurer, Godolphin, eager to see the event celebrated in some worthy manner, was reminded of the young poet. The courtier sent for him, found him in his uncomfortable lodgings, and applied to him to sing the glory of the English hero. *The Campaign*, written in 1704, was the result. The verses are stiff and artificial enough ; but Addison, abandoning the absurd custom of former poets, who paint a military hero as slaughtering whole squadrons with his single arm, places the glory of a great general on its true basis—the power of conceiving and executing profound intellectual combinations, the possession of calmness and imperturbable foresight in the hour of danger. The praises of Marlborough were none too lofty for the popular demand ; the town went wild over one passage, in which the hero was compared to an angel guiding a whirlwind.*

* " So when an angel by divine command,
　　With rising tempests shakes a guilty land
　　(Such as of late o'er pale Britannia passed),
　　Calm and serene he drives the furious blast ;
　　And, pleased the Almighty's orders to perform,
　　Rides on the whirlwind and directs the storm."

From the writing of that successful poem, the career of Addison was brilliant and prosperous. He was appointed Under-Secretary of State, and afterwards Chief Secretary for Ireland. Besides these high posts he held other lucrative and honorable offices. The *Campaign* was followed by his *Travels in Italy*, exhibiting proofs not only of his scholarship, but also of his delicate humor, and his deep religious spirit. In 1707 he published his pleasing and graceful opera of *Rosamond ;* and about this time he sketched the comedy of *The Drummer.*

Although Addison entered upon his literary career as a poet, he won his highest fame by writing prose for the earliest English periodicals.

A short account of Steele and of the early periodical literature may be appropriately given at this point. **Sir Richard Steele (186)** (1672 ?–1729) was of Irish parentage. He had been the schoolfellow of Addison, upon whom, both at the Charter-house and afterwards during a short stay at Oxford, he seems to have looked with veneration and love. His life was full of the wildest vicissitudes, and his character was one of those which it is equally impossible to hate or to respect. His heart was tender, his benevolence deep, his aspirations lofty; but his passions were strong, and his life was passed in getting into scrapes and in making projects of reformation. He lacked prudence and self-control. Fond of pleasure, and always ready to sacrifice his welfare for the whim of the moment, he caused himself to be disinherited by enlisting as a private in the Horse-Guards ; and when afterwards promoted to a commission, he astonished the town by his wild extravagance, in the midst of which he wrote a moral and religious treatise entitled *The Christian Hero*, breathing the loftiest sentiments of piety and virtue. He was a man of ready talents ; and being an ardent partisan pamphleteer, was rewarded by Government with the place of Gazetteer. This position gave him a monopoly of official news at a time when newspapers were still in their infancy.

The Tatler. Steele determined to profit by the facilities afforded him, and to found a new species of periodical which should contain the news of the day and a series of light and agreeable essays upon topics of universal interest, likely to improve the taste, the manners, and morals of society. It should be remarked that this was a period when literary taste was at its lowest ebb among the middle and fashionable classes of England. The amusements, when not merely frivolous, were either immoral or brutal. Gambling, even among women, was prevalent. The sports of the men were marked with cruelty and drunkenness. In such a state of things, intellectual pleasures and acquirements were regarded either with wonder or with contempt. The fops and fine ladies actually prided themselves on their ignorance of spelling, and any allusion to books was scouted as pedantry. Such was the disease which Steele desired to cure. He determined to treat it, not with formal doses of moral declamation, but with homœopathic quantities of good sense, good taste, and pleasing morality, disguised under an easy and fashionable style. *The Tatler* was a small sheet appearing three times a week, at the cost of 1*d*., each number containing a short essay, generally extending to about two octavo pages, and the rest filled up with news and advertisements. The popularity of the new journal was great; no tea-table, no coffee-house—in that age of coffee-houses— was without it; and the authors, writing with ease, pleasantry, and knowledge of life,—writing as men of the world, and as men about town, rather than as literary recluses, soon gained the attention of the people whom they addressed. *The Tatler* was published for nearly two years,— from April 12th, 1709, till January 2d, 1711. By that time

Steele had lost his position as Gazetteer. His success in writing under the *nom de plume* of Isaac Bickerstaffe,

1711.] prompted him to continue his addresses to the public. He soon established the famous *Spectator.*

This was like the *Tatler*, with the difference that it appeared six times a week. After reaching five hundred and fifty-five numbers, it was discontinued for about eighteen months, resuming its work in 1714. *The Guardian*, inferior to either of the other periodicals, though having Addison and Steele for contributors, was begun in 1713, and continued for one hundred and seventy-five numbers. Steele, though he was master of a ready and pleasant pen, was compelled to obtain as much assistance as he could from his friends. Many writers of the time, among them Swift and Berkeley, furnished hints or contributions.

Addison's Co-operation with Steele. But we must return to Addison. His constant and powerful aid was freely given to Steele. He entered warmly into the project, making the most valuable as well as the most numerous contributions. For *The Tatler* (**182**) he furnished one-sixth, for *The Spectator* (**183, 184**) more than one-half, and for *The Guardian* one-third of the matter. His papers are signed by one of the four letters, C. L. I. O., either the letters of the name of Clio, or the initials of Chelsea, London, Islington and the Office, the places where the essays were written.

The fertility of invention displayed in his charming papers published in the *Tatler*, *Spectator* and *Guardian*, the variety of their subjects, and the felicity of their treatment, will ever place them among the masterpieces of fiction and of criticism. Their variety is wonderful. Nothing is too high, nothing too low, to furnish matter for amusing and yet profitable reflection. From the patches and cherry-colored ribbons of the ladies to the loftiest principles of morality and religion, everything is treated with appropriateness and unforced energy. He was long held up as the finest model of elegant yet idiomatic English prose ; and now the student will find in him qualities that never can become obsolete—an unfailing clearness and limpidity of expression, and a singular harmony between the language and the thought.*

Addison's Delineations of Character. But his delineations of the characters of men are wonderfully delicate. That inimitable personage, Sir Roger de Coverley, is a perfectly finished picture, worthy of Cervantes or of Walter Scott. The manner in which the foibles and the virtues of the old squire are combined is a proof that Addison, who added most of the subtile strokes to the character, possessed humor in its highest and most delicate perfection. And the telling sketches of the squire's dependants, the chaplain, the butler, and Will Wimble, the poor relative,—all these delicate observations of character must ever place Addison high among the great painters of human nature.

His Poetry, though very popular in his own time, has since fallen in public estimation to a point very far below that occupied by his prose. His earlier and more ambitious poems, even including the once-lauded *Campaign*, have little to distinguish them from the vast mass of regular, frigid, irreproachable composition popular in that time. His lighter lyrical poetry, such as the songs in *Rosamond*, are pleasing and musical. His *Hymns* breathe a fervent and tender spirit of piety, and are in their diction and versification stamped with great beauty and refinement. This is especially true of the verses beginning,

" When all thy mercies, O my God,"

and of his well-known adaptation of the noble psalm, " The heavens declare the glory of God."

---

* " Whoever wishes to attain an English style, familiar but not coarse, and elegant but not ostentatious, must give his days and nights to the volumes of Addison."—*Samuel Johnson.*

The Tragedy of Cato. For several years four acts of an unfinished drama were tossed about among Addison's papers. During the suspension of *The Spectator* he improved the opportunity of completing the work, and in 1713, brought out his tragedy of *Cato* (**185**). It is cold, solemn and pompous, written with scrupulous regard for the classical unities. The story is without special interest. The characters, however, are full of patriotic and virtuous rhetoric. The play was a wonderful success on the stage. Night after night an applauding audience crowded the theatre, Whig and Tory finding delight in applying the political sentiments of the piece to the English politics of their own day; but after a few weeks the enthusiasm cooled, and the play was allowed to find its place in the library, and to exchange the unintelligent praises of the throng for the cool criticism of the reader.

Addison's Social and Political Career. Addison won no distinction as a member of the House of Commons, or as a public officer. His inveterate timidity prevented him from speaking with effect. His powers of conversation are said to have deserted him when in the presence of more than two or three hearers. The one blemish in his life may be ascribed to this diffidence, for in order to conquer it, and to give flow and vivacity to his ideas, he had recourse to wine. We must remember, however, that excessive drinking was the fashion of that age in England, and was not regarded as a vice.

In 1716 Addison married the Countess Dowager of Warwick, to whose son he had been tutor. The union does not seem to have added to the happiness of either the polished scholar or the dashing lady. He often would escape from the elegance of Holland House to spend his days and nights with old friends in the clubs and coffee-houses.

The year after his marriage, Addison reached the highest

point of his political career; he was made Secretary of State, and in this eminent position exhibited the same liberality, modesty, and genuine public spirit, that had characterized his whole life. Even in his political journals, *The Freeholder* and *The Examiner*, he never departed from a tone of candor, moderation, and good breeding. He retained his secretary-ship but a short time, retiring from it with a pension of fifteen hundred pounds a year. It was his determination to devote the evening of his life to the composition of an elaborate work on the evidences of the Christian religion; but his remaining days were few; and the work was left incomplete. He died at the early age of forty-seven. A distressing asthma had afflicted his closing years and other trials had attended him; but his serene and gentle spirit lost none of its patience, nor did his reverential faith desert him.

Addison's celebrated quarrel with Pope has been discussed. However painful it may be to find the highest spirits of the age embittered against each other, we can hardly regret that quarrel; for we owe to it one of the finest passages in Pope's works, the unequaled lines drawing the character of Atticus, which was unquestionably meant for Addison. Of all the accusations so brilliantly launched against him, Addison should plead guilty to none save the very venial one of loving to surround himself with an obsequious circle of literary admirers. The blacker portions of the portrait are traceable to the pure malignity of the satirist.

Thackeray's Estimate. "Addison wrote his papers as gayly as if he were going out for a holiday. When Steele's *Tatler* first began its prattle, Addison, then in Ireland, caught at his friend's notion, poured in paper after paper, and contributed the stores of his mind, the sweet fruits of his reading, the delightful gleanings of his daily observation, with a wonderful profusion. . . . . . He was six and thirty years old; full and ripe. He had not worked crop after crop from his brain, cutting and sowing and cutting again, like other luckless cultivators of letters. He had not done much as yet; a few Latin poems—graceful prolusions; a polite book of travels; a dissertation on medals, not very deep; four acts of a tragedy, a great classical exercise; and *The Campaign*, a large prize poem that won an enormous prize. But with his friend's discovery of the *Tatler*, Addison's calling was found, and the most delightful talker in the world began to speak. . . . . Addison was one of the most resolute clubmen of his day. He passed many hours daily in those haunts. Besides drinking, he indulged in that odious practice of smoking Poor fellow; he was a man's man, remember. The only woman he did know he did not write about. I take it there would not have been much humor in that story."

"When this man looks from the world whose weaknesses he describes so benevolently, up to the Heaven which shines over us all, I can hardly fancy a human face lighted up with a more serene rapture; a human intellect thrilling with a purer love and adoration than Joseph Addison's. Listen to him: from your childhood you have known the verses; but who can hear their sacred music without love and awe?—

> " ' Soon as the evening shades prevail,
> The moon takes up the wondrous tale,
> And nightly to the listening earth
> Repeats the story of her birth;
> And all the stars that round her burn,
> And all the planets in their turn,
> Confirm the tidings as they roll,
> And spread the truth from pole to pole.
> What though in solemn silence all
> Move round this dark terrestrial ball;
> What though no real voice nor sound,
> Among their radiant orbs be found;
> In reason's ear they all rejoice,
> And utter forth a glorious voice
> Forever singing as they shine,
> The hand that made us is divine,'

"It seems to me those verses shine like the stars. They

shine out of a great, deep calm. When he turns to Heaven, a Sabbath comes over that man's mind; and his face lights up from it with a glory of thanks and prayer. His sense of religion stirs through his whole being." *

JONATHAN SWIFT.

"The most unhappy man on earth."—*Bishop King.*

"The most agreeable companion, the truest friend, and the greatest genius of his age."—*Joseph Addison.*

"He moves laughter but never joins in it. He appears in his works such as he appears in society. All the company are convulsed with merriment, while the Dean, the author of all the mirth, preserves an invincible gravity and even sourness of aspect, and gives utterance to the most eccentric and ludicrous fancies, with the air of a man reading the commination service."—*T. B. Macaulay.*

"Swift was in person tall, strong and well made, of a dark complexion, but with blue eyes, black and bushy eyebrows, nose somewhat aquiline, and features which well expressed the stern, haughty, and dauntless turn of his mind. He was never known to laugh, and his smiles are happily characterized by the well known lines of Shakespeare,—indeed, the whole description of Cassius might be applied to Swift:—

> ' He reads much:
> He is a great observer, and he looks
> Quite through the deeds of men: . . . .
> Seldom he smiles, and smiles in such a sort
> As if he mocked himself, and scorned his spirit
> That could be mov'd to smile at anything.' "
>
> —*Walter Scott.*

"In humor and in irony, and in the talent of debasing and defiling what we hated, we join with the world in thinking the Dean of St. Patrick without a rival." —*Francis Jeffrey.*

"Dean Swift may be placed at the head of those that have employed a plain style. Few writers have discovered more capacity. He treats every subject which he handles, whether serious or ludicrous, in a masterly manner. He knew, almost beyond any man, the purity, the extent, the precision of the English language,"— *Hugh Blair.*

Jonathan Swift (1667–1745), a most original genius, holds an eminent place in the literary and political history of his time. He was born in Dublin; but his parents were Eng-

* Thackeray.

For further readings on Addison, the student is referred to **Johnson's** *Lives of the Poets*, Macaulay's *Essay*, Thackeray's *English Humorists.*

lish. His father died in poverty before Swift was born, and so the child became dependent upon the charity of relatives. His uncle sent him to school at Kilkenny, and then to Trinity College, Dublin. There Swift busied himself with irregular and desultory study, and at last received his degree with the unfavorable notice that it was conferred *"speciali gratia,"* indicating that his conduct had not satisfied the academical authorities. In 1688 he entered the household of Sir William Temple, a distant connection of his family, in whose service he remained as secretary for six years. His social position, midway between that of a member of the family and a servant, was galling to his proud spirit. His residence at Moor Park continued down to Temple's death in 1699, with, however, one interruption in 1694, caused by a quarrel with his patron, whose supercilious condescension Swift's haughty spirit could not brook. During his residence with Sir William, Swift was an industrious student. Steady and extensive reading corrected the defects of his earlier education. On Temple's death he became the literary executor of his patron, and prepared numerous works for the press. These he presented to William III. with a preface and dedication written by himself.

Failing to obtain any preferment from that sovereign, Swift went to Ireland in 1699 as chaplain to Earl Berkeley, the Viceroy. He made yearly visits to England, where he became the familiar companion of Halifax, Godolphin, Somers, and Addison, the most illustrious men of the time. His connection with William III. and Temple, as well as the predominance of Whig policy, naturally caused Swift to enter public life under the Whig banner. It was in the interests of this party that he wrote his first work, the *Dissensions in Athens and Rome,* a political pamphlet in favor of the Whig ministers who were impeached in 1701.

The Tale of a Tub, his first important work, was published in 1704. It is a savage and yet exquisitely humorous pasquinade, ridiculing the Roman Catholics and Presbyterians, and exalting the High Anglican party, the three churches being impersonated in the ludicrous and not very decorous adventures of his three heroes, Peter, Jack, and Martin. The *Tale* is that three brothers, Peter (the Roman Catholic Church), Martin (the Lutherans), and Jack (the Calvinists) received coats from their dying father. The coats were to last them as long as they lived, provided they kept them clean. But as fashions changed the coats changed with them. Embroidery, fringes and tinsel conceal the simple garments bequeathed by the father. Peter hides the will and assumes lordly dignities. Martin and Jack steal copies of the will, and leave Peter's house. Martin tries to remove some of the trappings from his coat and to leave some; but Jack, in his earnestness, rips off all the embroidery and tears away much of the coat.

Hallam regards this as Swift's masterpiece. It was published anonymously; and that is not strange, for the book contains passages to which no clergyman could becomingly put his name.

The Battle of the Books, though first published in 1704, appears to have been written as early as 1697, to support his patron, Sir William Temple, in the celebrated Boyle and Bentley controversy on the letters of Phalaris. This dispute arose out of the violently-contested question of the relative superiority of the Ancients and Moderns, a question started in England by Sir William Temple in 1692.* Swift

---

* The dispute had its origin in France, where Fontenelle and Perrault claimed for the moderns a general superiority over the writers of antiquity. A reply to their arguments was published by Sir William Temple in 1692, in his *Essay on Ancient and Modern Learning,* written in elegant language, but containing much puerile matter, and exhibiting great credulity. Not content with pointing out the undoubted merits of the great writers of antiquity, he undervalued the labors and discoveries of the moderns, and passed over Shakespeare, Milton, and Newton without even mentioning their names. Among other arguments for the decay of

became a champion of the Boyle faction, and in this work gave a foretaste of those tremendous powers of sarcasm which made him the most formidable pamphleteer that ever lived. The merits of the case he does not attempt to touch; but with grotesque invention, and with unscrupulous use of everything coarse and ludicrous in language, he strives to cover his opponents with contempt.

Swift's Political Pamphlets. In 1705 Swift was employed to negotiate with the English government in reference to the claims of the Irish clergy. He visited England on this mission, and though unsuccessful, displayed great activity and shrewdness. He had by this time made himself conspicuous both in his profession and in politics; he was known and feared as a powerful and unscrupulous pamphleteer, and was the familiar associate of those who were at the head of affairs. His advocacy of Whig principles, never very hearty, came to an end in 1710. He had long regarded Ireland with detestation, and was eager for a promotion that would enable him to reside in England, near the focus of literary and political activity. But his hopes of preferment were not fulfilled, and, when his patience was exhausted, he abandoned his party, and began to intrigue and to satirize on the side of the Tories. In this same year, Harley and Pope's friend, St. John, reached the head of affairs. Swift was received by them with open arms. He was caressed and

---

humor, wit, and learning, Temple maintained "that the oldest books extant were still the best in their kind ;" and in proof of this assertion cited the *Fables of Æsop* and the *Epistles of Phalaris*. This led to a publication of a new edition of the *Epistles of Phalaris* by the scholars of Christ Church, Oxford (1695). The nominal editor was Charles Boyle, who, in his Preface, inserted a bitter reflection upon RICHARD BENTLEY (1662-1742), the King's Librarian, on account of the refusal of the latter to grant the loan of a MS. in the King's Library. Bentley soon had an opportunity for retaliation. He proved that the author of the *Epistles of Phalaris* was not the Sicilian tyrant, but some sophist of a later age. Sir William Temple was incensed at Bentley's Dissertation ; and Swift, who then resided in Temple's house, made his first attack on Bentley in the *Battle of the Books*, in which he ridiculed the great scholar in the most ludicrous manner.

flattered by the great. With unexampled rapidity he poured forth squib after squib and pamphlet after pamphlet, employing all the stores of his fancy and powerful sophistry to defend his party and to blacken and ridicule his antagonists. The great object of his ambition was an English bishopric, and the ministers would have been willing enough to gratify him; but his authorship of the *Tale of a Tub*, and his lampoon on the Duchess of Somerset, proved fatal to him, and he was obliged to content himself with the Deanery of St. Patrick's, Dublin. He entered upon the duties of this office in 1713. This was the most active period of Swift's life. His *Public Spirit of the Whigs*, his *Conduct of the Allies*, and his *Reflections on the Barrier Treaty*, the ablest political pamphlets ever written, not only reconciled the nation to the peace policy of the Tory ministry, but also kindled a feeling of enthusiasm for the Tory statesmen among the people. Evil days, however, were at hand. Harley and St. John tore asunder their party with their dissensions; in spite of all Swift's efforts, the troubles became desperate; and Swift retired to Ireland, where he was received with contempt and execration.

During his frequent visits to London, Swift's company had been sought after by men of letters as well as by statesmen. With Pope, Gay and Arbuthnot, he formed what was called the Scriblerus Club, a company united by the closest intimacy, where each threw the ideas published in their famous *Miscellanies* into a common stock.

His Residence in Ireland. For twelve years Swift remained in Ireland. He was quiet, but thoroughly discontented. At last, in 1724, the opportunity came for him to speak his hatred for the English government, and he spoke in such a way as to raise himself from being an object of detestation to a height of popularity such as no other English churchman ever attained in Ireland.

The condition of Ireland was just then unusually deplorable; the manufacturing industry and the commerce of the country were paralyzed by the protective statutes of the English Parliament; the agricultural classes were reduced to the lowest abyss of degradation. Swift boldly proclaimed the misery of the country. His force and bitterness soon drew down the persecution of the ministers. But the highest point of his Irish popularity was attained by the seven famous *Drapier Letters.* These letters, signed *M. B. Drapier*, were written by Swift and inserted in a Dublin newspaper. The occasion was the attempt, on the part of the English ministry, to force the circulation of a large sum of copper money in Ireland. The contract for coining this money had been undertaken by William Wood, a Birmingham speculator. Swift endeavored to persuade the people that it was far below its nominal value; and he counselled all true patriots not only to refuse to take it, but to refrain from using any English manufactures whatever. The force of his arguments, and the skill with which he wore the mask of a plain, honest tradesman, excited the populace almost to frenzy. Swift was known to be the real author of the letters, and his defence of the rights of the Irish people made him from that moment the idol of that warm-hearted race. Two years later he visited England for the

1726.] purpose of publishing his famous *Gulliver's Travels.*

The work was received with delight and admiration, and was at once recognized as his greatest gift to literature. But applause could not soothe the griefs that were about to befall him. The death of Stella, one of the few beings whom he ever really loved, happened in 1728; and the loss of many friends further contributed to darken and intensify the gloom of his proud and sombre spirit. He had from an early period suffered occasionally from giddiness, and after Stella's death the attacks were more frequent and more severe. Deafness deprived him of the pleasure of conversation. Forebodings of insanity tormented him until they were cruelly verified.* In 1741 he passed into a state of idiocy that lasted without interruption till his death in 1745. He is buried in his own cathedral of St. Patrick; and over his grave is inscribed that terrible epitaph composed by himself, in which he speaks of resting " *ubi sæva indignatio ulterius cor lacerare nequit.*" But the most impressive monument of this sad life is the hospital for idiots and incurable madmen, built and endowed in accordance with the directions of Swift's will.

Stella and Vanessa. An account of Swift's career would be imperfect without some mention of the two unhappy women whose love for him was the glory and the misery of their lives. While residing in Temple's family, he became acquainted with Esther Johnson, a beautiful young girl, brought up as a dependent in the house, to whom, while hardly in her teens, Swift gave instruction. The acquaintance ripened into the deepest and tenderest passion. On his removal to Ireland, Swift induced Stella—such was the poetical name he gave her—to settle with her friend Mrs. Dingley in that country, where he maintained with both of them that long, curious, and intimate correspondence which has since been published as his *Journal to Stella.* There is little doubt that Swift intended to marry Stella, and that Stella's life was filled with the hope that she should be his wife. During one of his visits to London, Swift became intimate with the family of a rich merchant named Vanhomrigh, whose daughter Hester, to whom he gave the name of Vanessa, he unwittingly inspired with a deep and

---

* "I remember as I and others were taking with Swift an evening walk, about a mile out of Dublin, he stopped short; we passed on ; but perceiving he did not follow us I went back and found him fixed as a statue, and earnestly gazing upwards at a noble tree, which, in its upper branches, was much withered and decayed. Pointing at it, he said, 'I shall be like that tree; I shall die at the top.'"—*Dr Young.*

jealous love for him. On the death of her father, Miss Van-homrigh, possessing an independent fortune, retired to a villa in Ireland. There Swift continued his visits without explaining to either of the unhappy ladies the nature of his relations to the other. At last Vanessa, driven almost to madness by suspense and irritation, wrote to Stella to in-quire into the nature of Swift's relations to her. Stella gave the letter to Swift. In rage he carried it to Vanessa, and without a word, but with a terrible countenance, threw it down before her. The poor girl died soon after. Swift at this time was probably the husband of Stella. It is believed that they were privately married in the garden of the dean-ery, in 1716. He, however, never recognized her in public as his wife, nor did he ever live in the same house with her, nor did he allow her to meet him unless a third person were present. In reading his words when he was bereaved by her death, one must see that his love for her was real.

Gulliver's Travels. A few comments on his writings must close this essay. The greatest and most characteristic of his prose works is the *Voyages of Gulliver* (175), a vast and all-embracing satire upon humanity itself. The general plan of this book is as follows: a plain, unaffected, honest ship-surgeon, describes the strange scenes and adventures through which he passes, with an air of simple, straightfor-ward, prosaic good faith, such as Defoe displays in *Robinson Crusoe*. The contrast between the extravagance of the inventions and the gravity with which they are related, illustrates the peculiar humor of Swift. This admirable fiction consists of four parts or voyages: in the first Gulliver visits the country of Lilliput, whose inhabitants are about six inches in stature, and where all the objects, houses, trees, ships, and animals, are in exact proportion to the miniature human beings. The invention displayed in the droll and surprising incidents is unbounded; the air with which they

are recounted is natural, and the strange scenes and adventures are recorded with an appearance of simple, straightforward honesty altogether inimitable. The second voyage
is to Brobdingnag, a country of enormous giants, sixty feet
in height; and here Gulliver plays the same part that the
pigmy Lilliputians had played to him. As in the first
voyage the contemptible and ludicrous side of human
things is presented by showing how trifling they would appear in almost microscopic proportions, so in Brobdingnag
we are made to perceive how petty and ridiculous our
politics, our wars, and our ambitions would appear to the
perceptions of a gigantic race. The third part carries
Gulliver to a series of strange and fantastic countries. The
first is Laputa, a flying island, inhabited by philosophers
and astronomers; whence he passes to the Academy of
Lagado; thence to Glubbdubdrib and Luggnagg. In this
part the author introduces the terrific description of the
Struldbrugs, wretches who are cursed with bodily immortality without intellects or affections. Gulliver's last voyage
is to the country of the Houyhnhnms, a region where horses
are the reasoning beings; and men, under the name of Yahoos, are degraded to the rank of noxious, filthy and unreasoning brutes. The satire goes on deepening as it advances;
playful in the scenes of Lilliput, it grows more and more
bitter at every step, till in the Yahoos it reaches a pitch of
almost insane ferocity.

Miscellaneous Writings. Swift wrote pamphlets of a partly
religious character, such as his *Sentiments of a Church of
England Man*, *The Sacramental Test*, and others on local and
temporary subjects (**176**). They all exhibit the vigor of his
reasoning, the force of his style, and the fierceness of his
invective. Neither respect for his own dignity nor respect
for the candor of others ever restrained him from over-
whelming his opponents with ridicule or abuse. The pleas-

antest and most innocent of his writings are the papers written in the character of Isaac Bickerstaffe (174), where he shows up with exquisite drollery, the quackery of the astrologer Partridge. His letters are very numerous; those addressed to his intimate friends, Pope and Gay, and those written to Sheridan, half-friend and half-butt, contain choice specimens of his peculiar humor.

Swift's Literary Style. Swift will ever be regarded as one of the masters of English prose, and his poetical works will give him a place among the writers of his age. Yet they have no pretension to loftiness of language; they studiously preserve the familiar expression of common life. In nearly all of them he adopted the short octosyllable verse that Prior and Gay had rendered popular. The poems, like his prose, show wonderful acquaintance with ordinary incidents, intense observation of human nature, and a profoundly misanthropic view of mankind. Most likely to remain popular are the *Verses on my own Death,* describing the mode in which that event, and Swift's own character, would be discussed among his friends, his enemies, and his acquaintances; and there is no composition in the world which gives a more easy and animated picture, at once satirical and true, of the language and sentiments of ordinary society. But his fame rests wholly upon his wonderful prose. Vigor and perspicuity mark every page. There is no sign of pedantry in his style; every sentence is homely and rugged and strong. "He seems to have hated foreign words as he hated men." His vocabulary is thoroughly Saxon, and the variety of English idioms used in expressing his thought is greater than can be found in any other writer of his age.*

* For further readings on this topic see *The North American Review,* Jan. 1868, —Craik's *English Literature,* Vol. II., p. 208, seq.,—Macaulay's Essay on *Sir William Temple,*—Thackeray's *English Humorists,*—Jeffrey in the *British Essayists* —Scott's *Life of Swift,*—Hazlitt's Lectures on *The English Poets,* Lect. VI.

Dr. John Arbuthnot (1667–1735) was greatly esteemed by the brilliant society of which Pope and Swift were the chief luminaries. He was of Scottish origin, and enjoyed high reputation as a physician attached to the Court, from 1709 till the death of Queen Anne. He was one of the most learned wits of the day, and was the chief contributor to the *Miscellanies* spoken of in our discussion of Pope. He is supposed to have conceived the plan of that extensive satire on the abuses of learning, embodied in the *Memoirs of Martinus Scriblerus*, and to have executed the best portions of that work. But the fame of Arbuthnot is more intimately connected with the *History of John Bull*, in which the intrigues and Wars of the Succession are caricatured with much drollery. The object of the work was to render the prosecution of the war by Marlborough unpopular with the nation. The adventures of Squire South (Austria), Lewis Baboon (France) Nic. Frog (Holland), and Lord Strutt (the King of Spain), are related with fun, odd humor, and familiar vulgarity of language. The characters of the various nations and parties are conceived and maintained with spirit. The popular ideal of John Bull, with which Englishmen are so fond of identifying their personal and national peculiarities, was first stamped and fixed by Arbuthnot's amusing burlesque. Arbuthnot is always good-natured. He shows no trace of that fierce misanthropy which tinged every page of Swift. Of him Swift said, "Oh, if the world had a dozen Arbuthnots I would burn my [Gulliver's] Travels."

Henry St. John, Viscount Bolingbroke (1678–1751), remarkable for his career as a statesman and orator, was a prominent member of the brilliant coterie of Pope and Swift. After a stormy public life, he amused his declining years by the composition of political, moral, and philosophical essays. While an exile he wrote his *Reflections on Exile*, his *Letter to Sir William Windham* in defence of his political life, his papers *On the Study of History*, and *On the True Use of Retirement*. After his death a complete edition of his works was published in five volumes. His disbelief in the divine origin of Christianity is distinctly stated. The language of Bolingbroke is lofty and oratorical; but the thought is often feeble, and the tone of philosophical indifference to matters in which other men are interested seems to be affected. It was to Bolingbroke that Pope addressed *The Essay on Man*, and from him the poet derived many of his opinions (**189, 190**).

George Berkeley (1684–1753) was full of projects for increasing the virtue and happiness of his fellow-creatures. When fifty years of age he was made Bishop of Cloyne in Ireland. This position he continued to hold, obstinately refusing any promotion that would remove him from the people for whom he loved to work. His writings are numerous, embracing a wide field of moral and metaphysical discussion (**191**). He is one of the most brilliant, as well as one of the earliest advocates of the Ideal theory ; and therefore appears in contrast with Locke in the history of English philosophy. Locke traced ideas to external nature, teaching that the phenomena observed are the measure of ideas. Berkeley taught that the *ideas* themselves are the only things man can pronounce *real*. His first philosophical work was the *New Theory of Vision*, in which he announces his startling doctrine concerning knowledge of the properties of bodies. This was followed by *The Principles of Human Knowledge*, and by the *Three Dialogues*. What he aimed to do in his writings, was to refute the skepticism found in other philosophical works; but in the interpretation of much of his thought he is treated as though he were himself a reckless teacher of error.

Mary Wortley Montagu. Although Pope and many distinguished men of letters in this period assiduously cultivated epistolary composition, none of them could .equal Lady Mary Wortley Montagu (1690–1762) in brilliant letter-writing. She was the daughter of the Duke of Kingston, and was celebrated, even from her childhood, for the vivacity of her intellect, her mental acquirements, and the beauty and graces of her person. Her education had been far more extensive and solid than was then usually given to women. Her acquaintance with history, and even with Latin, was considerable, and her studies had been in some degree directed by Bishop Burnet. In 1712 she married Mr. Edward Wortley Montagu, and accompanied him on his embassy to the court of Constantinople. She described her travels over Europe and the East in those delightful *Letters* which have given her in English literature a place resembling that of Madame de Sévigné in the literature of France (**192**). Admirable common sense, observation, vivacity, extensive reading without a trace of pedantry, and a pleasant tinge of half-playful sarcasm, are qualities of her correspondence. She had seen so much, and had been brought into contact with so many remarkable persons, in a way that gave her such means of judging of them, that she is always sensible and amusing. The successful introduction of inoculation for the small-pox is mainly to be attributed to her intelligence and courage. She not only had the daring to try the experiment upon her own child, but with admirable constancy she resisted the furious opposition of bigotry and ignorance against the innovation. She was at one time the intimate friend of Pope, and the object of his most ardent adulation; but a violent quarrel occurred between them, and the spiteful poet pursued her for a time with an almost furious hatred. She is the Sappho of his satirical works.

In this chapter we have considered:—

Prose Writers of the first half of the Eighteenth Century.

1. *Joseph Addison,—a. His Early Writings,—b. A short account of Sir Richard Steele,—c. The Tatler,—d. Addison's Co-operation with Steele,—e. His Delineations of Character.—f. His Poetry,—g. The Tragedy of Cato,—h. His Social and Political Career,—i. Thackeray's Estimate of Him.*

2. *Jonathan Swift,—a. The Tale of a Tub,—b. The Battle of the Books,— c. His Pamphlets,—d. His Services to the Tories,—e. His Residence in Ireland,—f. Stella and Vanessa—g. Gulliver's Travels,—h. His Miscellaneous Writings,—i. His Literary Style.*

3. *Dr. John Arbuthnot.*

4. *Henry St. John, Viscount Bolingbroke.*

5. *George Berkeley.*

6. *Lady Mary Wortley Montagu.*

CHAPTER XX.

THE FIRST GREAT NOVELISTS.

PROSE FICTION was one of the latest departments of literature cultivated by English authors. It is true that Sidney's *Arcadia* was a chivalric form of this kind of writing, and Bacon's *Atlantis* and More's *Utopia*, written in Latin, were philosophical romances; but the use of prose narrative in the delineation of passions, characters, and incidents of real life was first developed by writers in the eighteenth century, among whom the names of Defoe, Richardson, Fielding, Smollett, and Sterne, are the most brilliant.

The literature of fiction divides itself into two great branches, —romances and novels. In the romance the characters and incidents are of a lofty or supernatural character; in the novel there is a recital of the events of ordinary life. "The romance lacks truth, and that in the worst of all ways, by insensible departures, by excessive coloring, by glaring and false lights. . . . . It is against the romance element, ever likely to appear in historical novels, as it appears in history itself, when it runs like a child after the glittering march and sonorous sounds of war, that most of the moral objections to works of fiction hold." * In the department of the novel, from its first appearance in our literature down to the present time, English writers have encountered few rivals and no superiors.

Daniel Defoe (1661–1731) was the founder of the English novel. He was the son of a London butcher named Foe, and not liking the family name he attached a prefix to suit his taste. He was an advanced reformer, even advocating, as early as 1698, the founding of insurance companies, savings banks for the poor, and colleges for the higher education of women. His interest in politics led him to

* Bascom's *Philosophy of English Literature*, p. 271.

take up the pen as a pamphleteer, and his radical **Protestantism** carried him to such extremes that he was frequently subjected to punishment. In spite of fines and imprisonment, he fearlessly pub-lished pamphlet after pamphlet, full of irony, logic, and patriot-ism. In *The True-born Englishman*, a poem written in tuneless rhymes, he defended William of Orange and the Dutch against the prejudices of his countrymen; in *The Shortest Way with the Dissenters* he gravely proposed as the easiest and speediest way of ridding the land of them, to hang their ministers and banish the people; * and when the House of Commons pronounced the pam-phlet a libel on the nation, and sentenced him to stand in the pillory, he coolly wrote his *Ode to the Pillory*, describing it as

> "A hieroglyphic state-machine
> Condemned to punish fancy in."

During one of his imprisonments he commenced *The Review*, the prototype of our semi-political, semi-literary periodicals, publish-ing it three times a week.

In 1719 the first part of *Robinson Crusoe* appeared. Its
1719.] success among the humble readers whom Defoe generally addressed was instantaneous. The simplicity and prob-ability of the events narrated, and the author's skill in identifying himself with the character of his recluse, gave the book an intense interest. The impression it leaves on the memory of every reader is deep and permanent. The hero is without pretensions to extra-ordinary knowledge, and is therefore such a person as every one, ignorant or cultivated, can sympathize with. The more thoughtful the reader, the more does he appreciate Defoe's wonderful art in throwing the air of reality over every part of his fiction.†

Among Defoe's other works of fiction, *The Memoirs of a Cavalier* deserves special mention. The work professes to have been written by one who had taken part in the great Civil War; and so success-fully was the pretence carried out, that it deceived even the great

---

* The Government advertised a reward for his arrest, and gave the following description of his person: "A middle-sized, spare man about forty years old, of a brown complexion and dark brown-coloured hair, but wears a wig; a hooked nose, a sharp chin, grey eyes, and a large mole near his mouth."

† "Let us think how a man of weak imagination would have solved the problem: given one man and an island, to make a story. In Defoe's story, all is life and action."—*Morley*.

Chatham into citing the volume as an authentic narrative. In *A Journal of the Great Plague in London* (**193**), he shows the same marvelous faculty for representing fiction as truth. The imaginary annalist, a respectable London shopkeeper, describes the terrible sights and incidents of that time with a vividness that is appalling. *The Adventures of Colonel Jack, Moll Flanders, Roxana,* and *Captain Singleton,* show the same power of feigning reality. His *True Relation of the Apparition of one Mrs. Veal* was one of the boldest experiments ever made upon human credulity, and yet so plausibly was the story told that searching inquiries were made concerning the facts alleged. It was long supposed that his object in telling the story was to promote the sale of a dull book; for several editions of *Drelincourt on the Fear of Death* rapidly quitted the bookseller's shelves after its advertisement by the ghostly visitation so plausibly narrated.

Defoe's success in fiction attracted the attention of other writers. The field was inviting; for the stage was not in favor, the periodical essays were written out, and the popular demand for literary entertainment was increasing. To supply the demand a company of story-tellers put themselves at work.

Samuel Richardson (1689–1761) was the pioneer in that branch of fiction which grows out of the incidents of commonplace affairs. His life presents little matter for comment; its main features belong to the ordinary career of a prudent and successful tradesman. He was born in Derbyshire,—the son of a poor carpenter. At fifteen years of age he went to London to become a printer's apprentice. The diligence with which he pursued his calling secured him rapid advancement; he was taken into partnership with his employer, and ultimately became the head of an extensive business. At fifty years of age, he stumbled into a path leading him to literary fame. Letter-writing, in those days, was regarded as an important branch of composition,—a means of literary culture. Richardson had been known from his youth as a fluent letter-writer; and a London firm, wishing to publish a series of model letters as an epistolary manual for the lower classes, applied to him as the suitable person to prepare them. After he had accepted the commission, he conceived the happy idea of making the letters tell a connected story. The result of his undertaking was his first novel, *Pamela;*

1740.] *or Virtue Rewarded.* The heroine is represented as a poor, beautiful, and innocent country girl, who enters the service of a rich gentleman. Most of the letters, in which the master's wickedness and the maid's virtue are narrated, are written by Pamela herself. Her minute descriptions of her situation and sur roundings, her trials and heart-conflicts, and the various events of her anxious life, are tedious to the modern reader. But they possess an air of reality, and often introduce exquisite touches of nature and pathos. The sensation made among readers of the old school of chivalric fable by this "romance of real life" was un paralleled. It captivated public fancy as *Hudibras* had done a century before. Fashionable circles made it the theme of their enthusiasm; grave moralists praised its fidelity to nature, and popular preachers applauded the high tone of its morality. Five editions were exhausted in a single year. Richardson suddenly found himself famous; but his was not a mind to be unsettled by success. He continued to exercise laudable and prosaic industry in his business. He was first Printer of the House of Commons; in 1754 he became Master of the Stationers' Company, and in 1760 he bought a half-share in the lucrative office of Printer to the King. In the intervals of business, however, writing in the parlor of his back shop, he assiduously labored to develop his new-found resources. *Clarissa Harlowe,* published in 1748, and *Sir Charles Grandison,* in 1753, gave fresh evidence of his literary talent, and attained a popularity equal to that of their predecessor. Richardson's pleasure in his own fame was somewhat alloyed by his over-sensitive temperament. He could not endure with complacency the free and sometimes caustic criticism passed upon his work. For some years before his death he withdrew himself from general society, and passed most of his time in his suburban home at Parson's Green, London. There he was the centre of a little group of admiring women. His published correspondence and literary remains give a curious picture of the enervating flattery which soothed his timidity and nourished his self-satisfaction.

Clarissa Harlowe is Richardson's greatest work. It is the tragic story of a young lady who falls a victim to the treachery and profligacy of a man of splendid talent and attractions, but of infamous character. Although Richardson is far more successful in the delineation of women than of men, yet Lovelace is one of the most perfect and finished portraits that literature has to show. In this, as in Richardson's other novels, the interest is generated by the accumulation of a thousand delicate, almost imperceptible touches, and the characters are elaborated with painful minuteness. It requires an effort to yield the attention to the gentle, equable current of incident and emotion; yet after a time its force is found to be irresistible.

In his three successive works Richardson portrayed three different orders in the social scale. *Pamela* dealt with the low, *Clarissa Harlowe* with the middle class of society. In *Sir Charles Grandison* he intended to represent an ideal hero who should combine the graces and accomplishments of the man of fashion with the perfection of mental and religious culture.

Henry Fielding. While Richardson was enjoying the praise of his first volume, Henry Fielding (1707–1754) set himself to work to ridicule Pamela and to rival the modest printer. In character the two men had little in common. Fielding was a gay, rollicking fellow, who laughed at virtue and hated all pretensions to dignity. He had inherited a broken-down estate and extravagant habits. At twenty years of age he found himself dependent upon his own resources, and at once betook himself to the stage, composing many inferior comedies, and writing busily for the journals of the day. His career for some years was a continuous struggle with fortune. He married an excellent lady, and squandered her property; he speculated in the Haymarket Theatre, and failed utterly; he then tried the law, and was called to the bar, but there too he was unsuccessful. He also took an active part in political controversy, and in numerous pamphlets and articles maintained liberal doctrines. It was not until the year 1742 that he struck out that vein of humorous writing in which he had no rival. His first novel, *Joseph Andrews*, was a powerful caricature of the timid and fastidious morality, the sentimentalism and the somewhat preaching style of *Pamela*. It at once received the honor due to a great original creation. In rapid succession he produced his *Journey from this World to the Next*, full of political allusions that have now lost their piquancy, and his remarkable satirical tale, *The Life of Jonathan Wild the Great*. In 1749 he had been appointed a police magistrate. While holding this office he composed the finest of his works, the incomparable *Tom Jones* (**194**), a story whose dramatic scenes and characters must have been drawn from the exhibitions of real life in his court.

Amelia, his third great novel, closes the list. Ruined in health by labor and excesses, he sailed for Lisbon in 1754, seeking benefit from a genial climate; but before the close of that year he was buried in the strange land.

Fielding was an accurate observer of character. With the vast and motley field of English society, so strongly marked at that time, he was minutely acquainted, and delighted in the reproduction of its oddities and eccentricities. He is intensely English. Hogarth himself is not more so. In the construction of his plots, Fielding was masterly. That of *Tom Jones* is perhaps the finest example to be met with in fiction, of a series of events probable, yet surprising, each leading to the ultimate catastrophe. He combined an almost childish delight in fun and ludicrous incident, with a philosophic analysis of character. In *Tom Jones* (**194**) it is difficult to know what most to admire—the artful conduct of the plot, the immense variety, truth, and humor of the personages, the gayety of the incidents, or the many acute remarks. Tom Jones himself and the fair Sophy, though elaborated by the author with peculiar care, as types of all that he thought attractive, are tinged with much coarseness and vulgarity; but the time when Fielding wrote was remarkable for the low tone of manners and sentiment. Sometimes he masks impressive moral reflections under a pleasant air of satire and irony. There is a freshness in his writing not found in Richardson; there is also boisterousness, coarseness of thought, and an evident delight in dealing with the nature of the depraved.

The most attractive character in *Joseph Andrews* is Parson Adams, whose learning, simplicity, and courage, together with his consistent oddities, make him a character as humorous as Sancho Panza himself. In the adventures of *Jonathan Wild the Great*, the exploits of a consummate scoundrel are related in a tone of ironical admiration; and the story contains powerful and humorous scenes.

The interest of *Amelia* is entirely domestic. The story was intended to portray Fielding's own follies and irregularities, and to pay a tribute to the virtues and love of his wife. The errors and repentance of Captain Booth, and the inexhaustible love and indulgence of the heroine, are strongly contrasted. Fielding had little power over the pathetic emotions; there are, however, in this novel several touching episodes and strokes of character exhibiting that peculiar characteristic of truly humorous conceptions, namely, the power of touching the heart while exciting the sense of the ludicrous.

Tobias George Smollett. Nearly contemporary with Fielding's novels, were the first efforts of another distinguished worker in the same field,—Tobias George Smollett (1721-1771) **(195)**. Smollett was of Scotch parentage. His family, though poor, gave him a university education. He undertook to support himself by the profession of medicine; but his attention was diverted from his studies by an uncontrollable desire for literary fame, and his life was almost as checkered and distressed as that of Defoe. At the age of nineteen he went to London, hoping to secure a publisher for a tragedy entitled *The Regicide*. Failing in this, he embarked in an expedition to Carthagena in the humble office of surgeon's mate. This gave him an opportunity of studying those grotesque features of sea-life which he afterwards reproduced in his fictions. Quitting the service after he had reached the West Indies, he resided there until he returned to London in 1746. For several years he divided his time between the practice of medicine and the pursuits of literature. He had produced several satires and poems of trifling merit before 1748; in that year *Roderick Random* opened to him a career as a novelist. Three years later it was followed by *Peregrine Pickle*, and in 1753 *The Adventures of Ferdinand, Count Fathom*, a counterpart to Fielding's *Jonathan Wild*, appeared. Previous to this Smollett had become discouraged with his small success as a physician, and had resolved to concentrate his energies in the efforts of his pen. He produced in rapid succession a translation of *Don Quixote*, a fourth novel entitled *Sir Lancelot Greaves*, and a *History of England*, in which he displayed his partisan prejudices. The experiences of two years spent in foreign travel were narrated in a *Tour in France and Italy*. His last political work was a satirical attack upon Lord Bute, entitled *The Adventures of an Atom*. At fifty years of age his health was completely broken down by agitation and incessant labor, and he was ordered to try the effect of a more genial climate. He resided a short time at Leghorn, and there, in spite of exhaustion and suffering, his genius gave forth its most pleasing flash of comic humor. This was the novel of *Humphrey Clinker*, the most genial and humorous of his works. Like Fielding, Smollett died and was buried in a foreign land. The two most intensely national of the great group of English character-painters were doomed to lay their bones, nearly at the same time, under the soil of the stranger,

Of Smollett's novels *Roderick Random* is in some respects the most vigorous. It is full of transcripts from the author's personal experience; the hero's miseries at school, his apprenticeship to the apothecary, his sufferings on board ship, bear every mark of pictures from life. The same may be said of his sailor-characters. As a rule his heroes have but little to attract the reader's sympathy, being generally hard, impudent, and selfish adventurers; but in the subordinate persons, and especially in those of whimsical but faithful dependents, he shows a greater warmth of sentiment. *Humphrey Clinker*, though running over with fun and grotesque incident, exhibits a riper and mellower tone of character-painting than is to be found in his preceding works. This novel contains much that is merely descriptive; it purports to be the travelling-journal of the droll and original party whose letters make up the work. The modern reader may gather many interesting details of life in the eighteenth century from Smollett's pictures of the various localities in England and Scotland which were visited in the imaginary tour.

The plots of Smollett's novels are not unfolded with the slow and logical coherence of Richardson, nor are the incidents combined and grouped with that masterly knowledge of effect which distinguishes Fielding. Each of his novels is a series of scenes—striking, grotesque, farcical, pathetic—with no bond of union save their common connection with two or three chief actors. Yet the lively succession of persons and events is a constant stimulus to the attention. Smollett's characters are numerous and sketched with great animation, but they are not analyzed with a profound knowledge of passion and motive. Having seized some prominent feature, or having placed some oddity of mind or person in a strong light, he ceased to care for development and consistency. Many of his most laughable scenes depend for their effect upon physical humor, —blows and kicks and extravagant terrors; but, unlike Fielding, he fails to make such episodes throw light upon interesting traits of human nature. With the laugh they have excited, Smollett's use of them is at an end. He "excels most as the lively carica-turist; Fielding as the exact painter and profound metaphysician."

We have already referred to Smollett's works as a political writer. He also possessed considerable poetical talent. His best effort in this department is entitled the *Tears of Scotland*. It expresses the patriotic indignation of a generous mind, horror-struck by the cruelties perpetrated by the English troops after the battle of Culloden.

Laurence Sterne (1713–1768) was as eccentric as his works. He was born in Ireland, but received his education at the University of Cambridge. He entered the church, and through the influence of his relatives secured a rich living. His private life was little in harmony with his profession; he appears to have been fanciful, vain, and self-indulgent, perpetually at war with his brother churchmen, and to have masked caprice and selfishness in his domestic relations under a pretence of extreme sensibility. In 1759 he published the first two volumes of a novel entitled *Tristram Shandy* (**196**). The freshness and oddity of his style, and the grotesqueness of his humor, captivated popular taste. Seven volumes more of the same story appeared during the next eight years. Sterne became the lion of fashionable society in London. For a time he indulged his morbid appetite for flattery and his pro-pensity to sentimental intrigue in the brilliant circles of the capital. He then went to the Continent; and during his travels through France and Italy accumulated the materials for his charming *Senti-mental Journey*. This was his best and last production; he took up his residence in London for the purpose of superintending its publication, and died in desolate lodgings, in the fifty-fifth year of his age.

Sterne's works consist of the novel of *Tristram Shandy*, of the *Sentimental Journey*, and of a collection of *Sermons*, written in the odd and fantastic style which he brought into temporary vogue. *Tristram Shandy*, though nominally a romance in the biographical form, is intentionally irregular and capricious. The hero makes no appearance on the scene of action, and the story consists of a series of episodes which introduce the reader to the home-life of an English country family. This family is one of the most amusing collections of odd individualities that ever genius has delineated. The mythical Tristram, and Yorick, a humorous clergyman in whom Sterne has idealized his own character, alternately carry on the narrative; and other prominent personages are Walter Shandy, a retired merchant, the father of Tristram, his wife, his brother, Toby Shandy, a veteran officer, and his servant, Corporal Trim. Mr. Shandy, the restless, crotchety philosopher, is drawn with consummate skill, and is contrasted with the simple benevolence and professional enthusiasm of the unequaled Uncle Toby, a creation of the order of Sancho Panza and Parson Adams. The *Sentimental Journey* was intended by its author to form a sequel to *Tristram Shandy*. It has glaring faults, both in taste and in morality; yet it abounds in charming descriptions and passages of quaint pathos. Acute observation of the minor traits of human nature seems to have been Sterne's strongest quality. He portrays his characters not by description, but by allusion, and fascinates the reader by incidental and unexpected revelations of their amiable eccentricities. He also shows himself a master in combining humor and pathos; although the one sometimes degenerates into buffoonery, and the other into sentimentality. Much may be forgiven the author, in consideration of his candid and appreciative tone in treating of foreigners and foreign institutions. Such a tone was equally rare and laudable, at a time when Englishmen regarded all other nations with the most bigoted prejudice and hostility.

In Sterne's writings there is a parade of obscure and quaint erudition. This tends to give an original flavor to his style, and at the time of his writing, when the elder authors were but little studied, it passed for an indication of extensive learning; but he is now known to have been the boldest of plagiarists, pillaging without scruple the pages of Burton, Rabelais, and the old lawyers and canonists.

In this chapter we have considered:—

The First Great Novelists.

　　1. Daniel Defoe ; 2. Samuel Richardson ; 3. Henry Fielding ; 4. Tobias George Smollett ; 5. Laurence Sterne.

CHAPTER XXI.

HISTORICAL WRITERS OF THE EIGHTEENTH CENTURY.

IN accordance with a law which seems at particular epochs to govern the appearance of great names in one department of art or literature, like the sculptors of the Periclean age, the romantic dramatists in that of Elizabeth, and the English novelists whom we have been discussing in the preceding chapter, the middle of the eighteenth century was signalized by a remarkable wealth of historical genius, and gave birth to Hume, Robertson and Gibbon.

David Hume (1711–1776), a Scotchman, was educated at the University of Edinburgh. A taste for literature and literary pursuits early declared itself as his ruling passion, but the limited circumstances of his family seemed to make its gratification impossible. However, after a vain attempt to devote himself to the law, and an equally unsuccessful trial of commercial life, Hume resolved "to make a very rigid frugality supply his deficiency of fortune, and to regard every object as contemptible except the improvement of his talents in literature." At the age of twenty-three he went to France with the intention of pursuing his studies in a country retreat. Three years passed very agreeably in close attention to philosophy and general literature. In 1737 he returned to Great Britain to publish the first-fruits of his pen, *A Treatise on Human Nature*. "Never," says Hume's autobiography, "was literary attempt more unfortunate. But being naturally of a cheerful and sanguine temper, I very soon recovered the blow." The first volume of *Moral and Philosophical Essays*, published in 1741, met with a more favorable reception; but the wavering fortunes of the next ten years would have chilled the aspirations of a less resolute soul. True to his resolve, Hume eked out his slender patrimony with genuine Scotch thrift; it was, however, hardly sufficient for his support, and as yet his receipts from the booksellers were very small. By acting for one year as tutor to an insane nobleman, and for two more as aid-de-camp of a military embassy, he obtained what seemed to his modest desires a competence. He then, in 1752, became Librarian of the Faculty of Advocates in Edinburgh. This position brought him no salary, but placed at his command a large and excellent collection of books. With the aid thus furnished he began his great work, the *History of England from the Accession of the Stuarts to the Revolution of 1688* (**203**). To this he afterwards added the earlier history, from the invasion of Julius Cæsar to the reign of James I. The first two volumes were received with the same neglect which had blighted his former publications; and indifference became general odium when the work was found to be an embodiment of high Tory principles. However, the great merits of the plan and the excellence of the style, revealed more and more with each successive volume, gradually overcame [1762.] prejudice. Before the time of its completion, the History had attained great reputation. One edition after another was rapidly bought up; and common consent named Hume the first of English historians. He now received a call to public service, and attended Lord Hertford on his embassy to Paris. Although he had neither the personal graces nor the conversational talents requisite for shining in the brilliant society of that capital, his literary reputation secured him abundant homage. His autobiography speaks with evident complacency of the "excessive civilities" he received from "men and women of all ranks and stations." After his return to Scotland, he for two years discharged the duties of Under-Secretary of State. The emoluments of his public offices, added to his income from the publishers, had by this time raised him to comparative affluence. He retired to his native city of Edinburgh, and passed the last years of his life in the tranquil enjoyment of his literary fame, and in the affection of his personal friends.

The *History of England* is a book of very high value. It has ease and vivacity of narration; and in the analysis of character and the appreciation of great events, Hume's philosophic view gives him a right to one of the foremost places among modern historians. But its defects are no less considerable. Hume's indolence induced him to remain contented with taking his facts from preceding writers, without troubling himself about accuracy, so that he must be read with distrust whenever he discusses questions that demand patient research.

As a metaphysical writer Hume deserves a distinguished place in the history of philosophy (**204**). He was a skeptic of the most logical and uncompromising type.

William Robertson. Naming them in the order of their birth, the second in this group of historians is William Robertson (1721–1793), the son of a Scotch clergyman. At twenty-two years of age he entered his father's profession, and began his public work in a quiet rural parish. There he remained for fifteen years, acquiring skill as a writer in the composition of his sermons, gaining reputation as a scholarly thinker, and devoting all the time he could spare to the study of history. In 1758 he was promoted to the charge of an important church in Edinburgh, and in the following year he introduced himself to the literary world by the publication of *A History of Scotland during the Reigns of Queen Mary and James the Sixth* (**205**). Three years later he was appointed Principal of the University of Edinburgh, and Royal Historiographer of Scotland. Ten years after the publication of his *History of Scotland*, his greatest work, *The History of the Emperor Charles the Fifth of Germany*, was ready for the press. Eight years more were spent in preparing his *History of America*.

Like Hume he is distinguished by the eloquence of his narrative, by the picturesque delineation of characters and events, and by the purity and dignity of his style. In all of his works there is richness and melody of expression, and vivid description; but there is lack of accuracy in research. Recent investigations made by Prescott and by English writers have dispelled some of the romance of Robertson. "The fault of this great historian was one common to the writers of his time. Filled with an exaggerated idea of the dignity of history, he trembles at the thought of descending to so mean a thing as daily life. The Emperor moves before us in all his grandeur, the rich velvet of his train sweeping in stately waves upon the marble that he treads. We know many of the laws he made, the wars he waged, the great public assemblies and pageants of which he was the brilliant central figure; but we know little of the man who dwelt within the gorgeous wrappings. . . . . Of

the many-hued life the people lived, we hear next to nothing." [*]
But in spite of his defects, Robertson's name will always hold an
honorable place among the historians of England.

Edward Gibbon (1737–1794) was the greatest historical writer
of this group. He was born at Putney, near London, and was the
grandson of a merchant of large fortune. As his health was delicate, his early education was neglected; but he acquired an insatiable appetite for reading, especially for historical literature.
When he had been at the University of Oxford a little more than a
year, he embraced the Roman Catholic faith. For this act he was
taken from the University and was sent to Lausanne, where he was
placed under the care of an eminent Swiss theologian. He subsequently re-entered the Protestant Church; but it is probable that
this change of faith was only a matter of form, about which he
was indifferent. In Switzerland he commenced that course of
systematic study which gradually filled his mind with stores of
sacred and profane learning; and there too he acquired a strong
sympathy with French modes of thought. Indeed, the first-fruits
of his pen actually appeared in French, an essay on the *Study of
Literature.* Between 1763 and 1765 he traveled over France, Switzerland, and Italy. His own words must be used in describing an
incident which occurred in 1764. "As I sat musing amidst the
ruin of the Capitol, while the barefooted friars were singing vespers
in the Temple of Jupiter, the idea of writing the Decline and Fall
of the city first started to my mind." [†]

Returning to England in 1765 he passed several years in comparative leisure, before setting himself at work on the composition
of his history. The first volume appeared in 1776, receiving the
applause of the learned, and the favor of the mass of
1776.] readers. Meanwhile Gibbon had taken a seat in Parliament and was interested in the political questions of the
day. His support was given to Lord North throughout the period
of our Revolutionary War. In 1781 the second and third volumes
of his history were published. He then retired from the service
of the government, sought his old retreat at Lausanne, and for
four years devoted himself to the completion of his work. He
thus describes the hour and the scene when the task was ended:

* Collier.   † Memoirs, p. 198.

"It was on the day, or rather night, of the 27th of June, 1787, between the hours of eleven and twelve, that I wrote the last lines of the last page, in a summer house in my garden. After laying down my pen, I took several turns in a *berceau* or covered walk of acacias, which commands a prospect of the country, the lake, and the mountains. The air was temperate, the sky was serene, the silver orb of the moon was reflected from the waters, and all nature was silent. I will not dissemble the first emotions of joy on the recovery of my freedom, and perhaps the establishment of my fame. But my pride was soon humbled, and a sober melancholy was spread over my mind by the idea that I had taken an everlasting leave of an old and agreeable companion; and that, whatsoever might be the future fate of my history, the life of the historian must be short and precarious." He died in London in 1794.

Scope of Gibbon's History. *The History of the Decline and Fall of the Roman Empire* (206–209) is one of the greatest monuments of human industry and skill. It begins with the reign of Trajan, A. D. 98, and closes with the fall of the Eastern Empire in 1453. These thirteen and a half centuries include not only the slow decline of the Roman Empire, but also the irruption of the barbarians, the establishment of the Byzantine power, the re-organization of the European nations, the foundation of the religious and political system of Mohammedanism, and the Crusades. The materials for much of the structure had to be patiently gathered from the rubbish of the Byzantine annalists, and from the wild stories of the Eastern chroniclers. To bring light and order out of this chaos, the historian had to make himself familiar with philosophy, religion, science, jurisprudence and war, as they contributed to the civilization of the nations and ages described by him. And when all this work was done, he had to set it forth in an attractive manner. For the influences exerted by the literature and civilizations of Greece and Rome, he had adequate appreciation; but he is not mindful of the important part played by the Teutonic races in contributing to the results of modern history, and is boldly skeptical concerning the power and purity of Christianity. He has been regarded as one of the most dangerous enemies by whom the Christian faith has been assailed. Earnest men have taken up weapons against him, and, in some instances, have been betrayed by their zeal into an unfair warfare upon him. The accusation of having intentionally distorted facts, or of garbling authorities, he has refuted in the Vindication in which he replied to his opponents; and the deliberate opinion of Guizot, whom no one can accuse of indifference to religion, will be conclusive as to Gibbon's merit on this point.

His style is elaborate and sonorous. There is something stately in his sentences. They lack simplicity; they abound in epigram and antithesis, and show a displeasing preponderance of the Latin over the Saxon element in their diction. He describes scenery and manners with the accuracy and vividness of an eye-witness. His chief fault is found in the fact that his imagination was sensuous, and led him to dwell upon material grandeur with a fonder enthusiasm than he could feel for moral elevation (**206-209**).

In this chapter we have considered:—

Historical Writers of the Eighteenth Century.

1. David Hume.

2. William Robertson.

3. Edward Gibbon.

CHAPTER XXII.

ETHICAL, POLITICAL, AND THEOLOGICAL WRITERS OF THE LATTER HALF OF THE EIGHTEENTH CENTURY.

SAMUEL JOHNSON.

"A mass of genuine manhood."—*Thomas Carlyle.*

"Johnson, to be sure, has a rough manner; but no man alive has a better heart. He has nothing of the bear but the skin."—*Oliver Goldsmith.*

"Rabelais and all other wits are nothing compared to him. You may be diverted by them; but Johnson gives you a forcible hug and squeezes laughter out of you, whether you will or no."—*David Garrick.*

"If it be asked, who first, in England, at this period, breasted the waves and stemmed the tide of infidelity,—who, enlisting wit and eloquence, together with argument and learning on the side of revealed religion, first turned the literary current in its favor, and mainly prepared the reaction which succeeded—that praise seems most justly to belong to Dr. Samuel Johnson."—*Lord Mahon: History of England.*

"The club-room is before us, and the table on which stands the omelet for Nugent and the lemons for Johnson. There are assembled those heads which live forever on the canvas of Reynolds. There are the spectacles of Burke and the tall thin form of Langton, the courtly sneer of Beauclerc and the beaming smile of Garrick; Gibbon, tapping his snuff-box, and Sir Joshua with his trumpet in his ear. In the foreground is that strange figure which is as familiar to us as the figures of those among whom we have been brought up; the gigantic body, the huge, massy face seamed with the scars of disease, the brown coat, the black worsted stockings, the gray wig with the scorched foretop, the dirty hands, the nails bitten and pared to the quick. We see the eyes and mouth moving with convulsive twitches; we see the heavy form rolling, we hear it puffing; and then comes the ' Why, sir!' and the ' What then, sir?' and the ' No, sir!' and the ' You don't see your way through the question, sir!'"—*T. B. Macaulay.*

WHILE the novelists and historians whose works we have been considering were busy with their pens, other writers of prose were making valuable contributions to letters in the departments of ethics, politics, and theology. The central figure of the literary men of the period is Samuel

Johnson (1709–1784). He was the son of a poor bookseller in Lichfield. From his childhood he had to struggle against disease, melancholy, and an indolent disposition. In 1728 he was sent to Oxford. There he remained three years, until his dying father had become unable to help him. Leaving the University without his degree, he attempted to support himself by teaching; but he was unsuccessful, and turned his attention to literary work. He was already married to a lady old enough to be his mother. Without fortune and friendless, he settled in London in 1737, beginning his twenty-five years of struggle with labor and want.* The profession he had chosen was then at its lowest ebb, and he was compelled to do its humblest work. He was a bookseller's hack, a mere literary drudge. Poverty attended him. Once, in a note to his employer, he subscribed himself, " Yours, *impransus*, S. Johnson." He wrote for various publications, and particularly for the *Gentleman's Magazine*, furnishing criticism, prefaces and translations. In 1738 he made a good name among the booksellers by the sale of his *London* (215), an admirable paraphrase of the third satire of Juvenal. In 1744 he published *A Life of Savage*, that unhappy poet whose career was so extraordinary, and whose vices were not less striking than his talents. Johnson had known him well, and they had often wandered supperless and homeless about the streets at midnight. Indeed, no literary life was ever a more correct exemplification than his own of the truth of his majestic line:

> " Slow rises worth by poverty depressed."

Johnson's Dictionary. From 1747 to 1755 Johnson was engaged in the preparation of his most famous work, A Dictionary of the English Language (211).
1755.] He had promised to complete it in three years ; but

---

* David Garrick, a young man who had been one of his pupils, accompanied Johnson to London, intending to study law at Lincoln's Inn ; but the stage attracted him away from the bar, and he soon began his famous career as an actor.

the labor was arduous, and seven years were spent in getting its pages ready for the printer. As there was no such work in English literature, it supplied a want that had been long felt. Its success was great, and its compiler was applauded far and wide. Many imperfections may be found in it, especially in its etymologies, for Johnson shared the general English ignorance of the Teutonic languages from which two-thirds of the words of our language are derived. But in the accuracy of its definitions and in the quotations adduced to exemplify the different meanings of words, it could not have been surpassed.

While at work upon his Dictionary he diverted his mind by the publication of *The Vanity of Human Wishes* (**216**), an imitation of the tenth satire of Juvenal; and at the same time he brought out upon the stage his tragedy of *Irene*, a work begun in his earlier years.

His Periodicals. Johnson founded, and carried on alone, two periodical papers in the style that Addison and Steele had rendered so popular. These were the *Rambler* (**212**), and the *Idler;* the former was published from 1750 until 1752, and the latter from 1758 until 1760. The ease, grace, pleasantry, and variety which gave such charm to the *Tatler* and *Spectator* are totally incompatible with the manner of Johnson; and his good sense, piety, and sombre tone of morality are but a poor substitute for the knowledge of the world displayed in his models. This species of periodical essay-writing, which exerted so powerful an influence on taste and manners in the eighteenth century, may be said to terminate with the *Idler*, though continued with gradually decreasing originality by other writers.

Rasselas. Johnson's mother died in 1759, and he was without the funds needed to pay the expenses of her funeral.

To raise this money, he spent the nights of one week in the composition of his once famous moral tale, *Rasselas, Prince of Abyssinia.* The manners and scenery of this story are neither those of an Oriental nor of any other country, and the book is but a series of dialogues and reflections, embodying the author's ideas on a great variety of subjects connected with art, literature, society, philosophy, and religion.

His Escape from Poverty. It was not until 1762, when he was fifty-three years of age, that he escaped from the poverty against which he had long and valiantly struggled. At the accession of George III. the government hoped to gain popularity by showing favor to art and letters. Johnson was recognized as holding a high position among literary workers, and was selected as one who should enjoy the royal bounty. A pension of three hundred pounds placed him above want, and enabled him to indulge his constitutional indolence. His good-fortune was shared with the poor. A blind old woman, a peevish old man, and other helpless people found a home in his dwelling, and in him a patient friend.   ·

His Acquaintance with Boswell. Johnson's earlier life, with its poverty, its affliction, its toil, is not distinctly pictured by his biographer. Its mingled romance and misery keep us from intimate acquaintance with him before the day of his good-fortune, but from that time he is known as is no other man of the past; * for the year after the pension

* "Johnson grown old, Johnson in the fullness of his fame and in the enjoyment of a competent fortune, is better known to us than any other man in history. Everything about him,—his coat, his wig, his figure, his face, his scrofula, his St. Vitus's dance, his rolling walk, his blinking eye, the outward signs which too clearly marked his approbation of his dinner, his insatiable appetite for fish-sauce and veal-pie with plums, his inextinguishable thirst for tea, his trick of touching the posts as he walked, his mysterious practice of treasuring up scraps of orange-peel, his morning slumbers, his midnight disputations, his contortions, his mutter

was decreed to him, he became acquainted with a young Scotchman, James Boswell, Esq., a vain, tattling, frivolous busybody, whose only claim to respect is that he produced the best biography that had been written in English,—and that was *Boswell's Life of Johnson.* From the beginning of the acquaintance Boswell revered the sage, listened to him as though his sentences were sacredly inspired, and treasured up every word that he could, as it came from the lips of his saint. Every night he wrote in his note-book the wise sayings of the philosopher, adding notes to the last detail of dialogue and of action, until, at last, his notes gave him the material with which to produce his famous book. He has given not only the most lively and vivid portrait of the person, manners, and conversation of Johnson, but also the most admirable picture of the society amid which he played so brilliant a part. Among the celebrated social meetings of that age of clubs was the society founded by Johnson, in which his friends, Reynolds, Burke, Garrick, Bishop Percy, Goldsmith, Bennet Langton, Beauclerc, and others, were prominent figures. Johnson's powers of conversation were extraordinary, and were freely used in that company. He delighted in argument, and, by constant practice, had acquired the art of expressing himself with pointed force and elegance. His ponderous style formed an appropriate vehicle for his weighty thoughts and for his immense stores of reading and observation.

In 1773 Johnson, in company with his friend Boswell, made a journey to the Hebrides (214), which enabled him to become acquainted with Scotland and the Scotch, and thus to dissipate many of his odd prejudices against the

---

ings, his gruntings, his puffings, his vigorous, acute, and ready eloquence, his sarcastic wit, his vehemence, his insolence, his fits of tempestuous rage, his queer inmates, old Mr. Levett and blind Mrs. Williams, the cat Hodge and the negro Frank,—all are as familiar to us as the objects by which we have been surrounded from childhood."—*T. B. Macaulay.*

country and the people. The volume giving an account of his impressions contains many interesting passages.*

The Thrales. He made the acquaintance of the family of a rich brewer named Thrale, a member of the House of Commons, whose wife was famous for her talents and for the intellectual society she gathered around her. Under their roof Johnson enjoyed all that friendship, respect, and great wealth could give. This acquaintance lasted sixteen years, and gave him the opportunity of frequenting refined society. In the company of the Thrales he made several excursions to different parts of England, and once to Paris.

His edition of Shakespeare appeared in 1765. It cannot be said to have added to his reputation. With the exception of an occasional happy remark, and a sensible selection from the commentaries of preceding annotators, it is quite unworthy of him.

The Lives of the Poets (213), published in 1781, was his last important work. Johnson had undertaken the task of preparing very brief biographical sketches, and a critical preface for a new edition of the English poets. His information was so abundant that the work grew into a volume abounding in passages of the happiest and most original criticism. But no reader should form his opinion of these poets from Johnson. His applause is given to the writers of the artificial school; Cowley, Waller, and Pope filled his vision. Others he could not understand. His criticisms

---

* The *Journey to the Hebrides* was a work re-written from private letters addressed to Mrs. Thrale. A comparison between the original letters and the version expressed in pompous language, such as Johnson considered essential to the dignity of literature, shows many amusing transformations. The following instance furnishes an illustration. " When we were taken up stairs," he says in one of the letters, " a dirty fellow bounced out of the bed on which one of us was to lie." In the *Journey*, the same incident is thus described,—" Out of one of the beds on which we were to repose, started up, at our entrance, a man black as a Cyclops from the forge."

on Milton, Gray, Thomson, Akenside, were denounced at the time as monstrous examples of injustice. In uttering his disapproval of Johnson's treatment of Milton, even the patient Cowper said, "I could thrash his old jacket till I made the pension jingle in his pocket."

Johnson's Style was so peculiar that it has received the distinguishing name of "Johnsonese." There is in it none of Addison's colloquial elegance, none of Swift's idiomatic terseness. Short words had no charm for him. Sonorous Latin derivatives, and carefully elaborated sentences, were marshaled in honor of his thoughts. Whether describing a scene in a tavern, or expatiating on the grandest of moral themes, the same display of language makes his writing monotonous. This was generally thought to be the sign of his genius by the men of letters who bowed before him; though Goldsmith once boldly declared to his face, "If you were to write a fable about little fishes, Doctor, you would make the little fishes talk like whales." "In fact, his phraseology rolls away in solemn periods, in which every substantive marches ceremoniously, accompanied by its epithet; pompous words peal like an organ ; every proposition is set forth balanced by a proposition of equal length ; thought is developed with the compassed regularity and official splendor of a procession.† . . . . . An oratorical age would recognize him as a master, and attribute to him in eloquence the primacy which it attributed to Pope in verse." * †

Johnson's Character shows a blending of prejudice and liberality, of skepticism and credulity, of bigotry and candor. He was an heroic struggler with misfortune. He was

* Taine.

† Johnson's famous letter to Lord Chesterfield (210) is in striking contrast with his general style.

one of the invincibles. Throughout his life he was an independent, resolute man; in boyhood he threw away the shoes which pity had sent to him, in manhood he threw away the tardy courtesies of Chesterfield. Among frivolous men, he was serious; among scoffers, he was reverent; among insincere men, he was sincere; among selfish men, he was generous. Of him Carlyle says, "As for Johnson, I have always considered him to be, by nature, one of th' great English souls." In common breeding he was utterly wanting; his dress, his motion, his voice, his face, his eating, —all were offensive. We think of him as a most ill-mannered man. The blending of greatness and meanness puzzles us until we remind ourselves that his severe schooling in poverty developed the noble and the boorish traits together. When, weary and lame, he reached the top of the ladder by which he had climbed from poverty and obscurity to competence and fame, he had brought with him the begrimed and offensive manners of his underground life. He was thoroughly a man of letters. No better specimen of the type appears in the eighteenth century.

On the 13th of December, 1784, this eminent man died, and a week afterwards he was buried in Westminster Abbey. For two years he had been suffering from dropsy and asthma, and had been haunted by his old melancholy.

Consult Carlyle's Essays,—Walpole's *Men of the Reign of George III.*,—Albert Barnes's *Miscellaneous Essays*,—Hazlitt *On the Periodical Essayists*,—Macaulay's Essay on *Samuel Johnson*,—Macaulay's Essay on *Croker's Edition of Boswell's Life of Johnson*, and *Boswell's Life of Johnson*.

Edmund Burke (1730–1797) was a man of such powerful and versatile genius that he has been likened to Bacon. He stands foremost among English political writers and orators. The fervor and imagery of oratory are found in his philosophical discussions, and the highest qualities of the statesman and the man of letters appear in all of his pages. He was the son of an Irish attorney, and spent many of his early days near the ruins of Spenser's famous castle of Kilcolman. Early in life he went to England to study law, but his tastes soon led him into literary work, and he became a regular writer for the magazines. His first reputation was gained by *The Vindication of Natural Society*, an ironical imitation of the style and sentiments of Lord Bolingbroke. In pursuing Bolingbroke's course of reasoning he reached the conclusion, that as wickedness has prevailed under every form of government, society itself is evil, and therefore, that only the savage state is conducive to virtue and happiness. The work was published anonymously; but so perfect was it as an imitation of the style and sentiment of Bolingbroke that the most eminent critics of the day, among them Samuel Johnson, did not detect its intense and delicate irony, and pronounced it a genuine posthumous work of the earlier philosopher and statesman.

A few months afterwards Burke published *An Essay on the Sublime and Beautiful* (**218**), which has since been regarded as one of the classics in our literature.

He began his political career as secretary to the Chief Secretary of Ireland. The position was not pleasing to him. He soon received an appointment from the Marquis of Rockingham, the Prime Minister, and at once began his long public life of honor and activity. He sat in the House of Commons, and was one of the most prominent debaters during the agitated periods of the American and French Revolutions. The Reign of Terror in France transformed Burke from a constitutional Whig into a Tory, but at the same time animated his genius to some of its noblest bursts of eloquence. His *Reflections on the French Revolution* (**220**) was written with the most anxious care, and with the most masterly skill. In going through the press its proofs were patiently criticised eleven times before he was satisfied to publish the work. When it appeared its success amply repaid his labor, for it was read far and wide, and was influential throughout Europe in checking the dangerous tendencies of that age. His *Letter to a Noble Lord* (**222**), provoked by an ungenerous assault, deservedly ranks high among the products of his pen. The culminating point of his political life was his action in the trial of Warren Hastings (**221**). In that majestic and solemn scene, where a great nation sat in judgment upon a great man, Burke played the most prominent part. He was among the managers of the impeachment, and acting in the name of the House of Commons he pronounced one of the sublimest philippics that ancient or modern oratory can show.

The Letters of Junius.

From 1769, with occasional interruptions down to 1772, there appeared in the *Public Advertiser*, one of the leading London journals, a series of brilliantly sarcastic letters, for the most part signed Junius (**223**). They attacked the public men of the day. They exhibited so much weight and dignity of style, so minute an acquaintance with the details of party tactics, and breathed so lofty a political tone, combined with such bitterness, even ferocity of personal invective, that their influence was unbounded. The annals of political controversy show nothing more fierce than these lampoons. Who Junius was still remains a mystery. Burke, Hamilton, Francis, Lyttleton, and Lord George Sackville have been fixed upon successively as their writer. The preponderance of evidence points towards Sir Philip Francis.

Adam Smith

(1723–1790) was the founder, in England, of the science of Political Economy. He was a Scotchman, a Professor of Logic and of Moral Philosophy in the University of Glasgow. His most important work is the *Inquiry into the Nature and Causes of the Wealth of Nations* (**224**). This discussion was the result of ten years of study and investigation. Upon the fact that the only natural process by which a nation can acquire wealth is labor, he laid the foundation for modern economic science. His clear and logical reasoning, and his abundant and popular illustration attracted much attention to his teachings, and exerted a beneficial influence on legislation and commerce. His moral and metaphysical theories are now forgotten, but his *Wealth of Nations* still presents the general principles of Political Economy in their most attractive form.

Sir William Blackstone.

What Adam Smith did for the students of Political Economy, Sir William Blackstone (1723–1780) did for the students of the Constitution and laws of England. He was a lawyer who mingled a strong taste for elegant literature with the graver studies of his profession. His *Commentaries on the Laws of England* was the first systematic work which gave the elementary and historical knowledge requisite for the study. The book is written in an easy and pleasant style, with a masterly analysis, and is the best outline of the history and the principles of the subject he discusses.

Butler and Paley. The most prominent names in the English theological literature of the eighteenth century are those of **Bishop Butler** (1692–1752) and **William Paley** (1743–1805). Butler is more remarkable for the severe and coherent logic with which he demonstrates his conclusions; Paley, for his consummate skill in popularizing the abstruser arguments of his predecessor Butler's principal work is *The Analogy of Religion, Natural and Revealed, to the Constitution and Course of Nature* (**181**). In it he examines the resemblance between the existence and attributes of God as proved by arguments drawn from the works of nature, and shows that existence and those attributes to be in no way incompatible with the notions conveyed to us by revelation.

Paley's books are numerous, and all excellent; chief among them are *Elements of Moral and Political Philosophy*, the *Horæ Paulinæ* (**225**), the *Evidences of Christianity*, and the production of his old age, the *Treatise on Natural Theology*. It will be seen from the titles of these works, over what an extent of moral and theological philosophy Paley's mind had traveled. For clearness, animation, and easy grace, his style has rarely been equaled.

Among the crowd of less noticeable writers whose names might be mentioned in this chapter, but few produced works that still have peculiar value. The *Elements of Criticism* by **Henry Home, Lord Kames,** and *The Philosophy of Rhetoric* by **George Campbell,** in spite of many publications on the same subjects since their time, continue to be standard authorities in their respective departments.

In this chapter we have considered:—

Ethical, Political, and Theological Writers of the Latter Half of the Eighteenth Century.

1. *Samuel Johnson.*

    a. *Johnson's Dictionary.*

    b. *His Periodicals.*

    c. *His Rasselas.*

    d. *His Escape from Poverty.*

    e. *His Acquaintance with Boswell.*

    f. *The Thrales.*

    g. *The Lives of the Poets.*

    h. *His Style.*

    i. *His Character.*

2. *Edmund Burke.*

3. *The Letters of Junius.*

4. *Adam Smith.*

5. *Sir William Blackstone.*

6. *Butler and Paley.*

7. *Henry Home, Lord Kames; and George Campbell.*

CHAPTER XXIII.

THE DAWN OF ROMANTIC POETRY.

THE mechanical perfection of the poetry of Pope and his school was so generally applauded that every common versifier imitated its tricks of melody and its neat antitheses. But a thoroughly artificial spirit cannot satisfy the demands of poetry. Even while Pope swayed the sceptre, there were indications of a disposition to seek for themes in a wider sphere. In **Matthew Greene's** poem *The Spleen*, in *The Minstrel* of **James Beattie,** and in *The Grave*, by **Robert Blair (226)**, this tendency is perceptible, and may be ascribed to a weariness coming from repetitions of far-off echoes of Pope.

James Thomson (1700–1748) was a leader in that revolution of popular taste and sentiment which supplanted the artificial by what is known as the romantic type in literature. He stands between the poets of the first and the poets of the third generation in the eighteenth century. In his fervid descriptions he enters a realm of poetry unknown to Pope; but he does not reach the poetry of emotion and passion in which Burns and later poets found their inspiration. Thomson was educated at the University of Edinburgh, and it was intended that he should be a preacher; but in the theological class-room he was so imaginative in his interpretation and paraphrase of Scripture that he was cautioned by his professor against the danger of exercising his poetic faculty in the pulpit. This caution diverted him from his calling, and turned him into the paths of literature. In 1725 he went to London, carrying with him an unfinished sketch of his poem on *Winter* **(228)**. After much discouragement he succeeded in selling it for three guineas, and in winning a handsome purse from the gentleman to whom he had dedicated it with flattering phrases. The

poem was received with favor. *Summer* was published in 1727
and Thomson then issued proposals for the completion of the c
of *The Seasons* (227). *Sophonisba*, the first of his tragedies, was
published in 1730. For two years he traveled in France, Switzerland and Italy, and on his return to England in 1733, was appointed
to a sinecure office. When he lost this office the Prince of Wales
honored him with a pension, and a lucrative position was assigned
him by the King. He purchased a snug cottage near Richmond,
and lived in modest luxury. It was a pleasure for him to live. He
was of an extremely kind and generous disposition, making him
self and all about him comfortable. In leisure he carried on his
literary work until his death, in the forty-eighth year of his
age. *The Seasons* is the corner-stone of Thomson's literary fame.
In plan and in treatment it is original. Its description of the
phenomena of nature during an English year is minute, and therefore it is a work much read by foreigners. The blank verse, though
seldom showing any of the Miltonic grandeur, is rich and harmonious. Occasionally the style is pompous. During his happy
retirement he composed *The Castle of Indolence* (229), the most
enchanting of the many imitations of Spenser's style His easy
daily life breathed itself into this charming poem, and favored a
display of the finest qualities of his poetic genius. In literary
finish *The Castle of Indolence* is superior to *The Seasons.* The
allegory of the enchanted "Land of Drowsihead," in which the
unhappy victims of Indolence find themselves hopeless captives,
is relieved with occasional touches of a sly and pleasant humor.

William Collins. The career of William Collins (1721–1759)
was brief and unhappy. He exhibited from very early years the
strong poetical powers of a genius which, ripened by practice and
experience, would have made him the first lyrical writer of his
age. But his ambition was fitful. He led a life of projects and
dissipation ; and the first shock of literary disappointment drove
him to despondency, despondency to indulgence and indulgence to
insanity. His first publication was a series of Eclogues, trans-
ferring the usual sentiments of pastoral verse to the scenery and
manners of the East. Although these eclogues exhibit traces of
vivid imagery and melodious verse, the real genius of Collins must
be looked for in his *Odes.* Judged by them, he will be found

entitled to a high place. The ode entitled *The Passions* is frequently quoted; and many of the less popular ones, as that addressed to *Fear* (**231**), to *Pity*, to *Simplicity*, and that *On the Poetical Character*, contain happy strokes, sometimes expressed in wonderfully laconic language, and in vivid portraiture. Some of the smaller and less ambitious lyrics, as the *Verses to the Memory of Thomson*, the *Dirge in Cymbeline*, and the exquisite verses *How Sleep the Brave*, are destined to a more enduring fame. All the qualities of Collins's finest thought and expression will be found united in the lovely little *Ode to Evening*, consisting merely of a few stanzas in blank verse, but so subtly harmonized that we may read them without observing the absence of rhyme.

Thomas Gray (1716–1771), a man of varied acquirements, whose life was devoted to the cultivation of letters, was greater than any former exclusively lyric poet of England. He received his education at Eton, and afterwards settled in learned retirement at Cambridge, where he became Professor of History in 1768. He acquired a poetical reputation through his beautiful *Ode on a Distant Prospect of Eton College* (**234**), published in 1747. This was followed, at intervals, by the *Elegy Written in a Country Churchyard* (**233**), the *Pindaric Odes*, and other brilliant productions. His industry was untiring, and his learning undoubtedly great; for he pushed his researches far beyond the usual limits of ancient classical philology, and was deeply versed in the romance literature of the Middle Ages, in modern French and Italian, and had studied the then almost unknown departments of Scandinavian and Celtic poetry. His finest lyric compositions are the Odes entitled *The Bard*, that on the *Progress of Poesy* (**235**), the *Installation Ode* on the Duke of Grafton's election to the Chancellorship of the University, and the short but truly noble *Ode to Adversity*. The *Elegy Written in a Country Church-yard* is a masterpiece from beginning to end. The thoughts indeed are obvious enough, but the dignity with which they are expressed, the range of allusion and description with which they are illustrated, and the finished grace of the language and versification in which they are embodied, give to this work somewhat of that perfection of design and execution which is seen in an antique statue. In *The Bard*, starting from the picturesque idea of a Welsh poet and patriot contemplating the victorious invasion of his country by Edward I., he passes in review the panorama of English History, from the thirteenth to the six teenth century. In the odes entitled *The Fatal Sisters* and *The Descent of Odin,* Gray borrowed his materials from the Scandinavian legends. The tone of the Norse poetry is perhaps not very faith-fully reproduced; but these early attempts to revive the rude and archaic grandeur of the Eddas deserve grateful appreciation.

Mark Akenside (1721–1770), like Arbuthnot and Smollett, was a physician as well as a writer. His chief work is the philosophi-cal poem entitled *The Pleasures of the Imagination* (232), in which he seeks to investigate and illustrate the emotions excited by beautiful objects in art and nature. The philosophical merit of his theories, indeed, is very often small, but the beauty of the imagery and language will ever secure for this thoughtful work the admiration of those readers who can content themselves with ele-vated thoughts, without looking for passages of strong feeling. Few English poets since Milton have been more deeply inspired by the spirit of classical antiquity.

The two brothers **Joseph Warton** (1722–1800) and **Thomas Warton** (1728–1790) were the sons of a Professor of Poetry at Oxford, and both brothers, especially the younger, deserve a place in the annals of our literature. Thomas, who was poet-laureate from 1785 until his death, rendered great service to letters by his *History of English Poetry.* That work unfortunately comes to an abrupt termination just as the author is about to enter upon the Elizabethan era ; but it is valuable for research and for a warm tone of appreciative criticism. The best of his own original verses are sonnets, breathing a tender feeling, and showing much picturesque fancy.

OLIVER GOLDSMITH.

"No man was more foolish when he had not a pen in his hand, or more wise when he had."—*Samuel Johnson.*

"He was a friend to virtue, and in his most playful pages never forgets what is due to it. A gentleness, delicacy and purity of feeling distinguish whatever he wrote, and bear a correspondence to the generosity of a disposition which knew no bounds but his last guinea."—*Walter Scott.*

"His elegant and enchanting style flowed from him with so much facility that in whole quires he had seldom occasion to correct or alter a single word."—*Bishop Percy.*

"Goldsmith is one of the most pleasing of English writers. He touched upon every kind of excellence, and that with such inimitable grace, that where he failed of originality most, he had ever a freshness and a charm."—*Mrs. S. C. Hall.*

"There was in his character much to love, but little to respect. His heart was soft even to weakness ; he was so generous that he quite forgot to be just ; he forgave injuries so readily that he might be said to invite them ; and was so liberal to beggars that he had nothing left for his tailor and his butcher. He was vain, sensual, frivolous, profuse, improvident."—*T. B. Macaulay.*

"Think of him reckless, thoughtless, vain, if you like—but merciful, gentle, generous, full of love and pity. His humor delighting us still ; his song fresh and beautiful as when first he charmed with it ; his words in all our mouths ; his very weaknesses beloved and familiar ; his benevolent spirit seems still to smile on us ; to do gentle kindnesses ; to succor with sweet charity ; to soothe, caress, and forgive ; to plead with the fortunate for the unhappy and the poor."—*W. M. Thackeray.*

Oliver Goldsmith (1728–1774) is the most charming and versatile writer of the eighteenth century. We place him among the poets, but we might as well name him with the novelists, with the historians, or with the ethical writers, for he belongs to each of these classes, and in each of them he has written for delighted readers. He was born in Ireland, the son of a poor curate of the Established Church. In childhood he was attacked by small-pox, and through life he bore the ugly scars. At seventeen years of age he obtained a servant's scholarship at the University of Dublin. He neglected his opportunities for study, and became somewhat notorious for his irregularities, his disobedience to authority, his improvidence and his morbid charity. After leaving the university he tried successively to enter the professions of the teacher, the clergyman, the lawyer, and the physician. In 1755–6 he traveled on foot through Holland, France, Germany, Switzerland, and Italy. Much of the way he journeyed playing his flute for the peasants, in order to gain a supper and a bed. While thus wandering in the guise of a beggar he sketched the plan of his famous poem, *The Traveller* (**199**). In 1756 he found his way back to England, and for eight years struggled against starvation, sometimes as a chemist's clerk, sometimes as an usher in boarding-schools, sometimes as a physician among the most

squalid, and much of the time as a plodding drudge for the
booksellers. His literary apprenticeship was passed in writing
school-books, tales for children, prefaces, indexes, reviews of
books, and occasional articles for the magazines. In this
period of obscure drudgery he composed the *Letters from a
Citizen of the World* (**197**), giving a description of English
life and manners in the assumed character of a Chinese
traveler; a *Life of Beau Nash ;* and a short and gracefully
narrated *History of England*, in the form of Letters from a
Nobleman to his Son. The publication of his beautiful
poem of the *Traveller* in 1764 was the beginning of his uninterrupted literary success. His writings were sought by
publishers who were ready to pay him generous prices.
But his folly and improvidence kept him plunged in debt.
In 1768 *The Vicar of Wakefield* appeared, that masterpiece
of gentle humor and delicate tenderness; and in the next
year his comedy, *The Good-natured Man*, though failing
upon the stage, brought him a purse of five hundred pounds.
Those earnings were quickly scattered, and Goldsmith put
himself at the task-work of writing a *History of Rome* for
the publishers. Such a work, hurriedly written, was, of
course, wanting in research, and valueless as an authority;
but it displayed the author's grace of style and vivacity of
narration. In 1770 he published his finest poem, *The
Deserted Village* (**200**), and by it won new fame. Five
editions were sold at once. Three years after, he wrote his
comedy, *She Stoops to Conquer*, one of the gayest, pleasant-
est, and most amusing pieces that the English stage can
boast.

Goldsmith was now one of the popular authors of his
time. His society was courted by the wits, artists, statesmen and writers who formed a brilliant circle round Johnson and Reynolds; and he became a member of the famous
Literary Club. His unconquerable improvidence, however,
still kept him the slave of booksellers, who obliged him

to waste his exquisite talent on works for which he neither possessed the requisite knowledge nor could make the necessary researches. Thus he wrote the *History of England*, the *History of Greece*, and the *History of Animated Nature*. He died at the age of forty-six, deeply mourned by the brilliant circle of friends to whom his very weaknesses had endeared him, and followed by the tears and blessings of many wretches whom his inexhaustible benevolence had relieved.

In everything Goldsmith wrote, prose or verse, serious or comic, there is a peculiar delicacy and purity of sentiment. His genius, though in its earlier years surrounded by squalid distress, was incapable of being sullied by any stain of vulgarity. No quality in his writings is more striking than the union of grotesque humor with pensive tenderness. While literature lasts, readers will linger over Goldsmith's sketches of the scenery and natural peculiarities of various countries, and over the details in his picture of "sweet Auburn."

The Vicar of Wakefield. The *Vicar of Wakefield*,* too, in spite of the absurdity of the plot, is one of those works that the world will not let die. It was colored with the hues of childhood's memory; and the central figure in the group of shadows from the past that came to cheer the poor London author in his lonely garret, was the image of his

---

* Dr. Johnson gives the following account of his first knowledge of *The Vicar of Wakefield* :—

"I received one morning a message from poor Goldsmith that he was in great distress, and, as it was not in his power to come to me, begging that I would come to him as soon as possible. I sent him a guinea, and promised to come to him directly. I accordingly went as soon as I was dressed, and found that his landlady had arrested him for his rent, at which he was in a violent passion. I perceived that he had already changed my guinea, and had got a bottle of Madeira and a glass before him. I put the cork into the bottle, desired he would be calm, and began to talk to him of the means by which he might be extricated. He then told me he had a novel ready for the press, which he produced to me. I looked into it and saw its merits ; told the landlady I should soon return ; and, having gone to a bookseller, sold it for sixty pounds. I brought Goldsmith the money and he discharged his rent, not without rating his landlady in a high tone for having used him so ill."—*Boswell's Life of Johnson.*

dead father : "For," says John Forster in his life of Goldsmith, "they who have loved, laughed and wept with the
man in black of the *Citizen of the World,* the Preacher of
The Deserted Village, and Doctor Primrose in the *Vicar
of Wakefield,* have given laughter, love and tears to the
Rev. Charles Goldsmith." The gentle and quiet humor
embodied in the simple Dr. Primrose, the delicate yet
vigorous contrasts of character in other personages, the
purity, cheerfulness, and gayety which envelop all the scenes
and incidents, insure the work its immortality.

His Comedies. Goldsmith's two comedies are written in
two different methods, the *Good-natured Man* being a
comedy of character, and *She Stoops to Conquer,* a comedy
of intrigue. The merit of the first piece chiefly consists in
the truly laughable personage of Croaker, and in the excellent scene where the disguised bailiffs are passed off on Miss
Richland as the friends of Honeywood, whose house and
person they have seized. But in *She Stoops to Conquer* we
have a choice specimen of the comedy of intrigue, where
the interest mainly depends upon a tissue of lively and
farcical incidents. The best proof of Goldsmith's success in
this drama is the constancy with which it has always kept
possession of the stage. Peals of laughter ever greet the
lively bustle of its scenes, the pleasant absurdities of Young
Marlow, Mr. and Mrs. Hardcastle, and the admirable Tony
Lumpkin.

Among Goldsmith's minor poems *The Haunch of Venison*
deserves special attention on account of its easy narrative
and its accurate sketching of commonplace society. In the
poem *Retaliation,* written as a reply to taunting epitaphs
on himself, he has given portraits of some of his distinguished literary friends, and he has painted them with a
hand at once refined and vigorous.

For further readings on this topic, see Irving's *Oliver Goldsmith,*—Forster's

Life and Adventures of Oliver Goldsmith,—Walter Scott's *Life of Goldsmith,*— *N A. Review,* Vol. XLV., p. 91,—De Quincey's works,—*Essays on the Poets,* Vol. IX.,— Macaulay's *Essays,* Vol. VI.

William Cowper (1731–1800) is eminently the poet of the domestic affections, and the exponent of that strong religious feeling which, towards the end of the eighteenth century, began to penetrate and modify all the relations of social life (**236, 240**). From his early childhood he was exceedingly sensitive. His mother died when he was six years of age, and he was sent to one of the English boarding-schools, where the bullies were allowed to abuse the younger boys, and there he was brutally persecuted for two years. For seven years he was at the famous Westminster School, and then he was apprenticed to an attorney. By the influence of his friends a desirable position was secured for him in the service of the House of Lords; but his sensitive nature was so terrified at the thought of presenting himself for a formal examination, that he fell into despondency and attempted suicide. A short confinement in an asylum restored him from his insanity; but he was so shaken by the attack that he was unfitted for active life. Four times during his life madness assailed him, and his last six years were continually shrouded in its pitiful gloom. Upon his recovery from the first attack he retired into the country, and placed himself under the care of the family of Mr. Unwin, a clergyman in Huntingdon. Cowper's virtues and accomplishments secured him the good-will of the family circle, and especially won the tender and life-long friendship of Mrs. Unwin. His mind, still smarting under its affliction, made him the victim of religious melancholy, and tormented him with despair concerning the salvation of his soul. As a pastime and as a means of escaping from his melancholy, he wrote a few hymns for Newton's collection, and cultivated his literary taste. The force, grace, and originality of his compositions soon acquired popularity, and he pursued as a profession what he had at first taken up as a diversion. His poetical talent did not flower until late. He was more than fifty years of age when his first volume was published. It contained long didactic and satiric poems entitled *Table Talk, The Progress of Error, Truth, Expostulation, Hope, Charity, Conversation,* and *Retirement.* The sale of his book was small. His sentiments, though sometimes genial, and always delicate, were too grave and desponding to receive the popular applause. At about this time Lady Austen formed his acquaintance, and urged him to trim his pen for gayer verse. At her suggestion the famous ballad of *John Gilpin* was written. She playfully gave him "The Sofa" as a theme, and thus started him in the composition of that humorous, graceful, reflective poem, *The Task* (**238**). His most laborious, but least successful undertaking, was the translation of the Iliad into English blank verse. He justly considered that the neat and artificial style of Pope had done scant justice to the father of Greek poetry; but in endeavoring to give greater force and vigor to his own version, he fell into a fault of which Pope could not be accused, and made his translation too harsh and rugged, without approaching one whit nearer to the true character of the original.

The longer and more important poems of Cowper are written in an original manner. They are a union of reflection, satire, description and moral declamation. Some of them are in blank verse, while in others he employed rhyme. His aim was to keep up a natural and colloquial style. His satirical sketches of the follies and absurdities of manners, and his indignant denunciations of national offences against piety and morality, are equally remarkable, in the one case, for sharpness and humor, and in the other for loftiness of sentiment.

Cowper's *Letters* are famous. They show the poet in his most amiable light and invest his character with a halo of goodness. Their style is free from all affectation. They should be studied carefully by all who would excel in this most elegant of accomplishments. Southey pronounces him the "best of English letter-writers."

Macpherson, Chatterton, and Ireland. The latter half of the eighteenth century was remarkable for several nearly contemporaneous attempts at literary imposture—the poetical forgeries of Macpherson, Chatterton, and Ireland. **James Macpherson** (1738–1796), originally a country schoolmaster, and afterwards in the service of the English and East India governments, professed to have accumulated, in his travels through the Highlands of Scotland, a mass of fragments of ancient poetry composed in the Gaelic or Erse dialect, common to that country and Ireland. The translations, which Macpherson claimed to have made from the originals, were composed in pompous and declamatory prose (**243**). Upon their publication a controversy arose as to their authenticity. The Highlanders, eager for the honor of their country, declared for the genuineness of the literature, and said that the name of Ossian, and the incidents of the stories, had been told in the familiar traditions of the Highlands. It was also urged in their support that Celtic traditions in Ireland strikingly resembled the sentiments of *Ossian*. The English critics, on the other hand, doubted the antiquity of the papers, and demanded a view of the original poems. This Macpherson refused to grant, on the ground that he had been treated with indignity by those who scorned his pretensions. They then cited against him his plagiarisms from the whole range of literature,—from Homer, the Bible, Shakespeare, Milton, and even from Thomson. But in spite of opposition and ridicule the papers were translated into the leading languages of Europe, and commanded the wondering attention of Goethe, Hume, and many other distinguished men of letters. In Germany the admiration of these productions has not subsided. The conviction lingers there, that they were the work of some grand old epic poet. Macpherson died without disclosing the originals of his professed discoveries, and was buried in Westminster Abbey.

The annals of literature hardly present a more extraordinary example of precocious genius than that of **Thomas Chatterton** (1752–1770), nor an instance of a career more brief and melancholy (**244**). He was born in 1752, the son of a poor sexton and parish schoolmaster at Bristol ; and he died, by suicide, before he had completed his eighteenth year. At eleven years of age he produced verses which will bear comparison with the early poems of any author; and though he had received little education beyond that of a parish school, he conceived the project of deceiving all the scholars of his age.

In the muniment room of a church at Bristol there was a chest called Canynge's coffer. (Canynge was a rich citizen who lived in the reign of Edward IV.) The coffer contained charters and other documents connected with Canynge's gifts to the church. The young poet familiarized himself with the sight of these antiquated writings, and determined to forge papers that could be palmed off upon the credulous. These he produced at intervals, generally taking advantage of some topic of public interest to contribute to the local newspapers or to his acquaintances, the pretended originals, or transcripts of pretended originals, having some relation to the subject. Thus, on the opening of a new bridge over the Avon, he produced an account of processions, tournaments, religious solemnities, and other ceremonies which had taken place on the opening of the old bridge. To Mr. Burguin, a pewterer of the town who had a taste for heraldry, he gave a pedigree reaching back to William the Conqueror. Horace Walpole was then writing his anecdotes of British Painters, and Chatterton furnished him with a long list of mediæval artists who had flourished in Bristol. Besides these documents he claimed to have discovered old poems in the chest. They are of great variety and unquestionable merit; and though modern criticism will instantly detect in them the most glaring marks of forgery, yet their brilliancy and their number were enough to deceive many learned scholars in an age when accurate antiquarian knowledge of the Middle Ages was much rarer th . at present. In his eagerness to incrust his diction with the rust of antiquity, he overlays his words with such an accumulation of consonants as belongs to the orthography of no age of our language. He has also, as was inevitable, sometimes made a slip in the use of an old word, as when he borrowed the expression *mortmal* found in Chaucer's description of the Cook, he employed it to signify, not a disease, the gangrene, but a dish. Burning with pride, hope, and literary ambition, the unhappy lad betook himself to London, where, after struggling a short time with distress and almost with starvation, he poisoned himself on the 25th of August, 1770.

William Henry Ireland (1777–1835) deserves mention only on account of his Shakespearean forgeries, imposed upon the public while he was yet a boy. Their success was due entirely to his skill in imitating old handwriting, and to the credulousness and the stupidity of those who were deceived by his work. He was soon compelled to acknowledge his guilt.

George Crabbe (1754–1832). Byron speaks of Crabbe as "Nature's sternest painter, yet the best." He was born in the little seaport town of Aldborough in Suffolk, where his father was a collector of customs; and after a dreamy and studious childhood, he was apprenticed to a surgeon and apothecary. Passionately fond of literature, he determined to seek his fortune in London, carrying with him several unfinished poems. After many disappointments he found himself reduced to despair; when he addressed a manly and affecting letter to Edmund Burke, who immediately admitted him to his house and his friendship. From this time Crabbe's fortune changed; he was assisted, both with money and advice, in bringing out his poem of *The Library*, and was induced to enter the Church. He became chaplain to the Duke of Rutland; but after marriage with a young lady to whom he had been long attached, he changed his position for the humbler but more independent life of a parish priest, and in this occupation he continued until his death.

It was not until the appearance of *The Village*, in 1783, that Crabbe struck out that path in which he had neither predecessor nor rival. The success of this poem was great, for it was the first attempt to paint the manners and existence of the laboring class, without dressing them up in the artificial colors of fiction. In his next work, *The Parish Register* (246), the public saw the gradual ripening of his vigorous and original genius; and this was followed, at comparatively short intervals, by *The Borough*, *Tales in Verse*, and *Tales of the Hall*. These, with the striking but painful poems, written in a different measure, entitled *Sir Eustace Grey* and *The Hall of Justice*, make up Crabbe's large and valuable contribution to the poetical literature of his country. Almost all these works are constructed upon a peculiar and generally similar plan. Crabbe starts with some description, as of the Village, the Parish Church, the Borough, from which he naturally proceeds to deduce a series of separate episodes, usually of middle and humble life, appropriate to the leading idea. Thus in *The Parish Register* we have the most remarkable births, marriages, and deaths that are supposed to take place in a year amid a rural population; in *The Borough* (245) we have the lives and adventures of the most prominent characters that figure on the narrow stage of a small provincial town. With the exception of *Sir Eustace Grey* and *The Hall of Justice*, which are written in a short-lined stanza, Crabbe's poems are in heroic verse. The contrast is strange between the neat, Pope-like regularity of the metre, and the deep passion, the intense reality, and the quaint humor of the scenes displayed. His descriptions of nature, too, are marked by power of interesting a

13

reader in the most unattractive features of the external world, by the sheer force of truth and exactness. The village-tyrant, the poacher, the smuggler, the miserly old maid, the pauper, and the criminal, are drawn with the same vivid force that paints the squalid streets of the fishing-town, or the fen, the quay, and the heath.

Hannah More. The movement in the direction of greater freedom can be detected in many minor poets of the time; and its influence is nowhere more noticeable than in the fact that, towards the close of the eighteenth century, women entered the walks of literature. Hannah More (1745--1833) was the most influential writer of her sex. Johnson considered her the best of "female versifiers," but her prose is equal, if not superior, to her verse. She was the daughter of a schoolmaster in Gloucestershire. Her first works were dramatic. *The Search after Happiness*, written at the age of sixteen, *The Inflexible Captive*, written a year later, and a few of her tales, had given her so good a name that when she removed to London, at about her twenty-eighth year, she was admitted to the literary circle of Johnson and Burke. A volume of her *Poems* was published in 1786, portions of which were termed by Johnson a great performance. Becoming weary of the life of London, she removed to Bristol. There her pen was busy,—prose and poetry flowing from it constantly. Her tales directed against Jacobins and Levellers reached a circulation of a million copies. Her best known works are—*Thoughts on the Manners of the Great*, 1788; *On Female Education*, 1799; *Cœlebs in Search of a Wife*, 1809; and *Practical Piety*, 1811. "She did, perhaps, as much real good in her generation as any woman that ever held a pen."

Mrs. More's* style is flowing, and often sparkles with the light of a pleasant humor. Her later works are of a more sombre cast, from the deeper impressions which religion seemed to be making upon her. *Cœlebs* is perhaps the chief of her works—a fiction of much beauty in style, with a mixture of quiet irony; the plot is well evolved, but the characters are too few, and the incidents too tame, to make it in the present day a readable book. It has been called a "dramatic sermon."

---

* Hannah More, though never married, was in her own day, and still is named *Mrs.* More. This title she acquired, in her dignified years, according to a courteous custom then observed in England.

Richard Brinsley Sheridan. A comic drama appeared contemporaneously with the more romantic poetry. With a single exception its writers were men who failed of an enduring fame. Richard Brinsley Sheridan (1751–1816) was a genius of versatile and brilliant powers. He was famous as a Parliamentary orator; but his highest fame was achieved as a dramatist. Byron says that " the intellectual reputation of Sheridan was truly enviable, that he had made the best speech—that on the Begums of Oude,—written the two best comedies, *The Rivals* and *The School for Scandal* (**253**), the best opera, *The Duenna*, and the best farce, *The Critic.*" His career was extravagant and imprudent. The ingenious shifts by which he endeavored to stave off his embarrassments, and the jokes with which he disarmed even his angriest creditors, would furnish materials for a most amusing jest-book. His repartees and witticisms made him the darling of society. He died in poverty, but was buried with princely pomp.

ROBERT BURNS.

"Burns is by far the greatest poet that ever sprung from the bosom of the people and lived and died in an humble condition."—*Professor Wilson.*

" O he was a good-looking fine fellow!—he was that; rather black an' ill-colored ; but he couldna help that, ye ken. He was a strong, manly-looking chap ; nane o' your skilpit milk-and-water dandies : but a sterling, substantial fellow, who wadna hae feared the deil suppose he had met him. An' then siccan an ee he had !"—*Memoir of Burns.*

" His person was strong and robust, his manners rustic, not clownish ; a sort of dignified plainness and simplicity which received part of its effect perhaps from one's knowledge of his extraordinary talents. . . . . I think his countenance was more massive than it looks in any of the portraits. . . . . There was a strong expression of sense and shrewdness in all his lineaments ; the eye alone, I think, indicated the poetical temperament. It was large and of a dark cast, and glowed (I say literally glowed) when he spoke with feeling or interest. I never saw such another eye in a human head, though I have seen the most distinguished men in my time. His conversation expressed perfect self-confidence without the slightest presumption."—*Sir Walter Scott.*

" None but the most narrow-minded bigots think of his errors and frailties but with sympathy and indulgence ; none but the blindest enthusiasts can deny their existence."—*James Hogg.*

" He has in all his compositions great force of conception, and great spirit and animation in its expression. He has taken a large range through the region of Fancy, and naturalized himself in all her climates."—*Francis Jeffrey.*

"As a poet Burns stands in the front rank. His conceptions are all original, his thoughts are new and weighty; his style unborrowed; and he owes no honor to the subjects which his muse selected, for they are ordinary, and such as would have tempted no poet, save himself, to sing about."—*Allan Cunningham.*

The greatest poet that Scotland has produced is **Robert Burns** (1759–1796) (**247–251**). He was born at the hamlet of Alloway in Ayrshire, and was the son of a peasant farmer of the humblest class. Popular education at that period was diffused in Scotland more generally than in any other country of Europe; and Burns received the training of the common school. Impelled by his eagerness for knowledge, he early became acquainted with some of the masterpieces of English literature. In this way he acquired the pure diction of classical English authors, and was able to use it with facility when he took up the poet's pen. *The Spectator,* and the volumes of Pope, Thomson, Shenstone and Sterne were on the shelf in his cabin. His early years were spent in laboring as a peasant on his father's farm. In the correspondence of his later years he says: "This kind of life, the cheerless gloom of a hermit, with the unceasing moil of a galley-slave, brought me to my sixteenth year, when love made me a poet." His "first performance," the song of *Handsome Nell,* revealed to him a talent by whose use he drove away some of the gloom of his youth. When his muse would not help him in writing song, she gave him expression for satire, or revery, or the poetic epistle. Until his twenty-eighth year he continued his weary struggle against poverty. He was driven from one farm to another in his attempts to improve his condition. At last, in despair, he determined to cross the ocean, and seek his fortune in the West Indies. In order to raise funds for the voyage he was induced to publish poems which had won local applause. The sale of the volume brought him twenty guineas. Out of the money he bought his passage, and then awaited the sailing of his ship.

His Summons to Edinburgh. On the last night that he expected to be in Scotland, he wrote what, he said, should be the last song he would ever measure in Caledonia,— "The gloomy night is gathering fast." But the clouds broke with the dawn; for a letter from a poetical critic gave him encouragement that an edition of his poems would be received with favor in Edinburgh. The voyage was abandoned. His own words are: "I immediately posted to Edinburgh, without a single acquaintance or letters of introduction. The baneful star which had so long shed its blasting influence upon my zenith, for once made a revolution to the nadir." But he needed no letters of introduction. His songs had gone before him. The literary and the gay of the capital welcomed the singer. The new edition of his poems was received with an enthusiasm that made "The Ayrshire Ploughman" the lion of the town.* This success put moeny in his purse; and he was able to gratify his desire to see the celebrated scenery and the places of historical interest in his native country. After spending the summer of 1787 in travel, he returned to Edinburgh with the reasonable expectation of securing from those whose praises and friendship he had won, such employment as would enable him to devote some of his time to his muse. While waiting for their help he joined in their

---

* "It needs no effort of the imagination to conceive what the sensations of an isolated set of scholars (almost all either clergymen or professors) must have been in the presence of this big-boned, black-browed, brawny stranger, with his great flashing eyes, who, having forced his way among them from the plough-tail, at a single stride, manifested in the whole strain of his bearing and conversation, a most thorough conviction that in the society of the most eminent men of his nation, he was exactly where he was entitled to be; hardly deigned to flatter them by exhibiting even an occasional symptom of being flattered by their notise; by turns calmly measured himself against the most cultivated understandings of his time, in discussion; overpowered the *bon mots* of the most celebrated convivialists by broad floods of merriment, impregnated with all the burning life of genius; astounded bosoms habitually enveloped in the thrice-piled folds of social reserve, by compelling them to tremble—nay, to tremble visibly—beneath the fearless touch of natural pathos."—*Lockhart.*

convivial revelries. His social nature led him into intemper-
ance. When his money was gone, and he was compelled
to find support, a place was given him as a gauger of liquors
in his old district. He rented a farm and lived upon a
meagre income. Now his spirit was buoyant and gleeful,
now despondent. His strong constitution, undermined by
excesses, soon broke down, and the poet died at Dumfries,
in the thirty-seventh year of his age.

His Poems. The highest poetical qualities—tenderness
the most exquisite, humor the broadest and most refined, the
most delicate perception of natural beauty, the highest
finish and the easiest negligence of style, are found in the
writings of Burns. They are chiefly lyrics of inimitable
charm; but he has also written narrative and satire. The
variety of his poetic talent is best displayed in *Tam
O'Shanter*. In no other poem of the same length can there
be found a blending of so much brilliant description, touching pathos, and quaint, sly humor; nor is there elsewhere
in our literature such a combination of the terrific and the
ludicrous. Another inimitable poem, half-narrative, but
set thick with glorious songs, is the *Jolly Beggars:* careless
vagabond jollity, roaring mirth and gipsy merriment, have
never been better expressed. In his *Address to the De'il,
Death and Dr. Hornbook, The Twa Dogs,* and the dialogue
between the Old and New Bridges of Ayr, Burns gives us
humorous and picturesque description with reflections and
thoughtful moralizing upon life and society. In the poem
descriptive of rustic fortune-telling on *Halloween,* in the
Vision of Liberty, where Burns gives such a sublime picture
of his own early aspirations, in the unequaled sorrow that
breathes through the *Lament for Glencairn,* in *Scotch Drink,*
the *Haggis,* the epistles to *Captain Grose* and *Matthew
Henderson,* in the exquisite description of the death of the
old ewe Mailie, and the poet's address to his old mare, we

find the same mixture of pathos and humor; that truest pathos which finds its materials in the common, every-day objects of life, and that truest humor which is allied to the deepest feeling. The famous lines *On Turning up a Mouse's Nest with the Plough*, and on destroying in the same way a *Mountain Daisy*, will ever remain among the gems of poetry. The Dialogue between the *Twa Dogs* is an elaborate comparison of the relative degrees of virtue and happiness granted to the rich and the poor. His description of the joys and consolations of the poor man's lot is perhaps even more beautiful in this poem than in the more generally popular *Cotter's Saturday Night* (**251**). Certainly there has never been a tribute paid to the virtues of the poor, nobler than has been given by Burns in these two poems.

Those of Burns's songs that are written in pure English, in some instances have a pretentious air. But there is no affectation in his verse when it flows in the rhythm of his native dialect. The list of subjects adapted to the purpose of the song-writer is always very limited—love, patriotism, and pleasure, constitute the whole. In the song *Ae Fond Kiss and then We Part* is concentrated the essence of a thousand love-poems; the heroic outbreak of patriotism in *Scots wha hae wi' Wallace bled* is a lyric of most stirring force; and in those of a calmer and more lamenting character, as *Ye Banks and Braes*, there is the union of personal sentiment with the complete assimilation of the poet's mind to the loveliness of external nature.

THE LITERATURE OF THE EIGHTEENTH CENTURY.

In reviewing the English literature of the eighteenth century the student will be reminded that it contains the most powerful satire and the most elegant light essays that have been produced. In it the first great works of fiction, the first distinctively pronounced skepticism, the first carefully written histories, are found coming from the pens of Englishmen. In it, too, our poetry of the fireside was first sung.

The literature of the century may be divided into three eras, and they are distinctly marked : I. The Augustan Age; so it was called by the men of the next generation, who felt that in it English literature had reached such paramount excellence as the literature of Rome attained in the age of Augustus. It closes with the reign of George I. The attitude of the government towards literary men was somewhat changed at the accession of George II.; a few writers of note appeared at that time, and at about that time some of the bright stars of the Augustan galaxy disappeared.—II. The Reign of George II. (1727–1760). It was not illumined by such brilliant men as Newton and Addison. There was less of elegance, but there was a gain in purpose. There was more earnest questioning than in the former age. Men were no longer satisfied with attacking the advocates of principles, they attacked the principles themselves. Hume published his philosophical essays, startled his readers by the audacity of his questioning, and prepared the way for study of German philosophy and skepticism. His example led the thinkers of a later generation to study Kant and to recognize German thought and literature. He also alarmed the theologians, so that they took up weapons of defence, and fought for the honor of English religious opinions, and for the sacredness of the Scripture record. A reaction from this boldly pronounced skepticism called forth earnest reformers. They demanded practical as well as theoretical deference to Christ's teachings. In sermon and treatise and song, the Wesleys and Whitefield and Watts charmed the saintly, and terrified the sinful. They created a demand for simple, fervent religious literature. A progressive seriousness shows itself in the essays that would rival the glory of the Spectator, in the philosophy that would secure firm foundation for the religious faith of the intellectual man, and, where it would be least expected, even in the poetry that is imitative of Pope.—III. The Reign of George III. (1760–1820). Here we find a poetry simpler than in either of the preceding generations. The song gave thrilling and laughing echoes. The imagination was revived, and poetic life was healthful. Philosophy turned the seriousness to practical account.

The century of literature under consideration was superficial in its thinking, and held itself in high esteem.* But it had a record to be pleased with; for it was opening new lines of literary work, and was producing earnest and original thinkers.

That century was the formative period of English prose style. It developed two distinct modes of literary expression. The first in order of time and in excellence is the style approaching the diction and idioms of elegant conversation. Addison is its best representative. The second style seeks harmonies of sound, avoids elliptical idioms, is scholastic, and is based upon the idea that there must be more dignity in writing than in the best speaking. Johnson is its exponent and champion. The former style is English; the latter is Latinic. They are both influencing the writing of our own time; but the simpler method commands the higher approval.

* The poor eighteenth century was critical, negative, and unpoetic. . . . It was one of those seasons of comparative diminution of the general vital energy of our species."—*Masson's Essays*, p. 350.

In this chapter we have considered:—

The Dawn of Romantic Poetry.

1. *Matthew Greene, James Beattie, Robert Blair.*
2. *James Thomson.*
3. *William Collins.*
4. *Thomas Gray.*
5. *Mark Akenside.*
6. *Joseph and Thomas Warton.*
7. *Oliver Goldsmith.*
    a. *The Vicar of Wakefield.*
    b. *His Comedies.*
8. *William Cowper.*
6. *Macpherson, Chatterton, and Ireland.*
10. *George Crabbe.*
11. *Hannah More.*
12. *Richard Brinsley Sheridan.*
13. *Robert Burns.*
    a. *His Summons to Edinburgh.*
    b. *His Poems.*
14. *The Literature of the Eighteenth Century*

ENGLISH LITERATURE,
FROM THE BEGINNING OF THE AUGUSTAN AGE TO THE CLOSE OF THE EIGHTEENTH CENTURY.
As discussed in the six preceding chapters.

THE ARTIFICIAL POETS
of the first half of the Eighteenth Century.
- ALEXANDER POPE,
- JOHN GAY,
- MATTHEW PRIOR,
- EDWARD YOUNG.

PROSE WRITERS
of the first half of the Eighteenth Century.
- JOSEPH ADDISON,
- RICHARD STEELE,
- JONATHAN SWIFT,
- JOHN ARBUTHNOT,
- HENRY ST. JOHN, Viscount Bolingbroke
- GEORGE BERKELEY,
- MARY WORTLEY MONTAGU.

THE FIRST GREAT NOVELISTS.
- DANIEL DEFOE,
- SAMUEL RICHARDSON,
- HENRY FIELDING,
- TOBIAS GEORGE SMOLLETT,
- LAURENCE STERNE.

THE FIRST GREAT HISTORIANS.
- DAVID HUME,
- WILLIAM ROBERTSON,
- EDWARD GIBBON.

ETHICAL, POLITICAL, AND THEOLOGICAL WRITERS
of the latter half of the Eighteenth Century.
- SAMUEL JOHNSON,
- EDMUND BURKE,
- ADAM SMITH,
- SIR WILLIAM BLACKSTONE,
- WILLIAM PALEY.

THE DAWN OF ROMANTIC POETRY.
- JAMES THOMSON,
- WILLIAM COLLINS,
- MARK AKENSIDE,
- WILLIAM SHENSTONE,
- JOSEPH WARTON,
- THOMAS WARTON,
- [OLIVER GOLDSMITH],
- WILLIAM COWPER,
- *The Literary Impostors.*
  - James McPherson,
  - Thomas Chatterton
  - William Henry Ireland
- GEORGE CRABBE,
- [HANNAH MORE],
- [RICHARD BRINSLEY SHERIDAN.]

ROBERT BURNS.

CHAPTER XXIV.

WALTER SCOTT.

" Blessings and prayers in nobler retinue
Than sceptred king or laureled conqueror knows,
Follow .his wondrous potentate."—*William Wordsworth*.

THE great revolution in literary taste which culminated in the poems and novels of Walter Scott, is traceable to the labors of **Bishop Thomas Percy** (1728–1811). In 1765 he published a collection of old ballads under the title of *Reliques of Ancient English Poetry*. Many of these ballads had been preserved only in manuscript, and others had been printed on loose sheets in the rudest manner for circulation among the lower orders of people. Many authors before him, as, for instance, Addison and Sir Philip Sidney, had expressed the admiration which cultivated taste must ever feel for the rude charms of the old ballad-poets ; but Percy was the first who undertook a systematic and general examination of the neglected treasures. He found, in collecting these compositions, that the majority of the oldest and most interesting were distinctly traceable to the frontier region between England and Scotland which had been the scene of the most striking incidents of predatory warfare, such as those recorded in the noble ballads of *Chevy Chase* and the *Battle of Otterburn*. Besides a very large number of these purely heroic ballads, Percy gave specimens of songs and lyrics extending down to a comparatively late period of English history, even to his own century. But the chief interest of his collection, and the chief service he rendered to literature by his publication, is in the earlier portion. It is impossible to exaggerate the influence exerted by the *Reliques*. This book has been studied with the utmost interest by each succeeding generation of English poets, and has given the first direction to the youthful genius of some of our most illustrious writers. The boyish enthusiasm of Walter Scott was stirred by the vivid recitals of the old Border rhapsodists. Percy's volumes* gave him the sentiment that culminated in the *Lady of the Lake,* and in *Waverley*.

A genius at once so vigorous and versatile, a productiveness so magnificent and so sustained as that of **B. 1771.]** **Walter Scott (254, 263)**, will with difficulty be **D. 1832.]** found, though we ransack the realms of ancient and modern letters. He was connected, both by the father's and mother's side, with several of those ancient, historic Border families whose warlike memories his genius was destined to make immortal. In consequence of delicate health in early life he passed much of his time at the farm of his grandfather near Kelso, where he was surrounded with legends, ruins, and historic localities. He was afterwards sent to the High School, and then to the University of Edinburgh. He was not distinguished as a student; but among his fellows he was famous for his talent in telling stories. After leaving the University, he entered the profession of law. It had little charm for him. English, German and Italian authors easily won him away from his law-books. The direction of his mind was towards the poetical and antiquarian works of the Middle Ages; but just at that time there had been awakened in the intellectual circles of Edinburgh a taste for German literature. Scott's

---

* "The first time I could scrape a few shillings together—which were not common occurrences with me—I bought unto myself a copy of these beloved volumes: nor do I believe I ever read a book half so frequently, or with half the enthusiasm." —*Scott, in Lockhart's Life.*

first appearance as an author was in translations from Bürger. Scott was now residing with his young wife at Lasswade. He formed the purpose of rescuing from oblivion the large stores of Border ballads still current among the descendants of the Liddesdale and Annandale moss-troopers, and he traveled into those picturesque regions, where he not only gathered a vast treasure of unedited legends, but also made himself familiar with the scenery and manners of that country over which he was to cast the magic of his genius. Three volumes of the *Minstrelsy of the Scottish Border* were soon published. The learning and taste of this work gave Scott a high reputation. His success was tempting him to abandon the profession of the law altogether, and to devote himself to literature, when an appointment as Sheriff of Selkirkshire brought him to a decision. He changed his residence to a pleasant farm at Ashestiel on the Tweed, and six years after he appeared before the public as an original romantic poet.

His Poems. In 1805 *The Lay of the Last Minstrel* was published. In rapid succession followed *Marmion*, *The Lady of the Lake*, *Rokeby*, and *The Lord of the Isles*, not to enumerate many less important works, such as *The Vision of Don Roderick*, *The Bridal of Triermain*, *Harold the Dauntless*, and *The Field of Waterloo*. We cannot overstate the rapture of enthusiasm with which these poems were received. They were written rapidly and with unstinted freshness. With *Rokeby* the popularity of Scott's poetry, though still very great, perceptibly declined. This may have been due in part to the fact that he was not fortunate in the choice of the theme for that poem, and in part to the eclipsing glory of Byron's genius. Aware of the declining public favor, he immediately and quietly abandoned poetry to enter the field of the novelist, where he could stand without a rival.

His Prose Writings.   Nine years earlier, *Waverley* had been sketched and thrown aside.   In 1814 it was published without the author's name,—the first of the inimitable *Waverley Novels*.   The town and the country were wild in its praise, and all were curious to know who the writer might be.   The secret was kept.   During the seventeen years between 1814 and 1831 he wrote his long series of novels, and wrote them with such inconceivable facility, that, on an average, two of the works appeared in one year. During this same period he also published many works in the departments of history, criticism, and biography ; among them, *A Life of Napoleon*, the *Tales of a Grandfather*, the amusing Letters on *Demonology and Witchcraft*, and extensive editions, with lives, of Dryden and Swift.   Such activity is rare indeed in the history of letters ; still rarer, when combined with such general excellence in the products.   The impulse to this prodigious industry was Scott's passionate and long-cherished ambition to found a territorial family, and to be able to live the life of a provincial magnate.   In 1811 he had purchased about one hundred acres of land on the banks of the Tweed, and now, encouraged by the immense profits accruing from his works, he purchased one piece of land after another, planted and improved the estate, and transformed his modest cottage at Abbotsford into a mansion crowded with the rarest antiquarian relics.   There he exercised a princely hospitality, "doing the honors of Scotland" to those who were attracted in crowds by the splendor of his name.   The funds needed for such a mode of life he supplied in part by engaging secretly in large commercial speculations with the printing and publishing firm of the Ballantynes, his intimate friends and school-fellows.

His Misfortunes.   By the failure of the Ballantynes in the commercial crisis of 1825, Scott found himself financially ruined. He might easily have escaped from his liabilities by taking advantage of the bankrupt law; but his sense of honor was so delicate that he asked only for time, and resolutely set himself to pay off, by unremitting literary toil, the vast sum of one hundred and seventeen thousand pounds. *Woodstock* was his first novel after his misfortune. It was written in three months, and brought him £8,228. The nine volumes of the *Life of Napoleon* followed, and for that work he received £18,000. Thus encouraged, he toiled on with unflagging energy, determined to pay the last guinea due to the creditors of his firm. Volume after volume came from his pen—not so joyous as the earlier ones had been—and he had all but reached the goal, when the tired body broke down. There is no more touching or sublime spectacle than that of this great genius, in the full plenitude of his powers, voluntarily and without a word of repining, abandoning the splendor he was so well qualified to adorn, and the rural life he so well knew how to appreciate, and shutting himself up in a small house in Edinburgh, to wipe out, by incessant literary toil, the liabilities which he had too much nobility to evade.

The *Waverley Novels*, though anonymously published, were universally ascribed to him, as the only man in Great Britain whose peculiar acquirements and turn of genius could have produced them. Nevertheless, the mystery of the true authorship, long a very transparent one, was maintained by Scott with great care. It was not until the failure of Ballantyne's house rendered longer concealment impossible that he formally avowed himself their author.* In the year 1830 his mind, exhausted by incessant toil, began to

* Robert Chambers, in the *Biographical Dictionary of Eminent Scotchmen*, suggests that Scott "kept the *Waverley* secret with such pertinacious closeness" because "unwilling to be considered as an author writing for fortune, which he must have thought something degrading to the baronet of Abbotsford." The suggestion is the most plausible that has been made, and well accords with Scott's foolish notions concerning the peculiar dignity of titled gentlemen.

show symptoms of weakness; and in the autumn of the next
year he was sent to Italy and the Mediterranean in the vain
hope of re-establishing his health. He returned to Scotland after an absence of six months; and after lingering in
a state of almost complete unconsciousness for a short time,
he died at Abbotsford on the 21st of September, 1832. His
body was buried in the old ruin of Dryburgh Abbey.

His personal character is almost perfect. High-minded,
generous and hospitable to the extreme, he hardly had an
enemy or a misunderstanding during the whole of a long and
active career. He was the delight of society; for his conversation, though unpretending, kindly, and jovial, was
filled with that union of old-world lore and acute and picturesque observation which renders his works so enchanting.
There perhaps never was a man so totally free from the
pettinesses and affectations to which men of letters are
prone.

Comments upon His Narrative Poems. The narrative
poems of Scott form an epoch in the history of modern
literature. In their subjects, their versification, and their
treatment, they were an innovation. The materials were
derived from the legends and exploits of mediæval chivalry;
and the actors were borrowed partly from history and partly
from imagination. He seems to move with most freedom
in that picturesque Border region with whose romantic
legends he was so wonderfully familiar. The greater of
these poems are, unquestionably, the *Lay of the Last Minstrel* (254), *Marmion* (256–258) and the *Lady of the Lake*
(259). According to Scott's own judgment, the interest
of the *Lay* depends mainly upon the style, that of *Marmion*
upon the descriptions, that of the *Lady of the Lake* upon
the incidents. The plots of these poems are in general
neither very probable nor very logically constructed, but
they allow the poet ample opportunities for striking situa-

tions and picturesque episodes. The characters are discriminated by broad and vigorous strokes, rather than by any attempt at moral analysis or strong delineation of passion. In his vivid descriptions of scenery, Scott sometimes indulges in a quaint but graceful vein of moralizing, in which he beautifully associates inanimate nature with the sentiments of the human heart. A charming instance of this may be found in the opening description of *Rokeby*.

The action of the *Lay of the Last Minstrel* is drawn from the legends of Border warfare; and necromancy, the tourney, the raid, and the attack on a strong castle, are successively described with unabating energy. The midnight expedition of Deloraine to the wizard's tomb in Melrose Abbey, the ordeal of battle, the alarm, the feast, and the penitential procession, are painted with the force and picturesqueness of real scenes. In *Marmion* the main action is loftier and more historical, and the catastrophe is made to coincide with the description of the great battle of Flodden. It is indeed "a fearful battle rendered you in music;" and the whole scene, from the rush and fury of the onset down to the least heraldic detail or minute trifle of armor and equipment, is delineated with the truth of an eyewitness. In the *Lady of the Lake* he broke up new and fertile ground; he brought into contact the wild, half-savage mountaineers of the Highlands and the refined and chivalrous court of James V. The exquisite scenery of Loch Katrine became, when invested by the magic of the descriptions, the chief object of the traveler's pilgrimage; and it is no exaggeration to say, as Macaulay has said, that the glamour of the great poet's genius has forever hallowed even the barbarous tribes whose manners are here invested with all the charms of fiction. In no other of his poems is that gallant spirit of chivalric bravery and courtesy which pervades Scott's poetry, as it animated his personal character, so powerfully manifested.

Though the tale of *Rokeby* contains many beautiful descriptions, and exhibits strenuous efforts to draw and contrast individual characters with force, the epoch—that of the Civil Wars of Charles the First's reign—was one in which Scott felt himself less at home than in the feudal ages.

The last of the greater poems, *The Lord of the Isles,* went back to Scott's favorite epoch. The voyage of Robert Bruce, the scenes in the Castle of Artornish, the description of the savage and terrific desolation of the Western Highlands, show little diminution in his picturesque power. The Battle of Bannockburn reminds us of the hand that drew the field of Flodden. Scott's ardent patriotism must have found a special pleasure in delineating the great victory of his country's independence.

The Vision of Don Roderick, though based upon a striking and picturesque tradition, is principally a song of triumph over the recent defeat of the French arms in the Peninsula; but the moment he leaves the mediæval battle-field, Scott seems to lose half his power ; in this poem, as in *Waterloo,* his combats are neither those of feudal knights nor of modern soldiers, and there is painfully visible, throughout, a struggle to be emphatic and picturesque. Indeed it may be said that almost all poems made to order, and written to celebrate contemporary events, have a forced and artificial air.

The Waverley Novels may be divided into the two main classes of *Historical,* or such as derive their principal interest from the delineation of some real persons or events ; and *Personal,* or those entirely or principally founded upon private life or family legend. According to this method of classification, we shall range seven works under Scottish history, seven under English, and three will belong to the Continental department ; while the novels mainly assignable to the head of private life—sometimes, it is true, more or less connected, as in the cases of *Rob Roy* and *Red-*

gauntlet, with historical events—are twelve in number. The latter class deal for the most part with purely Scottish scenery and character. The following arrangement will assist the memory in recalling such a large and varied cycle of works:—

I.—HISTORICAL.

I.—SCOTTISH........*Waverley.* The Period of the Pretender's attempt in 1745.

The Legend of Montrose. The Civil War in the seventeenth century.

Old Mortality. The Rebellion of the Covenanters.

The Monastery, ⎫ The deposition and imprisonment of
The Abbot. ⎭ Mary Queen of Scots.

The Fair Maid of Perth. The Reign of Robert III.

Castle Dangerous. The time of the Black Douglas.

II.—ENGLISH..........*Ivanhoe* (263). The return of Richard Cœur de Lion from the Holy Land.

Kenilworth. The Reign of Elizabeth.

The Fortunes of Nigel. Reign of James I.

Peveril of the Peak. Reign of Charles II.; period of the pretended Catholic plot.

Betrothed. The Wars of the Welsh Marches.

The Talisman. The Third Crusade: Richard Cœur de Lion.

Woodstock. The Civil War and Commonwealth.

III.—CONTINENTAL....*Quentin Durward.* Louis XI. and Charles the Bold.

Anne of Geierstein. The epoch of the Battle of Nancy.

Count Robert of Paris. The Crusaders at Byzantium.

II.—PERSONAL.

Guy Mannering.
The Antiquary.
Black Dwarf.
Rob Roy.
The Heart of Midlothian (262).
The Bride of Lammermoor.

The Pirate.
St. Ronan's Well.
Redgauntlet.
The Surgeon's Daughter.
The Two Drovers.
The Highland Widow.

In this unequaled series of fictions, the author's power of bringing near to us the remote and historical, whether of persons, places, or events, has something in common with that of Shakespeare, as shown in his historical dramas. Scott was careless in the construction of his plots. He wrote with great rapidity, and aimed at picturesque effect rather than at logical coherency. His imagination was so powerful that the delight he felt in developing the humors and adventures of one of those inimitable persons he had invented, sometimes left him no space for the elaboration of the pre-arranged intrigue. His style, though always easy and animated, is far from being careful or elaborate. Scotticisms will be found in almost every chapter. Description, whether of scenery, incident, or personal appearance, is abundant in his works; but few of his readers will be found to complain of his luxuriance in this respect, for it has filled his pages with bright and vivid pictures. His sentiments are invariably pure, manly, and elevated; and the spirit of the true gentleman is seen as clearly in his deep sympathy with the virtues of the poor and humble, as in the knightly fervor with which he paints the loftier feelings of the educated classes. In the delineation of character, as well as in the painting of external nature, he faithfully reflects the surface. He simply sets before us so brightly, so vividly, all that is necessary to give a distinct idea, that his images remain in the memory.

For further reading concerning Scott's life and writings the student is referred to Prescott's *Biographical and Critical Miscellanies*,—Irving's *Abbottsford*,—Lockhart's *Life of Scott*,—articles in *Harper's Magazine*, Vols. 3, 26, 33, 36, 43, 44,—Carlyle's *Essays*,—Jeffrey's *Essays*,—*North American Review*, Vol. 87,—Leslie Stephen's *Hours in the Library*,—Hazlitt's Miscellaneous Works, Vol. V.,—Bayne's Essays on *Biography and Criticism*, First Series.

In this chapter we have considered:—

The Revolution in Literary Taste.

1. Bishop Percy.
2. Walter Scott, — a. His Poems, — b. His Prose Writings,—c. His Misfortunes,—d. Comments upon His Narrative Poems,—e. The Waverley Novels Classified.

CHAPTER XXV.

BYRON, MOORE, SHELLEY, KEATS, LEIGH HUNT, LANDOR, HOOD, BROWNING.

LORD BYRON.

"Never had any writer so vast a command of the whole eloquence of scorn, misanthropy, and despair."—*T. B. Macaulay.*

"I found Lord Byron in the highest degree courteous, and even kind. We met for an hour or two almost daily in Mr. Murray's drawing-room, and found a great deal to say to each other. . . . His reading did not seem to me to have been very extensive, either in poetry or history. Having the advantage of him in that respect, and possessing a good competent share of such reading as is little read, I was sometimes able to put under his eye objects which had for him the interest of novelty."—*Walter Scott.*

"Byron's poetry is great—great—it makes him truly great : he has not so much greatness in himself."—*Thomas Campbell.*

"To this day English critics are unjust to him. . . . . . If ever there was a violent and madly sensitive soul, but incapable of being otherwise ; ever agitated but in an enclosure without issue ; predisposed to poetry by its innate fire, but limited by its natural barriers to a single kind of poetry—it was Byron's."—*H. A. Taine.*

THE influence exerted by Byron on the taste and senti- ment of Europe has not yet passed away, and, though far from being so pervading as it once was, it is not likely to be effaced. He called himself, in one of his poems, "the grand Napoleon of the realms of rhyme;" and there is some similarity between the suddenness and splendor of his literary career, and the meteoric rise and domination of the first Bonaparte. They were both, in their respective de- partments, the offspring of revolution ; and both, after reigning with absolute power for some time, were deposed from their supremacy. Their reigns will leave traces in the political, and in the literary history of the nineteenth cen-

tury. **George Gordon, Lord Byron** (1788–1824) **(264–277)**,
was born in London, and was the son of an unprincipled
profligate and of a Scottish heiress. His mother had a
temper so passionate and uncontrolled that, in its capricious
alternations of fondness and violence, she seemed insane.
Her dowry was speedily dissipated by her worthless husband, and she, with her boy, was obliged to live for several
years in comparative poverty. He was about eleven years
old when the death of his grand-uncle, an eccentric and
misanthropic recluse, made him heir-presumptive to the
baronial title of one of the most ancient aristocratic houses
in England. With the title, he inherited large, though
embarrassed estates, and the noble, picturesque residence of
Newstead Abbey, near Nottingham. He was sent first to
Harrow School, and afterwards to Trinity College, Cambridge. At college he became notorious for the irregularities of his conduct. He was a greedy though desultory
reader; and his imagination was especially attracted to
Oriental history and travels.

While at Cambridge, in his twentieth year, Byron made
his first literary attempt, in the publication of a small
volume of fugitive poems entitled *Hours of Idleness, by Lord
Byron, a Minor*. An unfavorable criticism of this work in
the Edinburgh Review threw him into a frenzy of rage.
He instantly set about taking his revenge in the satire,
English Bards and Scotch Reviewers, in which he involved
in one common storm of invective, not only his enemies of
the Edinburgh Review, but almost all the literary men of
the day,—Walter Scott, Moore, and many others, from
whom he had received no provocation whatever. He soon
became ashamed of his unreasoning violence; tried, but
vainly, to suppress the poem; and, in after life, became the
friend and sincere admirer of some whom he had lampooned.
Byron went abroad to travel, and filled his mind with the
picturesque life and scenery of Greece, Turkey and the

East, accumulating those stores of character and description which he displayed with splendor in his poems. The first two cantos of *Childe Harold* (264–267) took the public by storm, and placed the young poet at the summit of social and literary popularity. "I awoke one morning," he says, "and found myself famous." These cantos were followed in rapid succession by *The Giaour* (268, 269), *The Bride of Abydos* (270), *The Corsair* (271), and *Lara.* Scott had drawn his material from feudal and Scottish life ; Byron broke up new ground in describing the manners, scenery, and wild passions of the East and of Greece—a region as picturesque as that of his rival, and as new and fresh to readers. Returning to England in his dawning fame, the poet became the lion of the day. His life was passed in fashionable dissipation. He married Miss Milbanke, a lady of fortune ; but the union was an unhappy one. In about a year Lady Byron suddenly quitted her husband. Her reasons for taking this step remain a mystery. Deeply wounded by the scandal of this separation, the poet again left England ; and thenceforth his life was passed uninterruptedly on the Continent, in Switzerland, in Italy, and in Greece, where he solaced his embittered spirit with misanthropical attacks upon all that his countrymen held sacred. While at Geneva he produced the third canto of *Childe Harold*, *The Prisoner of Chillon* (273), *Manfred*, (274), and *The Lament of Tasso.* Between 1818 and 1821 he was residing at Venice and Ravenna ; and was writing *Mazeppa*, the first five cantos of *Don Juan*, and most of his tragedies, as *Marino Faliero*, *Sardanapalus*, *The Two Foscari*, *Werner*, *Cain*, and *The Deformed Transformed.* In many of these poems the influence of Shelley's literary manner and philosophical tenets is traceable. At this time he was grossly dissipated. In 1823 he determined to devote his fortune and his influence to the aid of the Greeks, then struggling for their independence. He arrived at Missolonghi at the beginning of 1824; where, after giving striking indications of his practical talents, as well as of his ardor and self-sacrifice, he died on the 19th of April of the same year, at the early age of thirty-six.

Childe Harold. Childe Harold, his most remarkable poem, consists of a series of gloomy but intensely poetical monologues, put into the mouth of a jaded and misanthropic voluptuary, who seeks refuge from his misery in the contemplation of lovely and historic scenes of travel. The first canto describes Portugal and Spain ; the second carries the wanderer to Greece, Albania and the Ægean Archipelago ; in the third, the finest of them all, Switzerland, Belgium and the Rhine, give opportunities not only for splendid pictures of the beauty of nature, but also for musings on Napoleon, Voltaire, Rousseau, and the great men whose renown has thrown a new glory over those enchanting scenes ; in the fourth canto the reader is borne successively over the fairest part of Italy—Venice, Ferrara, Florence, Rome, and Ravenna—and the immortal dead, and the masterpieces of painting and sculpture, are described to him with an intensity of feeling that had never before been shown in descriptive poetry.

The first two cantos are somewhat feeble and tame as compared with the strength and massive power of the two latter, which are the productions of his more mature faculties. The third canto contains the magnificent description of the Battle of Waterloo. The poem is written in the Spenserian stanza. To the beginning the poet makes an effort to give somewhat of the quaint and archaic character of the Fairy Queen ; but he soon throws off the useless and embarrassing restraint. In intensity of feeling, in richness and harmony of expression, and in an imposing tone of gloomy, skeptical, and misanthropic reflection, *Childe Harold* stands alone in our literature.

Qualities of His Poems. The romantic tales of Byron are all marked by similar peculiarities of thought and treatment, though they differ in the kind and degree of their respective excellences. *The Giaour* (**268**), *The Siege of Corinth, Mazeppa, Parisina, The Prisoner of Chillon* (**273**), and *The Bride of Abydos*, are written in that irregular and flowing versification which Scott brought into fashion; while *The Corsair, Lara,* and *The Island*, are in the regular heroic measure. These poems are, in general, fragmentary. They are made up of intensely interesting moments of passion and action. Neither in these nor in any of his works does Byron show the least power of delineating *variety* of character. There are but two personages in all his poems—a man in whom unbridled passions have desolated the heart, and left it hard and impenetrable; a man contemptuous of his kind, skeptical and despairing, yet occasionally feeling kindly emotions with a singular intensity. The woman is the woman of the East—devoted and loving, but loving with the unreasoning attachment of the lower animals. These elements of character, meagre and unnatural as they are, are, however, set before us with such power that the young and inexperienced reader invariably loses sight of their contradictions. In all these poems we meet with tender, animated or profound descriptions ; thus the famous comparison of enslaved Greece to a corpse in *The Giaour,* the night-scene and the battle-scene in *The Corsair* and *Lara,* the eve of the storming of the city in *The Siege of Corinth*, and the fiery energy of the attack in the same poem, the exquisite opening lines in *Parisina*, besides a multitude of others, might be adduced to prove Byron's extraordinary genius in communicating to his pictures the coloring of his own feelings and character.

In *Beppo* and *The Vision of Judgment* Byron has ventured upon the gay, airy, and satirical. The former of these
poems is not over-moral ; but it is exquisitely playful and
sparkling. The *Vision* is a severe attack upon Southey, and
though somewhat ferocious, is exceedingly brilliant. Among
the less commonly read of Byron's longer poems we may
mention *The Age of Bronze,* a vehement satirical declamation; *The Curse of Minerva,* directed against the spoliation
of the frieze of the Parthenon by Lord Elgin ; *The Lament
of Tasso,* and *The Prophecy of Dante,* the latter written in
the difficult *terza rima,* the first attempt of any English poet
to employ that measure. *The Dream* is in some respects
the most touching of Byron's minor works. It is the narrative, in the form of a vision, of his early and unfortunate
passion for Mary Chaworth.

His Dramatic Works. The dramatic works of Byron are in
many respects unlike what might have been expected from
the peculiar character of his genius. In form they are cold,
severe, and lofty. Artful involution of intrigue they have
not; and though singularly destitute of powerful passion,
they are full of sentiment. The finest of them is *Manfred,*
a poem consisting not of action represented in dialogue, but
of a series of soliloquies, in which the mysterious hero
describes nature, and pours forth his despair and his self-
pity. In this work, as well as in *Cain,* we see the expression
of Byron's skeptical spirit, and the tone of half-melancholy,
half-mocking misanthropy, which was in him partly sincere
and partly put on for effect. The more exclusively historical pieces—*Marino Faliero, The Two Foscari*—are derived
from Venetian annals; but in neither of them has Byron
clothed the events with living reality. There is in these
dramas a complete failure in variety of character ; and the
interest is concentrated in the obstinate harping of the
principal personages upon one topic—their own wrongs and

humiliations. In *Sardanapalus* the remoteness of the epoch chosen, and our total ignorance of the interior life of those times, remove the story into the region of fiction. *Werner,* a piece of domestic interest, is borrowed bodily, as regards its incidents, and even much of its dialogue, from the Hungarian's Story in Miss Lee's *Canterbury Tales;* indeed, Byron's share in its composition extends little farther than the cutting up of Miss Lee's prose into tolerably regular lines.

Don Juan is the longest, and in some respects the most characteristic, of Byron's poems. It is, indeed, one of the most significant productions of the age of revolution and skepticism which preceded its appearance. The outline of the story is the old Spanish legend of *Don Juan de Tenorio,* upon which have been founded so many dramatic works, among the rest the *Festin de Pierre* of Molière and the immortal opera of Mozart. The fundamental idea of the atheist and voluptuary, enabled Byron to carry his hero through various adventures, serious and comic, to exhibit his fine powers of description, and remain unfettered by any necessities of time and place. Even in its unfinished state, it consists of sixteen cantos, and there is no reason why it should not have been indefinitely extended. It was the author's intention to bring his hero's adventures to a regular termination, but so desultory a series of incidents has no real coherency. The merits of this poem are its richness of ideas, thoughts, and images; its witty allusion and sarcastic reflection; and above all, its frequent and easy transitions. The morality is throughout very low and selfish; but, in spite of much superficial flippancy, this poem contains profound and melancholy satire.

Angus's Estimate of Byron. "The genius of Lord Byron is one of the most remarkable in our literature for originality, versatility, and energy. It is true that his quick sense of beauty made him a mimic of other poets; it is true that as the wealth of his own resources raised him above the suspicion of unfair copying, he never scrupled to imitate whatever he most admired; but it is no less true that he is on the whole one of the most original writers of his age. His versatility is perhaps less obvious. The monotony of his motives and of his characters strikes every reader; but characters and tone apart, his style and imagery and sentiments are endlessly diversified, nor has he treated a single subject in which he has not excelled. His energy, however, is his most striking quality; ' thoughts that breathe, and words that burn ' are the common staple of his poetry. He is everywhere impressive, not only in passages, but through the whole body and tissue of his compositions.

" With all this we cannot but concur in Lord Jeffrey's judgment: ' *the general tendency* of Lord Byron's writings we believe to be in the highest degree pernicious; though his poems abound in sentiments of great dignity and tenderness, as well as in passages of infinite sublimity and beauty, it is their tendency to destroy all belief in the reality of virtue, and to make all enthusiasm and consistency of affection ridiculous.' His sarcasm blasts alike the weeds of hypocrisy and cant, and the flowers of faith and of holiest affections. ' His plan of blending in one and the same character lofty superiority and contempt for commonplace virtue, heroism and sensuality, great intellectual power and a mocking, profane spirit, is as unnatural as it is mischievous.' " *

For discussions of Byron and his works, see Moore's *Life of Byron,—Edinburgh Review*, Vol. XXVII.,—*North American Review*, Vols. V., XIII., XX. and LX.,—*The British Essayists*, Jeffrey,—E. P. Whipple's *Essays*, Vol. I.,—and Taine's English Literature.

* Angus Eng. Lit., p. 249.

Thomas Moore (1779–1852), the personal friend and biographer of Byron, though living for a quarter of a century after Byron Shelley, and Scott, is associated with them in literature. This is accounted for by the fact that his best works were written early in the century. He was an Irishman, born in Dublin, and received an education such as was called for by his extraordinary talents. Being a Catholic, many of the avenues to public distinction were then closed to him by the invidious laws that oppressed his country and his religion. After distinguishing himself at the University of Dublin he passed over to London, nominally with the intention of studying law in the Temple, but he soon began his long and brilliant career as a poet. He first appeared as the translator of the *Odes of Anacreon*. The work, published by subscription, and dedicated to the Prince Regent, immediately introduced Moore into gay and fashionable life. He had, both in his personal and poetical character, everything calculated to make him the favorite of society; great conversational talents, an agreeable voice, and a degree of musical skill that enabled him to give effect to his tender, voluptuous or patriotic songs. During his whole life he was the spoiled child of popularity. In 1804 he obtained a small government post in the island of Bermuda. His visit to America and the Antilles drew from him some of the most sparkling of his early poems. Nearly the whole of his long life was devoted to the production of a rapid succession of compositions, both in prose and verse. As an Irishman and a Catholic, Moore's sentiments naturally supplied the biting and yet pleasant sarcasm found in his political pasquinades. He spent the latter part of his life in a cottage near Bowood, the residence of the Marquis of Lansdowne, whose friendship he had won.

His Poetry. Moore's poetical writings consist chiefly of lyrics, serious and comic, the most celebrated collection among them being the *Irish Melodies*. The version of *Anacreon* is far too brilliant and ornamental in its language to give a correct idea of the manner of the Greek poet. In his juvenile poems, as well as in the collection published under the pseudonym of *Thomas Little*, in the productions suggested by his visit to America and the West Indies, and in the *Odes and Epistles*, we see invention, and also a strongly voluptuous tendency of sentiment, sometimes carried beyond the bounds of good taste and morality.

The *Irish Melodies*, a collection of about one hundred and twenty-five songs (**279–282**), were composed in order to furnish appropriate words to beautiful national airs, some of great antiquity, which had been degraded by becoming gradually associated with lines often vulgar and not always decent. Patriotism, love, and conviviality form the subject-matter of these charming lyrics; their versification has never been surpassed for melody and neatness; the language is always clear, appropriate, and concise, and sometimes reaches a high degree of majesty, vigor, or tenderness. Though Moore is destitute of the sincerity of Burns, yet like Burns he appeals to the universal sentiments of his countrymen, and his popularity is proportionally great. "Burns and Moore stand side by side as the lyrists of two kindred nations. But the works of the latter, polished and surpassingly sweet as they are, have something of the drawing-room sheen about them, which does not find its way to the heart so readily as the simple grace of the unconventional Ayrshire peasant. The Muse of the Irish lawyer is crowned with a circlet of shining gems; the Muse of the Scottish peasant wears a garland of sweet field-flowers." *

The political squibs of Moore were directed against the Tory party in general, and were showered with peculiar vivacity and stinging effect upon the Regent, afterwards George IV., and upon all who were opposed to the granting of any privileges to the Irish Catholics. His *Odes on Cash, Corn, and Catholics*, his *Fables for the Holy Alliance*, show an inexhaustible invention of quaint and ingenious ideas, and the power of bringing the most remote allusions to bear upon the person or thing selected for attack. Some of the most celebrated of these brilliant pasquinades were combined into a story ; as for example *The Fudge Family in Paris*, purporting to be a series of letters written from France at the time of the Restoration of the Bourbons. These poetical epistles are seasoned with such a multitude of personal and political allusions, that *The Fudge Family* retains its popularity, as a social and political sketch of a most interesting episode in modern European history.

The longer and more ambitious poems of Moore are *Lalla Rookh* and the *Loves of the Angels*, the former being immeasurably the better, both in the interest of the story and in the power of its treatment. The plan of *Lalla Rookh* is original; it consists of a

* Collier.

little prose love-tale, describing the journey of a beautiful Oriental princess from Delhi to Bucharia, where she is to meet her betrothed, the king of the latter country. The prose of the work is inimitably beautiful; the whole style is sparkling with Oriental gems, and perfumed as with Oriental musk and roses; and the very profusion of brilliancy and of voluptuous languor, which in another kind of composition might be regarded as meretricious, only adds to the effect. The story forms a setting to four poems: *The Veiled Prophet*, *The Fire Worshippers*, *Paradise and the Peri* (**278**), and *The Light of the Harem;* all, of course, of an Eastern character, and the first two in some degree historical. The first, written in the rhymed heroic couplet, is the longest and most ambitious, while the others are composed in that irregular, animated versification, brought into fashion by Walter Scott and Byron.

His Prose Writings. The chief prose works of Moore are the three biographies of Sheridan, Byron, and Lord Edward Fitzgerald, and the tale of *The Epicurean*. The last, a narrative of the first ages of Christianity, describes the conversion of a young Athenian philosopher, who travels into Egypt, and is initiated into the mysterious worship of Isis. Moore's biographies, especially that of Byron, are of great value. His memoir of his friend and fellow-poet is the best that has yet appeared.

Percy Bysshe Shelley (1792–1822) was of a wealthy family, and was born at Field Place, in Sussex (**283**-**285**). At Eton his sensitive mind was shocked by the sight of boyish tyranny; and he went to Oxford full of abhorrence for the cruelty and bigotry which he fancied pervaded all the relations of civilized life. He filled his mind with arguments against Christianity; and having published a tract avowing atheistic principles, he was expelled from the University. This scandal, together with his marriage to a beautiful girl, his inferior in rank, caused him to be renounced by his family. After a few years his wife left him, and subsequently ended her life by suicide. He then married Mary Wollstonecraft Godwin, and having induced his family to make him an allowance, he was relieved from pecuniary difficulties. The delicate state of his health rendered it advisable that he should leave England for a warmer climate, and the remainder of his life was passed abroad, with only one short interruption, In Switzerland he became acquainted with Byron, upon whom he exerted a powerful influence. He afterwards migrated to Italy, where he kept up an intimate companionship with Byron, still continuing to pour forth his strange and enchanting poetry. He resided at Rome, and composed there many of his finest productions. His death was early and tragic. Boating had always been a passion with him. As he was returning in a small yacht from Leghorn, in company with a friend and a single sailor, his vessel was caught in a squall, in the Gulf of Spezzia, and went down with all on board. His body was washed ashore some days afterwards, and in accordance with the quarantine laws of that locality was burned. The ashes were deposited in the Protestant cemetery at Rome.

Shelley, both as a poet and as a man, was a dreamer, a visionary. The very intensity of his sympathy with his kind clouded his reason ; and he fell into the common error of enthusiasts, of supposing that, if the present organization of society were swept away, a millennium of virtue and happiness must ensue. As a poet he was gifted with genius of a high order, with richness and fertility of imagination, an intense fire and energy in the reproduction of what he conceived, and a command over all the resources of metrical harmony such as no English poet has surpassed. His career commences with *Queen Mab*, written by the poet when but eighteen years old, a wild phantasmagoria of beautiful description and fervent declamation. The defect of the poem, and indeed of many of Shelley's other compositions, is a vagueness of meaning often becoming absolutely unintelligible.

The finest and most distinct of his longer poems is *Alastor, or the Spirit of Solitude.* In its blank verse he depicts the sufferings of such a character as his own,—a being of the warmest sympathies, and of the loftiest aspirations, driven into solitude and despair by the ingratitude of his kind, who are incapable of understanding and sympathizing with his aims. Its descriptions are beautiful : woodland and river scenery are painted with a wealth of tropical luxuriance that places Shelley in the foremost rank among pictorial poets. *The Revolt of Islam, Hellas,* and *The Witch of Atlas,* are violent invectives against kingcraft, priestcraft, religion, and marriage, alternating with airy and exquisite pictures of scenes and beings of unearthly splendor.

Two important works of Shelley are dramatic in form—*Pro*

metheus Unbound and *The Cenci*. The *Prometheus* is wild and unintelligible; still it contains passages of beauty and sublimity. It breathes hostility to social systems, and love for humanity in the abstract. Many of the descriptive passages are sublime; and bursts of lyric harmony alternate with the wildest personifications and the strongest invective. *The Cenci* is founded on the famous crime of Beatrice di Cenci. Driven to parricide by the wickedness of her father, she suffered the penalty of death at Rome. In spite of several powerful and striking scenes, the piece is of a morbid and unpleasing character, though the language is vigorous.

Shelley had a desperate hostility to marriage; and his narrative poem of *Rosalind and Helen* is an elaborate plea against that institution. In the poem of *Adonais* he has given us a touching lament on the early death of Keats. One of the most imaginative, and at the same time one of the obscurest, of Shelley's poems is *The Sensitive Plant*. It combines the qualities of mystery and fancifulness to the highest degree, perpetually stimulating the reader with a desire to penetrate the meaning symbolized in the brilliant description of the garden and the plant. Many of his detached lyrics are of inexpressible beauty. The *Ode to a Skylark* (**283**) breathes the very rapture of the bird's soaring song. Wild and picturesque imagery abounds in the poem of *The Cloud*.

John Keats (1795-1821) was born in Moorfields, London, and, in his fifteenth year, was apprenticed to a surgeon. During his apprenticeship he devoted most of his time to poetry, and in 1817, he published a juvenile volume. His long poem, *Endymion*, followed in 1818 (**289**). It was severely censured by *The Quarterly Review*, and the attack has been erroneously described as the cause of his death. He had a constitutional tendency to consumption, which would have developed itself under any circumstances. For the recovery of his health he went to Rome, where he died. In the previous year he had published another volume of poems, and a fragment of his remarkable poem entitled *Hyperion* (**287**).

It was the misfortune of Keats to be either extravagantly praised or unmercifully condemned. What is most remarkable in his works is the wonderful profusion of figurative language, often exquisitely beautiful and luxuriant, but sometimes fantastical and far-fetched. One word, one image, one rhyme suggests another, till we lose sight of the original idea, smothered in its own luxuriance. Keats deserves high praise for one very original merit: he has treated the classical mythology in a way absolutely new, representing the Pagan deities not as mere abstractions of art, nor as mere creatures of popular belief, but giving them passions and affections like our own, though highly purified and idealized. In *Hyperion*, in the *Ode to Pan* (which appears in "Endymion"), in the *Verses on a Grecian Urn* (288), we find a strain of classic imagery, combined with a perception of natural loveliness inexpressibly rich and delicate. If we consider his extreme youth and delicate health, his solitary and interesting self-instruction, the severity of the attacks made upon him by hostile and powerful critics, and, above all, the original richness and picturesqueness of his conceptions and imagery, even when they run to waste, he appears to be one of the greatest of young poets.

Thomas Campbell (1777–1844) was born at Glasgow, and was educated at the University in that city, where he distinguished himself by his translations from the Greek poets. In his twenty-second year, he published his *Pleasures of Hope* (290), and was encouraged by having it received with hearty enthusiasm. Shortly afterwards he traveled abroad, where the warlike scenes he witnessed, and the battle-fields he visited, suggested several noble lyrics. To the seventh edition of *The Pleasures of Hope*, published in 1802, were added the verses on the battle of *Hohenlinden* (293), *Ye Mariners of England* (292), the most popular of his songs, and *Lochiel's Warning*. In the following year he settled in London, married, and began in earnest the pursuit of literature as a profession. In 1843 he retired to Boulogne, where he died in the following year. His body was returned to England and interred in Westminster Abbey.

In the circle of poets with Byron, Shelley, and Keats, outliving them by many years, the names of Leigh Hunt and Walter Savage Landor must be mentioned.

James Henry Leigh Hunt (1784–1859) was born at Southgate, Middlesex, and received his education at Christ's Hospital. In 1805 he joined his brother in editing a paper called *The News*, and shortly afterwards established *The Examiner*. A conviction for libel on the Prince Regent detained him in prison for two years. Soon after leaving prison he published the *Story of Rimini*, an Italian tale in verse (1816), containing some exquisite poetry. About 1818 he started *The Indicator*, a weekly paper, in imitation of *The Spectator;* and in 1822 he went to Italy, to assist Lord Byron and Shelley in their projected paper called *The Liberal*. Shelley died soon after Hunt's arrival in Italy ; and though Hunt was kindly received by Byron, and lived for a time in his house, there was no congeniality between them. Returning to England, he continued to write for periodicals, and published various poems. His poetry is graceful, sprightly, and full of fancy. Although not possessing much soul and emotion, here and there his verse is lit up with wit, or glows with tenderness and grace. His prose writings consist of essays, collected under the titles of *The Indicator* and *The Companion; Sir Ralph Esther*, a novel ; *The Old Court Suburb;* his lives of *Wycherley, Congreve, Vanbrugh*, and *Farquhar*, prefixed to his edition of their dramatic writings.

Walter Savage Landor (1775–1864) entered Rugby at an early age, and thence went to Trinity College, Oxford ; but he left the University without a degree. As a poet he stands with Leigh Hunt between the age of Scott and Byron and the age of Tennyson and Browning. In 1795 his first work—a volume of poems—appeared, followed early in the present century by a translation into Latin of *Gebir*, one of his own English poems. Landor had facility in classical composition, and he appeared to have the power of transporting himself into the times and sentiments of Greece and Rome. This is clearly seen in the *Heroic Idyls* in Latin verse ; and the reproduction of Greek thought in *The Hellenics* is one of the most successful attempts of its kind. Shortly after the death of his father, the poet took up his abode on the Continent, where he resided during the rest of his life, making occasional visits to his native country. The republican spirit which led him to take part as a volunteer in the Spanish rising of 1808 continued to burn fiercely to the last. He even went so far as to defend tyrannicide, and boldly offered a pension to the widow of any one who would murder a despot. Between 1820 and 1830 he was engaged upon his greatest work, *Imaginary Conversations of Literary Men and Statesmen*. This was followed in 1831 by *Poems, Letters by a*

Conservative, Satire on Satirists (1836), *Pentameron and Pentalojus* (1837), and a long series in prose and poetry, of which the chief are *The Hellenics Enlarged and Completed, Dry Sticks Fagoted,* and *The Last Fruit off an Old Tree.* He died at Florence, an exile from his country, misunderstood by the majority of his countrymen, but highly appreciated by those who could rightly estimate the works he has left.

Thomas Hood (1798–1845) has unfortunately been regarded only as a humorist; but "pathos, sensibility, indignation against wrong, enthusiasm for human improvement—all these were his." "His pen touched alike the springs of laughter and the sources of tears." He was associated with the brilliant circle who contributed to *The London Magazine;* among whom were Lamb, Hazlitt, the Smiths, and De Quincey. His magazine articles were followed by *Whims and Oddities.* Hood became at once a popular writer; but in the midst of his success a business house failed, involving him in its losses. The poet, disdaining to take refuge in bankruptcy, emulated the example of Scott, and determined by the economy of a life in Germany to pay off the debt thus involuntarily contracted. In 1835 the family took up their residence in Coblenz; thence removed to Ostend; and returned to London in 1840. He was editor of the *New Monthly* from 1841 until 1843, when the first number of his own Magazine was issued. A pension was obtained for him in 1844; and he died in the following year.

Hood has given little indication of the highest imaginative faculty; but his fancy was delicate, and full of graceful play. He possessed in a remarkable degree the power of perceiving the ridiculous and the odd. His words seemed to break up into the queerest syllables. His wit was caustic; it was never coarse. An impurity even in suggestion cannot be found in Hood's pages With the humor was associated a tender pathos. *The Death-bed* (**323**) is one of the most affecting little poems in our language, and is equaled by another of his ballads entitled *Love's Eclipse.* Amongst his larger works, the *Plea of the Midsummer Fairies* and *Hero and Leander,* are the most elaborate. The descriptive parts in both are full of careful observation of nature, and most musical expression of her beauties. The best known of his poems are *The Bridge of Sighs* (**322**), *Eugene Aram,* and the *Song of the Shirt.* In them the comic element is entirely wanting. His poems usually have a blending of humor and pathos; and in their humor there is an earnest purpose. "He tempts men to laugh, and then leads them to pity and relieve."

Elizabeth Barrett Browning. The most eminent poet among women is Elizabeth Barrett Browning (1809–1861). She was the daughter of a wealthy merchant of London, and by good fortune received what had been allowed to few of her sex, a good education. In the Latin and Greek literature she was well versed. The delicacy of her health prevented her from doing the toilsome work of the most laborious students; yet her acquirements were so great, that in her youth she was as famous for her learning as for her genius. Illness did not keep her from books. By a varied and extensive course of reading, and by her meditation, she prepared herself for her place among the poets. Her first acknowledged work was a translation of the *Prometheus Bound*, published in 1833. Next appeared a collection of poems, in 1844. In 1846 she was married to Robert Browning, and went with him to Italy for the improvement of her health. From that time her sympathies with Italian aspirations were so intense that they colored nearly all of her writings. Her *Casa Guidi Windows* gives her impressions of what she saw of Italian life from her home, the Casa Guido, in Florence. Her greatest work, and in the estimation of some critics the finest poem of the present century, is *Aurora Leigh*. This she herself pronounces "the most mature of my works, and the one into which my highest convictions upon Life and Art have entered." In 1856 she left England for the last time, dying at Florence in 1861.

This woman of emotion, of thought, of devout spirit, shut in her darkened chamber, reading "almost every book worth reading in almost every language," mingling with a few friends, her heart going forth in sympathy with the wretched and down-trodden, gathered up her strength and put her soul into her verse, now with all the passion of *Aurora Leigh*, and now in tenderer sonnets full of pathos and love. It is not to be wondered at, that some of her writing has been called *spasmodic*. Mrs. Browning has not the calm, unfailing flow of thought and feeling found in Tennyson, her only modern superior in England. Her style is often rugged, unfinished, and at times utterly without rhythm.

The sadness pervading all the writings of Mrs. Browning is what might be expected from such a life as hers. Her own idea of the poet's work seems to bear this view: " Poetry has been as serious a thing to me as life itself; and life has been a very serious thing. I never mistook pleasure for the final cause of poetry, nor leisure for the hour of the poet." From such a view of poetry and life, we cannot wonder at the moral purpose found in all her writing (**324**)

It is fitting that the literary chronicles of **Robert Browning** (1812–1889) should be closely linked with those of his gifted wife. Theirs was one of the ideal marriages of history; the kinship of their studies and sympathies exerted marked influence upon the writings of both. Our great poets have often manifested their genius in spite of the most adverse surroundings; but with Browning, as with Milton, the culture of native gifts was assisted from earliest years by the sympathy of friends. He was born at Camberwell, a suburb of London; his father is said to have possessed poetic power as well as appreciation; and although, as a Dissenter the young man was not destined for either of the great universities, his student life was happy and earnest. Byron was his first inspiration and model; in fact, in 1824, the year of the older poet's death, a volume of verses was ready for the publisher, whom Browning's friends sought in vain. A year later he came by chance under the spell of Shelley and Keats, then neglected and almost unknown. The result was a complete revision of his poetic standards. For several years he wrote little, though planning much; his mind was set upon gigantic undertakings, midway between drama and epic in their scope. Some of these were sketched, but only one saw the light. *Pauline, a Fragment of a Confession*, was anonymously published in 1833, through the generosity of an aunt. It attracted no general notice, although such thinkers as J. S. Mill, John Forster, and D. G. Rossetti at once marked the strong note of the unknown singer. At this time Browning's *Wanderjahre* began; for being arrived at man's estate, and assured of receiving a moderate fortune from his parents, he had resolved, with their full concurrence, to devote his life to study, travel, and letters. He made a long stay at St. Petersburg, and thence went to Italy, beginning that ardent study of Italian history and literature which was to prove a dominating influence in his thought. Returning to England, he finished *Paracelsus*, which was published (1835) at his father's expense. It was sufficiently read and talked about to bring its author much friendly encouragement from literary circles. He has said himself that he was nearly fifty years old before his writings became popular enough to secure him income. But his position as a "poet's poet" was certain before he was twenty-five. *Strafford*, an historical tragedy (1837), was prepared for the stage at the instance of the tragedian Macready, who himself assumed the leading part. *A Blot in the Scutcheon* (1843) and *Colombe's Birthday* (1852) were composed with the same design. All had enough of success to excite enthusiasm among Browning's friends, and to this day the reason of their short stage-life remains matter of dispute. Judging them as acting plays, one can see, in the abstract nature of their themes and their tendency to lengthy recitative, abundant counterpoise to their beauties,—eloquent passages, occasional strong characterization, and genuine dramatic insight. To this period also belong several dramas which were never acted: *Pippa Passes* (1841), by common consent the most perfect of Browning's dramas; *King Victor and King Charles* (1842); *The Return of the Druses* (1843); *Luria* and *A Soul's Tragedy* (1846). *Sordello* (1840) had received much of the sweeping censure and unqualified praise, whose contradictions were destined to become so familiar to the poet; *Dramatic Lyrics* (1842) contained a number of the striking and beautiful short poems with which his name is associated in the popular mind: *How they Brought the Good News from Ghent to Aix*, *Incident of the French Camp*, *Cavalier Tunes*, and the inimitable *Pied Piper of Hamelin*. To this period belongs also a popular edition of his works under the fanciful title of *Bells and Pomegranates* (1841–46). In 1846, after a brief acquaintance brought about by poetic sympathy, Browning won and married Elizabeth Barrett. For the next fifteen years the two poets found a congenial home in Italy, amid the stirring scenes of the Italian struggle for national unity. Although Robert Browning published comparatively little at this time, later years proved that he felt, thought, and studied deeply. *Christmas Eve* and *Easter Day* appeared in 1850; and *Men and Women* (1855) contained, among reprinted pieces, many strong new poems.

After the death of his wife (1861) Browning returned to England, residing mainly in London during the last and most productive years of his life. "Casa Guidi," his Florentine home, had long been a Mecca to literary pilgrims of every race; and Browning now became one of the most familiar and cherished figures of London society. His personal relations were singularly delightful. Recognized as a connoisseur in art and letters, and a brilliant talker, he was also a genial, generous friend. Many writers, famous and obscure, have borne witness to the modesty and the unspoiled kindliness of his nature. Freedom from egotism seems truly noteworthy in a poet who lived to see learned societies organized under his name, for the purpose of justifying the alleged defects and extolling the beauties of his verse. It must be owned that he gave them abundant material for elucidation. *Dramatis Personœ* (1864) was heavily weighted with metaphysical disquisition, which was by no means absent from the *Ring and the Book* (1868–69), generally pronounced the masterpiece among his long poems. This numbers 20,000 lines of blank verse, and its foundation narrative is told and retold eleven times. *Balaustion's Adventure* (1871) embodies a beautiful rendering of the *Alkestis* of Euripides, whose *Herakles* is freely translated in *Aristophanes' Apology* (1875). A noble and accurate rendering of the *Agamemnon* of Æschylus (1877) was found difficult reading even by scholarly critics. *Prince Hohenstiel-Schwangau* (1871), *Fifine at the Fair* (1872), *Red Cotton Night-cap Country* (1873), *The Inn Album* (1875), *Dramatic Idyls* (1879–80), *Jocoseria* (1883), *Ferishtah's Fancies* (1884), *Parleyings with Certain People of Importance in their Day* (1887), *Asolando* (1889), although warmly received by the inner circle of Browning's admirers, have as yet added little to the general estimate of his powers.

Browning died in Venice, during one of his frequent visits to Italy; and the city sent a wreath to be placed upon his bier. Westminster Abbey received his remains amid manifestations of a nation's grief, which were echoed by the elect spirits of two continents. Recalling the stately obsequies of Spenser, where "mournful elegies, with the pens that wrote them," were thrown into the tomb, the critic queries whether Browning, like Spenser, is destined to a select and limited immortality, bounded by the refined understanding of a literary class. The decision cannot yet be pronounced. Browning's greatness, like his faults, can ill be resolved into a brief summary. Only careful study and judicial comparison can define the scope of his powers.   His work repays serious thought, not only as a reflection of the many influences exerted upon artists in the nineteenth century, but as an epitome of poetic method—possibly mistaken, certainly original.   He did not himself pose as a lawgiver; he has frankly disclaimed many of the subtleties praised by his commentators.   To those who value the laws of melodious versification, which have been followed by the greatest masters from Chaucer to Tennyson, Browning seems great in spite of frequent deviations, rather than because the necessities of his genius have transcended them.   In his best writing he has proved himself a master of fluent, musical, impressive verse, and this deepens our regret that he has so often thought it superfluous. But making every allowance for the blemishes which repel conventional critics,—his obscurities and remote allusions, his prolixity, his frequent errors of taste, and the crude, commonplace diction which masks many of his noblest thoughts,—we must still concede him creative originality, vast fertility, and imagination of a high order.   He has often proffered his readers rather the raw material of poetry than poetry itself, yet we are sure of finding in his most unpolished masses beauties of thought and diction sufficient to assure the fame of an ordinary poet.   Moreover, he has fulfilled the moral mission of the poet in a high sense.   His religious faith is expressed without dogmatism or sentimentality; he believes in the high destiny of man, in the "soul of goodness in things evil," in the noble ends of Art and of Love.   Chaucer himself is not freer from cynicism.   His sympathy no less than his insight has made him a cosmopolitan, while his interest in the individual, the exceptional type, has enabled him to portray for us race, epoch, caste, sect, even eccentricity and crime, with realistic fidelity.   If we acknowledge, furthermore, the virile quality of his genius, the sympathetic breadth of his humor, the variety of his character-study, we shall not ridicule the comparisons with Shakespeare which are so frequently preferred by his disciples.   He himself considered his genius to be dramatic in its bent.   But no company of scholars can subject him to those tests which three centuries have applied to Shakespeare. The dramatic monologue, his chosen vehicle of expression, is of itself less easily understood than the drama which interprets thought by action; and Browning's themes are frequently foreign to the knowledge and to the interest of English readers.   More-

exception in the annals of literature, that their results demand thoughtful analysis. Embodying the influences of refined heredity and systematic scholarly training, Tennyson's poetry is no less the product of art than of inspiration. Such brief comments as the present limits allow, can only direct the student's further investigation. His first appearance as a literary artist, destined to bring English verse to a perfection hitherto unparalleled, was in 1830. In France this was the *annus mirabilis* of modern painting. We can hardly doubt that the coincidence had influence in stimulating and developing Tennyson's art-sense. Chaucer, Spenser, the Elizabethan dramatists, Burns, Byron, Scott, Shelley and Keats had severally and occasionally revealed certain capabilities of English vocables and English metres. Tennyson was the first to exemplify all; greatest in the poet's art of 'marrying music to immortal verse.' Lyric lightness and grace, epic sublimity, pastoral smoothness, the picturesque ruggedness of dialect, the stormy energy of dramatic passion—he has perfectly attained each of these in its own place. Many of his followers have perverted his method, and well-nigh lost their thought in the mere joy of fluent verse-making. But Tennyson's intellectual range is as wide as his mastery of form. Withal, into the melody, the flexibility of his measures, he has infused the true artist's charm of color. He is the most exquisite word painter who has used the English language. His choice of subject has been extensive; yet seldom has he failed to win commanding excellence in his chosen field. To praise the perfection of his lyrics, one need only cite *Break, Break, Break*, the exquisite songs in *Maud, The Princess* and *Queen Mary. Enoch Arden, Dora, The Grandmother, The Gardener's Daughter*, are but types of a class wherein he has hardly been surpassed by Burns or Wordsworth. *The Idyls of the King* constitute an epic which may challenge comparison with *The Fairy Queen*, if not with *Paradise Lost. In Memoriam* has been criticised as too measured in its grief, incomplete in its revelation of religious faith. Yet it is the most sympathetic, the most suggestive, the most elevated of English elegiac poems. In the most perfect of his shorter psychological poems, such as *The Palace of Art, The Two Voices, The Vision of Sin, The Lotos-Eaters*, Tennyson embodies profoundest insight, sometimes undervalued by captious critics, only because the perfect verse discloses the contained thought without labor or artifice. In his dramas, the chosen work of his later years, he has been least successful. They vary greatly in power and vividness of effect. Most of them have proved unsuitable for the modern stage. Yet such eminent scholars as Edward Freeman and George Eliot have owned a debt to their power of historic imagination.

Tennyson is, in fact, essentially a modern thinker and a national poet. So we find in him the genuine British faults and excellencies, and many of the nineteenth century limitations. Restrained force and dignity characterize him as truly as John Milton. He is never bombastic or extravagant; he never gives loose rein to passion or fancy. Expressing the English mind in its highest development, his poetry discloses Grecian, Gothic Italian, French influences, mellowed in the alembic of his understanding to a chastened and harmonious splendor. His judgment is the curb-rein of his genius Of the results many critics have complained, with ill-judged emphasis. They have found the virtues of *The Blameless King* stilted and mechanical; the tempered pathos of *In Memoriam* mere convential mourning; *Oenone* and *Ulysses* successful archæological exercises. Even his finished verse has been a blemish to such as love to smelt subtle thought out of rugged ore, like Browning's *Sordello*. Accident, moreover, has unduly emphasized some of his least perfect productions. *Maud*, *The Princess*, *The Lover's Tale*, *The Promise of May*—each chancing to appear at a flood-tide of his renown, show neither richness of thought nor symmetry of form equal to less-quoted works. The *Idyls of the King* appeared in a disjointed series, perhaps in the reverse order of their excellence. They are seldom read in connection, save by careful critics. When familiar with the poet's guiding plan, the student does justice to their cumulative effect.

We may justly pronounce Tennyson's work deficient in humor— that most sympathetic of intellectual qualities. Consequently, he fails in completeness of dramatic insight in many of the finer touches of character-painting. He made himself a recluse, unwilling and at last unable, to deal with men or their passions at close range. But his powers, like those of every son of genius, must be estimated by an appeal to the law of his own nature, not by any fanciful standard of poetic completeness.

See Stedman's *Victorian Poets,* and Henry Van Dyke's *Poetry of Tennyson.* Appended to the latter work is a valuable chronology of Tennyson's productions, and the critical commentaries which they have evoked.

In this Chapter we have considered:—

    1. Lord Byron.
        a. Childe Harold.
        b. His Dramatic Works.
        c. Don Juan.
        d. Angus's Estimate of Byron.
    2. Thomas Moore.
        a. His Poetry.
        b. His Prose Writings.
    3. Percy Bysshe Shelley.
    4. John Keats.
    5. Thomas Campbell.
    6. James Henry Leigh Hunt.
    7. Walter Savage Landor.
    8. Thomas Hood.
    9. Elizabeth Barrett Browning.
   10. Robert Browning.
   11. Alfred Tennyson.

CHAPTER XXVI.

THE LAKE SCHOOL—WORDSWORTH, COLERIDGE AND SOUTHEY

WILLIAM WORDSWORTH.

"Him who uttered nothing base."—*Alfred Tennyson*.

"I do not know a man more to be venerated for uprightness of heart and loftiness of genius."—*Walter Scott*.

"To feel for the first time a communion with his mind, is to discover loftier faculties in our own."—*Thomas N. Talfourd*.

"Whatever the world may think of me or of my poetry is now of little consequence; but one thing is a comfort of my old age, that none of my works written since the days of my early youth, contains a line which I should wish to blot out because it panders to the baser passions of our nature. This is a comfort to me; I can do no mischief by my works when I am gone."—*William Wordsworth*.

WILLIAM WORDSWORTH (1770–1850), the founder of the so-called Lake School of poetry, was born in the north of England (294-300). He was left an orphan very early in life. In his ninth year he was sent to a school at Hawkshead, in the most picturesque district of Lancashire, where his love for the beauties of creation was rapidly developed. After taking his degree at Cambridge in 1791, he went to France, and eagerly embraced the ideas of the champions of liberty in that country. His political sentiments, however, became gradually modified, till in later life they settled down into steady conservatism in all questions of church and state. In 1793 he published two little poems, *An Evening Walk*, and *Descriptive Sketches*. Their metre and language are of the school of Pope; but they are the work of a promising pupil, and not of a master. In the following year he completed the story of *Salisbury Plain; or, Guilt and Sorrow*. In regard to time it is separated from the *Descriptive Sketches* by a span, but in merit they are parted by a gulf. He had ceased to write in the style of Pope; and composed in the stanza of his later favorite, Spenser. There is an exquisite simplicity and polish in the language. In his twenty-sixth year, just as he was finding it necessary to enter some regular business for the purpose of earning a livelihood, he found himself placed in what was affluence to him, by receiving a legacy of £900 from his friend Raisley Calvert, with the request that he would devote himself to literary work. Thoughts of the law, and attempts to earn money by writing for the newspapers were abandoned. He settled with his sister in a quiet country place in Somersetshire, and began his long devotion to the muse. His second experiment was the tragedy of *The Borderers*, a work considered an unqualified failure when it first appeared. In 1797 Coleridge went to live in the neighborhood, and formed a close friendship with Wordsworth and his sister. The following year they started on a tour in Germany. To furnish funds for the journey they published a volume together, entitled *Lyrical Ballads*. The first poem was Coleridge's *Ancient Mariner*, and the other pieces were by Wordsworth. Of these, three or four were in Wordsworth's finest manner; but they did not save his name from ridicule and censure.

Returning to England, Wordsworth and his sister settled at Grasmere, in the Lake District. Coleridge and Southey resided near them. From this fact they came to be spoken of as the Lake School. The name, originally applied contemptuously, came to be the distinguishing title of these friends. Wordsworth now set himself to work to inculcate his peculiar views of poetry. Not disheartened by the unpopularity of his first attempt, he promptly issued a new edition of Lyrical Ballads, adding thirty-seven pieces to the original collection. At this time he was working on a biographical poem, *The Prelude*, published a half-century after its composition.

A debt of £8500 due to his father at the time of his death, was paid to the poet in 1802. This increase of his fortune enabled him to marry. In 1807 he published two new volumes of *Poems*, containing the *Song at the Feast of Brougham Castle*, and many more of his choicest pieces. Here appeared his first sonnets, and several of them are still ranked among his happiest efforts. Wordsworth's next publication was in prose. His indignation arose at the grasping tyranny of Napoleon; and in 1809 he put forth a pamphlet against the Convention of Cintra. The sentiments were stirring, but the manner of conveying them was not, and his protest passed unheeded. His great work, *The Excursion*, appeared in 1814. This is a fragment of a projected great moral epic, discussing the mightiest questions concerning God, nature, and man, our moral constitution, our duties, and our hopes. Its dramatic interest is exceedingly small; its structure is very faulty; and the characters represented in it are devoid of life and probability. On the other hand, so sublime are the subjects discussed, so lofty is their tone, and so deep a glow of humanity is perceptible throughout, that no honest reader can study this composition without reverence and delight.

The White Doe of Rylstone, published in 1815, is Wordsworth's only narrative poem of any length. The incidents are of a simple and mournful kind. *Peter Bell* was published in 1819, and was received with a shout of ridicule. The poet stated in the dedication that the work had been completed twenty years, and that he had continued correcting it in the interval to render it worthy of a permanent place in our national literature. It is meant to be serious, and is certainly not facetious, but there is so much farcical absurdity of detail and language that the reader revolts. Between 1830 and 1840 the tide which floated him into favor rose to its height. Scott and Byron had in succession entranced the world. They had now withdrawn, and no third king arose to demand homage. It was in the lull that the less thrilling notes of the Lake bard obtained a hearing. It was during this time that he published his *Ecclesiastical Sonnets* and *Yarrow Revisited;* and in 1842 he brought forth a complete collection of his poems. His fame was now firmly established. On the death of Southey in 1843 he was made Poet Laureate. He died April 23, 1850, when he had just completed his eightieth year.

The Defects and Merits of His Poetry.

The poetry of Wordsworth has passed through two phases of criticism; in the first his defects were chiefly noted, and in the second his merits. We have arrived at the third era, when the majority of readers are just to both. A fair estimate of Wordsworth's poetry is given by an acute writer in the *Quarterly Review :* * " It is constantly asserted that

* Vol. XCII., p. 233, seq.

he effected a reform in the language of poetry, that he found the
public devoted to a vicious and flowery diction, which seemed to
mean a great deal and really meant nothing, and that he led them
back to sense and simplicity.   The claim appears to us to be
a fanciful assumption, refuted by the facts of literary history.
Feebler poetasters were no doubt read when Wordsworth began to
write than would now command an audience, however small; but
they had no real hold upon the public, and Cowper was the only
popular bard of the day.   His masculine and unadorned English
was relished in every cultivated circle in the land, and Wordsworth
was the child and not the father of a reaction, which, after all,
has been greatly exaggerated.   Goldsmith was the most celebrated
of Cowper's immediate predecessors, and it will not be pretended
that *The Deserted Village* and *The Traveller* are among the specimens
of inane phraseology.   Burns had died before Wordsworth had
attracted notice.   The wonderful Peasant's performances were admired by none more than by Wordsworth himself: were they not
already far more popular than the Lake-poet's have ever been—
or ever will be? . . . .   Whatever influence Wordsworth may
have exercised on poetic style, be it great or small, was by deviat-
ing in practice from the principles of composition for which he
contended.   Both his theory, and the poems which illustrate it,
continue to this hour to be all but universally condemned.   He
resolved to write as the lower orders talked ; and though where
the poor are the speakers it would be in accordance with strict
dramatic propriety, the system would not be tolerated in serious
poetry.   Wordsworth's rule did not stop at the wording of dialogues.   He maintained that the colloquial language of rustics was
the most philosophical and enduring which the dictionary affords,
and the fittest for verse of every description. . . . .   When
his finest verse is brought to the test of his principle, they
agree no better than light and darkness.   Here is his way of
describing the effects of the pealing organ in King's College
Chapel, with its 'self-poised roof, scooped into ten thousand cells:'

> ' But from the arms of silence—list ! O list—
>   The music bursteth into second life ;
>   The notes luxuriate, every stone is kissed
>   With sound, or ghost of sound, in mazy strife !'

This is to write like a splendid poet, but it is not to write as rus tics talk. A second canon laid down by Wordsworth was, that poetic diction is, or ought to be, in all respects the same with the language of prose; and as prose has a wide range, and numbers among its triumphs such luxuriant eloquence as that of Jeremy Taylor, the principle, if just, would be no less available for the advocates of ornamental verse than for the defence of the homely style of the *Lyrical Ballads.* But the proposition is certainly too broadly stated; and, though the argument holds good for the adversary, because the phraseology which is not too rich for prose can never be considered too tawdry for poetry, yet it will not warrant the conclusions of Wordsworth, that poetry should never rise above prose, or disdain to descend to its lowest level."

The following references note interesting discussions of Wordsworth and his poetry: Reed's *British Poets*, Lecture XV.,—Wilson, in the *British Essayists,—The North American Review*, Vol. C., p. 508,—Craik's *English Literature and Language*, Vol. II., p. 453,—De Quincey's *Essays on the Poets*,—Coleridge's *Biographia Literaria*, Chap. XIV.,—Hazlitt's *Lectures on the English Poets*,—Jeffrey, in the *British Essayists*,—Talfourd, in the *British Essayists*,—Taine's *English Literature*, Vol. II.

Samuel Taylor Coleridge (1772–1834). Carlyle paints Coleridge's portrait in these words: " Brow and head were round and of massive weight; but the face was flabby and irresolute. The deep eyes, of a light hazel, were as full of sorrow as of inspiration; confused pain looked mildly from them, as in a kind of mild astonishment. The whole figure and air, good and amiable otherwise, might be called flabby and irresolute; expressive of weakness under possibility of strength. He hung loosely on his limbs, with knees bent, and stooping attitude; in walking, he rather shuffled than decisively stepped; and a lady once remarked, he never could fix which side of the garden-walk would suit him best, but continually shifted, in cork-screw fashion, and kept trying both. A heavy-laden, high-aspiring, and surely much-suffering man."

This strange man had a strange childhood. At three years old he read the Bible; at six he had devoured " Belisarius," " Robinson Crusoe," " Philip Quarll," and the " Arabian Nights." In 1782 he was entered as a pupil at Christ's Hospital, where, though he won the position of Senior Grecian, or first scholar, his life was, on the whole, a dreary one. He spent his time in moping and reading.

By turns the restless energy and roving inclination of the inspired "Charity boy" settled upon shoemaking, surgery, and metaphysics as a means of escaping school and getting a living; but the judicious Doctor Bowyer flogged out each determination, with an extra cut for his being such an ugly fellow. In 1791 he went to Jesus College, Cambridge. A debt of less than £100 drove him from the University in the second year. He enlisted in the dragoons, under the name of Comberbacke. After four months' service, his friends procured his discharge, and he returned to Cambridge, leaving again in June, 1794, without taking a degree. He formed a friendship with Southey, and together they planned a model republic, to be located on the Susquehanna and called the "Pantisocracy"; but when it was found that not one of the directors could pay his passage to America, the plan was abandoned. In 1795 he married Miss Sarah Fricker, a sister of Southey's wife, and during the first three years of his marriage, he lived in Wordsworth's neighborhood. In 1796 he took opium to allay severe neuralgic pain, and this laid the foundation of a habit which was to exert a baneful influence over his life. To this period belong the ten numbers of the *Watchman* and the publication of the *Juvenile Poems*. In 1798 he wrote his share in the *Lyrical Ballads*. About this time, the Wedgwoods, of Staffordshire, settled on him £150 a year for life. This made him independent of the "bread-and-cheese question" and enabled him to visit Germany, where he studied the language and heard lectures at Göttingen. After his return he went to live in the Lake District, near Wordsworth and Southey. In 1804 he went to Malta for his health, and became confirmed in the use of opium. From 1801 to 1816 he produced only one work of importance, *The Friend*, a periodical which appeared in numbers from June, 1809, to March, 1810. In 1814 he tried to lecture in Bristol, but he was completely under the dominion of opium, and was unable to command his powers, or meet his engagements. He struggled against his infirmity with all the force which his nerveless will could bring to bear; but the odds were hard against him. He wrote in reply to the remonstrances of his old friend and publisher, Cottle: "You have poured oil in the raw and festering wounds of an old friend's conscience, Cottle! but it is oil of vitriol! I have prayed with drops of agony on my brow, trembling not only before the justice of my Master, but even before the mercy of my Redeemer : ' I gave thee so many talents; what hast thou done with them?'" At last he became convinced that single-handed he was unequal to the struggle, and in 1816, he took up his residence in the house of Mr. Gillman, a physician, where he died July 25, 1834.

It ought never to be forgotten that the struggles of the man were often responsible for the sins of the author. At fifteen, Coleridge was a master of abstract thought, but had lost the ability to tread in beaten paths—to use common methods; at twenty-four, he displayed wonderful powers of genius, but they soon passed into the long eclipse of a diseased will. And yet, from fifteen years old to the day of his death, this weak character, this irresolute man, was a power in his own country and age; nor has his influence been unfelt in ours. The wonderful charm of his conversation, the spell of his enthusiasm, influenced the opinions of all the young men of his day who were worth influencing. Carlyle, Julius Hare, John Sterling, De Quincey, and John Stuart Mill bear testimony to the good which he accomplished in the midst of the disaster of his own life.

His Literary Character. The literary character of Coleridge resembles some vast but unfinished palace; all is gigantic, beautiful and rich, but nothing is complete, nothing compact. He was all his days, from his youth to his death, laboring, meditating, projecting; and yet all that he has left us bears marks of imperfection. His mind was dreamy, his genius was multiform, many-sided, and for this reason, perhaps, could not at once seize upon the right point of view. No man, probably, ever thought more, and more intensely, than Coleridge; few ever possessed a vaster treasury of learning and knowledge ; and yet how few of his works are in any way worthy of the undoubted majesty of his genius! Materials, indeed, he has left us in enormous quantity—a store of thoughts and principles, golden masses of reason, either painfully sifted from the rubbish of obscure and forgotten authors, or dug up from the rich depths of his own mind; but these are still in the state of raw materials, or only partially worked.

But the literary character of Coleridge must be judged by its manifestations in four very different departments of thought, while in each of these departments he has left only fragments by which to judge him. As poet, critic, philosopher, and theologian, he has added to the force of English thinking and to the beauty of English expression what it could ill afford to lose.

The Poet. His poetry seems only a prophecy of what he might have done, and yet some of it is what he alone could do. Fancy, beautiful imagery, exquisite versification, are characteristic of nearly all Coleridge's poems, and now and then a daring flight of his imagination is attended by the boldest measures. The best known of his poems are *Religious Musings, Lines on Sunrise in the Valley of Chamouni, Love, Kubla Khan, The Ancient Mariner*, and *Christabel*. His translation of Wallenstein has the reputation of being the finest translation in the English language; and yet it fell almost dead from the press in 1799.

The Critic. As a critic, Coleridge was the leader in the reaction against the deadening influence of the theories of the eighteenth century. The Edinburgh critics had almost persuaded the English readers to believe that Pope was a better poet than Shakespeare. In such a time, a new and original work needs a doughty champion to defend it against the assaults of criticism. But for Coleridge, Wordsworth might have been another Keats. Coleridge was a sympathetic man. In Wordsworth's first attempts, he felt the poetry which Jeffrey could not see, and he set himself at work to find out the principles which must alike underlie his interpretations and Jeffrey's rules. These he set in order, and at once magnified the philosophy of criticism and freed literature from the bondage to which such men as Jeffrey had reduced it. Coleridge was the first who taught that a successful criticism of Shakespeare must depend not upon dogmatic judgment, but upon reverent investigation; and thus he brought it about that Englishmen can admire Shakespeare without the fear of the "dramatic unities" before their eyes.

The Philosopher. As a philosopher, Coleridge began by being a materialist and a Whig,—he ended as a follower of Kant and a Tory. His theories of government and of mental science are characterized by the same sympathy, the same acuteness, and the same lack of method which mark his other thinking. Mr. Mill praises his philosophy as one of moral goodness, and true insight. *The Friend*, the *Aids to Reflection*, the *Church and State*, and the *Lay Sermons*, are the sources from which most of his opinions on these subjects are to be gathered.

The Theologian. As a theologian, Coleridge made perhaps the most definite and sustained effort of his life; but his thought is so fine-spun, and his expression is so involved that it is very hard to understand him. In early youth a Unitarian, he came to be a firm believer in all the doctrines of the Evangelical Christian Church. It is in his religious philosophy that he shows his nearest approach to the common method and practical doctrine of ordinary men; for his own experience had taught him that a man's thinking may have little influence on his action. A fragmentary poet, a careless critic, an unscientific philosopher, a mystical theologian, and an irresolute man, " he suffered an almost life-long punishment for his errors, whilst the world at large has the unwithering fruits of his labors, and his genius, and his sufferings."

Robert Southey (1774–1843) was born at Bristol, where his father carried on the business of a draper (**308–311**). At the age of fourteen he was sent to the famous Westminster School. After spending four years there, he was expelled for writing an article against flogging in public schools and publishing it in a periodical conducted by the boys. The following year he went to Oxford. His friends wished him to take orders in the church, but his religious opinions prevented him. He lingered at Oxford, until Coleridge appeared with his scheme of " Pantisocracy." Quitting Oxford, Southey attempted to raise funds for the enterprise by authorship, and in 1794 published a small volume of poems, which brought neither fame nor profit. His chief reliance, however, was on his epic poem *Joan of Arc*, for which Joseph Cottle, the patron of Coleridge, offered him fifty guineas. After spending six months in Spain, he returned to England, and in 1795 began a life of patient literary toil. He had from the outset an allowance of one hundred and sixty pounds a year, yet he was constantly on the verge of poverty, and not even his philosophy and hopefulness were always proof against the difficulties of his position. In 1804 he took up his residence in Cumberland, where he continued to reside for the remainder of his life. Coleridge and Wordsworth were already there. From being a skeptic and a republican, Southey became a firm believer in Christianity, and a staunch supporter of the English Church and Constitution. In 1813 he was appointed poet-laureate; * and in 1835 received a pension of three hundred pounds a year from the government. During the last four years of his life he had sunk into a state of hopeless imbecility. He died March 21, 1843.

Southey's industry was prodigious. His life was very quiet, and all his time was given to literary labor. One of his letters to a friend tells how his days were spent: "Three pages of history after breakfast; then to transcribe and copy for the press, or to make any selections and biographies, or what else suits my humor till dinner-time. From dinner-time till tea I read, write letters, see the newspaper, and very often indulge in a siesta. After tea I go to poetry, and correct and re-write and copy till I am tired; and then turn to anything else till supper. And this is my life." The list of his writings numbers *one hundred and nine* volumes. In addition to these he contributed to the *Annual Review* fifty-two articles, to the *Foreign Quarterly* three, to the *Quarterly* ninety-four. The composition of these works was a small part of the labor they involved: they are all full of research.

His Poetry. Southey's success as a poet fell far short of his ambition. *Joan of Arc*, a juvenile production, was received with favor by most of the critical journals on account of its republican doctrines. *Madoc*, completed in 1799, was not published till 1805. Upon this poem he was contented to rest his fame. It is founded on one of the legends connected with the early history of America. Madoc, a Welsh prince of the twelfth century, is represented as making the discovery of the Western world. His contests with the Mexicans, and the ultimate conversion of that people from their cruel idolatry, form its main action. Though the poem is crowded with scenes of more than possible splendor,—of more than human cruelty, courage, and superstition,—the effect is languid. *Thalaba* was published in 1801, and the *Curse of Kehama* in 1810. The first is a tale of Arabian enchantment, full of magicians, dragons, and monsters; and in the second the poet has selected for his ground-

* The honor was offered to Walter Scott at this time, and he declined it.

work the still more unmanageable mythology of the Hindoos. The poems are written in irregular and wandering rhythm—the *Thalaba* altogether without rhyme; and the language abounds in an affected simplicity, and in obtrusions of vulgar and puerile phraseology. *Kehama* was followed, at an interval of four years, by *Roderick, the Last of the Goths*, a poem in blank verse, more modest and credible than its predecessors.

The tone of Southey's poems is exaggerated. His personages, like his scenes, have something unreal, phantom-like, dreamy about them. His robe of inspiration sits gracefully and majestically upon him, but it is too voluminous in its folds, and too heavy in its texture for the motion of real existence.

His Prose. Southey's prose works are valuable on account of their learning. The *Life of Nelson* (**311**), written to furnish young seamen with a simple narrative of the exploits of England's greatest naval hero, has perhaps never been surpassed for the perfection of its style. In his principal works—*The Book of the Church, The Lives of the British Admirals, The Life of Wesley,* a *History of Brazil,* and a *History of the Peninsular War*—we find the same clear, vigorous English; we find also the strong prejudice and political and literary partiality, which detract from his many excellent qualities as a writer and as a man.

In this chapter we have considered:—

The Lake School — Wordsworth, Coleridge, and Southey.

1. *William Wordsworth.*
    a. *The Defects and Merits of His Poetry.*
2. *Samuel Taylor Coleridge.*
    a. *His Literary Character.*
    b. *The Poet.*
    c. *The Critic.*
    d. *The Philosopher.*
    e. *The Theologian.*
3. *Robert Southey.*
    a. *His Poetry.*
    b. *His Prose.*

CHAPTER XXVII.

THE ENGLISH LITERATURE OF THE NINETEENTH CENTURY.

THE early years of the present century were years of conflict and excitement. The mind was wrought to the highest pitch, now of fear, and now of triumph. England fought for the liberties of Europe; at times the struggle seemed to be for her own existence. The literature of a people always reflects something of the prevalent tone of its age, and we may therefore expect to find the chief compositions of the first thirty years of this century marked by intense feeling. There is no other age in English history which exhibits such an array of masters of song. At the close of the reign of George III., in 1820, there were living in England ten poets whose writings commanded the attention of all English readers. Then Crabbe, Wordsworth, Coleridge, Southey, Scott, Campbell, Moore, Byron, Shelley, and Keats were stars in the literary firmament. They gave voice to the passionate states of the mind of society which demand expression in song. "The Victorian age" following this group of poets is distinguished by an unusual number of dignified writers of prose. The calmer inquiries into politics, philosophy, art, and physical science, have been prosecuted in the more tranquil period.

Poetry is the earlier expression of every literature. The first writers whose works are preserved are the writers of verse. The rhythm of their song, the pictures of their excited fancy, the stories they tell, catch and enchain the popular attention. Until our century, the patronage of the English court, the heartiest sympathies of the English scholar, and the applause of the people had been given to the writer of song. Prose is now in the ascendant over poetry. An illustration of the fact is at hand. Two elaborate works were recently published in England ; both written to face the test of scholarly criticism, and to gain the interest of the common readers. One is in prose; it gives strange opinions on puzzling historical questions, and packs twelve duodecimo volumes. The other has the fascination of rhythmic verse, of scholarship, of mythical story, and has conceded to it a high place among the masterly poems of the century. But Morris's *Earthly Paradise* has a limited sale, and comparatively few readers; while every public library, and thousands of private libraries, have well-thumbed copies of Froude's *History of England*. It is not that the culture of the poet has declined; the tact of the writer of prose and the thoughtfulness of the masses of readers have improved. Spenser, Milton and Byron are not read as they once were. What has brought about the change? There is the same lofty theme, there is the same resounding line, there is the same poetic inspiration. But the taste and thought of the readers have changed. They are in sympathy with what is called the practical spirit of the age. They lead to the instructive novel, to books of travel, to biography, to history. They compel readers to seek for information, as well as for entertainment and elegant culture in literature.

Forces which have wrought this change in popular thought and taste should be noted. (1.) The newspaper, the mightiest social force of this century, by publishing the interesting facts of the day, has created a desire for information, and has led thoughtful people to search after knowledge of facts in history, in commerce, in geography. (2.) The growth of manufactures, and the improvements in the methods of agriculture, by increasing the number of prosperous workmen has increased the number of alert thinkers. (3.) Extended intervals of peace have been favorable to the sobriety of national thought. (4.) The general acquaintance of English scholars with the thought and literature of other nations has broadened and deepened the English thinking. And (5.) fitted to the more practical thought of our time, is the fact that the writers of the previous century had developed an artistic style in prose, so that the prose-writers of to-day have at their command such charms of expression as were not dreamed of even in the days of John Milton and Jeremy Taylor.

The writers of this century, then, are supplying what is demanded by an increasing number of thoughtful readers, and in so doing, are marking out a literary epoch. The chief external influence has come from Germany. Coleridge introduced it largely, and he has been followed in the work by Thomas Carlyle. In former pages we have spoken of the Elizabethan age as under Italian influence, of the Augustan age as under French influence, and our age, doubtless, will be regarded by the future historian as the age of German influence.

The New Literature of History. During this century greater progress has been made in History than in any other department of letters. A new impulse was given to the study by the publication of the first volume of Niebuhr's *Roman History* in Germany, in 1811. This remarkable work taught scholars not only to estimate more accurately the value of the original authorities, but also to enter more fully into the spirit of antiquity, and to think and feel as the Romans felt and thought. In the treatment of Modern History the advance has been equally striking. An *historical sense* has grown up. A writer on any period of modern history is now expected to produce in support of his facts the testimony of credible contemporary witnesses; while the public records of most of the great European nations, now rendered accessible to students, have imposed upon historians a labor, and opened sources of information, quite unknown to the historical writers of the preceding century.

Bishop Connop Thirlwall and George Grote are the most eminent English writers upon Ancient History, both having produced *Histories of Greece*, superior to any existing in other European languages. Thirlwall's work is dry and unattractive to the general reader; but it is scientific, thorough, and liberal in its spirit. Grote's history was written under peculiar circumstances. The author was a banker, and during part of his career he was an active radical politician. His sentiments were democratic, and his sympathies, throughout his work, are heartily enlisted on the side of the Athenian democracy. He had not received a university education. While a clerk in a banking-house, he set himself at work to master the Greek language and literature, to make himself a scholar in Greek geography, antiquities and history. His toilsome work was so well done that all readers came to look upon him as the most competent of Englishmen to deal with Grecian history and letters.

A prominent place among the historians of England belongs to **John Lingard** (1771–1851). Born at Winchester, he pursued his studies at the College of Douay, received holy orders in the Church of Rome, and passed the last forty years of his life in scholarly retirement, holding the small preferment belonging to the Catholic Church at Hornby, in Lancashire. Beloved for his sincere piety and his genuine worth, his Church honored in him a zealous and able champion. High ecclesiastical preferment was warmly urged upon him, but was steadfastly refused, out of devotion to his historical labors. To these he brought signal abilities and unflagging industry. *A History of England from the First Invasion by the Romans to the Accession of William and Mary* (1819–30) is his finest contribution to literature, though his *Antiquities of the Anglo-Saxon Church* and a number of controversial essays exhibit the same dignity of thought, learning, and mental acumen. Dr. Lingard was a student of original authorities and a master in clear and forcible narration. His field of research was nearly the same as that of Hume ; and while his style is less graphic and brilliant, the material of his work is far more scholarly and original. Disclosing as he does a consistent Catholic view of England's religious and political development, he could hardly escape the oft-repeated charge of partisanship. His opponents did not accuse him of negligence or of superficiality. They took issue chiefly with his account of the Anglo-Saxon period of English History, and with the coloring which he gave to his portraits of eminent ecclesiastical and political characters. The harsh strictures of those earlier critics, the reviewers of the *Edinburgh* and the *London Quarterly*, were characteristic of the state of feeling then prevailing among the upholders of the Established Church. Lingard defended himself with dignity and fortified his disputed positions anew in a revised version of his *History*. This received from him a prodigious amount of care and labor ; it was published in 1839–40, and is highly esteemed by all competent authorities. During the later years of Dr. Lingard's life, he enjoyed an annual pension of £300 from the Queen, in itself no slight witness to his learning and character.

Lord Macaulay. The most versatile writer of the century is Thomas Babington Macaulay (1800–1859). In descriptive poetry **(325)**, in criticism, in essay-writing, in political papers, in oratory, and especially in historical narration, he has shown himself to be a master. He was born in England, but his lineage was Scotch. His father, Zachary Macaulay, a merchant, was an ardent philanthropist and one of the earliest opponents of the slave trade. At Cambridge, Macaulay won high honors. Leaving the university, he began the study of the law, but, while at his books, he suddenly achieved a literary reputation by an article on **1825.]** Milton **(341)** in the *Edinburgh Review*. This was the first of a long series of brilliant literary and historical essays contributed to the same periodical. His career as a member of Parliament was brilliant, and his work in the East Indian service was significant, but it is as a man of letters that his name will be longest remembered.

His *Lays of Ancient Rome* are the best known of his poems; but the lines upon his political defeat at Edinburgh in 1847 are the finest. His Essays and his History will always give him a high place among English classics. His style has been well described by Dean Milman. "Its characteristics were vigor and animation, copiousness, clearness ; above all, sound English, now a rare excellence. . . . . As to its clearness, one may read a sentence of Macaulay twice to judge of its full force, never to comprehend its meaning. His English was pure, both in idiom and in words, pure to fastidiousness."

Macaulay's *Essays* **(341, 342)** are philosophical and historical disquisitions, embracing a vast range of subjects ; but the larger number, and the most important, relate to English History. These Essays, however, were only preparatory to his *History of England*. In the opening chapter of that grand work, he says : "I purpose to write the *History of England* from the accession of King James the Second down to a time which is in the memory of men still living." His purpose was not carried out, for the narrative is brought down only to the death of William the Third, and the latter portion of what is written is fragmentary. In a review of Sir James Mackintosh's *History of the Revolution*, Macaulay observed that a "*History of England*, written throughout in this manner, would be the most fascinating book in the language. It would be more in request at the circulating libraries than the last novel." The unexampled popularity of his own History verified the prediction.

Henry Hallam (1778–1859) **(337)**, though inferior in graces of style, was superior to Lord Macaulay as a judicial historian. He was one of the early contributors to the *Edinburgh Review*. His criticism in that journal, in 1808, of Sir Walter Scott's edition of Dryden's works was marked by that power of discrimination and impartial judgment which characterized all his subsequent writings.

The result of his long-continued studies first appeared in his *View of the State of Europe during the Middle Ages*, published in 1818, exhibiting, in a series of historical dissertations, a comprehensive survey of the chief circumstances that can interest a philosophical inquirer during the period usually denominated the Middle Ages. Mr. Hallam's next work was *The Constitutional History of England from the Accession of Henry VII. to the Death of George II.*, published in 1827; and his third great production was *An Introduction to the Literature of Europe, in the Fifteenth, Sixteenth and Seventeenth Centuries*, which appeared in 1837–39. His latter years were saddened by the loss of his two sons, the eldest of whom is the subject of Tennyson's *In Memoriam.*

Henry Hart Milman. The oft-repeated reproach once directed against the English people, that Gibbon was their only ecclesiastical historian, has been removed by Henry Hart Milman (1791–1868), Dean of St. Paul's, one of the best-balanced and most highly cultivated intellects that England has produced. For many years he held the professorship of Poetry at Oxford, and at different times he published *The Martyr of Antioch*, the *Fall of Jerusalem*, and other poems. But it is upon his historical productions that his fame rests. The *History of the Jews*, the *History of Christianity*, and the *History of Latin Christianity*, have taken their place among English classics. Certain indispensable qualities of a great historian,—a mind free from prejudice, keen critical sagacity, and a faculty for determining the value of evidence — were possessed by him to a remarkable degree. He grappled with a subject extending over a vast period of time, and a wide area of human activity, and dealing with the subtlest and most intricate phenomena. His themes present difficulties from which any but the boldest would shrink.

Henry Thomas Buckle (1821–1862) was the son of a prosperous merchant. As a child he was delicate in health, and backward in his studies. At his own request, he was taken from school in his fourteenth year. From this time his education was carried on by means of foreign travel and reading. The death of his father, in 1840, had left him in independent circumstances. The influence of his mother combined with a peculiar self-confidence to awaken in Buckle a literary ambition to which he consistently devoted his life. At the age of nineteen, the idea of his history was already dimly before his mind, and he set about preparing himself for its execution by studying the literature and languages of the countries through which he traveled. In 1850 he knew nineteen languages, and in seven of them he could talk or write with ease. The first volume of the *History of Civilization in England* was published in 1857, at the author's expense, the second in 1861. The book met with quick success. It attracted readers by the clearness and beauty of the style, as well as by the novelty of its views, and was the topic of discussion in all the leading Reviews. Buckle's claim to lasting fame is not based upon his popularity, nor upon the striking character of his opinions, but upon the purpose of his work. It was an attempt to put into elaborate and scientific form the scattered theories and vague guesses which, until his day, stood for a science of history.

The book is open to many criticisms; its argument is often inadequate; its statements inaccurate. Two facts should be kept in mind while attempting to form a just estimate of Buckle's work : first, he is dealing with generalizations, which he applies only to the mass of mankind, avowedly leaving the individual out of account. Nearly all the criticism urged against him, as an opponent of religious belief and moral conduct, misapprehends his true position in this respect. Secondly, his work is but a fragment of a fragment — only two volumes in the civilization of one country, when his original plan had been for the history of civilization itself. He worked with untiring industry, until the strain of intense application, constant attacks of sickness, and grief for the death of his mother, necessitated change of scene. In October, 1861, Buckle left England for the East. He died in Palestine, in May, 1862.

The eminent modern historians have shown not only unflagging zeal in research, but also that sustained imaginative power which can truly re-create past epochs. **John Richard Green** (1837-

1883), perhaps the most gifted writer of the school of Froude, Stubbs, and Freeman, passed away in the fullness of his intellectual powers. His life was nurtured by scholarly influences. Born, educated, and esteemed at Oxford, he slighted university honors to devote himself to varied and systematic reading. Receiving his degree in 1860, he took holy orders, and for several years gave his best and most loving energies to pastoral labors, mainly among the London poor. By 1867, incessant self-devotion had brought him to the early stages of consumption. Through the friendship of Archbishop Tait, he was made honorary librarian at Lambeth Palace, and was enabled to give himself exclusively to historical research. Although rapidly failing health soon forced him to divide the seasons between England and Southern Europe, his pen was busy and his intellectual activity ceaseless. His contributions to the *Saturday Review*, afterwards republished as *Stray Studies from England and Italy*, showed the nervous, graphic style and keen yet genial analysis of men and things which marked his later work. When *A Short History of the English People* was published (1875), the master hand of the true historian was recognized at once. Scholars, critics, and readers united in almost unqualified praise, and Green was inspired to loftier aims. His *History of the English People* (1878) was the fruit of more extended studies and of laborious revision. Green was a patriot of an unusual type. His industry, his philosophical insight, his versatility, his power of clear, vivid portraiture were all concentrated and quickened by his ardent longing to make Englishmen share his belief in the grand future of a nobly-descended race. Full of this ambition, he prepared his *Making of England* (1881), which portrays the obscure era between 449 and 827 A. D. Writing "under the shadow of death," his high literary standard was in no wise relaxed, and he eagerly went on through months of growing weakness to compose the *Conquest of England*. So clearly had he conceived its scope, and so systematic and thorough-going were his notes, that his widow was able, with slight assistance, to edit and publish it after his death.

Edward A. Freeman (1823–1892), one of the most industrious and productive of English historians, has also been among the most influential. Born of a good Staffordshire family, he received his university training at Oxford, becoming a scholar of Trinity in 1841, and a Fellow in 1845. Having inherited a com-

fortable fortune and made a happy marriage early in life, he adopted
no profession, but established himself on an estate in Somerset, amid
the typical surroundings of an English country gentleman.   The
Tractarian movement, all-important to the university world at that
time, had incited him to the study of architecture and church history.   His first important publication was a *History of Architecture*
(1849), rapidly followed by other archæological writings.   Extending his field of labor, he produced a long series of historical works.
The History and Conquests of the Saracens (1856); *A History of Federal
Government* (1863); *The History of the Norman Conquest* (1867–76);
The Growth of the English Constitution (1872); three series of *Historical Essays* (1872–9); *Comparative Politics* (1873); *The Ottoman
Power in Europe* (1877); *Subject and Neighboring Lands of Venice*
and *The Historical Geography of Europe* (1881); *The Reign of William
Rufus and the Accession of Henry I.* (1882); *Greater Greece and Greater
Britain* (1888), and a *History of Sicily*, for which he was still collect-
ing material at the time of his death, are perhaps the most important.   During many years he was a constant contributor to the
Saturday Review.   In 1881 he visited the United States, delivering
courses of lectures, and observing American local institutions with
keen and friendly interest.   In 1884 he was made a Fellow of Oriel
College, Oxford, and succeeded Bishop Stubbs as Regius Professor of
Modern History.   His industry and power of accomplishment were
prodigious.   No less keen than his enthusiasm for research was his
interest in every-day affairs.   His convictions were positive—even
dogmatic; and he was intolerant of differences in intellectual method,
whether exhibited in the past or the present.   His judgment of
events was always influenced by his firm belief in the historic unity
of the English nation, in the logical developments of Church and
State.   All these characteristics are disclosed in his historical writing.   Conscientious in research, and candid in dealing with the
materials of history, he was also firm in maintaining his conclusions,
and never flinched from controversy.   His style is usually clear and
forcible, although the habit of the journalist sometimes makes him
prolix and diffuse.   The student of history must own a great debt to
his minute accuracy, his originality and courage, and his faithfulness in tracing the original sources of our knowledge.   He was a
comprehensive thinker as well as a zealous antiquarian.   The men
of his school have made it impossible for the historian to vaunt
himself in second-hand information, or deliberately to maintain a
partisan bias.

James Anthony Froude (1818–1894) the most brilliant of modern English historians, was reared under influences stimulating to
mental development.   Entering Oxford University in 1837, he was
drawn into intimate association with Keble, Pusey, and Newman.
He soon recoiled from their theological views.   His religious life

moved towards independence. *Shadows of the Clouds*, his first publication, describes varying phases of spiritual doubt. Becoming a
Fellow of Exeter College in 1842, he took deacon's orders in the
Established Church. Shortly after, his second book, *The Nemesis
of Faith*, was published. It was so boldly iconoclastic as to make
his university position untenable. In 1849 he sacrificed his flattering prospects and beloved associations, leaving Oxford, and forsaking
the secure paths of the church for the precarious field of literature.
Writing for the *Westminster Review* and other periodicals, he began
serious historical studies in preparation for his *magnum opus*, *The
History of England from the Fall of Wolsey to the Defeat of the Spanish
Armada* (1856–1869). The period chosen is rich in material for controversy. Froude made a brilliant study of the spirit, the growth,
and the results of the Protestant Reformation. Every question affecting that movement had absorbing interest for him. In a clear, rapid,
direct style, often dramatic and picturesque, always forcible and suggestive, he strove to portray events as they had appeared to contemporary observers, to estimate personages according to their motives.
The criticism called forth by this method has amounted to denunciation. Every fault, from wilful perversion to careless inaccuracy, has
been ascribed to Froude by those who disagree with his inferences; but
even those whose taste he offends by his high lights and deep shadows,
acknowledge profound obligation to him as an honest thinker, a great
and daring historical painter. He was a painstaking and industrious
worker. For several years he was editor of *Fraser's Magazine*. He
also edited the voluminous Carlyle memorials (1881–1882), and he
was the historian and apologist of Julius Cæsar (1879). These writings and the *Short Studies on Great Subjects*, in four volumes (1867–
1877), show the wide range of his literary interests. In 1872, he
made a lecturing tour in the United States. Expeditions of semi-
official nature to Africa, Australia, the West Indies, and other colonies, emphasized his influence as a literary statesman. Froude's last
historical work was called into form by a curious, even dramatic,
reversal of popular judgment. Professor Freeman had been his
virulent critic for years. When Freeman died, in 1892, Oxford
University invited Froude to succeed him as Regius Professor of
Modern History. *The Life and Letters of Erasmus* embodied his first
professional lectures, and gave his mature views of many questions
which were hotly debated when he left Oxford in 1849.

THE LITERATURE OF PHILOSOPHY.

Many contributions have been made to the English literature of Philosophy during the period under consideration. The centers of philosophical influence have been at the Universities of Glasgow and Edinburgh in Scotland, at Oxford and Cambridge in England. In later years the scientific schools of Sheffield and Birmingham have made their influence felt, as one after another their graduates have been rewarded for their industry by distinction at home and abroad.

The Scottish School. The thinking of the Scottish philosophers of this century is a protest against the skepticism which was prevalent in religion and philosophy during the eighteenth century. This Scottish thinking presents very little that is striking or original. Certain well-defined features, however, are characteristic, to a greater or less extent, of all the writers of this school. They adopt systematically the method of induction, they pursue their investigation by means of consciousness, and they believe in the existence of principles prior to and independent of experience. The practical merit of the school lies in the fact that it once more enlisted talent and scholarship on the side of morality and religion.

Thomas Reid (1710–1796), the best representative of the Scottish school, lived in the last century. His life was a singularly quiet one. At the age of twelve he entered Marischal College, Aberdeen, and was graduated in 1726. He remained in the college as its librarian for ten years, spending his time in hard study. In 1737 he took charge of a country parish. At the age of thirty-eight, he published in the Transactions of the Royal Society of London, *An Essay on Quantity*. In 1752 he was elected to the chair of Moral Philosophy in King's College, where he was influential in bringing about many improvements in the system of university education. The professorship of Moral Philosophy in the University of Glasgow was given to him in 1763. The following year the *Inquiry into the Human Mind on the Principles of Common Sense* was published, and at once fixed his reputation and determined the course of subsequent Scottish Philosophy. Occasional

essays and reviews in the publications of the Glasgow Literary
Society are all that he wrote before 1785, when his *Essays on the
Intellectual Powers of Man* appeared, followed by *Essays on the Active
Powers* in 1788. He died October 7, 1796.

Reid's philosophy has been the object of almost equally exaggerated praise and blame. His admirers have tried to find in his
works much that he certainly never accomplished, while his critics
have discovered incongruities where he had attempted nothing.
He was a patient, industrious thinker, whose sphere of greatest
usefulness was in clearing up what was vague and contradictory in
the theories of his predecessors. Reid was no rhetorician; he
was a shrewd, sagacious Scotchman, whose literary style was simple
and unadorned, but very clear, and characterized by a purity of
English idiom quite uncommon in writers of philosophy.

Dugald Stewart (1753–1828) was the son of the Edinburgh
Professor of Mathematics, and connected on the side of both father
and mother with two of the most influential classes in Scotland—
the Presbyterian ministry and the Edinburgh bar. His education in Scotland was intended to fit him for a further course at
Oxford, but the latter part of this plan was never carried out. In
1775 he was elected assistant and successor to his father, and in
1785, on the resignation of Dr. Adam Ferguson, he was appointed
to the chair of Moral Philosophy in the University of Edinburgh.
This office he retained until 1810, when he retired in favor of
Dr. Thomas Brown. His principal works are:—*Elements of the
Philosophy of the Human Mind* (1792, 1814, 1827), *Outlines of Moral
Philosophy*, *Account of Adam Smith* (1793), *Account of Reid* (1802),
Philosophical Essays (1810), *Dissertations* (1815, 1821, 1827), *Active
and Moral Powers* (1828). His lectures on *Political Economy* were
published in 1856.

Stewart was the expounder of the doctrines of Reid, and any
claim of his to philosophical reputation can rest on very little else.
He had elegant taste and reliable judgment. He was a man eminently fitted to be a disciple; for the caution which would have
been a fatal weakness in an investigator, made him an admirable
commentator.

As a teacher, Stewart exercised a wide and powerful influence.
His dignified treatment of his subject recommended it to the

attention of his critical hearers, and the genial character of the man himself emphasized and made permanent the first impression. Among the young men who listened to his lectures on philosophy and political economy, were many who were afterwards distinguished—Lord Brougham, Lord Palmerston, and Lord John Russell, in politics; Sir Walter Scott, Francis Jeffrey, and Sydney Smith, in literature. Some of them have carried out in practical measures the doctrines he taught them, while nearly all have borne testimony to the inspiration which they received in his class-room.

Thomas Brown (1778–1820) entered the University of Edinburgh in 1792, where Stewart was then lecturing, and in the following year had the courage to wait upon his professor and read to him some critical observations upon his philosophy. Stewart declined to enter into any controversy, but from that time took a paternal interest in the career of the brilliant scholar. Brown began to study law, but abandoned it for medicine, with which he occupied himself from 1798 to 1803. At twenty years of age he published a volume refuting Erasmus Darwin's *Zöonomia*. The first edition of his *Essay on Cause and Effect* appeared in 1804. In 1810 Brown was chosen to assist Stewart in his professorship at the Edinburgh University, and from that time he discharged all the duties of the position. With the exception of a few essays and four volumes of forgotten poems, Brown's writings were, from this time, limited to the lectures which he delivered to the students of the University. He died in 1820.

The philosophy of Brown is a combination of that of Reid and Stewart, with the analysis of the sensational school in France. For a time his popularity as a teacher and thinker was unbounded. His brilliant rhetoric, his ingenious analysis, his enthusiastic temperament, made his personal influence very great, and even kept alive the interest in his published lectures for twenty years. Brown's philosophy never met the expectations which his brilliant boyhood raised; his theories were nearly always the premature hints of his youth, elaborated and adorned by his powers of analysis and rhetoric. He lacked the conscientious industry of Reid and the critical erudition of Hamilton, but he was able to inspire young men with an elevated idea of literary taste and with a firm belief in the spirituality of the soul.

William Sterling Hamilton (1788-1856) was the son of the Professor of Anatomy and Botany in the University of Glasgow. He went to Oxford in 1807. His habits of study and research had been early formed, and even during his undergraduate years, he was known as the most learned Aristotelian in the University, but he owed little to the actual teaching of Oxford. Up to the year 1812 he had intended to practice medicine, but suddenly decided in favor of law, and, in 1813, passed his examination as Advocate at the Edinburgh Bar. In 1816 he was adjudged heir to Sir Robert Hamilton, of Preston. Sir William Hamilton's career at the bar was not brilliant. In 1820 he offered himself as candidate for the professorship of moral philosophy in the University of Edinburgh, left vacant by the death of Dr. Thomas Brown. The election was in the hands of the Edinburgh Town Council, and was conducted on strict party principles, so that in spite of his undoubted superiority of attainments, Sir William Hamilton was rejected in favor of Professor Wilson, who was a Tory. In 1821 Hamilton was appointed Associate Professor of Civil History at the University. The duties of this position were very light, the compensation in proportion, and during part of his time, Sir William was not paid at all; nevertheless, he did his work with energy and enthusiasm. In 1836 Hamilton was elected to the professorship of logic and metaphysics in the University of Edinburgh. This position he held for more than twenty years. In 1844 he was struck down by paralysis. The remaining twelve years of his life were passed in great physical weakness and suffering, but his intellectual power seemed unabated. It was during this period that he published his edition of Reid's works, gathered together his materials for a treatise on Logic and for a life of Luther, and undertook the editing of Stewart's works. He died May 6, 1856.

Sir William Hamilton, like Brown, taught a philosophy which differed from the tenets of Reid and Stewart, but like Brown again he never completed his own system. His fame is, to a very great extent, the victim of the habit of procrastination. He always put off writing until forced to the effort by some outward necessity. Then, too, the peculiar discursiveness of his mind made him look at his subject from so many points of view that his researches in all directions overwhelmed him with a quantity of material too great for him to set in order. Besides his lectures to his classes on logic and metaphysics, his notes in the editions of Reid and of Stewart, and the *Discussions of Philosophy*, Sir William Hamilton has written very little; and yet we find him in 1840 elected Corresponding Member of the Institute of France, while the University of Leyden conferred upon him the title of Doctor of Divinity. Until 1839 Sir William contributed occasional articles to the *Edinburgh Review* on education, medicine and philosophy; but after his appointment to the professorship of logic, he was occupied by the duties of his position.

Hamilton's metaphysics is, in the main, an application of the Kantian method to the premises of the Scottish philosophy. His immense learning and critical taste made him often prefer exactness to clearness of style, and hence he is often accused of unnecessary obscurity. Of this charge, M. Cousin emphatically declares him guiltless. As a teacher, Sir William Hamilton was successful rather from the white heat of his own enthusiasm than from any intrinsic good in his method. As a man he was resolute in holding a position, dogmatic and controversial. His influence upon the life and thought of his time, was to give an impulse towards profounder thinking, and towards a higher estimate of the mind of man.

The English School. While the Scottish Philosophy in the hands of Brown and Hamilton was tending more and more to identify itself with metaphysics, a wider movement was going on in England. James Mill, a pupil of Dugald Stewart, may be named as the first of the group of thinkers who, from the same starting-point of Common Sense as the Scottish school, have extended the jurisdiction of philosophy to all the important social, political, and scientific problems of the day. In this movement are found men of the most contrasted character, and of interests the most opposed; but they are united here by an earnest desire to reach the truth, by a strong impulse of practical benevolence, and by the patient use of scientific investigation.

James Mill (1773–1836) was the author of the *History of British India*, (1817–18), and of the *Analysis of the Human Mind* (1829). The history displayed such stores of information that it caused the directors of the East India Company, in spite of the author's censure of their conduct of affairs, to give him a place in their home establishment. He eventually became head of the department of Indian correspondence. James Mill was a man of strong character. Although his name is intimately associated with that of Bentham, he was no servile follower, but a man of acute and independent views. The *Analysis of the Human Mind* is the first elaborate and scientific exposition of the sensational and associational philosophy. It resolves all mental exercises into sensations and ideas, with laws of association connecting and combining them. He wrote articles in the *Encyclopædia Britannica*, and was an important contributor to the *Westminster Review*. His *Elements of Political Economy* was published in 1821–22, and presented in a precise and clear style the views of Ricardo, who was at that time unknown to the majority of English readers. James Mill, as a critic and as an original thinker, was strongly tinctured by the influences of the eighteenth century, of which, indeed, he may be called the last representative. He was a man of remarkable conversational ability, and his personal influence kept about him a score or young men who came to be known as the Westminster Review school. They followed Bentham in morals, and Mill in metaphysics. From the narrow, the partial, and the fanatical part of Mill's teaching they gradually fell away; but to his earnestness, sincerity and enthusiasm, the careers of men like George Grote, John Arthur Roebuck, and Mr. Grant, still bear grateful testimony.

Jeremy Bentham (1748–1832). The founder of the "Utilitarian School" was born in London, where he spent most of his life. His father was a shrewd attorney, who took great pride in the mental precocity displayed by his son, and cherished the hope of seeing him some time Lord Chancellor. At the age of twelve, Bentham was so far recovered from the ill health of his earlier years that he was entered as a commoner at Oxford. His life there was not happy, for his high estimate of his own ability, and his sensitiveness to the opinion of others, were constantly subjecting him to suffering. He took his degree of A. B. in 1763, and shortly afterward commenced the study of law. He listened to Blackstone's lectures with feelings of protest, though he did not at that time set himself up as a critic. Bentham took his degree of A. M.

at the age of eighteen, and at twenty-four was called to the bar. The hopes of a successful career, which his remarkable attainments had inspired, were all disappointed; his temperament utterly unfitted him for the practice of English law as it then stood, and he employed himself in planning for the reconstruction of English jurisprudence on the basis of Utility. His fierce attacks on law abuses and on lawyers naturally raised against him a great deal of prejudice, and it was forty years before he gained the respectful attention of the English public. During all this time he worked with an unwavering faith in himself and in the ultimate triumph of the principles which he advocated. He became the acknowledged head of a school of young men who were Radicals in politics and Utilitarians in morals, and although nearly every one of his disciples found subsequent reasons to differ with him in his most important doctrines, he was for many years one of the great influences in English thought. In 1823 he supplied the money to set up the *Westminster Review* as the Radical organ. The first editor of the *Review*, Sir John Bowring, has compiled Bentham's works in eleven volumes (1843). Bentham was a Utilitarian to the last; for he bequeathed his dead body to his friend Dr. Smith, for the purpose of dissection.

As a philosopher Bentham's keen sense of justice made him quick to see abuses in practical life; his critical power enabled him to discover incongruities in schemes of philosophy; but his self-esteem and lack of sympathy made him too ready to believe that what he did not see did not exist. It is limited to utility, and stops short with the business interests of the individual and society. As a system it is inadequate. But the principles which were utterly insufficient to account for a moral nature in man or for character in a nation were well adapted to practical reform in the science and method of jurisprudence. In this field Bentham has been the direct or the indirect source of nearly every improvement of the present century. His pages are the storehouses from which modern legislators and jurists pilfer. The work from which the general reader will obtain the best idea of Bentham's system is the *Theory of Legislation*.

John Stuart Mill (1806-1873). The childhood of this acute thinker was made aged by a pedantic training; the happiness of his early manhood was almost destroyed by the excessive development of his analytical powers, and his whole life was a pathetic attempt to find satisfaction for the cravings of an ardent nature in the habits of thought which an artificial education had imposed.

In 1823 Mill became a clerk in the East India Company. There he remained until he was appointed examiner, only two years before the abolition of the Company in 1858. In 1865, under somewhat peculiar circumstances, he was elected to the House of Commons from Westminster. He refused to take any part in the canvass or to incur any expense; he declined to give any of his time or labor to the interests of the election, and declared his belief that women were entitled to representation in Parliament on the same terms with men. Mr. Mill's career as a member of the House was the rather unattractive one of the man who makes it his business to do what is left undone or thought not worth the doing by others. He was prominent in his advocacy of the Irish interests, and of Northern principles in the Civil War of the United States. On the dissolution of Parliament in 1868, he was not re-elected, and from that time he took no active part in public business.

His career as an author began with frequent contributions to journals committed to liberal views in politics and philosophy. He gained access to the *Westminster Review* through his connection with Bentham, and was one of its most laborious supporters, although its management was not in accordance with his personal views. From 1834 to 1840, as the *London and Westminster*, he conducted it himself. Mr. Mill's reputation was established by his *System of Logic* (1843). The *Principles of Political Economy* appeared in 1848, and his *Examination of Sir William Hamilton' Philosophy* in 1865. In the *Logic* his acceptance of the tenets of the sensational school leads him to lay great stress upon induction, and makes him utterly unsatisfied with the theories of the syllogism offered by Whately and others. The *Political Economy* is not confined to abstract theories, but treats of practical applications as well. Able discussions of most of the questions of the day which are to be found in its pages make it the most satisfactory treatise on the subject.

Mr. Mill's vigorous criticism of Sir William Hamilton's *Philos ophy* demands attention on account of its polemical as well as its philosophical value. The rival schools of Intuition and Experience are here represented by two acknowledged champions, and the various points at issue are stubbornly contested. The *Essay on Liberty* was written to emphasize the importance of variety in types of character, and has been one of the most influential of Mr. Mill's efforts. The essay on *The Subjection of Women* is an eloquent plea for greater freedom of effort for the sex, and shows in a clear light the ardor of sentiment which was hidden under Mr. Mill's uncompromising logic.

George Henry Lewes (1817–1878) occupies a somewhat anomalous position in the literature of the nineteenth century. His education was desultory, his career erratic. His taste for philosophical research seems to have displayed itself early, but as it was coupled with the necessity of earning his own living, he could indulge it only in the intervals of other employments. He began the study of medicine, but could not overcome a constitutional horror of the dissecting-room, and therefore studied anatomy and physiology only as a part of his general education. Gradually he drifted into a literary career as that for which he was best fitted. His early works—plays, poems, and novels—were written to gain a subsistence for himself while he went on with the studies which were to fit him for work in the more serious departments of thought. From 1841 to 1878 he supplied articles on topics of general interest to nearly all the leading magazines of England, and twice in that time he filled the position of editor (*The Leader*, 1851–1854; *Fortnightly*, 1865–6). Mr. Lewes endeavored to make philosophy popular and practical. He was a Positivist, and held the social opinions of an advanced Liberal. His work is always original, bold, and suggestive; he insists upon doubt and experiment as necessary steps in scientific method, and is a most painstaking illustrator of his own doctrine. His efforts have been fragmentary, and have gone over much ground. To the last he was a man of promise rather than of accomplishment. His principal writings are:—*Biographical History of Philosophy* (1857), *Comte's Philosophy of the Sciences* (1853), *Life of Goethe* (1855), *Aristotle* (1864), *Problems of Life and Mind:* I. *The Foundations of a Creed* (1874), II. (1875), III. (1877).

Influence of the Clergy.—The nineteenth century has favored the diffusion of thought. It has thereby increased the number of questions which have clamored for solution, because they have involved the interests of the common people. In all attempts at settling these questions the clergy of England have borne an honorable and important part. With patient industry some of them have worked to bring knowledge within the reach of the people, and with large-hearted sympathy they have tried to lighten the burdens which increased intelligence sometimes seemed to render only more intolerable. With earnest self-devotion others have labored to adjust the relations between Church and State—between private judgment and authority.

Richard Whately (1787–1863).—While still a fellow of Oriel, Whately was the representative of a class of able and philanthropic men who had set themselves the task of improving the teaching and discipline in the Oxford colleges. Even at that early day the struggle between the reason of the individual and the authority of the Church was dimly shadowed forth in the subtle disputations which took place in the Oriel Common Room. Even then, men like Keble thought that others like Whately were not free from "pride of reason;" but the practical temperament and active industry of Whately found plenty to occupy him in the discharge of obvious duty without turning aside to what he could not but consider fine-spun distinctions. His elevation to an archbishopric was the cause of great rejoicing to Dr. Arnold and the other members of the Church Reform Party, but their hopes were disappointed. Whately, while working for reform, did not become its eminent champion. His great service was his support of the national school system; he was also largely concerned in the reform of the Poor Laws, and he did much to bring about the abolition of penal transportation and the admission of Jews to Parliament. His first work, published anonymously, was the once famous argument entitled *Historic Doubts Relative to Napoleon Bonaparte.* It was an illustration of the fact that the principles of reasoning used by infidels against the teachings of the New Testament are just as effective in seeming to disprove the best authenticated facts of history. While Professor of Political Economy at Oxford he published his well-known works on *Logic* and *Rhetoric*

To enumerate all the publications of this diligent man would not be possible in this sketch. " He was always either writing himself or helping some one else to write." His best essays are : *New Testament Difficulties*, *The Sabbath*, and *Romanism*. His lectures on *Political Economy* (**346**) appeared in 1831, and later he published other works on social and economical questions. His work in annotating an edition of Bacon's essays has received much deserved praise. Whately had a mind of great logical power, with little imagination and fancy. His views of questions are always practical. His style is luminous, easy, and well adorned with every-day illustrations.

John Keble (1792–1866).—In the year 1833 Oxford became the center of a religious movement which found expression in the famous *Tracts for the Times*. This *Tractarianism* was marked by the self-denial of its originators—by the lofty aims of its supporters. If its spirit was sometimes too exclusive, its meaning too mystical, it must always be admitted that it made worldly old men thoughtful and young men serious. The prominent supporters of this movement were men versed in dialectics, who were able to parry and return every thrust of their opponents. The leader of it all was a quiet man living as a curate at Fairford. This man was John Keble, the author of *The Christian Year* and of the *Summer Assize Sermon* at Oxford, afterward published under the title of *National Apostasy*. Years before, he had been one of the Oxford celebrities. In 1810 he had obtained double first-class honors, and shortly afterward he was elected to an Oriel fellowship. Copleston, Davidson, and Whately, Arnold, Newman and Pusey were his companions ; but the brilliant intercourse of such intellects was unsatisfactory to him, and after five years of residence at Oriel, during which he took part in the college tuition and acted as an examiner, he was ordained, and left the University. For nearly twenty years he was content to be his father's curate, and bounded his earthly ambition by the duties of a son and brother. He was called from time to time to serve his College and University, but his sincere desire was for the peace and serenity of a country parish. This meditative life resulted in the publication of *The Christian Year* in 1827. The Catholic Emancipation disturbed his serenity. He came to Oxford, and in his assize sermon attempted to defend the English Church against Lord Grey by reviving her claims to heavenly origin and divine prerogative. He sounded the alarm, and then went back to his quiet parish, leaving it for others to reduce to logical form the principles which were part of his nature. But when, in 1845, John Henry Newman went over to the Church of Rome, the burden of defence fell back upon Keble and Dr. Pusey. Keble accepted his share of the uncongenial task, and worked until his death in 1866 with unwearying energy and affectionate devotion.

Of all Keble's literary works *The Christian Year* is the one which has appealed most to the popular heart and experience. It is marked by the simple expression of genuine poetic feeling, by unaffected piety, and love of nature. Of the *Tracts for the Times*, he wrote Nos. 4, 13, 40, and 89.

Considerable understanding of the religious and social reactions of the present century is needful to appreciate the commanding influence exerted by **John Henry Newman** (1801–1890). His contributions to our permanent literature have been overshadowed by the power which he exercised upon contemporary thought and action. Matriculated at Oxford before he was sixteen, he distinguished himself in 1822 by winning an Oriel Fellowship, then a prime goal of academic ambition. Keble was accounted the brilliant light of the university; Whately was still an active influence there; Pusey, Hurrell Froude, and Robert Wilberforce became Newman's close friends. The deep interest in theological matters which he had felt from early boyhood was stimulated and defined by these associations. Questions of the government, functions and sacraments of the English Church soon acquired for him, as for his friends, all-absorbing importance. When he took holy orders (1824) he entered upon his clerical duties with apostolic fervor. His high ideal of the pastoral function extended to his university relations. Like others of his circle, he had always waged war on the dissipation and religious torpor which were prevalent at Oxford; and when, in 1826, he was appointed a Public Tutor, he regarded his duties as a means of moral elevation to his pupils. This had a twofold result: it brought him into close personal relations with many active, aspiring young minds; and it set him at variance with the general policy of the university. The latter circumstance led him, in 1832, to relinquish his tutorship. From a visit to the Continent, he returned in 1833, just as Keble preached his famous sermon on National Apostasy, and joined with fervor in the preparation of the *Tracts for the Times*, being himself the author of Tract 90. This called out the formal prohibition of the Bishop of Oxford, and ended the series. Newman's sermons and correspondence early foreshadowed that movement towards the Church of Rome, of which he himself long remained unconscious. As Curate of St. Clement's, Vicar of St. Mary's (1828–1843), and one of the University's Select Preachers, he won reputation and influence. But in 1843 his theological position seemed so doubtful to his own conscience that he relinquished his university functions. He entered the Roman communion in 1845. That step not only severed many personal ties, but cut him off from his former intellectual associations. However, he bore temporal consequences as unflinchingly as he had followed the dictates of his reasoning. He had early said of himself that he was "not a person to take the head of a party;" his withdrawal from public affairs during the latter half of his life contrasted singularly with his early activity. After receiving holy orders in Rome (1847) he introduced into England a branch of the Congregation of the Oratory. Save for an interval of seven years, which he spent in Dublin as Rector of the Irish Catholic University, he resided at Birmingham with the brethren of the Oratory until his death. The rank of Cardinal was conferred on him in 1879. When he died, the sharp controversy of earlier times had well-nigh faded from contemporary recollection; he was mourned by all sects and parties as "a great Englishman, whose beauty of life shed its light of purity over his own century, but belongs to all ages."

More powerful even than Newman's published writings was his conversation. Abundant witness has been borne to his wonderful blending of simplicity and strength of character, of sweetness of spirit with profound inward conviction. These qualities made him a venerated force in the seclusion of the Oratory, and drew thitherward pilgrims of every class. Before Newman had left the Anglican Church his *Parochial Sermons, Lectures on the Prophetical Office of the Church*, and similar writings, had been widely read. Several volumes of *Sermons* (1843–5), an *Essay on the Development of Christian Doctrine* (1845), *Loss and Gain* (1848),

Discourses Addressed to Mixed Congregations (1849), *Lectures on the Present Position of Catholics in England* (1851), *Lectures on the History of the Turks in its Relation to Christianity* (1853), expounded his modified views in a prose style which has been justly pronounced unique. Directness, flexibility, an effect of polish which seems rather a result of clear thinking than of literary effort, characterize whatever he has written. It is to this style, the admiration of critics and the despair of imitators, much more than to the subject-matter which it conveys, that Newman owes his place in English literature. The *Apologia pro Sua Vita*, a dignified vindication of his transition from the Anglican to the Roman Church, and the *Grammar of Assent*, which expounds his view of the relation between syllogistic reasoning and Christian faith, are the most famous of his distinctively polemic writings.

Nicholas Wiseman (1802–1865), S.T.D., won his place among English men of letters through the versatility and power which he exercised as a champion of the Catholic faith. The scion of an old English family, he was born in Spain, where his father had business interests. He became one of the first members of the English College at Rome, took holy orders, passed rapidly through various phases of ecclesiastical preferment, and in 1835 resumed his residence in England. In 1850 he was nominated by the Pope as Archbishop of Westminster and was also named Cardinal, being the seventh Englishman to receive the latter dignity since the Reformation. Early in life he won reputation as a linguist and student of Church History. From the time of his return to England until his death he was prominent as a public lecturer. During these years religious controversy was very active in England. The re-establishment of the Catholic hierarchy, the Ecclesiastical Titles Bill, and the later phases of Tractarianism, gave constant occasion for advocacy of Roman Catholic tenets. Wiseman's oratory, his personal presence, his varied culture and power of clear and attractive statement, were employed so effectively as to win him national celebrity. His published works exhibit a wide range of study and interest. *Horæ Syriacæ*, a work of much learning, was largely derived from manuscripts in the Vatican; *Essays on Various Subjects* were republished from the *Dublin Review*, of which Dr. Wiseman was one of the founders and chief contributors; Lectures *On the Connection between*

of literature, and helped to lessen the distance between the rich and the poor. Robertson was never able to shut his eyes to the fact that the self-indulgence of the lower classes was, after all, answerable for most of the hardships of their condition; so that while he was their constant friend, he never ceased to be their critic. His life proved that a man could retain his individuality and still be a clergyman of the Church of England; that a man might oppose the demands of the working people and yet be the only minister of his Church who would vote for the Radicals in 1852. His influence has not ceased with his life; he is to-day perhaps better understood than when his voice was still heard in Brighton This subtler recognition began on the day when frivo-lous Brighton closed her shops and wore mourning; when her tradespeople, workingmen, and literary societies went together to his funeral.

Robertson's sermons and lectures have gone through many editions in England and America, and have been printed in the Tauchnitz edition of English authors.

John Frederick Denison Maurice (1805–1872) was the friend of John Sterling and the co-laborer of Charles Kingsley. A man of great sensitiveness of conscience in respect to his own action, he exercised the broadest charity toward the shortcomings of others. His active career was marked by two purposes—one, to make the theology of the Church of England minister to the needs of man-kind; the other, to ameliorate the condition of the working classes. In the first he co-operated with Dr. Arnold of Rugby; in the second with Kingsley. He met with opposition and misunder-standing in both attempts, but gradually recognition of his generous intentions and ardent love for truth was given to him. He was made Professor of Theology in King's College, London. In 1866 he became Professor of Moral Philosophy at Cambridge. He has written much on the history of philosophy, the philosophy of religion, the critical study of the Scriptures, the condition of the working people, and social morality. Charles Kingsley has said that, although Maurice was a great and rare thinker, he was greatest in his personal influence. Perhaps the verdict of less partial critics would deny the first statement. There is very little originality in his thinking, no great subtlety in his intellect. He was the principal of the Workingmen's College in Red Lion Square; he was the founder of Christian Socialism; he was the "Master" to whom Charles Kingsley looked up with love and reverence.

Charles Kingsley (1819-1875).—Kingsley's name is so closely associated with some of the greatest political movements and religious issues of this century that his writings have an historical interest quite apart from their artistic value. The Chartist excitement and the Newman controversy both occurred during his lifetime, and both were influential in determining the character of his work. He was the friend of Maurice, of Bunsen, of Mill, and of Carlyle, an old-fashioned High Churchman, and a Chartist. He was ordained in 1842, and in the same year accepted the curacy of Eversley; two years afterward he received the living. Here he spent his life in active parish work, and in the churchyard he is buried.

The literary life of Kingsley is divided into two parts, each characterized in the main by one of the two influences which held his mind in balance. In his youth and early manhood he was self-assertive, impatient of abuses, destructive in his tendencies. *Yeast*, published as a serial in *Fraser* in 1848, was the outcome of his interest in the Chartist Riots of that year, and gives some of the most powerful delineations of the sufferings of the poor which are to be found in English literature. *Alton Locke* (1850) deals with the same general subject, though the literary tone of the book is more dignified. As a parish clergyman, Kingsley was particularly interested in the intellectual and sanitary condition of the poor. He found Eversley without schools, and its poor people in the squalor of ignorance; his struggle with dirt, sickness, and unbelief during the attacks of cholera which visited England in these years was the motive for his novel of *Two Years Ago*. In 1851 he published *Hypatia* as a serial in *Fraser*. He says of it: "My idea in the romance is to set forth Christianity as the only really democratic creed and philosophy; above all, spiritualism as the most exclusively aristocratic creed." In 1855 appeared *Westward Ho*, an historical novel, relating to Elizabethan English history. During this period of his life, Mr. Kingsley was constantly suffering from the ill-feeling and opposition which his bold sympathy with the working classes had roused in the minds of his clerical superiors and brethren. As compensation for this, he seems to have enjoyed the confidence of workingmen to a degree hardly excelled by any other man in England.

As Kingsley grew older, as the rights of the poor found more champions, his opinions seemed less singular, and the prejudice created by his way of stating them lessened. The reverence of the man for sacred things now found a voice in sermons, lectures, and essays, which he published from time to time.

The regius professorship of modern history at Cambridge he held from 1860 until his resignation in 1869. In this position he was very successful in rousing the interest of the undergraduates, although the character of his work received much criticism, on the ground that it was unscholarly, and not sufficiently formal in method. In 1869 he was made a Canon of Chester Cathedral, and in 1873 he accepted a vacant stall in Westminster.

Besides his contributions to religious, social, and political literature, Mr. Kingsley was a poet of a low order. The pathos of some of his ballads will long make them dear to the hearts of the simple folk who were their inspiration. Two of the most popular are *The Three Fishers* and the *Sands o' Dee*.

One important result of theological agitation in the Anglican Church was the formation, towards the middle of the century, of the group of clergymen known as Broad Churchmen. By their opponents of Ritualistic and Evangelical parties they were styled latitudinarians; but their zealous, practical Christianity combined with their intellectual prominence to compel respect for their views. Conspicuous among them was **Arthur Penrhyn Stanley** (1819-1881). He sprang from ancient and illustrious English stock: his father, a Bishop of Norwich, was his forerunner in the effort to liberalize Church practices. Arthur Stanley was a pupil and devoted friend of Dr. Arnold, whose biography (1846) was his first important literary work. His connection with Oxford was marked by many distinctions. Although his judicial attitude in religious matters subjected him to bitter partisan attacks, the sweetness and elevation of his character, not less than the vigor of his pen, brought him ever-widening influence. As Canon successively of Canterbury and of Christ Church, regius professor of Ecclesiastical History at Oxford, and finally as Dean of Westminster, he sought to vitalize Church history and institutions, while keeping himself abreast of modern thought. He wrote much and ably, besides taking an active share in common affairs. From boyhood to age an enthusiasm for historical study dominated all his intellectual pursuits, and although not especially given to antiquarian research, he possessed the rare gift of historical imagination. In *Sinai and Palestine, Sermons and Essays on the Apostolic Age, The Early Christians of Northumbria, Historical Memorials of Canterbury, Historical Memorials of Westminster Abbey*, he has shown remarkable power in interpreting the spirit of remote ages and tracing the eras of progress. He was a frequent contributor to periodicals, and several volumes of his sermons attained wide circulation. But his greatest work was the *History of the Jewish Church* (1863–1876). This is comprehensive in plan, vivid, strong, and graceful in style, and marked throughout by the most enlightened and catholic Christian spirit. Maurice said of his early work : " Stanley has done more than any living man to make the Bible a reality in English homes." This praise might fitly be extended to the labors of his lifetime; and his thought has probably been as influential in America as in England.

The Influence of the Scientists.—The science of the nineteenth century has been developed in two very different directions—one of them practical, the other speculative, so that our time boasts its great discoverers as well as its able thinkers. For the most part, the two influences have gone on side by side. Literature has received an impetus from minds which have been roused into activity by the questions and answers of experimental science.

William Whewell (1794–1866) was a man of whom it was said, " Science is his forte and omniscience is his foible." He graduated from Cambridge in 1816, received a fellowship, and from 1828 to 1832 was professor of mineralogy. He was elected Professor of Moral Theology in 1838, master of Trinity in 1841, and in 1855 vice-chancellor of Cambridge.

Dr. Whewell was a man of strong convictions, fond of argument and inclined to self-assertion. His friendships with the scientific men of his time were numerous and cordial. As an officer of Cambridge he was eminently conservative.

His contributions to literature cover a large number of subjects. Sir John Herschel says of him that " a more wonderful variety and amount of knowledge in almost every department of human inquiry was perhaps never in the same interval of time accumulated by any man." Political economy, education, mathematics, and architecture have all been the subjects of formal treatises, but the works upon which his literary reputation mainly rests are four: *The Bridgewater Treatise* (1833), *History of the Inductive Sciences* (1837), *Philosophy of the Inductive Sciences* (1840), and *Lectures on the History of Moral Philosophy in England* (1852). In all his writings it was one of Dr. Whewell's objects to reconcile science with the orthodox religious views of his time.

Sir John Frederick William Herschel (1792–1871).—A graduate of Cambridge in 1813, he was distinguished for his mathematical genius and for his studies in physical science.

His service to literature lies in what he has done to make the fruits of abstruse research in his profession available to the ordinary reader. He wrote for the Encyclopædia Metropolitana, for Lardner's Cyclopædia, and for the Edinburgh and London quarterlies. Clear, vigorous English, vivid and happy illustration are found in all his writing, but the work displaying the best merits of his style is the *Preliminary Discourse on the Study of Natural Philosophy*.

Michael Faraday (1791–1867), one of the most original and distinguished scientists of the age, was a lecturer of great popularity, and a contributor to scientific journals. His works are almost entirely records of experiments and investigations. The style is clear and simple, often rising into fervor when the author treats of the wonders of nature or calls attention to a moral truth.

Hugh Miller (1802–1856) was a descendant of buccaneers and Highland chiefs. He grew up in Cromarty in daily contact with a people as untamed as the sea, as rugged as their coast. Refusing to [study for the Church, he was apprenticed to a stone-mason. Until he was thirty-four he lived in the midst of continual toil, journeying through different parts of Scotland in search of work. Meanwhile his education did not stop ; his hammer was always at

hand, his quick eyes always alert for a chance to use it. The gangs of workmen with whom he lived had to get used to the silent fellow who spent hours in meditation. He made himself master of the best English and Scotch literature, beginning with nursery stories and Border ballads, but ending with Locke and the Scotch Philosophy, thus laying the foundation of that literary style which combines the excellences of the eighteenth and the nineteenth centuries—a style of which Dr. Buckland said that he would give his left hand to possess its powers of description. In 1829 Miller published a volume of poems, but his best poetry after all is in his prose. Miller was a strong Presbyterian, and took a prominent part in the "non-intrusion" controversy. His efforts were rewarded by an appointment to the editorship of the *Witness*. His position among the Edinburgh journalists was deservedly high. The articles which came from his pen are remarkable for thoughtfulness, high morality, and 'iterary finish. *The Old Red Sandstone* appeared in a series of papers in the *Witness* during the first year of his editorship, and revealed his discovery of fossils in a formation which up to that time had been deemed almost destitute of them. *The Footsteps of the Creator* was written to oppose the development theory as embodied in the *Vestiges of the Natural History of Creation*. Miller was intimately associated with Dr. Chalmers in the councils of the Free Church, and worked constantly in its interests in spite of increasing ill health. His overworked brain at last began to show signs of disease, but he toiled on in his efforts to finish the *Testimony of the Rocks* until he had written the last page, and awoke to the consciousness that his mind was ruined. The strong man was not strong enough to meet such a future, and he shot himself Dec. 26, 1856.

The character of Hugh Miller's early life and education has left its imprint upon his scientific work and his literary style. The solitude of his unshared tastes through so many years forced him to be independent in his investigations, and gave a rugged strength to the language in which he described the experiences of his life.

Reviewers and Essayists.—The cheapness of printing and the increasing readers have promoted the success of "periodicals." They range from the valuable quarterlies, through the various forms of magazine and review down to the daily paper, the peculiar feature of the literature of the times. Some of the most valuable essays of our literature have appeared in these publications. Every shade of politics, every school of philosophy, every sect of religion, has its paper or its magazine. To give a sketch of these periodicals is of course impossible, but the *Edinburgh* and *Quarterly Reviews* and *Blackwood's Magazine* imparted such an impulse to literature as to demand a few words.

The *Edinburgh Review* was established in 1802 by a small party of young men, — Brougham, Jeffrey, Sydney Smith, Horner, — obscure at that time, but ambitious and enterprising, who **1802]** were all destined to attain distinction. It founded its claim to success upon the boldness and vivacity of its tone, its total rejection of all precedent and authority, and the audacity of its discussions. It was conducted from 1803 to 1829 by **Francis Jeffrey (333)** (1773–1850), a Scotch advocate, who was subsequently raised to the bench. He wrote critical articles, marked by vigor and elegance of style, and usually by keen discrimination. Another of the most important of the early contributors to the *Review*, who indeed edited the first number, was **Sydney Smith (331, 332)** (1771–1845), an English clergyman, and in the later period of his life Canon of St. Paul's. He wrote chiefly upon political and practical questions with a richness of comic humor and dry sarcasm, which is not only exquisitely amusing, but is full of truth as well as pleasantry.

The *Edinburgh* was reckless of fear or favor, and with a dashing and attractive style it fiercely advocated liberal opinions. To counteract its influence, and to defend the Tories, *The Quarterly Review* was started in 1809. It was warmly welcomed by the friends of the government, and immediately obtained a literary reputation at least equal to its rival. The editorship was intrusted to **William Gifford** (1757–1826), the translator of Juvenal, and the author of *Baviad* and *Mœviad*, two powerful satires — the former aimed at the second-rate authors, the latter at the dramatists of his day. Gifford was a self-taught man, who had raised himself, by dint of almost superhuman exertions and admirable integrity, to a high place among the literary men of his age.

He was succeeded in the editorship of the *Quarterly*, after a short interregnum, by **John Gibson Lockhart (319)** (1794–1854), the author of several novels, and one of the earliest and ablest contributors to *Blackwood's Magazine*. Many of the best articles in the

Quarterly were written by himself. In 1820 he married the eldest daughter of Sir Walter Scott, and in 1837–39 he published his charming Life of his father-in-law. He deserves the fame he has as a biographer. His *Life of Napoleon,* which appeared without the author's name, is far superior to many more ambitious performances.

Blackwood's Magazine first appeared in 1817, and was distinguished by the ability of its purely literary articles, as well as by the violence of its political sentiments. Among the many able men who wrote for it, the most eminent was **John Wilson (318)** (1785–1854), the son of a wealthy merchant. After studying at Oxford, he took up his abode on the banks of the Windermere, attracted thither by the society of Wordsworth, Southey, and Coleridge. Wilson was an ardent admirer of Wordsworth, whose style he adopted, to some extent, in his own poems, the *Isle of Palms* and *The City after the Plague.* The year before the publication of the latter poem, Wilson had been compelled, by the loss of his fortune, to remove to Edinburgh, and to adopt literature as a profession. Though Mr. Blackwood was the editor of his own magazine, Wilson was the presiding spirit, and under the name of Christopher North and other pseudonyms he poured forth article after article. His *Noctes Ambrosianæ,* in which politics, literary criticism, and fun were intermingled, gained great popularity. His pathetic tales, the *Lights and Shadows of Scottish Life,* and a novel, *The Trials of Margaret Lindsey,* show the gentle, genial spirit of this eloquent author. In 1820, as a competitor of Sir William Hamilton, he was elected Professor of Moral Philosophy at Edinburgh.

William Hazlitt (338) 1778–1830, son of a Unitarian minister, was educated for an artist, but lived by literature. He was one of the best critics in the earlier part of this century. His paradoxes are a little startling, and sometimes lead him astray ; but there is a delicacy of taste, a richness of imagination, and a perceptive power that make him a worthy second to De Quincey. His style is vivid and picturesque, and his discernment of character is clear. His chief works are *Principles of Human Action, Characters of Shakespeare's Plays, Table Talk, Lectures* on various authors, *Essays* on English novelists in the *Edinburgh,* and a *Life of Napoleon* in four volumes.

It would be impossible in our limits to give an account of the many other writers who distinguished themselves by their contributions to the Reviews and Magazines; but in addition to those already mentioned two essayists stand forth pre-eminent—Charles Lamb and Thomas De Quincey.

Charles Lamb (334, 335) (1775–1834), a poor man's son, was educated at Christ's Hospital. He was a *Londoner:* London life supplied him with his richest materials, and his mind was imbued with the spirit of the older writers. During the early and greater part of his life, Lamb, poor and unfriended, was drudging as a clerk in the India House; and it was not until late in life that he was released from the desk. There was a dark shadow above his path, for his beloved sister Mary, ten years older than himself, was subject to fits of insanity. In one of these fits she had killed her mother. That sad event, and the sad care which Lamb gave to his sister, imparted a tender melancholy to his writings, even where they seem to abound in good humor. The brother and sister lived together for thirty-eight years after the death of their mother, each devotedly attached to the other. They shared in the authorship and publication of four juvenile works—*Mrs. Leicester's School, Tales from Shakespeare, The Adventures of Ulysses,* and *Poetry for Children.* In Lamb's earliest compositions, such as the drama of *John Woodvil,* and subsequently in the *Essays of Elia,* although the world at first perceived a mere imitation of the quaintness of expression of the old writers, there was in reality a revival of their very spirit. The *Essays of Elia,* contributed by him at different times to *The London Magazine,* are surpassingly fine for humor, taste, penetration, and vivacity. Where shall we find such intense delicacy of feeling, such unimaginable happiness of expression, such a searching into the very body of truth, as in these unpretending compositions? The style has a peculiar and most subtle charm; not the result of labor, for it is found in as great perfection in his familiar letters—a certain quaintness and antiquity, not affected in Lamb, but the natural garb of his thoughts. As in all true humorists, his pleasantry was allied with the finest pathos; the merry jest on the tongue was but the commentary on the tear which trembled in the eye. The inspiration that other poets find in the mountains, in the forest, in the sea, Lamb could draw from the crowd of Fleet-street, from the remembrances of an old actor, from the benchers of the Temple,

Lamb was the schoolfellow, the devoted admirer and friend of Coleridge. Coleridge says of him: "Believe me, no one is competent to judge of poor dear Charles who has not known him long and well, as I have done. His heart is as whole as his head. The wild words which sometimes come from him on religious subjects might startle you from the mouth of any other man; but in him they are mere flashes of firework. . . . . Catch him when alone, and the great odds are you will find him with the Bible or an old divine before him, or may be, and that is the next door in excellence, an old English poet; in such is his pleasure."

There never was a man more beloved by all his contemporaries, by men of every opinion, of every shade of literary, political and religious sentiment. His *Specimens of the Old English Dramatists* first showed to modern readers what treasures of poetry lay concealed in the unknown writers of the Elizabethan age. Indeed, Lamb's mind, in its sensitiveness, in its mixture of wit and pathos, was eminently Shakespearean; and his intense and reverent study of the works of Shakespeare doubtless gave this tendency. In his poems, as, for instance, the *Farewell to Tobacco*, the *Old Familiar Faces*, and his few but beautiful sonnets, we find the very essence and spirit of this quaint tenderness of fancy, the simplicity of the child mingled with the learning of the scholar.

Thomas de Quincey (1785–1859) was one of the masters of English prose. He was the son of a wealthy Manchester merchant. After leaving Oxford he settled at Grasmere, and became intimate with Wordsworth, Southey, and Coleridge. There he became a slave to the habit of opium-eating. After many years of indulgence, and by a most desperate struggle, he broke the chain that had bound him. The last thirty-eight years of his life he was a resident of Glasgow and Edinburgh.

The best known of his writings, the *Confessions of an Opium-eater* (329, 330), made a great sensation upon its publication in 1821. The sketches of his experience with the drug are fearfully vivid and picturesque, while in places the ridicule of himself is keen and amusing. His language sometimes soars to astonishing heights of eloquence. Some of his essays are almost exclusively humorous, among which *Murder Considered as One of the Fine Arts* is the best known. An able critic, in the *London Quarterly Review*, No. 219, thus sums up his literary merits:—"A great master of English composition ; a critic of uncommon delicacy ; an honest and unflinching investigator of received opinions; a philosophic inquirer, second only to his first and sole hero (Coleridge), De Quincey has left no successor to his rank. The exquisite finish of his style, with the scholastic rigor of his logic, form a combination which centuries may never reproduce, but which every generation should study as one of the marvels of English literature."

Thomas Carlyle (1795–1881)—a man unlike all other men of letters ; so out of sympathy with the epoch in which he has written that he is called " the censor of his age ; " so versatile in talent that he may be classed among philosophers, cr historians, or biographers, or essayists—shall stand by himself in our discussion. He was the son of a Scotch village mason. He was reared to a thorough hatred of insincerity. His early studies gave him special pleasure in mathematics ; for in them he found the satisfaction of dealing with demonstrable truth. His education was intended to fit him for the work of a clergyman in the Scottish Kirk; but he did not take kindly to that calling, and, after pitiful mental struggles, he resolved to forego it, and devote himself to literature. His first publication was a translation of Legendre's *Geometry*, with an original " Essay on Proportion." This was followed by a *Life of Schiller*. Its unlikeness to conventional biography—its freedom from minute narration, its brilliant analysis of character, attracted critical attention, and won much applause for the anonymous author. From first to last, Carlyle wrote uncompromising and vigorous criticism of his fellow-men. Alert to detect shams and meannesses, he assailed them unsparingly, often unjustly. In 1826 he was married to Miss Jane Welsh, a descendant of John Knox. To her patience with his temperament, and to her ambition, devoted to him, he owes much of his success. Before his name was known in literary circles he had become weary of life among men, and had removed his home from Edinburgh to a small estate belonging to his wife, at Craigenputtoch, a lonely place in Dumfriesshire. "I came hither," he said, "solely with the design to simplify my way of life, and to secure the independence through which I could be enabled to remain true to myself." From his hermitage his busy pen sent forth essay after essay, some of them brilliant translations from the German, some of them original and bold biographical studies.

Sartor Resartus ("The Tailor Done Over") was written in 1831. Carlyle met many discouragements in seeking its publisher. He was even constrained to take up his residence in London in order that he might the more faithfully prosecute the search. When *Fraser's Magazine* published the work as a serial in 1833–4, it aroused much ridicule and rebuke. A few thoughtful readers found it a delight. In style it was barbarous, in thought it was fresh and stimulating. The number of its attentive readers steadily increased, until it was recognized as having an influence over English thought greater than any other work of that generation. The underlying idea of the book is that social organizations are but the garments of social life, and that they are so outworn as to be unsightly and almost worthless. Humor, pathos, satire, poetic sentiment give charm to its pages.

The French Revolution, a History (1837) was the first of Carlyle's works which bore the author's name. As a history it is unique. There is not even continuity of narrative. Characters seen in a flash of light, incidents, epochs are selected and portrayed with thrilling vividness.

In the three years following Carlyle delivered before small audiences of his admirers courses of lectures on literary, historical, and philosophical themes. The reporter's notes of one course of these lectures were written out into the volume of *Heroes and Hero Worship* (1841). *Past and Present*, published in 1843, was an attack upon the unheroic spirit of the English aristocracy. The *Life and Letters of Oliver Cromwell, with Elucidations*, published in 1845, was the attempt of a Cromwell in literature to give vindication of the character and achievements of the Protector. In 1864 the *History of Frederick II., commonly called Frederick the Great*, appeared. Preparation for writing it had cost Carlyle fifteen years of labor. Publications relating to his theme, unpublished records of state correspondence, minute points of scenery—all details of record and of scenery had been studied to fit him for the narration of his story. His respect for Frederick II. had attracted him to this task, and yet he gives his reader to understand that Frederick should command admiration not for greatness, but for the reason that "he managed *not* to be a liar and a charlatan as his century was."

Carlyle's last years were given to quiet ways. His pen was seldom used. Those who had access to him found him one of the most entertaining men in conversation. His thoughts were those of a rugged Scotchman who revered intellectual worth. His speech had the attractiveness of a broad and emphatic Scotch accent.

Carlyle's literary style has been loudly and justly condemned. It is usually jagged and intricate, a mixture of terse English vocabulary with involved German structure of sentence. At first it seems like the belching of a volcanic mind; but after careful scrutiny it is found to be the studied expression of a mighty rhetorician who seeks not grace, but vividness; not elegance, but power.

Matthew Arnold (1822-1888).—The literary worth of Matthew Arnold will perhaps be estimated the less highly by posterity because of those qualities which have made him potent and stimulating among his contemporaries. We may count him the foremost English critic of the century. His incisive analysis and wide range of vision have influenced education, theology, literature and manners. The son of Thomas Arnold of Rugby, he was heir to the richest and broadest intellectual influences that English life could give. His university degree was taken at Oxford, where he also won honors which foreshadowed his future distinctions. In 1845 he became a Fellow of Oriel College. From 1847 to 1851 he was private secretary to Lord Lansdowne. Resigning this post upon his marriage, he was appointed lay inspector of schools, in which office he continued until his death. During ten years (1857-1867) he was Professor of Poetry at Oxford, and he received honorary degrees at Oxford, Cambridge, and Edinburgh. Valuable reports to the Government summarized the researches involved by his educational functions, and he greatly advanced the scope and methods of middle-class education. His first poems were published in 1848, and although his offerings to the Muse have not been lavish, they comprise many numbers for which critics prophesy permanent fame. "Sohrab and Rustum," a narrative poem, "Thyrsis," an elegy on the death of Arthur Hugh Clough, "Urania," "The Last Word," "The Scholar Gypsy," "The Forsaken Merman," "Verses in Rugby Chapel," all evince a chastened but exquisite fancy, refined pathos, and subtle understanding of the doubts and longings, the griefs and pensive introspection peculiar to our time. Tried by Milton's canon, which Arnold himself applies to other poets, the "simple, sensuous, impassioned," is seldom character istic of his verse. Steeped to the lips in Hellenic culture, he has little of Greek joyousness or free objectivity. In like manner, his prose writings, polished, exact, everywhere revealing clear insight and honest analysis, are sometimes marred by an exacting, subtle self-consciousness. The avowed apostle of culture, he was occasionally hampered by a spirit of high exclusiveness akin to the Philistinism which he decried—a petulance close bordering upon dogmatism. These defects, however, are but flaws in the crystal; and many of his essays—" On Translating Homer," " Literature and Dogma," " God and the Bible," " Culture and Anarchy," " Last Essays on Church and Religion "—have exercised deep and inspiring influence. His intellect was essentially critical rather than creative, but his ideals were high and pure. We mark his limitations the more accurately because of the changes in traditional standards wrought through his single-minded warfare against materialism, pedantry and cant.

In this chapter we have considered:—

The English Literature of the Nineteenth Century.
1. *The New Literature of History.*
    Thirlwall, Grote, Lingard, Macaulay, Hallam, Milman, Buckle, Green.
2. *The Literature of Philosophy.*
    a. *The Scottish School; Reid. Stewart, Brown, Hamilton.*
    b. *The English School; The Mills, Bentham, Lewes.*
3. *Influence of the Clergy.*
    Whately, Keble, Newman, Wiseman, Robertson, Maurice, Kingsley, Stanley.
4. *Influence of Scientists.*
    Whewell, Herschel, Faraday, Miller.
5. *Reviewers and Essayists.*
    Smith, Gifford, Lockhart, Wilson, Hazlitt, Lamb, De Quincey, Carlyle, Arnold.

CHAPTER XXVIII.

THE MODERN NOVELISTS.

THE department of English literature which has been cultivated during the latter half of the last and the first half of the
present century with the greatest assiduity and success, is prose
fiction. Its authors and their productions should be classified
under the two general divisions of fiction as they were set forth in
a preceding chapter, viz. : I. Romances properly so called, *i. e.*, the
narration of picturesque and romantic adventures; II. Novels, or
pictures of real life and society.

I. ROMANCES.—The impulse to this branch of composition was
first given by **Horace Walpole** (1717–1797) (**326**), the fastidious
dilettante and brilliant chronicler of the court scandal of his day ;
a man of singularly acute penetration, of sparkling epigrammatic
style, but devoid of enthusiasm and elevation. He retired early
from political life, and shut himself up in his little fantastic Gothic
castle of Strawberry Hill, to collect armor, medals, manuscripts,
and painted glass; and to chronicle with malicious assiduity, in
his vast and brilliant correspondence, the absurdities, follies, and
weaknesses of his day. *The Castle of Otranto* is a short tale, written with great rapidity and without preparation. It was the first
successful attempt to take the Feudal Age as the period, and the
passion of mysterious, superstitious terror as the motive in the
action of an interesting fiction. The manners are absurd and unnatural, the character of the heroine being one of those portraits in
which the sentimental languor of the eighteenth century is added
to the gentlewoman of the Middle Ages—in short, one of those
contradictions to be found in all the romantic fictions before Scott.

Mrs. Ann Radcliffe.—The success of Walpole's original and
cleverly-written tale encouraged other and more accomplished artists to follow in the same track. The most popular of this class
was Mrs. Ann Radcliffe (1764–1823), whose numerous romances ap-

peal with power to the emotion of fear. Her two greatest works are *The Romance of the Forest* and *The Mysteries of Udolpho.* The personages of these stories have no more individuality than the pieces of a chess-board; but they are made the exponents of such terrible and intense fear, suffering, and suspense, that we sympathize with their fate as if they were real. At the beginning of the century her romances were held in the highest esteem by all readers. Men of letters—Talfourd, Byron, Scott—applauded her: but her fame is declining, and she is now known only by the students of literature. The effect of this kind of writing was so powerful that it was attempted by a crowd of authors. Most of them are forgotten; but there a:e two other names worthy of special mention.

Matthew Gregory Lewis (1775–1818), a good-natured, effeminate man of fashion, the friend of Byron, and one of the early literary advisers of Scott, was the first to introduce into England a taste for the German literature of that day, with its spectral ballads and enchantments. He was a man of lively imagination; and besides his metrical translations of the ballads of Bürger, he published in his twentieth year a prose romance called *The Monk,* one of the boldest of hobgoblin stories.

Mrs. Shelley (1798–1851), the wife of the poet, and the daughter of William Godwin, wrote the powerful tale of *Frankenstein.* Its hero, a young student of physiology, succeeds in constructing, out of the horrid remnants of the churchyard and dissecting-room, a monster, to which he afterwards gives life. Some of the chief appearances of the monster, particularly the moment when he begins to move for the first time, and towards the end of the book, among the eternal snows of the Arctic Circle, are managed with a striking and breathless effect, that makes us for a moment forget the extravagance of the tale.

II. The Novel.—No field of literature can be compared in fruitfulness with the English novel of the century just passed. A story of human life appeals to human sympathy as nothing else can; and the novelist has but to take advantage of that fact. Moreover, he finds inexhaustible resources. Each one of the possible localities for the scene of a story, and each one of the infinite variations of human character are ready to answer his summons. The romance appeals to the credulity, to the curiosity of a reader ; the novel may speak to the tenderest and most intelligent sympathies.

In this vast field of authorship we merely glance at a few writers who have been most popular. Richardson, Fielding, and Smollett, the first great English novelists, and Walter Scott, poet and novelist, have already found their appropriate places in our discussion.

Frances Burney (1752–1840) was the daughter of Dr. Burney, author of the *History of Music*. While yet residing at her father's house, she, in moments of leisure, composed the novel of *Evelina*, published in 1778. She did not even communicate to her father the secret of her having written it, until the astonishing success of the fiction rendered her avowal triumphant and almost necessary. *Evelina* was followed in 1782 by *Cecilia*, a novel of the same character. In 1786 Miss Burney received an appointment in the household of Queen Charlotte, where she remained till her marriage with Count d'Arblay, a French refugee officer. She published after her marriage a novel entitled *Camilla*, and two years after her death her *Diary and Letters* appeared.

An eminent place in this class of writers belongs to **William Godwin** (1756–1836), a man of powerful and original genius, who devoted his whole life to the propagation of social and political theories—visionary, indeed, and totally impracticable, but marked with the impress of benevolence and philanthropy. His long life was incessantly occupied with literary activity. The first and finest of his fictions is *Caleb Williams* (1794). Its aim is to show the misery and injustice arising from the present imperfect constitution of society, and the oppression of defective laws, not merely those of the statute-book, but also those of social feeling and public opinion. Caleb Williams is an intelligent peasant-lad, taken into the service of Falkland. Falkland, the true hero, is an incarnation of honor, intellect, benevolence, and passionate love of fame, who, in a moment of ungovernable passion, has committed a murder, for which he allows an innocent man to be executed. This circumstance, partly by accident, partly by his master's voluntary confession, Williams learns, and is in consequence pursued through the greater part of the tale by the unrelenting persecution of Falkland, who is now led, by his frantic and unnatural devotion to fame, to annihilate, in Williams, the evidence of his guilt. The adventures of the unfortunate fugitive, his dreadful vicissitudes of poverty and distress, the steady pursuit, the escapes and disguises of the victim, like the agonized turnings and doublings of the hunted hare—all this is so depicted that the reader follows the story with breathless interest. At last Caleb is accused by Falkland of robbery, and naturally discloses before the tribunal the dreadful secret which has caused his long persecution, and Falkland dies of shame and a broken heart. The interest of this tale is indescribable; the various scenes are set before us with something of the minute reality and simplicity of Defoe. " There is no work of fiction which more rivets the attention—no tragedy which exhibits a struggle more sublime, or suffering more intense, than this; yet to produce the effect, no complicated machinery is employed, but the springs of action are few and simple." *

Maria Edgeworth (1767–1849) passed nearly all of her long and useful life in Ireland. Many of her earlier works were produced in partnership with her father, Richard Lovell Edgeworth, a man of eccentric character, and of great intellectual activity. The most valuable series of Miss Edgeworth's educational stories were the charming tales entitled *Frank, Harry and Lucy, Rosamond*, and others combined under the general heading of *Early Lessons*. These are written in the simplest style, and are intelligible and interesting even to very young readers; while the knowledge of character they display, the naturalness of their incidents, and the practical principles they inculcate, make them delightful even to the adult reader. The first, the most original, and the best of her stories is *Castle Rackrent*. Abounding in humor and pathos, it sets forth with dramatic effect the follies and vices of the Irish landlords, who have caused so much of the misery of the Irish people. In the novels of *Patronage*, and *The Absentee*, other social errors, either peculiar to that country or common to many countries, are powerfully delineated. Miss Edgeworth has done for her countrymen what Scott did with such loving genius for the Scottish people. The services rendered by her to the cause of common sense are incalculable. Walter Scott says that " Some one has described the novels of Miss

* T. N. Talfourd.

Edgeworth as a sort of essence of common sense, and the definition is not inappropriate." The singular absence of enthusiasm in her writings, whether religious, political, or social, only makes us wonder at the force, vivacity, and consistency with which she has drawn a large and varied gallery of characters.

Jane Austen (1775–1817), was the daughter of a clergyman, well connected. Miss Austen's life was marked by elegant moderation. Thousands of women of her rank in England lived as she did, mastering the intricacies of needlework and endearing themselves to their families. Miss Austen's letters show little interest in the exciting politics or in the literary questions of her day. So completely did she identify herself with the class to which she belonged, that few of her acquaintances suspected her power. Many of them would have echoed the question of the verger who, pointing to her grave, asked, "Pray, sir, can you tell me whether there was anything particular about that lady?" The recognition of her literary worth, which came tardily, has been hearty. Lord Macaulay is only the most illustrious of the critics who have assigned to her a high rank as a novelist. She is pre-eminently the literary artist of the commonplace. Under her skilful hand the conventional English drawing-room becomes a theatre, where oddities, foibles, and sterling worth have their well-appointed parts. The reader is not worked up to a pitch of enthusiasm by delineations of passion, or by the analysis of emotions; but he is often amused and always interested by the exercise of an art so perfect that it is almost unsuspected. The most brilliant of Miss Austen's novels is *Pride and Prejudice* (1813). Her other works are *Sense and Sensibility* (1811), *Mansfield Park* (1814), *Emma* (1816). *Northanger Abbey* and *Persuasion* were not published until after her death, although the former was the first novel she wrote.

Charlotte Bronte (1816–1855) was the daughter of a clergyman of Haworth in Yorkshire. Her career is an illustration of the influence of early impressions and surroundings upon the mind. Of six motherless children left to the care of the Rev. Patrick Brontë, only four lived long enough to see in him anything but a stern and self-occupied man, who set them tasks or interrupted their play with horrid stories that made them afraid to go to bed at night.

The scenery of Yorkshire was bleak and forbidding, the house in which the family lived damp and unhealthy—its outlook the parish graveyard; but the children growing up amid such surroundings were sensitive to every change in the face of the stern landscape, and came to love it with a passionate devotion. Their few opportunities for gaining culture threw them back with a despairing reliance upon their own resources. Of these six children, three have been known as the writers of remarkable books. One of them, Charlotte, gained a literary success which has put her name in the list of the most powerful writers of fiction. Her books were all written in the stress of mental suffering, the materials were taken from her own limited experience, thus making it almost necessary that whatever of force or of originality existed in the writer should be reproduced in the words. Charlotte Brontë's words are protests against the conventionality which has from time to time threatened to destroy the vigor of English thinking, the health of its social life, and the power of its religion. While Thackeray's satire was uncovering the shams of society, Miss Brontë gave a powerful delineation of the realities which society was ignoring. Her influence began and ended abruptly. The popular admiration which exaggerated her merits, and the popular criticism which blackened her faults, have both died away, and the critic may make a calm and fair estimate of the services of the woman who was the literary forerunner of George Eliot.

The tenor of Miss Brontë's life was uneventful. For years sickness and death were almost the only variations in the monotonous story of the Haworth parsonage. *Jane Eyre* was published in 1847 over the name of Currer Bell, and made a sensation. *Shirley* was published in 1849, and *Villette* in 1853. *Shirley* is the only one of Miss Brontë's works which displays any humor, while *Villette* is by far the most deserving of praise for artistic finish. In 1854 Miss Brontë married Mr. Nicholls, her father's curate, and gave up all literary ambition. She died in 1855. Her life has been written by Mrs. Gaskell, herself a novelist of great merit.

The charming sketches of **Mary Russell Mitford** (1789–1855), a lady who has described the village life and scenery of England with the grace and delicacy of Goldsmith himself, seem destined to hold a place in our literature long after the once popular novels of her famous contemporaries shall have been forgotten. *Our Village* is one of the most delightful books in the language. Miss Mitford describes with the truth and fidelity of Crabbe and Cowper, but without the moral gloom of the one, or the morbid sadness of the other.

Frederick Marryat.—The immense colonial possessions of Great Britain, and the Englishman's passion for knowing about foreign nations, have turned the attention of English novelists to the delineation of the manners and scenery of ancient and distant countries. They have also found ready applause for stories of sea-life. England's cherished pride over her long supremacy on the sea has given the masses of her readers admiration for the sailor, and sympathy with the hardships of his life. Captain Marryat (1792–1848), one of the most easy, lively, and truly humorous story-tellers, stands at the head of the marine novelists. High, effervescent, irrepressible animal spirits characterize everything he has written. He seems half-tipsy with the gayety of his heart, and never scruples to introduce grotesque extravagances of character, language, and event, provided they are likely to excite a laugh. Nothing can surpass the liveliness and drollery of his *Peter Simple*, *Jacob Faithful*, or *Mr. Midshipman Easy*. Marryat's narratives are often improbable ; but we read on with delight, never thinking of the story, solicitous only to follow the adventures and laugh at the characters. In many passages he has shown a mastery over the pathetic emotions. Though superficial in his view of character, he is generally faithful to reality, and shows an extensive if not very deep knowledge of what his old waterman calls "human natur." There are few authors more amusing than Marryat.

William Makepeace Thackeray (1811–1863) was one of the greatest among modern novelists. He was born in Calcutta, the son of an English official. In his very early years he was sent away from his Eastern home to receive his education in England. After a careful training he was admitted to the University of Cambridge. He did not remain there long; for the death of his father had left him wealth, and freedom to direct his own course of study. His desire was to become an artist. He left the University without his degree, and spent four or five years in France, Italy, and Germany.

His study of the masterpieces of the great painters made him distrust his own abilities. But his life abroad gave him stores of knowledge valuable for his later literary work. On returning to London he continued his art studies; but the loss of his fortune compelled him to throw himself with all his powers into the field of literature. He was first known by his articles in *Fraser's Magazine*, contributed under the names of Michael Angelo Titmarsh and George Fitzboodle, Esq. Tales, criticism, and poetry appeared in great profusion, and were illustrated by the author's own pencil. The chief of his contributions to the magazine was the tale of *Barry Lyndon, The Adventures of an Irish Fortune-hunter*. This was full of humor and incident, but the reading public was not yet expecting a great future for this unknown writer. In 1841 *Punch* was commenced, to which Thackeray contributed the *Snob Papers*, *Jeames's Diary*, and many other papers in prose and verse. In 1846 and the two following years *Vanity Fair* appeared, by many supposed to be the best of his works—certainly the most original.

1846⟩ The novel was not complete before its author took his place among the great writers of English fiction. The writer of satirical sketches and mirthful poems had shown himself to be a consummate satirist, and a great novelist.

Vanity Fair, the first of Thackeray's famous works, is called "A Novel without a Hero." It has, however, two heroines—Rebecca Sharp, the impersonation of intellect without heart, and Amelia Sedley, who has heart without intellect; the former is one of the most brilliant creations of modern fiction. As a whole the book is full of quiet sarcasm and rebuke; but a careful reading will perceive the kindly heart that is beating under the bitterest sentence and the most caustic irony.

Pendennis, published in 1849 and 1850, was the immediate successor of *Vanity Fair*. Literary life presents scope for description, and is well used in the history of Pen, a hero of no very great worth. As *Vanity Fair* gives us Thackeray's knowledge of life in the present day, so *Esmond* exhibits his intimate acquaintance with the society of the reigns of the later Stuarts and the earlier Georges. Like *Vanity Fair*, it is without plot, and gives in an autobiographical form the history of Colonel Henry Esmond. The style of a century and a half ago is reproduced with marvelous fidelity.

The Virginians is the history of the grandsons of Esmond. It consists of a series of well-described scenes and incidents in the reign of George III. The most popular of Thackeray's novels is *The Newcomes.* " The leading theme or moral of the story is the misery occasioned by forced or ill-assorted marriages." The noble courtesy, the Christian gentlemanliness of *Colonel Newcome* is perhaps a reflection of the author himself. *Ethel Newcome* is Thackeray's favorite womanly character. The minor personages are most life-like, while throughout the whole there is a clear exhibition of the real kindliness of Thackeray's heart.

His two courses of lectures *On the English Humorists* and *The Four Georges*, are models of style and criticism.

Charles Dickens (1812–1870) was the most popular novelist of his day. The two men, Dickens and Thackeray, stood side by side, each industrious, each effective in his work, each appreciating and applauding the other. Dickens's father intended that he should follow the profession of the law ; but it was distasteful to him, and he abandoned it for the busy life of a reporter to one of the London newspapers. This work gave him opportunities for observing the characters and habits of the poorer classes. His mind was quick to notice eccentricities of human nature. He could not refrain from the delineation of what he saw in men and women, and so he was soon furnishing " Sketches of Life and Character " to the columns of his journal. These papers were afterwards published as *Sketches by Boz.* The volume had a ready sale. Its author was called upon to write a book representing the adventures of a company of Cockney sportsmen, which Mr. Seymour, a comic artist of the day, was to furnish with illustrations. The volume was published in monthly parts ; and the first number appeared in 1836, bearing the title of *The Posthumous Papers*

1836 *of the Pickwick Club.* It was hailed with delight. The author's fame began, and he was regarded by all classes of readers as a writer of the most radiant humor. Everybody was merry over Mr. Pickwick and Sam Weller, and everybody was eager to read this entertaining author. Volume after volume came from his pen. There seemed to be no limit to his power of caricature, no weariness to him in observing the drolleries of life, no blunting to his sense of fun. After writing *Nicholas Nickleby*

Oliver Twist, The Old Curiosity Shop, and *Barnaby Rudge,* he made his first visit to America. His fame here was as great as in England, and he was received with hearty welcome. The visit furnished him with material for two new works, *American Notes for General Circulation* and *Martin Chuzzlewit.* The keen satirist had witnessed some of our national follies, and he was most severe in his exposure of them. Americans then thought, and still think, that he exaggerated our faults. It was natural for him to do that. All of his creations are exaggerations. The dominant faculty of his mind is his observation of peculiarities, and in painting them he distorts and misrepresents the unpeculiar qualities of a character. After his visit to America he spent a year in Italy, and then, returning to London, he entered upon the busiest years of his active life. He established and edited *The Daily News;* but finding the work uncongenial, he began again the writing of fiction. *Dombey and Son, David Copperfield,* and *Bleak House* appeared, to delight his rapturous readers. In 1850 Dickens took charge of a weekly paper, called *Household Words,* and gained for it a large circulation. Afterwards he started his own *All the Year Round,* and contributed to it, in instalments, his later novels. Among the most charming of Dickens's works are his *Christmas Stories.* One came from his pen each year after 1843. The children and the old folk will probably read *A Christmas Carol, The Cricket on the Hearth,* and *The Chimes* long after his more elaborate stories have been forgotten. Dickens's vigorous constitution broke down from desperate overwork, and he died suddenly in 1870.

"No one thinks first of Mr. Dickens as a writer. He is at once, through his books, a friend. He belongs among the intimates of every pleasant-tempered and large-hearted person. He is not so much the guest as the inmate of our homes. He keeps holidays with us, he helps us to celebrate Christmas with heartier cheer, he shares at every New Year in our good wishes; for, indeed, it is not in his purely literary character that he has done most for us, it is as a man of the largest humanity, who has simply used literature as the means by which to bring himself into relation with his fellow-men, and to inspire them with something of his own sweetness, kindness, charity, and good-will." *

Sir Edward George Bulwer-Lytton (1805–1873) was the son of General Bulwer. In 1844, upon inheriting his mother's estates, he was granted the privilege of adding her family name, Lytton, to his surname. In boyhood he made his first contribution to the shelves of the English libraries, and throughout his youth and manhood he was an unceasing writer. A few poems, a few dramas, occasional political papers, and a multitude of novels, have come from his pen. His principal novels are *Eugene Aram, The Last Days of Pompɛii, Rienzi, My Novel, The Caxtons*, and *The Parisians*. "The special ability of Bulwer appears to lie in the delineation of that passion with which the novel is so deeply concerned, the passion of love. All true and manly passions, let it be said, are honored and illustrated in his pages. But he stands alone among novelists of his sex in the portraiture of love. The heroism, the perfect trust, the strength in death, are painted by him with a sympathetic truth for which we know not where to seek a parallel."*

Not one of the wits who have written in this century for the theater deserves higher praise than Bulwer-Lytton. His "Richelieu" and "Lady of Lyons" have literary excellence as well as adaptation to the stage.

It may reasonably be doubted whether **Benjamin Disraeli,** Ear of Beaconsfield (1805–1880), does not owe his place among men of letters to the fact that he was Prime Minister of England and a peer of the realm. His many novels have, however, kept his name constantly before the reading public. They reflect his career in a measure, for they expound his political and social theories, and sketch the prominent personages of his time. All are characterized by a fluent but incorrect style, by daring flights of fancy, and florid, somewhat bombastic rhetoric. *Vivian Grey ; The Young Duke ; Tancred, or the New Crusade ; Coningsby, or the New Generation*, are the best of them. *Lothair* and *Endymion*, published when their author, as leader of the English Conservatives, was at the height of his political fame, attracted much attention because of their many portraitures of distinguished people. Lord Beaconsfield was an industrious writer. He produced many political pamphlets, a Life of Lord George Bentinck, several poems, and edited most of the works of his father, **Isaac Disraeli** (1776–1848).

* Bayne.

Anthony Trollope (1815–1883) may be styled the great photog-rapher of English society in the nineteenth century. Born of a respectable but impoverished family, he experienced during his boyhood as much neglect and hardship as fell to the lot of Johnson or Dickens. In his early manhood he entered the service of the Post-Office Department, where he slowly worked his way upward to an honorable position. At the age of thirty-two he published his first novel, and, not discouraged by its lack of success, he con-tinued to write until he won the regard of a public which has since given kindly hearing to scores of his productions. His aim was to represent life as he found it, without exaggeration, without false col-oring. He has neither great creative power nor deep poetic feeling but his kindly spirit and perfect purity of sentiment make his writ-ings invariably healthy in tone; and he has the remarkable gift of nar-rating everyday occurrences in an entertaining manner. His *Auto-biography* (1883) gives a frank account of the struggles which finally lifted him to wealth and literary distinction, also a chrono-logical list of his writings,—essays, books of travel, and novels. Among these last it is hard to particularize because of their general excellence in their own line. Perhaps *Orley Farm, La Vendée, The Bertrams, Is He Popenjoy?* and the so-called "clerical series," begin-ning with *The Warden* and closing with *The Last Chronicles of Barset,* most favorably represent his powers.

Charles Reade (1814–1884), like Trollope, represents the realis-tic school of fiction. Born in Oxfordshire, he was graduated at the neighboring university, and held one of its fellowships throughout his life. He was educated for the law; but his thoughts turned towards literature, and in 1850, when his story of *Peg Woffington* appeared, he was recognized as a novelist of power. *Christie John-stone* was received with yet heartier applause. Among his famous stories are *The Cloister and the Hearth; Very Hard Cash; Griffith Gaunt, or Jealousy; Put Yourself in His Place; Never Too Late to Mend;* and *A Terrible Temptation.* These novels, written in a style rugged and often crude, are full of energy, and are marked by strong moral purpose. They attack abuses in the English prison system, or the mismanagement of hospitals, or the tyranny of trades unions. Abounding in striking incidents and in dramatic fire, they have been found easily adaptable to the uses of the stage.

Reade wrote a few dramas, and believed them to be the best productions of his pen.

Mary Ann Evans (George Eliot). The biography of George
Eliot (1819–1880), the most admired of modern English novelists,
has been, until very recently, clouded with as much uncertainty
as surrounds the great dramatist of the sixteenth century. The highest praise she has received compares her genius with Shakespeare's;
like his, it won recognition independently of social position and personal influence. Like Shakespeare, again, she was a native of Warwickshire, and sprung from the rugged, strong-brained, upward-
pushing English middle class. The youngest of five children, diffidence and self-consciousness held her somewhat apart from youthful
companions; but her childhood seems to have been rather serene than
otherwise, and as she grew into womanhood, unusual love and veneration marked her relations to her widowed father, the prototype
of her *Adam Bede*. She was carefully educated in schools of local
repute, and received especial training in Latin, French, and English
composition. In 1841, when her father removed to Foleshill, near
Coventry, Mary Ann was already a student of books, of nature, and
of men. She continued her study of music and modern languages,
learned Greek "in order to read Æschylus," and even taught herself
something of Hebrew. Through converse with cultured friends she
was drawn towards metaphysics and history, and began to investigate
their bearing upon religion. By nature she was earnest and devout;
however, her speculative tendencies soon put her into a critical
attitude towards her inherited Calvinism. Her doubt and question
eventually grew into agnosticism; but her reverence for sincere
belief of all shades is evinced in many of her noblest creations.
Her first literary essay was a spirited and scholarly translation of
Strauss's *Life of Jesus* (1846); it won her the applause of many distinguished thinkers, and though an equally able translation of
Feuerbach's *Essence of Christianity* (1854), aroused less general interest, it confirmed the first estimate of her ability. At thirty-two
years of age, when her talents had long ripened in "the still air
of delightful studies," and she had attained an almost Miltonic
range of knowledge, came the turning-point in her career. The
death of her father (1849) had broken her local attachments and
deeply unsettled her spirit, and in 1851 she gladly accepted an

invitation to go up to London and become the assistant editor of the *Westminster Review*. Through its pages she gave to the world a long and brilliant series of essays on topics critical, literary, biographical, artistic, and ethical. Her labors were brightened by intercourse with choice friends, among whom were James and Harriet Martineau, Herbert Spencer, and George Henry Lewes. It was in 1854 that she entered upon her life-long union with Mr. Lewes, influenced by the recognition of mutual helpfulness, and by a conscientious dissent from certain stipulations of the English law of marriage.* The abstract morality of the step, and its ultimate influence upon her happiness, are still matters of fierce dispute. It certainly marked the great crisis of her life. Many of her friends were shocked and alienated; she was thrown back more than ever before upon her own moral resources. On the other hand, her husband's vivacious, appreciative criticism was of infinite service to her intellectual life. He first discerned in her the novelist's powers, and at his instance her *Scenes of Clerical Life* were published in Blackwood's Magazine (1857) over her since famous pseudonym. They set the reading world on fire with admiration and curiosity; and when *Adam Bede* appeared, in 1859, the note of enthusiasm became so strong as to beget spurious claims to its authorship. Mrs. Lewes now revealed her identity to Mr. Blackwood, and the next year her mask was entirely thrown aside. *The Mill on the Floss* (1860), followed by *Silas Marner, the Weaver of Raveloe* (1861), firmly established her popularity. Her girlhood's associates had been astonished by her exquisite portrayal of familiar provincial scenes and personages; her next work, *Romola* (1862–1863), embodied equally conscientious studies of Florentine life in the fifteenth century. Critics have differed widely concerning its artistic perfection, but universal consent ranks it high as an historical study—a grand narrative.

Appreciative publishers and eager readers now welcomed every effort of Mrs. Lewes's toilsome but productive pen. *Felix Holt, the Radical,* (1866), the dramatic poem entitled *The Spanish Gypsy* (1868), *Middlemarch* (1871), *The Legend of Jubal and other Poems* (1874), *Daniel Deronda* (1876), though varying in their command of popular sympathy, all gave evidence of profound observation, of deep poetic and philosophic insight, of a truly Shakes-

---

* Mr. Lewes, although separated from his first wife upon just and sufficient grounds, could not, according to English law, be divorced from her.

pearian range of creative power. Mrs. Lewes's literary fame had long since lifted her above social proscription, but the last years of her life were destined to be the most checkered. In 1878, the death of Mr. Lewes drew all hearts toward her in sympathy, which changed to amazement when, scarcely two years later, she married John Walter Cross, a London banker many years her junior. Half a year more, and sudden illness had closed her life, and filled the English-speaking world with a sense of bereavement.

George Eliot's latest publication was *Theophrastus Such* (1879), a volume of essays prepared before Mr. Lewes's death. The common verdict found it perceptibly lacking in freshness and vigor. Undoubtedly its author's enduring fame will rest upon her novels. They have made and marked an epoch in the development of English thought; no others have been so much discussed by eminent critics. More symmetrical and finished than any other English fiction, they are also superior in dramatic force, in variety of types, in subtle, life-like blending of pathos and humor. In them, as in the Elizabethan drama, development of character, not intricacy of plot, is the motive. But the author shared the limitations of her age. Her noblest efforts bear the marks of a sometimes too-labored synthesis. Her admirers often miss in her the *naïveté*, the fresh spontaneity of a Fielding or a Scott. For this reason, also, George Eliot's poetry, though lofty in sentiment and perfect in structure, takes rank below her prose. And her agnosticism, while it is tempered with sweet humanity and unselfish courage, is the mournful exponent of a world which has unlearned its simple faith.

In this chapter we have considered:—

The Modern Novelists.

1. Horace Walpole; 2. Ann Radcliffe; 3. Matthew Gregory Lewis; 4. Mrs. Shelley; 5. Frances Burney; 6. William Godwin; 7. Maria Edgeworth; 8. Jane Austen; 9. Charlotte Bronte; 10. Mary Russell Mitford; 11. Frederick Marryat; 12. William Makepeace Thackeray; 13. Charles Dickens; 14. Sir Edward George Bulwer-Lytton; 15. Benjamin Disraeli; 16. Anthony Trollope; 17. Charles Reade; 18. George Eliot.

WALTER SCOTT.

BYRON, MOORE, SHELLEY, KEATS, CAMPBELL, HUNT, LANDOR, and HOOD:
MRS. BROWNING, ROBERT BROWNING, TENNYSON.

"THE LAKE SCHOOL."
- WILLIAM WORDSWORTH,
- S. T. COLERIDGE,
- ROBERT SOUTHEY.

THE HISTORIANS.
- CONNOP THIRLWALL,
- GEORGE GROTE,
- THOMAS BABINGTON MACAULAY,
- JOHN LINGARD,
- HENRY HALLAM,
- HENRY HART MILMAN,
- HENRY THOMAS BUCKLE,
- JOHN RICHARD GREEN,
- EDWARD A. FREEMAN.

THE PHILOSOPHERS.
- THOMAS REID,
- DUGALD STEWART,
- THOMAS BROWN,
- SIR WILLIAM HAMILTON,
- JAMES MILL,
- JEREMY BENTHAM,
- JOHN STUART MILL,
- GEORGE HENRY LEWES.

THE CLERGY.
- RICHARD WHATELY,
- JOHN KEBLE,
- J. H. NEWMAN,
- NICHOLAS WISEMAN,
- THOMAS ARNOLD,
- F. W. ROBERTSON,
- J. F. D. MAURICE,
- CHARLES KINGSLEY,
- A. P. STANLEY.

THE SCIENTISTS.
- WILLIAM WHEWELL,
- SIR JOHN HERSCHEL,
- MICHAEL FARADAY,
- HUGH MILLER.

THE ESSAYISTS.
- FRANCIS JEFFREY,
- SYDNEY SMITH,
- JOHN GIBSON LOCKHART,
- JOHN WILSON,
- WILLIAM HAZLITT,
- CHARLES LAMB,
- THOMAS DEQUINCEY,
- THOMAS CARLYLE,
- MATTHEW ARNOLD.

THE MODERN NOVELISTS.
- HORACE WALPOLE,
- ANN RADCLIFFE,
- MATTHEW GREGORY LEWIS,
- MRS. SHELLEY,
- FRANCES BURNEY,
- WILLIAM GODWIN,
- MARIA EDGEWORTH,
- JANE AUSTEN,
- CHARLOTTE BRONTE,
- MARY RUSSELL MITFORD.
- FREDERICK MARRYAT,
- WILLIAM MAKEPEACE THACKERAY,
- CHARLES DICKENS.
- SIR EDWARD GEORGE BULWER LYTTON
- BENJAMIN DISRAELI,
- ANTHONY TROLLOPE,
- CHARLES READE,
- GEORGE ELIOT.

THE ENGLISH LITERATURE
Of the NINETEENTH CENTURY, as discussed in the five preceding chapters.

THE RULERS OF ENGLAND.

THE RULERS OF ENGLAND.

THE SAXON LINE.
- EGBERT, (King of the West Saxons, commonly called the first king of England), A. D. 827—836.
- ETHELWOLF, 836—857.
- ETHELRED, 857—871.
- ALFRED THE GREAT, 871—901.
- EDWARD, 901—925.
- ATHELSTAN, 925—941.
- EDMUND, 941—948.
- EDRED, 948—955.
- EDWY, 955—959.
- EDGAR THE PEACEABLE, 959—975.
- EDWARD II., 975—979.
- ETHELRED THE UNREADY, 979—1016.
- EDMUND IRONSIDES, 1016—1017.

THE DANISH LINE.
- CANUTE THE GREAT, 1017—1035.
- HAROLD, 1035—1039.
- HARDICANUTE, 1039—1041.

THE SAXON LINE RESTORED.
- EDWARD THE CONFESSOR, 1041—1066.
- HAROLD, 1066.

THE NORMAN LINE.
- WILLIAM THE CONQUEROR, 1066—1087.
- WILLIAM II. (Rufus), 1087—1100.
- HENRY I., 1100—1135.
- STEPHEN OF BLOIS, 1135—1154.

THE PLANTAGENETS.
- HENRY II., 1154—1189.
- RICHARD I., 1189—1199.
- JOHN, 1199—1216.
- HENRY III., 1216—1272.
- EDWARD I., 1272—1307.
- EDWARD II., 1307—1327.
- EDWARD III., 1327—1377.
- RICHARD II., 1377—1399.
- HENRY IV., 1399—1413.
- HENRY V., 1413—1422.
- HENRY VI., 1422—1461.
- EDWARD IV., 1461—1483.
- EDWARD V., 1483.
- RICHARD III., 1483—1485.

THE TUDORS.
- HENRY VII., 1485—1509.
- HENRY VIII., 1509—1547.
- EDWARD VI., 1547—1553.
- MARY, 1553—1558.
- ELIZABETH, 1558—1603.

THE STUARTS.
- JAMES I., 1603—1625.
- CHARLES I., 1625—1649.

THE COMMONWEALTH, 1649—1660.

THE STUARTS AFTER THE RESTORATION.
- CHARLES II., 1660—1685.
- JAMES II., 1685—1688.

THE HOUSE OF NASSAU.
- WILLIAM III., 1688—1702. and MARY, (died 1694).

THE LAST OF THE STUARTS.
- ANNE, 1702—1714.

THE HOUSE OF BRUNSWICK.
- GEORGE I., 1714—1727.
- GEORGE II., 1727—1760.
- GEORGE III., 1760—1820.
- GEORGE IV., 1820—1830.
- WILLIAM IV., 1830—1837.
- VICTORIA, 1837—

A LIST OF THE POETS LAUREATE.

EDMUND SPENSER	1591—1599
SAMUEL DANIEL	1599—1619
BEN JONSON	1619—1637

(*Interregnum*)

WILLIAM DAVENANT, Knight	1660—1668
*JOHN DRYDEN	1670—1689
THOMAS SHADWELL	1689—1692
NAHUM TATE	1692—1715
NICHOLAS ROWE	1715—1718
†LAWRENCE EUSDEN	1718—1730
COLLEY CIBBER	1730—1757
WILLIAM WHITEHEAD	1757—1785
THOMAS WARTON	1785—1790
‡HENRY JAMES PYE	1790—1813
ROBERT SOUTHEY	1813—1843
WILLIAM WORDSWORTH	1843—1850
ALFRED TENNYSON	1850—1892

* Though Dryden did not receive his letters-patent until the year 1670, he never-theless was paid the salary for the two preceding years.

† For Eusden see " Dunciad," Book I., line 63; and for Colley Cibber, see same work *passim*.

‡ "Better to err with Pope than shine with Pye," says Lord Byron, in his 'Hints from Horace.' And again in the 'Vision of Judgment,' the same poet repre-sents the ghost of King George as exclaiming, on hearing Southey's recitation of *his* 'Vision'—

> "What, what!
> Pye come again? no more—no more of that!"

It is by these notices alone that poor Pye stills hangs on the human memory.

ENGLISH LITERATURE IN AMERICA.

INTRODUCTORY.

DURING half a century after the people of the United States had gained their political independence from Great Britain they had to bear tauntings for their lack of originality and for their unproductiveness in literature. The reproaches cast upon them were plausible (at first thought, seem to have been just), inasmuch as the Americans had not poets, or historians, or novelists to be compared with the writers of the mother country. There was not an American author living whose fame had passed beyond his own country. Still, national resentment may have had its influence in prompting the English critics to cast ridicule and reproach upon us; for a friendly disposition would have found excuse for our shortcomings in the peculiar history of our people. That history is naturally divided into three periods—viz., the colonial, the revolutionary, and the national.

Throughout the colonial period our people were in a condition most unfavorable to the production of literature. They had no cities. They lived in villages scattered along a thousand miles of sea-coast. They were beset by savages; were ravaged by pestilence; were pinched by poverty. They were hindered in their national growth by their own sectional jealousies, and were far removed from the helping influences of European civilization. They had no special impulses to literary work, nor was there any need for them to write books, since books were supplied in abundance in their own language.*

The revolutionary period of our history, beginning with the war and lasting until the adoption of the Constitution in 1787, was equally unfavorable to authorship. At the outset there were the seven years of warfare, in which the national life was taxed to the utmost. The army absorbed the national forces. No man was spared for the pursuit of literature. When the war was over, the land was stripped and desolate, and poverty swayed the sceptre, compelling her people to toil for their daily bread. Literature does not thrive where there is no leisure class, nor where the people have not quiet confidence in the security of their government. Both of these essentials to literary prosperity were wanting throughout the revolutionary period of our history.

When the adoption of the Constitution came to mark the beginning of national prosperity, the same unfavorable conditions existed which had been in the way of literary achievement during the colonial period. The people were poor; they had no credit abroad; they had no real money. Exchange was mere barter, such as we expect to find only in rude civilization. And when the people began to emerge from their poverty, they came upon an epoch of astonishing activity in material industries. Agriculture had rich rewards for all who would come to her service ; manufacture was even more alluring; highways were to be built, rivers to be bridged; the laborer commanded such wages as were offered in no other market of the world, and the educated man was driven by the public necessity into the professions of the engineer, of the architect, of the lawyer, of the politician. Moreover, the nation has

---

* " Literature, the Americans have none ; no native literature we mean. * * *
But why should the Americans write books when a six weeks' passage brings them,
in their own tongue, our sense, science, and genius in bales and hogsheads ?"—
Edinburgh Review, Vol. XXXI., p. 144.

absorbed immigration from all countries of Europe, until it has grown from a population of about 3,000,000 at the beginning of the century to more than 60,000,000. The center of population in 1800 was in Carroll County, Md., and it has been crowded westward, until to-day it is found in Indiana. It would seem that amid these bewildering forces there could not be the leisure and quietude essential to the production of literature. Reflecting upon the stupendous results achieved in the material affairs of our country it would seem that all men must have been busied in building our cities, or that all must have been at work in bridging our rivers and in making the highways of commerce, or that all men must have been helping on the conquests of agriculture. It seems unreasonable to look for a display of literary effort and success. Not the colonial period, nor the revolutionary, nor the national period has been favorable to the production of literature. And yet for a quarter of a century the best writers of England and of America have been working side by side, with equal industry and with equal skill, making vast additions to the noble literature of their common language. Sydney Smith's question, "Who reads an American book?" is not repeated, and the criticism of the English reviewer upon the sterility of our national literature is silenced. That criticism, though ungenerous, was helpful, inasmuch as it added the incentive of patriotism to the personal ambition of American authors.

While the attacks made upon us were ungenerous, they were unjust as well; for, despite the most unfavorable conditions, there were writers even in the colonial and the revolutionary periods of our history who made noble and enduring contributions to English literature.

CHAPTER I.

THE COLONIAL PERIOD.

NO period could have been more favorable to the trans-
planting of healthful English life than the years
between 1607 and 1682. During that period the twelve
principal American colonies were founded. At its beginning, Bacon, the greatest of English thinkers, and Shakespeare, the greatest of English authors, were yet living and
were calling into activity the forces of the national thought;
as the period advanced, political turmoil made it easier for
Englishmen to break the ties which bound them to their
native land. And so it was possible to find great numbers
of men, eager in spirit, intellectual, representatives of
learned professions, graduates of the universities, who were
ready to become colonists in the early settlements of
America.

The settlers in Virginia and in Maryland were chiefly
adventurers intent upon making fortunes, but they brought
with them traditions of "the spacious times of great Elizabeth"; and, though they did not plan for permanent residence in this country, they introduced a generous way of
living which in later times enriched the national life, and
went far towards correcting the somewhat grim and ascetic
thought of New England.

On the other hand the exiles of Plymouth, Salem, and
Massachusetts Bay had come to these shores to find a home.
Among them there were men of the Miltonic type—statesmen and preachers in whom pure morality, religious consecration, mental toughness and activity abounded.

The colonists were Englishmen, who had love for English literature, but they were so much absorbed in maintaining existence that they were unable to keep themselves under such literary influences as were at work in Old England. Still, those influences were felt among the colonists. They produced writers answering to almost every variety of contemporaneous English authorship. The wit of Donne, the dignity of Hooker, the fancy of Jeremy Taylor, and later, the trained sense of Dryden and Pope—all have their counterparts within the neglected volumes of our colonial authors.

The first writings in the New World took the form of messages sent to England. They gave tidings to the friends in the Old Country, called for recruits from the adventurous, and contributed not a little to feed the imagination of English authors and readers. Allusions, and sometimes whole passages in the Elizabethan writers—in Bacon, Raleigh, and Shakespeare—prove the interest which they felt in the writers of the New World.*

The Virginians, pursuing gain and adventure, naturally took the lead in colonial literature. Their heroic John Smith wielded his pen in behalf of the colony with as much vigor and invention as he displayed in managing the disheartened and mutinous settlers at Jamestown. His alert, intrepid and sanguine spirit shines all through the pages of his first book, *A True Relation of Virginia.* "We doubt not," he writes, "but by God's gracious assistance, and the adventurous willing minds and speedy furtherance to so honorable an action in after times, to see our nation enjoy a country, not only exceedingly pleasant for habitation, but also very profitable for commerce in general, no doubt pleasing to Almighty God, honorable to our gracious sovereign, and commodious generally to the whole kingdom." An

---

* Spenser dedicated his *Faerie Queene*, the first great poem of modern English literature, to "Elizabeth the Queene of England, France, and Ireland, and *Virginia.*"

uncultured soldier, who handles his pen with the rough and ready boldness which his sword has learned in the vicissitudes of his stormy career, he has the fire, the directness, the sustained thought and the rich vocabulary of the best prose of the Elizabethan age.

Nor were the muses neglected in the early colony of Virginia. George Sandys, a man whom Dryden has praised as the best versifier of his age, while a resident upon the banks of the James River, made a pleasing translation of Ovid's *Metamorphoses*, which was printed in London in 1621.

Until the close of the seventeenth century, literary expression on this continent was mainly confined to Virginia and New England. The other colonies were so young, or so feeble, or so much engaged in the struggle for existence, that only here and there an individual found disposition to perpetuate his thought in print.

In New England, schools and colleges were established in the early days of the colonies, intellectual life was highly cultivated within narrow lines, and writings abounded. The governors of colonies—Winthrop of Massachusetts Bay (10), and Bradford of Plymouth—made valuable contributions to our literature. The clergymen of the day were eminent for their learning, and frequently published sermons, and discussions relative to the common weal. The people were devout and fond of disputation, and were not disposed to look with favor upon other than serious and controversial writings. The first book printed in America, *The Bay Psalm Book*, came from the press at Harvard College in 1640, and is itself a specimen of the literature for which the popular demand was strongest.

Thomas Hooker (1586–1647), known in his own time as "Minister Hooker," was one of the most influential of the early writers of New England. He was born in England, graduated at the University of Cambridge, and ordained as a preacher of the Established Church. Having been silenced by Archbishop Laud, for non-conformity, he spent a short time in Holland, and then came to Massachusetts, in 1633, with the reputation of being "without an equal either in preaching or in disputation." In 1636 he removed from Cambridge, Mass., to help in the founding of the colony of Connecticut, making his residence at Hartford, where he spent the rest of his life. His writings are exclusively religious. From a large number of his sermons about one hundred were selected, after his death, for publication in London. *A Survey of the Summe of Church Discipline* was his most notable work; the most popular was *The Poor Doubting Christian Drawn to Christ.*

Thomas Shepard (1605–1649), like Hooker, was a native of England, a graduate of Cambridge, a Nonconformist preacher, a man obnoxious to Archbishop Laud, and an exile to America. He arrived at Cambridge, Mass., in 1635, and in the following year was chosen to be Hooker's successor as pastor of the church in that town. In England he had been famous as a preacher; in the colonies he was revered as a man of great learning and piety. His pen was prolific in religious treatises, written in a style full of energy, and sometimes startling with eloquence. Among his writings the following deserve special mention: *The Clear Sunshine of the Gospel Breaking forth upon the Indians of New England, First Principles of the Oracles of God, New England's Lamentations for Old England's Errors.* Much deference was paid to Shepard by the colonial writers of his time, and he, more frequently than any other author, was quoted by them.

John Cotton (1585–1652), like Hooker and Shepard, was of English birth, educated at Cambridge, and driven from England by Laud for Nonconformity. He had won fame in England as the most scholarly and powerful of Puritan preachers, and upon his arrival in Massachusetts, in 1633, he was ordained to fill the most conspicuous pulpit of the colony. For twenty years, preaching all of the time in Boston, he was recognized as the masterly man of New England. He was full of energy, of magnetism, most positive in his opinions, bent upon making the government of New England a theocracy. His scholarship was so varied and so great, and his studies were so untiringly pursued, that he commanded the admiration of his fellow-clergymen; while his success as a preacher, and his shrewdness as a man of affairs, gave him unmatched influence over the laity. No other man of America has been so nearly an autocrat.

It was the man rather than his writings that made John Cotton's influence so great. As a writer he was far less accomplished than either Hooker or Shepard, and yet, in his own time, his writings were applauded as much as theirs. He wrote *Of the Holiness of Church Members, Of Set Forms of Prayer, A Practical Commentary upon the First Epistle of John, Spiritual Milk for Babes, A Treatise of the New Covenant, The Kings of the Kingdom of Heaven,* and many other publications bearing similar religious or theological titles. But the writing which attracted most attention to him in his own day and since was a controversial paper entitled *The Bloody Tenent Washed,* written in a vain attempt to confute the doctrine taught by Roger Williams, that the Civil Magistrate had not the right to interfere in matters of religious faith.

" Of all the great preachers who came to New England in our first age, there were three who, according to the universal opinion of their contemporaries, towered above all others—Thomas Hooker, Thomas Shepard, and John Cotton. These three could be compared with one another, but with them could be compared no one else." *

Although the great mass of early writing in New England was marked by Puritan sternness, there were men profoundly interested in the advancement of liberty who gave bold and powerful expression to their convictions.

Roger Williams (1606–1683) (1) † was the most conspicuous critic of the popular intolerance. A native of Wales, a graduate of Oxford, he was, for a time, a clergyman of the English Church. Convinced that any national Church must be bigoted, he resigned his orders. In 1631 he came to Massachusetts. His preaching at Salem, and his charity for the Indians, were so obnoxious, that he was arraigned in 1635, tried, and banished from the colony. He

---

* Tyler's *History of American Literature,* Vol. I., p. 193.
† The heavy-faced figures throughout this sketch of American Literature refer to selections in Professor B. N. Martin's Choice Specimens of American Literature.

sought the hospitality of the Indians, made it his "soul's desire to do the natives good," and became their most honored friend. Having founded the city of Providence as a haven of religious liberty, he secured a charter for the province of Rhode Island, became its president, and devoted his life to establishing the first of civil governments that allowed freedom of opinion. For this he holds a most honored place in American history. His writings are numerous, teaching that civil authority has no right to interfere with the conscience of its citizens, that the State should never punish violations of the first four Commandments of the Decalogue, and that there should be thorough tolerance in all matters of religion. "Persecutions of men's bodies," he declared, "seldom or never do these men's souls good;" and again, he pronounced it "a monstrous paradox that God's children should persecute God's children, and that they that hope to live eternally together with Jesus Christ in the heavens should not suffer each other to live in the common air together." The most famous of his writings, a strong and noble argument and plea for "soul-liberty," bears the defiant title, *The Bloody Tenet of Persecution for Cause of Conscience*. It was published in London, in the same year with Milton's *Areopagitica*.

John Eliot (1604–1690), a graduate of Cambridge, came to Massachusetts in early manhood and settled at Roxbury as a preacher. "The Apostle to the Indians," a title by which he was known in his own time, is still given to him. His fame as a literary man is chiefly due to his translation into the Indian language of the Bible, the Bay Psalm Book, Baxter's *Call to the Unconverted*, and other religious works. He wrote in English, *The Christian Commonwealth*, *The Harmony of the Gospels*, and *The Communion of Churches*.

Anne Dudley Bradstreet (1612–1672), a lady born in England, the contemporary of John Milton, was the first of our professional poets, and won fame above all other American writers of her time. Daughter of one Puritan governor (Dudley) and wife of another governor, she had every opportunity for influence that eminent social position could give. Moreover, she had heroic qualities. In spite of feeble health she reared a large family amid the trials of the wilderness, and by her industry and talents compelled the austere Puritans to recognize in her the most accomplished and most influential woman of New England. Their praise of her was lavish; they named her "The Tenth Muse." The first edition of her writings, printed in 1650, aroused such pride among the colonists as no other writings had called forth. The volume contained a series of poems, with four related themes in each poem. Its title, worthy of attention for its unique stateliness, reveals ambitious effort. The title is "The Tenth Muse lately sprung up in America; or, Several Poems, compiled with great variety of wit and learning, full of delight, Wherein especially is contained a complete discourse and description of the four elements, constitutions, ages of man, seasons of the year; together with an exact epitome of the four monarchies, viz., the Assyrian, Persian, Grecian, Roman; also a dialogue between Old England and New concerning the late troubles; with divers other pleasant and serious poems By a gentlewoman of those parts."

The sombre quality of Mrs. Bradstreet's verse was not peculiar to her; it was the mannerism belonging to all the Puritan writers. Her themes, historical and scientific, give her frequent opportunity for religious reflection. In "Contemplations," a poem written later in life, she rids herself of some of her earlier mannerism, and displays greater freedom of poetic feeling.

The Mathers. A father, son, and grandson,—Richard, Increase, and Cotton Mather, were men of immeasurable influence in Massachusetts. Their power was wielded from the early days of the colony until the close of the first quarter of the eighteenth century. They were men of great mental power, of self-assertion and self-esteem, of profound learning, of the severest Puritanism in theology and in manner of life; and these traits, pronounced in the father, were stronger in the son, and yet stronger in the grandson. "This fact is recorded in an old epitaph, composed for the founder of the illustrious tribe:

'Under this stone lies Richard Mather,
Who had a son greater than his father,
And eke a grandson greater than either.'"

Richard Mather (1596–1669), after leaving Oxford, became a preacher of the English Church, but, for the crime of preaching without his surplice, he was silenced by the Archbishop, and soon after, disguised, he set sail for Boston. An accomplished scholar and a powerful preacher, his services were in great demand. He settled at Dorchester in 1636, and there lived till the end of his days. His writings were voluminous, consisting of published sermons, controversial papers, and religious treatises. He was the author of the Preface to the Old Bay Psalm Book.

Increase Mather (1639–1723), was the first of the eminent scholars of New England who was born on this continent. He was a native of Dorchester, a student at Harvard in his thirteenth year, a graduate at seventeen. In his twentieth year he declined a fellowship at Trinity College, Dublin, where he had been winning scholarly distinction, and then, for three years, was a powerful preacher in England. Returning to America in his twenty-fifth year, he accepted the pastorate of the North Church in Boston. He was more than an eloquent preacher; he was a man of rare learning, of untiring industry, of unyielding will, of towering ambition, and of great political shrewdness. He was the autocrat of Massachusetts. While pastor of the North Church, he spent some years at the courts of James II. and of William and Mary, as the diplomatist of the colony, and during sixteen years of his pastorate he held the Presidency of Harvard College, then the goal of Puritan ambition. For more than fifty years of his life he was the most prolific of American authors. The best known of his works is a volume entitled *An Essay for the Recording of Illustrious Providences.* In literary style Increase Mather is more exact, simple, vigorous, and vivid than either his father or his son.

Cotton Mather (1663–1728 (**2**) was the consummate flower of a stock of scholarly and mighty men. Besides his inheritance from the Mathers he was the grandson of the " great John Cotton." At fifteen years of age he graduated with distinction at Harvard College. Then he was a teacher for five years, receiving ordination as a preacher when he became of age. His first sermon was preached at Dorchester, in his grandfather's pulpit; his second sermon was for his father's pulpit at North Church, Boston; his third sermon for his grandfather, John Cotton, in Boston. Thus introduced to the pulpit of New England, and already famous for his precocious

scholarship, the young man was in the line of succession for pre-
eminence among the Puritans. His learning was marvelous; he
knew all classical and theological literature, and was able to command his knowledge at a moment's warning. Of himself he says,
"I am not unable, with a little study, to write in seven languages.
I feast myself with the secrets of all the sciences which the more
polite part of mankind admiringly pretend unto. I am entertained
with all kinds of histories; ancient and modern." The people of
his time placed him before all other men in greatness and godli-
ness, and by their praise helped him to a very high opinion of himself. Three hundred and eighty-two publications are ascribed to
him, some sermons, some ponderous tomes. His *Magnalia Christi
Americana : or the Ecclesiastical History of New England from its
first Planting in the year 1620, unto the year of our Lord 1698,* is the
most bulky of his works, and although full of pedantry and error
it is the most valuable of colonial historical writing. He was the
last eminent writer of the Puritan style.

Later Colonial Writers.—At the beginning of the eighteenth
century the people of the New World had mastered many of the
difficulties which beset them in their earlier history. Their settlements had permanence assured to them ; agriculture and commerce
were well started ; the colonies had formed alliances with each
other, and the weaker colonies had developed strength.

The theocratic spirit of Massachusetts no longer dominated New
England. In the northern colonies friends and laymen, as well as
the orthodox clergy, were using their pens. **Captain Benjamin
Church** (1639–1718), who commanded the forces against King
Philip, wrote a valuable history, entitled *Entertaining Passages Relating to King Philip's War.* **Robert Calef,** a merchant of Boston,
had the courage to publish, in 1700, a book attacking the Mathers
and others of the clergy who had fanned the flame of the witchcraft delusion. **Benjamin Thompson** (1640–1714), "the learned
schoolmaster" of Boston, and **Roger Wolcott** (1679–1767), governor of Connecticut, won distinction as poets. **James Logan**
(1674–1751), chief justice of the colony of Pennsylvania, and
founder of the Loganian Library in Philadelphia, wrote many
scientific papers, which were republished in England and on the
Continent. **Cadwallader Colden** (1688–1776), (6), a physician, and

lieutenant-governor of New York, was the author of many scientific papers, and of *A History of the Five Indian Nations*. **Thomas Clap** (1793–1767), President of Yale College, a thoughtful and accomplished writer, was the author of religious, speculative, and historical works. **Jonathan Dickinson** (1688–1744), the first President of the College of New Jersey, was a man of such power as an orator, of such lofty character, that he had commanding influence throughout the middle colonies. He ranked next to Jonathan Edwards as a logician and theologian, having a European reputation. His most popular work was a volume of *Familiar Letters to a Gentleman upon a Variety of Seasonable and Important Subjects in Religion*.

Virginia was no longer the home of adventurers. Her citizens had established themselves as permanent residents, were founding schools and colleges, and were contributing to American literature. **Robert Beverley**, a young Virginian, the earliest of our Southern historians, published a history of his native colony in 1705. His work, like *The Present State of Virginia*, written by **Hugh Jones**, was intended to correct the prejudices which had been created in England against the colony and its territory by the malcontents who had returned to the mother country. But the man deserving most praise among the writers of Virginia was **James Blair** (1656–1743), the first President of William and Mary College. He was a Scotchman, a clergyman of the English Church, who came to Virginia in compliance with the urgent solicitations of the Bishop of London. His greatest service to the Southern colonies was his success in awakening an interest in education, and this success was won by untiring effort. He wrote important papers pertaining to Virginia and its college, but he made his best literary reputation in England and in America by publishing a series of one hundred and seventeen sermons on *Our Saviour's Divine Sermon on the Mount*.

JONATHAN EDWARDS.

"The metaphysician of America."—*Sir James Mackintosh.*

"The most subtle reasoner that America has produced."—*Prof. A. C. Fraser.*

"I consider Jonathan Edwards the greatest of the sons of men. He ranks with the brightest luminaries of the Christian Church, not excluding any country or any age since the apostolic."—*Robert Hall.*

"His works will live as long as powerful reasoning, genuine religion, and the science of the human mind continue to be objects of respect."—*William Orme.*

"I do not think our age has produced a divine of equal genius or judgment."—*Dr. Erskine.*

"America may boast of one metaphysician, who, in logical acuteness and subtlety, does not yield to any disputant bred in the universities of Europe. I need not say that I allude to Jonathan Edwards."—*Dugald Stewart.*

"We do not scruple to say that he is one of the acutest, most powerful, and of all reasoners the most conscientious and sincere."—*William Hazlitt.*

"On the arena of metaphysics he stood the highest of all his contemporaries, and we know not what most to admire in him, whether the deep philosophy that issued from his pen, or the humble and child-like piety that issued from his pulpit."—*Dr. Chalmers.*

Jonathan Edwards (1703–1758) (**3**), the son of a Congregational clergyman, was born at Windsor, Connecticut. He entered Yale College in his thirteenth year, and at nineteen was settled as a preacher in the city of New York. The year following he was elected a tutor at Yale. After two years of teaching he began his famous career as a preacher at Northampton, Massachusetts. There, for twenty-four years, he toiled with such success as to win the foremost place among the scholars and preachers of America; but he was compelled to leave his beloved pulpit, for dissension arose in his church on account of the plainness and severity of his preaching, and a large majority of his congregation were against him. He then went as a missionary to the Indians at Stockbridge, in western Massachusetts, and there, finding leisure at his command, he began the systematic statement of his philosophy. For eight years, with his wife and their ten children, living upon the frontier and among the Indians, in great poverty, this godly man found his duty and his delight in philosophical thought. From

this obscure place he was summoned, in 1758, to the presidency of the College of New Jersey. He assumed the duties of his office in February, and was received with great enthusiasm; but a month later he died.

No religious or speculative writer of our colonial period can be compared favorably with Edwards. He was a profound metaphysician, and he declared the Calvinistic philosophy with a clearness which no other writer had equaled. His works were more voluminous than those of any other author of the eighteenth century; and the profoundest of them, the *Freedom of the Will*, which was also the profoundest discussion of his time, was written while he was toiling amid severe privations as a missionary among the Indians.

His moral and intellectual qualities are equally admirable. Humility, patience, tolerance, piety, fervor, reverence, sincerity, unfaltering faith, the courage of his convictions, and a most solemn consecration to duty, are among the virtues of his character, while clearness and incisiveness of thought, sustained powers of reasoning, the light of imagination, the closest analysis of thought, keen observation of man and of nature, and literary ardor, are intellectual forces which he displays. His life and his works are full of solemn awe for the sovereignty of God.

The development of his character was precocious, for even in his boyhood he had firmly established the principles that governed him, and those principles were written into the famous "seventy resolutions" to "regulate his heart and life."

The first five of those resolutions may serve as samples of the rigorous discipline which he exercised over himself:

1. *Resolved*, That I will do whatsoever I think to be most to the glory of God, and my own good, profit, and pleasure, in the whole of my duration, without any consideration of the time, whether now, or never so many myriads of ages hence.

2. *Resolved*, To do whatever I think to be my duty and most for the good of mankind in general.

3. *Resolved*, Never to lose one moment of time, but to improve it in the most profitable way I possibly can.

4. *Resolved*, To live with all my might while I do live.

5. *Resolved*, Never to do anything which I should be afraid to do if it were the last hour of my life.

In his sixteenth year Edwards read Locke's Essay on the Human Understanding. It gave him "far higher pleasure than the most greedy miser finds when gathering up handfuls of silver and gold from some newly discovered treasure." His enthusiasm for metaphysical thinking never abated; but all of his speculations were directed towards theology.

Not even an enumeration of his many publications can be given in this sketch. Among his famous writings are *The History of the Work of Redemption*, *An Account of the Life of the Late Rev. David Brainard, Missionary to the Indians*, *A Treatise concerning Religious Affections*, and an *Inquiry into the Freedom of the Will*.

The *Treatise Concerning Religious Affections*, written during his pastorate at Northampton, was the product of long-continued study. It is written in careless style, but its thoughts are profound, and its analysis of the affections of mind under religious influence, and its characterizations of hypocrisy, are masterly.

After his removal to Stockbridge, Edwards had opportunity to give his time almost wholly to study, and there, from notes of his former thinking, he developed and arranged the argument by which he defended, upon metaphysical grounds, the theology of Calvin against the opposing views of Arminianism, and after five months of writing he had completed his famous *Inquiry into the Freedom of the Will*. That work made him eminent among the metaphysicians of the world.

BENJAMIN FRANKLIN.

"Franklin was the greatest diplomatist of the eighteenth century."—*George Bancroft*.

"His genius ranks him with the Galileos and the Newtons of the Old World."—*Lord Brougham*.

"Antiquity would have raised altars to this mighty genius."—*Mirabeau*.

"Science appears in his language in a dress wonderfully decorous, best adapted to display her native loveliness."—*Sir Humphrey Davy*.

Benjamin Franklin (1706–1790), (**13—16**), the son of a poor man, was taken from school at ten years of age, and set at work to help his father in making candles. The boy had a passion for reading and for the sea. At twelve, he was bound an apprentice to an older brother in the printer's trade. This apprenticeship was intended by the father to prevent the boy from running away; it was welcomed by the boy, inasmuch as it gave him access to books. In four years he was an expert in his business, and resenting the lack of appreciation, and the tyranny of his brother, he escaped his indenture, and fled to Philadelphia. There he worked at his trade, was thrifty and studious, and watchful for any chance that might help him. The governor of the colony professed great interest in him, and persuaded him to go to England for the purpose of buying the outfit for a new printing-office in Philadelphia; but the governor proved to be a faithless friend. After working a year at his trade in England, Franklin returned to Philadelphia and became the proprietor of the *Pennsylvania Gazette*. Success attended him. He was popular with all classes, and was especially influential among young men of studious habits. At this time he devised a plan for a library, and founded what has grown to be the "Library Company of Philadelphia." In 1732 he published the first number of *Poor Richard's Almanac*, a publication of great popularity for a quarter of a century. At thirty years of age he was prominent in all movements for the public welfare, was made clerk of the provincial General Assembly, and postmaster of Philadelphia. As commissioner to the Indians, as member of the Assembly, as founder of the American Philosophical Society, as one of the founders of the first hospital in the land, as an investigator in science, and as an author, he won an eminent place in his city and in the colony. His fame went abroad. Scholastic degrees were conferred upon him by Yale and Harvard and the universities of Edinburgh and Oxford, he was elected a "Fellow of the Royal Society," and in 1757 the king appointed him Postmaster General of America. During one of his visits to England he was summoned before the bar of the House of Commons to be interrogated in regard to the government

of the colonies. His influence on that occasion secured the
repeal of the Stamp Act. When the national impulse
started in this country he was one of its leaders, and was
a signer of the Declaration of Independence. During the
War of the Revolution he was our Minister Plenipotentiary
at the Court of France, where he won great fame as a
diplomatist. His country revered him, and in his old age
he won fresh laurels as a statesman of wonderful sagacity.
He was made Governor of Pennsylvania in 1785, and represented his State in the Federal Convention of 1787. In
1790, at the age of eighty-four, then being the special object
of his country's veneration, he died.

Striking points of contrast appear between Edwards and
Franklin, the two gigantic thinkers of our colonial period.
The son of an eminent divine, thoroughly trained in all the
learning of his day, called to active work in his profession
while yet in his teens, applauded by admiring colleagues,
Edwards could not have had better help in the cultivation
of his great natural gifts; while Franklin, among the
youngest of a family of seventeen children, reared in poverty, without early instruction, an exile from his home, had
a dreary way to travel, alone, unguided, and beset by many
hindrances. In their later years, Edwards, having left the
most conspicuous pulpit in New England, dwelt in the solitude of the wilderness ; while Franklin, emerging from the
obscurity of the printer's shop, became the most conspicuous social gentleman of England and America. Their
mental characters are as dissimilar as their careers. Edwards, eager to serve mankind, spent all his energy in the
work of a metaphysician; equally devoted to the service of
his fellow-men, Franklin displayed the forces of his versatile genius as a moralist, a philosopher, a diplomat, a statesman, a philanthropist. Edwards wrought to establish the old
faiths; Franklin developed new ideas; the theologian was
the strictest of his sect ; the philosopher was latitudinarian.

Both were men of measureless power, of tireless industry, of unswerving integrity; and both were animated by a sacred purpose to do good in the world.

Franklin's writings, edited by Dr. Jared Sparks in ten volumes octavo, are classified as follows:—1. *Autobiography.* 2. *Essays on Religious and Moral Subjects and the Economy of Life.* 3. *Essays on General Politics, Commerce, and Political Economy.* 4. *Essays and Tracts, Historical and Political, before the American Revolution.* 5. *Political Papers during and after the American Revolution.* 6. *Letters and Papers on Electricity.* 7. *Letters and Papers on Philosophical Subjects.* 8. *Correspondence.*

The clearness, force and naturalness of his style give charms to every page; shrewdness of thought and power of concise expression made him the author of a great number of our proverbs. "At all times, and in everything he undertook, the vigor of an understanding at once original and practical, was distinctly perceivable. But it must not be supposed that his writings are devoid of ornament or amusement. The latter especially abounds, in almost all he ever composed, only nothing is sacrificed to them. On the contrary, they come most naturally into their places, and they uniformly help on the purpose in hand, of which neither writer nor reader ever loses sight for an instant. Thus his style has all the vigor, and even conciseness, of Swift, without any of his harshness." *

In this chapter we have considered:—

The Colonial Period of American Literature.
1. *Thomas Hooker, Thomas Shepard, John Cotton, Roger Williams.*
2. *Anne Dudley Bradstreet.*
3. *The Mathers.*
4. *Jonathan Edwards.*
5. *Benjamin Franklin.*

* Lord Jeffrey.

CHAPTER II.

THE REVOLUTIONARY PERIOD.

From the Declaration of Independence to the Adoption of the Constitution.

THE literature of our Revolutionary period is vigorous and profound in its discussion of the political rights of man. There had been preparation for such writing. A century and a half of fighting against the savages and of resisting the oppressive legislation of England, had made the colonists forgetful of their mutual jealousies. They were ready to unite in asking their king for redress of grievances. Their petitions were ignored, and they made their Declaration of Independence, appealing to the King of kings for their rights. The sacred right to rebel against tyranny had never been fully broached till then; but our fathers declared it with all the emphasis that strong convictions could give. They drew their swords for a political conviction. "The Parliament of Great Britain asserted a right to tax the colonies in all cases whatsoever; and it was precisely on this question that they made the Revolution turn. The amount of taxation was trifling, but the claim itself was inconsistent with liberty, and that was in their eyes enough. It was against the recital of an act of Parliament, rather than against any suffering under its enactments, that they took up arms. They went to war against a preamble. They fought seven years against a declaration. They poured out their treasures and their blood like water, in a contest in opposition to an assertion which those less sagacious and not so well schooled in the principles of civil liberty would have regarded as barren phraseology or mere parade of words." * Men who had the heroism to take such a position were capable of producing noble political literature. Orators began to clothe the thoughts of the people in eloquent words, and writers produced many vigorous pamphlets. Already for half a century the weekly newspapers, small folios of four pages, had been publishing and discussing political news in the colonies, and three or four monthly magazines had been sustained for a decade by American authors and readers, so that the way had been prepared for the reception of new political writing. And there were educated men who had been trained in the early American colleges.

The presidents of these colleges were eminent among religious and political thinkers, and one of them wielded great political influence. **John Witherspoon, D.D., LL.D.** (1722—1794), president of the College of New Jersey, a signer of the Declaration of Independence, was a member of the General Congress during the Revolutionary War, and was one of its most active workers. A brilliant debater, a ready, humorous, and argumentative writer, his voice and pen were helpful in securing the independence of America. **Ezra Stiles, D.D., LL.D.** (1727—1795), of whom Channing said in 1835, "This country has not, perhaps, produced a more learned man," was president of Yale College for nearly a quarter of a century. His writings were usually scholastic or theological, but a few of them gave inspiration to the patriotism of his times.

The earliest of the great orators who led the way to freedom was **James Otis** (1725-1783), of Massachusetts. He was a scholarly lawyer, who wrote treatises on Latin and Greek prosody at the time when he was winning renown in his profession. In 1761 he made his powerful argument against "writs of assistance,"

* Daniel Webster.

and committed himself as an uncompromising foe to arbitrary British rule in America. His eloquence was a "flame of fire." Among his political writings are *A Vindication of the Conduct of the House of Representatives of Massachusetts Bay, The Rights of the British Colonists Asserted and Proved,* and *A Vindication of the British Colonists.*

Alexander Hamilton (1757–1804), **(66–67)**, was a native of the West Indies. At sixteen years of age he entered King's College, at New York. A year later, at a mass meeting in the city, he displayed astounding precocity as an orator, and at once was recognized as a leader of the revolutionists. In his nineteenth year he was placed in command of the company of artillery which had been raised by the Provincial Committee of New York, and began his career as a soldier. Washington quickly recognized his gifts, and summoned him to the staff of the commander-in-chief. He was Washington's "most confidential aide," and served him as secretary, writing many valuable military papers. At the close of the war he practiced law in New York, and was leader of the bar of that city. In securing the adoption of the Constitution of the United States, besides making the most brilliant forensic arguments, he wrote many papers of masterly power. He was the author of fifty-one numbers of the *Federalist*, and his share in that work was so much esteemed that it was promptly translated into French, and was widely read in Europe. De Tocqueville said of it that "it ought to be familiar to the statesmen of every nation." As Secretary of the Treasury under Washington, Hamilton was author of the most famous state papers which have been written in our country. At the same time his brilliant pen wrote the letters of "Camillus," a profound series of papers on questions of international law.

In serving his country Hamilton had thwarted the ambition of Aaron Burr. The antipathy felt by Burr forced a duel between them, and Hamilton fell. Fisher Ames, Hamilton's rival as an orator, wrote, "My soul stiffens with despair when I think what Hamilton might have been."

Thomas Jefferson (1743–1826), **(61–64)**, lacking the gifts of an orator, aspired to literary honors. His radicalism belonged to his religion and his morals as well as to his politics, so that novelty of thought and force of expression abound in his writing. In addition to papers of the State, he was the author of a *Parliamentary Manual*, of *Notes on the State of Virginia*, and of voluminous and interesting correspondence; but no literary work could add to the fame won by him as author of the *Declaration of Independence*.

George Washington (1732–1799), (**249**), is not ranked among the authors of his times, and yet his writings fill twelve octavo volumes. They contain official papers, selected letters, and now and then an essay on some agricultural topic. Writing was not a pleasure to him, but, like everything which he attempted, it was carefully done. It has been said that there was "a certain considerate, moral tone which distinguished all Washington's writing. It is stamped by the position, the character, the very turns of phrase of the great man who gave it to his country."

John Adams (1735–1826), (**56, 57**) wrote *A Dissertation on Canon and Feudal Law, A History of the Quarrel between Great Britain and the American Colonies, A Defense of the Constitution of the United States of America, Discourses on Davila, a series of Papers on American History*. Two volumes of *Letters*, addressed to his wife, have a permanent place in literature.

John Jay (1745–1829), (**65**), **James Madison** (1751–1836), (**72, 73**), **James Monroe** (1758–1831), and **William Livingston** (1723–1790), belonged to the group of eminent statesmen whose pens wielded mighty influence over the national thought during the Revolutionary period, and their writings add luster to our political literature.

Hardship and solicitude did not quench the humor of our forefathers. The same Revolutionary period which inspired the earnest writings of the statesmen abounded in humorous and satiric writings. **Francis Hopkinson,** of New Jersey (1737–1791), "a poet, a wit, a patriot, a chemist, a mathematician, and a judge of the admiralty," wielded a powerful influence as a humorous teacher of political independence. **Hugh Henry Brackenridge**, of Philadelphia (1748–1816), teacher, editor, preacher, and lawyer in turn, had literary fame in his day. His *Modern Chivalry; the Adventures of Captain Farrago*, still gives him reputation as a humorist. **John**

Trumbull, of Connecticut (1750–1831), **(316)**, a voluminous author, published in 1775 *McFingal, A Modern Epic Poem,* in imitation of Hudibras, to " satirize the follies and extravagances of my country-men as well as of their enemies." . The success of the poem made him the most conspicuous literary character of his day in this country. **Benjamin Rush** (1745–1813), **(101)**, an eminent surgeon of Philadelphia, wrote many scientific and social papers of great value. **David Ramsay** (1745–1815), **(114)**, of South Carolina, was the most distinguished of early American historians.

In this chapter we have considered:—

The Revolutionary Period of American Literature.

1. John Witherspoon, Ezra Stiles.

2. James Otis.

3. Alexander Hamilton, Thomas Jefferson, George Washington, John Adams, and minor writers.

CHAPTER III.

THE NATIONAL PERIOD.

THE war of 1776 gave to Americans an independent political existence, and it is fitting that this fact should be marked in their literary annals ; but it must never be forgotten that the adoption of the Constitution in 1787 did not bring with it a new and original literature. Our modes of thought, our style of expression, remained for many years distinctively English ; nor is any change which we may observe at present to be attributed to the influence of our national institutions, so much as to the enforced contact with Continental thought and customs brought to us by the stream of immigration. Nobody believes any longer in America's peculiar literary mission,— a mission fairly described in the words of the late Sidney Lanier as "* * * going to give a great new revolutionized democratic literature, which will wear a slouch hat and have its shirt open at the bosom, and generally riot in a complete independence of form." The ablest critic of to-day, and the impartial historian of our past, must alike admit that the highest claim for our literature, as well as its truest description, is that of being English written on this side of the Atlantic.

Although we disclaim for our literature any nationality that consists in a novelty of theme or treatment which might properly be considered the outgrowth of our polit-ical theories or the expression of " our vastness," we would emphasize the fact that there has been a continuous prog-

ress in the scope and delicacy of our literary art. Necessary toil, constant privation, poverty, and the thousand
other adverse circumstances that stunted literature during
the Colonial and Revolutionary periods, have given way
before the softening influences of time, of prosperity, and of
assured government, thus making leisure and contemplation
increasingly within the reach of all classes. The first result
of this change is to be noticed in the fact that our writers
are no longer so exclusively ministers and women. Their
literary responsibility seems to have been at first shared
with the Congressmen who went to debate at Washington,
and the Senators and Representatives who formed the State
legislatures. As the uprightness of the individual had been
the burden of Colonial literature, so the integrity of the
State was the first care of the young nation, and it was not
until the ardor of this labor had somewhat spent itself that
more artistic claims asserted themselves.

The last fifty years have brought significant changes, all
tending to emphasize the lines of distinction between professions; and we look back on the men of two generations
ago with the feeling that they must have been giants. Even
legislative business was idealized, and its record became
heroic. The speeches which Webster (85—88), Calhoun
(82—84), and Clay (80—81), wrote in support of measures
that are utterly forgotten still stir our blood. But the
lengthening lines of our national perspective have already
dwarfed many reputations that once seemed towering.

During the opening years of this period the influence of
French thought was very distinctly marked. **Thomas Paine**,
the author of the pamphlet *Common Sense*, which had been
so influential in deciding the colonists to enter upon the
struggle for independence, published in 1791 and 1792 a
vindication of the French Revolution under the title of *The
Rights of Man*. *The Age of Reason*, a later work of Paine's,
has been the armory from which the weapons for most sub-

sequent attacks upon revealed religion and conventional morality have been taken.

Philip Freneau (1752–1832), **(317)**, was the first American poet whose verses were much read in England ; but in spite of this, and the fact that his first volume, published in 1786, celebrated the events of the Revolution and narrated the author's own experience in a British prison-ship, it is as the editor of the *National Gazette* and the opponent of Hamilton that he is chiefly remembered in history. Freneau was a warm advocate of French political opinions.

Joel Barlow (1775–1812), minister, psalm-writer, lawyer and politician, was also a disciple of French republicanism. He projected a history of the French Revolution, and one of the United States, but never carried out either plan. He was a friend of the Girondins, opposed Washington's government, and was Minister to France under Monroe. His *Vision of Columbus* was published in 1787; the *Columbiad* in 1808.

Timothy Dwight (1752–1817), **(20—21)**, met with success in civil affairs, in poetry, and in theology. As president of Yale College for twenty-one years before his death, he seems to have added teaching to his other gifts. He is perhaps most widely known as a poet, in his version of the One Hundred and Thirty-seventh Psalm, "I love thy kingdom, Lord." His contribution to theology was in five volumes, published after his death under the title *Theology Explained and Defended*, a work very influential in the Congregational denomination. His satirical poem, *The Triumph of Infidelity*, was dedicated to Voltaire.

Charles Brockden Brown (1771–1810), **(276)**, the first American novelist, and the first of our authors to adopt literature as a profession, was a man of remarkable scope of mind, but weak in body. During his short life, which was a constant struggle with ill health, he wrote a succession of fictions, essays, political papers, and fragments of works on history, geography, and architecture. *Wieland*, published in 1798, gives evidence of the strong influence of Godwin, who had published his *Caleb Williams* four years earlier in England.

Arthur Mervyn, his third novel, is still read for its realistic description of the yellow fever in Philadelphia. Brown made several
attempts to establish a magazine, under the names of the *Monthly
Magazine and American Register* (1799), *The Literary Magazine and
American Register* (1803), *The American Register*, a semi-annual
(1807). His literary style is remarkable for its clearness, strength,
and melancholy; his character for its gentleness and equanimity
under misfortune.

The names of **Hannah Adams, David Ramsay, Jeremy Bel-
knap (113),** and **Abiel Holmes** are connected with the historical
research of this period. **Wirt's** *Life of Patrick Henry* and **Chief
Justice Marshall's** *Life of Washington* are still read.

Most of our early science, best represented by the labors **of
Rush** and **Wilson,** has comparatively little literary value.

Almost simultaneously with the outbreak of the war of 1812 the
literary activity of the country took on a controversial aspect, resulting in the formation of groups of writers associated by moral or artistic
principles. New York and Boston became the headquarters of the
rival claimants for public hearing. Historically, and perhaps artist-
ically too, Boston established her precedence. In that city, in the
midst of the "hard times" of the first year of the war, Nathaniel
Willis (father of the poet) was employed by Dr. Jedediah Morse
(father of the electrician) to print several editions of a pamphlet
entitled *American Unitarianism*, which attracted much attention,
and led to the famous Unitarian controversy. The Park Street
lectures by Dr. Griffin, sermons, addresses, and magazine articles by
all the ministers of ability in the neighborhood of Boston, testified
to the awakened interest. Foremost among those upholding the
Unitarian doctrine were Dr. Channing, Dr. Ware, and Professor Nor-
ton, while Dr. Morse, Moses Stuart, Leonard Woods, and Dr. Worces-
ter were equally stanch in their support of the orthodox views.

The First Religious Newspaper. Dr. Morse and Mr. Willis
have both claimed that the Boston *Recorder*, established in 1816,
was the first religious newspaper ever published; but there seems
to be little doubt that, although the original idea was the property
of Mr. Willis, the credit of actually publishing the earliest is due
to John Andrews, of Chillicothe, Ohio, whose paper, also the *Recorder*, was issued from 1814 to 1817, inclusive.

The most prominent literary figure among these earnest and learned men was **William Ellery Channing** (1780–1842), (**24—26**). The characteristics of his writings are enthusiasm and moral energy. By his direct and uncompromising treatment of the subjects of slavery, war, temperance, and education, he gained a remarkable influence over the opinions of the young people of his generation. He had profound respect for personal liberty and responsibility. In spite of his small stature and feeble health, his oratory was by turns powerful and winning. His best known essays are the *Moral Argument against Calvinism* (1820), *Remarks on the Character and Writings of John Milton* (1826), *Napoleon Bonaparte*, *Fénélon*, and *Self-Culture*.

The influence of this controversy has been felt down to our own day, and has been the animus of much of the writing of Lyman Beecher (**23**), Charles Hodge, President Hopkins, on the orthodox side, of James Freeman Clarke, Dr. Bellows, Dr. Peabody, and Theodore Parker among the liberals.

Theodore Parker (1810–1860), (**168—171**), was born in 1810 at Lexington, Mass. He was the grandson of a Revolutionary soldier, and seems to have inherited a good deal of the spirit of resistance which fired his sturdy ancestor. His literary work consists largely of sermons written on questions of slavery, war, social and moral reforms; of lectures, a few critical essays, and papers on theological subjects. His scholarship, though hardly profound, was encyclopædic; his temper courageous and energetic. The influence of his incisive thought was great, both on antagonists and on adherents. He was proscribed by the Unitarian societies of Boston for his extreme theological opinions, and organized some time about 1844 a congregation which met in the Melodeon, and later in the Music Hall. He died in Florence in 1860.

In this chapter we have considered:—

1. Thomas Paine; 2. Philip Freneau; 3. Joel Bar-
low; 4. John Trumbull; 5. Timothy Dwight;
6. Charles Brockden Brown; 7. William
Ellery Channing; 8. Theodore Parker.

CHAPTER IV.

WASHINGTON IRVING AND THE KNICKERBOCKER WRITERS.

"I have had a friend of your Mr. Irving's, . . . and talked with him much of Irving, whose writings are my delight."—*Byron.*

"Few, very few, can show a long succession of volumes so pure, so graceful, and so varied, as Mr. Irving."—*Mary Russell Mitford.*

"I have never read anything so closely resembling the style of Dean Swift as the *Annals of Diedrich Knickerbocker.*"—*Sir Walter Scott.*

"Mr. Washington Irving is one of our first favorites among the English writers of this age, and he is not a bit the less so for having been born in America."— *J. G. Lockhart.*

WHILE Boston was the arena in which the most philosophical minds of America were fighting the battles of theology, New York was the scene of a much milder and more genial display of mental activity. Local traditions were revived and given to the public in the pages of magazines that attempted to reproduce the ease and grace of the *Spectator* and *Tatler.* Young poets threw off their copies of verses in the intervals of business, witty lawyers indulged themselves in parodies and good-natured lampoons. Much of all this had only a passing value, but the possession of certain gifts in the lines indicated marked out a group of writers, most of whom were afterward employed on the *Knickerbocker Magazine* (1833) under the editorship of Charles Fenno Hoffman (**362**). They have sometimes been known as the Knickerbocker School, but there was hardly organization enough among them to deserve so sounding a name. Moreover, their experiments had been tried some time before by Joseph Dennie (**150**) and his friend Royal Tyler, in the *Farmers' Museum* of Walpole, N. H. (1796–1799), and in the *Porte Folio* of Philadelphia (1800–1812). The greater success of the Knickerbockers would seem to be due rather to the growing interest of the public in literature than to the superior merits of most of their productions. Aside from the crowd of writers who are already forgotten, the names of Irving, Paulding, Verplanck, Drake, and Halleck deserve somewhat extended notice.

Washington Irving (1783–1859), (**178—185**), was born in New York, not too late to be impressed by the natural beauty of his native city, not too late to receive a smile and blessing from Washington himself. In spite of these advantages, however, he experienced great difficulty in learning the alphabet, and never took kindly to regular study. At ten he loved to read a translation of Ariosto, and throughout his school days was more faithful to Chaucer and Spenser than to arithmetic, which he hated so much that he used to write the other boys' compositions while they did his "sums." Later, his indifferent health and application com-bined to keep him from attempting the course of study at Columbia College, and at the age of sixteen he entered his name as a student of law in an attorney's office. At nine-teen he wrote a series of essays for a paper called the *Chronicle*, edited by his brother Peter. These papers discussed social topics, in a light and humorous manner, over the signature of Jonathan Oldstyle. In 1804, Irving sailed for the south of France in search of health. A stay of two years in Europe, loitering about in Italy, Belgium, and Holland, was not likely to increase his love of legal pursuits. Indeed, while at Rome, in the society of Washington All-ston, he planned a future devoted to art, but the close of the year 1806 found him back in America and admitted to the bar. The young lawyer's first success was not in his profession, but in the line of his long-cherished tastes. *Salmagundi* was the joint production of William and Washington Irving and James K. Paulding, the elder Irving contributing the poetry, while the two younger men wrote nearly all the prose. The fortnightly issue of this period-ical, and the general tone of its comments, were strongly suggestive of the *Tatler* and *Spectator*, but the tales and scenes were of Tammany Hall, the Battery, and Wall Street.

From childhood Irving had been fond of wandering about New York, learning every corner of the quaint Dutch city, lingering by every bluff or knoll along the Hudson to study its beauty or its history. The school-boy who might have learned more Greek, and the young attorney who might have been pettifogging, were justified in 1809 by the publication of *Diedrich Knickerbocker's History of New York.* Everybody read it, and everybody laughed—excepting always the critic of the London Quarterly, who could not get "the point of many of the allusions in this political satire." The laughter came with a little effort, perhaps, from some of the Knickerbocker families who saw their honored names and customs thus satirized; but the delicate and kindly apology of the author in his second edition healed all fancied wounds. In 1810 his memoir of the poet Campbell appeared; three years later he tried journalism in Philadelphia, editing the *Analectic Magazine*, to which Paulding and Verplanck both contributed. Soon after the publication of the *History of New York* he was established in Liverpool, at liberty to indulge his taste for wandering about in picturesque neighborhoods.

Meantime his fortune had been lost in the business reverses which followed the peace of 1815, and it became necessary for him to set about some work that would yield an income. He began the *Sketch Book*, sending the numbers over to New York to be published by Van Winkle, in octavos of from seventy to a hundred pages. The great London publisher, Murray, was induced to buy the copyright of the entire work for £400. This bargain was brought about by the friendly mediation of Sir Walter Scott, an instance of international courtesy which found a later parallel in the business relations of Carlyle and Emerson. *Bracebridge Hall* and the *Tales of a Traveller* followed, for which Murray gave him £1,000 and £1,500 respectively. But they did not arouse such enthusiasm as had hailed the fun of *Knickerbocker* and the soberer fancy of the *Sketch Book*. Americans found nothing in the studies of English country life to compare with *Rip Van Winkle* and the *Legend of Sleepy Hollow*, while English critics openly accused him of truckling to their national vanity in his choice of subject, and taunted him with the fact that Brockden Brown had braved criticism and died poor. The fault-finding from both sides of the Atlantic seems to have been overstrained. The genius of Irving was essentially appreciative; his satire that of the humorist, not of the critic ; his imagination the artist's, not the reformer's. He felt a generous admiration for all that was noble and beautiful in England, and he never dreamed of being misunderstood.

In 1825, Irving was invited by Alexander H. Everett American Minister at Madrid, to visit Spain. A second visit, in 1827, resulted in the *Life and Voyages of Christopher Columbus*. The *Chronicles of the Conquest of Granada*, the *Voyages of the Companions of Columbus*, and the *Alhambra*, followed close upon his third tour in Spain.

Seventeen years were thus spent in acquiring "a European reputation" and a competency. His residence in Europe did not render his countrymen unappreciative of his work, nor did it impair his love for his country. Upon his return to America, in 1832, a public banquet was given in his honor in the City Hall in New York, and the occasion called forth expressions of the national pride in his success. As he replied to Chancellor Kent's address of welcome,— "I am asked," he said, "how long I mean to remain here, They know little of my heart who can ask me this question. I answer, as long as I live." This, however, was the exaggeration of strong feeling; for an account of his tour through the West, appearing in 1835 in *Crayon Miscel-*

lany, Astoria, and numerous contributions to the *Knick-erbocker Magazine,* barely sufficed to occupy him until his appointment as Minister to Spain, in 1842.   On his return to America, in 1846, he fitted up his bachelor quarters at "Sunnyside," on the Hudson, wrote his *Life of Oliver Gold-smith,* and was ready, in 1850, to publish *Mahomet and his Successors.*   Three months before his death he finished the *Life of Washington.*   This work was the most laborious of his life, being undertaken at an age when most authors are thinking of laying aside the pen.   It was accomplished in a way that commands the highest admiration for simplicity of style, proportion of parts, and unity.   Having gained the pre-eminent position among American men of letters, he died on the 28th of November, 1859.

James Kirke Paulding (1778–1860), (**280—281**), was a self-made man, shrewd and patriotic.   His works had the distinction of being fiercely reviewed by the English Quarterlies.   A large part of his life was spent in the United States civil service, and he was made Secretary of the Navy by President Van Buren.   As brother-in-law of William Irving, he was early introduced to the literary circles of New York.   He had a hand in the composition of *Salma-gundi;* and about the time of the second war with England he wrote *The Bulls and the Jonathans,* in which he satirized the English policy.   *The Dutchman's Fireside* (1831) is the one of all his works that retains most popularity, though his *Life of Washington* is still read.

Gulian Crommelin Verplanck (1786–1870), (**121**), had Dutch pedigree and Yankee wit—a combination which made it equally natural for him to lampoon dignitaries and sorrowfully to object to the freedom which Washington Irving displayed in treating of Knickerbocker traditions.

Verplanck entered Columbia College at eleven years of age, and was graduated in 1801.   He studied law, but disliked to practice his profession, and devoted himself to Greek, to antiquated reports of law cases in Norman French, and to reading Rabelais.   Meantime, the young men of his acquaintance—the Irvings, Paulding, and Gouverneur Kemble—amused themselves with literary pranks of all sorts. In these Verplanck never joined. His writings contain essays on a variety of subjects, including *Revealed Religion*, the *Doctrine of Contracts*, *Copyright*, and the *Use of Liberal Studies*. In 1844 he published an edition of *Shakespeare's Plays*. As an editor, Verplanck was fitted for his task by his wide scholarship, careful judgment, and severe taste; as a critic he was perhaps rather too unsympathetic, but his criticism is really an addition to the literature of the subject.

Joseph Rodman Drake (1795–1820), (**344**), the most precocious of American authors, experienced the extremes of fortune during his short life of twenty-five years. He was born in New York. Halleck and Cooper were his intimate friends. He was the author of *Culprit Fay*, the *American Flag*, and of satirical verses over the signature of *Croaker*.

Fitz-Greene Halleck (1795–1867), (**345-346**). A visitor to the Central Park may notice the statue erected in honor of this poet. The prim figure, rather carefully disposed in a drawing-room chair over a pile of volumes equally suggestive of gift books and ledgers, is a striking comment on the man's life and tastes. Halleck was pre-eminently the poet of the town, versed in its fashions, curious of its doings, and familiar enough with its society to be satirical. He was the lyric poet of the group of writers we have been describing; loved them when they were living, and wrote sonnets to their memory when they were dead. Halleck was born in Guilford, Connecticut, 1795, but his manhood was spent in New York, keeping intricate accounts for Jacob Barker and John Jacob Astor. Besides his contributions to the *Croakers*, his best known poems are *Marco Bozzaris*, written for W. C. Bryant's periodical, the *New York Review*, and *Fanny*. Halleck's visit to England in 1822 was the occasion of *Alnwick Castle* and the poem on *Burns*, although the latter appeared after his return to America. On the receipt of a pension of two hundred dollars a year from the will of John Jacob Astor, and a liberal addition from his son, Wm. B Astor in 1849, the poet retired to his birthplace, and there died in 1867.

The Knickerbockers had used poetry, essays, and fiction as the media of their gay or caustic comment on the life of the day, but none of them had made any important venture in the writing of novels. This department of literature was reserved for an author whose writings, from the outset, attracted universal attention.

James Fenimore Cooper (1789–1851), (**282—286**), lived among the stirring scenes of frontier life until he was thirteen, when he entered Yale College. He did not graduate. In 1805 he entered the navy as midshipman, and remained in the service six years. He had left the sea, however, and was living in Mamaroneck, N. Y., when a chance boast that he could write as good a novel as one that he was reading aloud to his wife led to his first literary attempt. *Precaution* was the result, a tame story, badly printed. It was followed by *The Spy*, in 1821, which drew upon the author's vast storehouse of information, and appealed to the public in Europe and America by its delineation of Washington, and Harvey Birch, the Revolutionary patriot. *The Pioneers*, published two years later, treated of the frontier life with which Cooper was so familiar. The same key was struck later in *Lionel Lincoln*, and in *The Last of the Mohicans* (1826), which is considered one of the best of the series called the Leatherstocking Tales. *The Pilot* (1823) and *The Red Rover* (1827) exchanged the woods for the ocean with no loss of interest to the reader. *The Prairie* was written in 1827, while the author was in Europe. There he found that translations of his works had everywhere gained him friends and critics. His novels number thirty-four in all, most of them being continuations or renewed treatment of themes already described. The last story he wrote, however, *The Ways of the Hour*, was a criticism of the method of trial by jury. His *Naval History of the United States*

(1839) cost him a lawsuit to defend his accuracy in describing the battle of Lake Erie.

It is sometimes urged that Cooper is never read now except by schoolboys and foreigners; that since a more intimate acquaintance has dispelled the belief that Indians, buffaloes and backwoodsmen, in equal parts, make up our population, the painstaking and vigorous delineation of these figures has ceased to interest. This may all be, and yet it must not be forgotten that the literary world is Cooper's debtor for a new sensation. Leatherstocking and Long Tom Coffin are his invention. They may seem artificial now, but they were vivid characters once, and the most superior of us read their stories with breathless interest.

In this chapter we have considered:—

Irving and the Knickerbockers.
   1. Washington Irving.
   2. James Kirke Paulding.
   3. Gulian C. Verplanck.
   4. Joseph Rodman Drake.
   5. Fitz-Greene Halleck.
   6. James Fenimore Cooper.

CHAPTER V.

WILLIAM CULLEN BRYANT AND THE EARLY POETS.

THE literary activity of Boston was by no means confined to the theological subjects which had been first discussed there.

The *North American Review* was established in 1815 by the Anthology Club, under the editorship of **William Tudor** (1799–1830), a Harvard graduate, and author of the *Life of James Otis* (1823), and *Gebel Teir* (1829). The latter is a clever description of the politics of nations, under the allegory of a council of birds on a mountain in Africa. Mr. Tudor was the author of three-fourths of the first four volumes of the *North American.*

Richard Henry Dana (1787–1879), **(329)**, a descendant of Anne Bradstreet, was born at Cambridge. He was a member of the Anthology Club, and from the first took an interest in the *North American*, being associate editor with his cousin, Edward T. Channing, in 1818. He began a periodical called *The Idle Man* in 1824, but stopped after the first six numbers, discouraged by lack of recognition. Bryant and Washington Allston generously helped him in his efforts to raise a higher American standard of literary excellence. The creative instinct in the poet was not strong enough to overcome his sensitiveness and reserve. *The Buccaneer* **(328)**, a poem of somber theme in the ballad style, was published in 1827, and two volumes of miscellaneous writings appeared in 1850, comprising most of his essays and review articles. Mr. Dana took an active part in the Unitarian controversy, 1825–35, and delivered a course of eight lectures on Shakespeare in the principal cities of the United States, 1839–40. He has written two novels, *Tom Thornton* and *Saul Fenton.*

Various influences at this time combined to develop a number of poets, who endeared themselves to the public by their sentiment or their patriotism. They sprang up in all parts of the country.

James Gates Percival's *The Coral Grove* **(327)**, *New England,*

and *Seneca Lake;* Charles Sprague's *Shakespeare Ode,* and the poem on *Curiosity* (**333**); the poems of N. P. Willis (**364, 365**), and George P. Morris (**350**); the lyrics of E. C. Pinkney (**355**), and C. F. Hoffman (**362**), have all received merited admiration. *The Star Spangled Banner* (**323**) was written by Francis Scott Key during a short imprisonment in the war of 1812. *The Old Oaken Bucket,* by Samuel Woodworth; *Home, Sweet Home,* by John Howard Payne; *My Life is Like a Summer Rose* (**329**), by R. H. Wilde; and *I Would not Live Alway,* by William Augustus Muhlenberg, keep alive the memory of their authors among the readers of American lyric verse.

BRYANT.

" His poetry overflows with natural religion—with what Wordsworth calls ' the religion of the woods.' "—*Christopher North.*

" Bryant's writings transport us into the depths of the solemn, primeval forest, to the shores of the lonely lake, the banks of the wild, nameless stream, or the brow of the rocky upland rising like a promontory from amidst a wild ocean of foliage, while they shed around us the glories of a climate fierce in its extremes, but splendid in its vicissitudes."—*Washington Irving.*

William Cullen Bryant (1794–1878), (**337-342**). The village doctor of Cummington, Mass., was the father of a precocious boy who wrote verses at nine years of age, and in his fifteenth year published a volume of them in Boston, under the title, *The Embargo; by William Cullen Bryant.* The young poet went to Williams College, but left before graduating in order to study law. In the *North American Review* of September, 1817, appeared his *Thanatopsis,* of which an English critic says: " Had Bryant written nothing else, this poem would have embalmed his memory. Wordsworth has written nothing of the same sort to surpass it." *The Ages* was delivered before the Phi Beta Kappa Society in 1821. The poet abandoned the law in 1825, went to New York, edited successively the *New York Review and Athenæum Magazine,* and the *United States Review and*

Literary Gazette. In these publications much of his criticism and some of his best poems appeared. Among them were *The Death of the Flowers*, *The Disinterred Warrior*, *The African Chief*, and the *Indian Girl's Lament*. In 1826 Bryant became connected with the *Evening Post*, in whose columns, till the end of his years, he earnestly advocated good government, free trade, and a hearty support of literature and art. He varied his laborious days by tours in Europe, the Southern States, and the West Indies. The English edition of Bryant's poems in 1832 was brought about by the joint efforts of Verplanck and Irving. Irving wrote a preface, and consented to have his name appear on the title page as the editor, although he was at the time personally unacquainted with Bryant. Bryant's translation of the Iliad is due to the generous importunity of his brother poets, Longfellow and Lowell, who found a fragment that had appeared in the pages of the *Atlantic* so good that they strongly advised the undertaking, serious as it seemed to a man of seventy. It was successfully finished in 1869, and was followed by the Odyssey in 1871.

Mr. Bryant stands almost alone among American authors in the finish and repose of his poetry, although the reader has no consciousness of mechanism. He shows a love of nature so great that it has everything of passion except the warmth. The poet made a precise and pitiless critic. He has rendered substantial services to American prose by refusing to countenance some of our national sins against rhetoric—notably those of slang and exaggeration. His clear, exact, and pure English is appreciated when it is compared with the slashing style of other hard-beset editors.

It would be difficult to find a more complete contrast to the strong, self-sustained, and yet sensitive man just described, than is afforded by the life and character of **Edgar Allan Poe**. Born in Baltimore in 1809, he lost his parents while he was a mere boy.

and ever afterward displayed an unrivaled power in making friends, and a fatal inability to keep them. The real character of Poe has come to be almost as much of a problem as the identity of the Man in the Iron Mask, but the surface facts are singularly unfortunate. A gambler, a drunkard, sensitive and melancholy, he wasted his genius and threw away his life. His first work, published in 1829 under the title of *Al Aaraaf, Tamerlane, and Minor Poems,* shows some features that marked all his later efforts. There is an intricate machinery of words without much thought to justify it, a surfeit of sweet sounds, which the reader meets again in *The Raven* (1845), *The Bells,* and *Annabel Lee.* His prose stories are all full of mysticism. Whether tales of metempsychosis, of weird crime, of strange retribution, or of fantastic discovery and marvelous invention, they are well-sustained extravaganzas, with an undercurrent of cool skepticism that sometimes appears as a kind of grim humor. Poe's wonderful knowledge of the mechanism of composition ought to have placed him among the first of critics, but he used it only to astonish, or to support some whimsical judgment. *The Philosophy of Composition* is an interesting compendium of the artificial subtleties in which this strange man delighted. He died in 1849.

LONGFELLOW, WHITTIER, HOLMES.

" Longfellow, in the Golden Legend, has entered more closely into the temper of the Monk, for good and for evil, than ever yet theological writer or historian, though they may have given their life's labor to the analysis."—*Ruskin.*

" His poems are of an order to which we have none akin. Germany, more than England, has been the source of his inspiration."—*London Metropolitan.*

" One of the most pleasing characteristics of this writer's works is their intense humanity."—*Gilfillan.*

" Mr John Greenleaf Whittier is the lyrical poet *par excellence* of America, and the best of his lyrics have a nerve, swing, and fire which imparts to the reader a share of the writer's enthusiasm."—*North British Review,* 1867.

" Holmes, the most cultivated wit, if not the chief humorist, America has ever produced."—*Westminster Review,* 1870.

Henry Wadsworth Longfellow (1807–1882), **(206—369).** It has fallen to the lot of some American poets to be more admired than Longfellow, to some, perhaps, to be more praised, but to none to be better loved. His lyrics have found their way to homes and hearts the world over. Men, women, and children read his poetry because it tells, in simple, direct fashion, the story of the common experiences of life. It is a pleasure to remember that the man lived what the poet sang, that his courtesy and gentle dignity were the habits of a lifetime, and that his own scholarly attainments never made him exacting toward others.

Longfellow was born in Portland, Maine, "in an old, square, wooden house upon the edge of the sea." His mother was a descendant of the John Alden whose wooing he celebrated; his father's family came from Hampshire, England. He went to Bowdoin College, where, in the later years of his course, a few poems testify to his love of nature and of legend. He was a classmate of Nathaniel Hawthorne, George B. Cheever, and J. S. C. Abbott. Like most of the literary men of his time, he intended to be a lawyer; but the offer of the professorship of modern languages in his college, determined him to go abroad and fit himself for the work. His stay covered two years. From 1829 to 1835, when he was chosen to succeed Mr. Ticknor at Harvard, Longfellow lectured to Bowdoin students and wrote for the North American Review. Allen & Ticknor, in 1833, published his first book, containing an essay on the Moral and Devotional Poetry of Spain, and some translations of Lope de Vega's sonnets. Before entering on his duties at Harvard, Longfellow paid another visit to Europe, lingering in Switzerland and Scandinavia. The beneficial effect of European culture at this period of the poet's development has been questioned; and indeed, if *Outre-Mer* (1835) and *Hyperion* (1839) had been its only outcome, the public would have reason for regret that he ever left his native shores. These two books, although they were once very popular, mark a time when he exchanged sentiment for sentimentality, and accepted mannerism for style. But the *Voices of the Night*, also published in 1839, contains some of the very best of his less pretentious work—*The Reaper and the Flowers, Woods in Winter*, and *The Psalm of Life*—poems whose simple truth and natural expression render them popular. The small volume of *Ballads, and other Poems*, appeared in 1841. The poet's return from Europe, in 1842, was marked by the *Poems on Slavery*, dedicated to Channing. About this time Longfellow gave a series of lectures on Dante, illustrating them by translations from the work of the great Italian poet. By the end of the year 1846 he had published the *Spanish Student*, a collection of translations called *The Poets of Europe*, and *The Belfry of Bruges*. The next year is marked by the appearance of *Evangeline*, the poet's favorite of all his works, and the one perhaps that is most dear to the public, although even it could not succeed in the mission of naturalizing the hexameter among us. The subject was one suggested to Hawthorne by a friend, but he rejected it as unfit for a story, and handed it over to Longfellow, who saw its possibilities. *Kavanagh*, a novel of little power, and a volume of poems called *The Seaside and the Fireside*, were published in 1849; *The Golden Legend*, a drama, in 1851. *Hiawatha* (1855) raised a storm of enthusiasm and literary controversy as to the cause of its success and its probable permanence. Longfellow called the poem "An Indian Edda;" the scene was among the Ojibways, near Lake Superior; the meter is rhymeless trochaic tetrameter. Dr. O. W. Holmes has given an ingenious explanation of the popularity of this meter on physiological grounds. The European critics attribute its success to the fact of its being modified from the common Finnish measure. *The Courtship of Miles Standish* was another successful essay in hexameter, followed by *The Tales of a Wayside Inn*, a collection of poems on various subjects; *The New England Tragedies, The Divine Tragedy*, and *The Hanging of the Crane* (1874).

Mr. Longfellow had resigned his professorship in 1854. He continued his residence in the " Craigie House," famous as the headquarters of Washington in Cambridge. There he was, as he says, "too happy," and there, in 1861, the tragedy of his life occurred. His wife's dress caught fire as she sat among her children, and she was burned to death. The translation of the *Divine Comedy* of Dante (1867) was the poet's refuge in his sorrow. It is extremely literal, and has been both praised and blamed on that account. The closing years of Longfellow's life were rich in friendship and success, but there is an increasing seriousness in all his work. The poem, *Morituri Salutamus,* which he read at the fiftieth anniversary of his graduation at Bowdoin, is weighty with feeling. In 1880 came *Ultima Thule ;* in 1881 a sonnet on the death of President Garfield. *Hermes Trismegistus* was his last poem. He died in 1882, and was buried near the "three friends"—Charles Sumner, Louis Agassiz, and Cornelius Felton—whom he had loved so dearly and mourned so sincerely. England has honored his genius by giving his bust a place in Westminster Abbey.

John Greenleaf Whittier (1808–1892), (**371—374**). The symmetry of Longfellow's life forms a strong contrast to the somewhat strait limits of Whittier's culture. The poetic taste that lived for eighteen years in the " spells " of farm work, shoemaking, and " schooling " that made up his life in a New England village—the fancy that found play in Quaker history and Indian superstition— had need to be strong as well as peculiar. Whittier was a characteristic product of New England influences, and he has been their worthiest poet. Upright, patriotic and talented, the man has had the rare fortune of remaining unsophisticated in life, manners, and verse. He was born in 1808, of Quaker parentage, in Haverhill, Mass. His literary career began with journalism in Boston in 1829, and was continued in Hartford, Haverhill, Philadelphia, and Washington until 1847. His early poems, *Mogg Megone* (1836) and the *Burial of Pennacook,* are Indian stories derived from early colonial records, and adorned with some of Whittier's most beautiful descriptions of scenery. From the very first he was an outspoken and ardent supporter of the anti-slavery movement. The signing of his name to the Anti-slavery Declaration in 1833 seems to have been a kind of dedication of his muse to the cause which he believed inseparable from justice and humanity. Until the close of the Civil War he was busy in writing and publishing in newspapers, magazines, and books the series of stirring lyrics and moral denunciations whose titles tell their own story: *Voices of Freedom* (1841), *The Panorama, and other Poems* (1856), *In War Time* (1863). After the war the beauty of New England's scenery, and the sober charm of her rural life, were the inspiration of his poetry. *Snow-Bound* (1865) is a masterpiece. It was followed by *The Tent on the Beach* (1867), *Among the Hills, Miriam,* and a number of other slight poems, all showing the author's purity of spirit and lyric grace. Mr. Whittier also published two volumes of his collected prose writings, besides editing John Woolman's *Journal.*

Oliver Wendell Holmes (1809–1894), descended from six famous colonial families, was born in Cambridge, Massachusetts. After being graduated at Harvard, he read law for a year. Then he adopted medicine as a profession, and went to Europe to study in Paris. In 1836 he returned to America after an absence of nearly three years, took his degree at Cambridge, recited *Poetry, A Metrical Essay,* before the Phi Beta Kappa Society, and published his first volume of poems. *Old Ironsides* and *The Chambered Nautilus* are choice specimens of Dr. Holmes's lyric power. His prevailing characteristic is a deftness of touch that produces sudden changes from pathos to humor under the reader's very eye. He is the merriest of satirists, and the foe of sentimentality and pretense. *The Autocrat of the Breakfast Table,* the work of a wisely humorous thinker, was written in 1857, for the opening numbers of the *Atlantic Monthly.* It is a book to be familiar with. The wit, satire, and sentiment of its colloquies gained for them immediate and lasting popularity. *The Professor at the Breakfast Table* and *The Poet* followed *The Autocrat,* and still the readers of the *Atlantic* showed no signs of weariness. The medical studies and the Puritan heredity of Dr. Holmes influenced him in much of his writing. Two powerful books testify to the interest he took in subjects that few pens could treat successfully. *Elsie Venner* (1860) is a dramatic statement of the problem growing out of a personality hampered, and yet preserved, by prenatal influences. *The Guardian Angel* (1867) is a healthful and characteristic American novel. We are also indebted to Dr. Holmes for a biography of the historian Motley.

As a lecturer, after-dinner speaker, and companion, he was unrivaled among contemporary men of letters. Trained as a scientific man, he kept the poet's keenness of spiritual vision. His fancy suggests striking images, and his unfailing good taste clothes them in faultless style. He is a rare instance of a character whose business is always his pleasure. During part of each year he lived in Boston; the rest of the year, in rural retirement. Emerson, Longfellow, Whittier, Lowell, Bancroft, and Motley were his life-long friends.

A number of our genuine poets have written very modestly or sparingly, relying apparently for recognition on the genuineness of their poetical sentiment. Their work extends over three or four decades. The first volume of poems by **Alice** and **Phœbe Cary** was published in 1856, when one was thirty and the other twenty-six years old. The sisters gained respect and admiration for their dignity of character as well as for the patient industry and careful workmanship of their lyrics and prose articles. Their authorship extended over a period of twenty years, and filled several volumes. Edgar Allan Poe has testified to the musical perfection of Alice Cary's *Pictures of Memory*, and Mr. Whittier gives his impressions of the author in a poem called *The Singer*. Alice Cary died in 1870; Phœbe in 1871.

Christopher Pearse Cranch (1813–1892), began preparation for the business of life in the Harvard divinity school, but, in 1842, devoted himself to landscape painting and poetry. From 1846 to 1863 he was in Europe most of the time, where he was successful in his chosen art. He has, however, published both prose and poetry from time to time. In 1854 a volume of his poems appeared; in 1856 and 1857 *The Last of the Huggermuggers* and *Koboltozo*, illustrated stories for children; and in 1872 a blank verse translation of the Æneid was published.

William Wetmore Story, born in Salem, Mass. (1819), has filled his days with the varied work of lawyer, sculptor, and poet. His first volume of poems appeared in 1847; his second in 1856. Readers of the *Atlantic* remember his charming sketches under the title *Roba di Roma*. A *Roman Lawyer* (1870) is a plea for Judas, as the mis-guided religious enthusiast instead of the sordid betrayer of Christ. A play called *Nero* was published in 1875. Mr. Story's latest contri-bution to literature is an artistic little brochure entitled *He and She; or, An Artist's Portfolio*, made up of exquisite poems connected by graphic prose.

John James Piatt (born 1835), and his wife, **Sarah Morgan Bryan Piatt** (born 1836), may both be termed poets of tempera-ment. In a stanza or two they succeed in giving an impression of exquisite delicacy and perfection. Mr. Piatt published, in 1860, with W. D. Howells, *Poems of Two Friends;* and in 1864, with his wife, *The Nests at Washington*. Other volumes of his are *Poems in Sunshine and Twilight*, *Western Windows and Landmarks* (1871). Mrs. Piatt has published *A Woman's Poems* and *A Voyage to the Fortunate Isles*. There is a melancholy about her sentiment that sometimes amounts to gloom.

Sidney Lanier (1842–1881) was born in Macon, Ga., but spent most of his life in Baltimore. In 1879 he was appointed lecturer on English Literature for the Johns Hopkins University. In 1875 he published *Florida*, a prose work; and in 1876 claimed the hearing of the whole country by his cantata, *From this Hundred-terraced Height*, sung at the opening of the Centennial Exposition. He also published in this year a small volume of poems of marked originality. They were not always either clear or musical to ears untrained in complicated verse, but they were often wonderfully graceful, tender, and heroic. *The Stirrup Cup* and *To ——, with a Rose*, are examples of his simpler poems. *The Science of English Verse* (1880), and *The Theory of the English Novel* (1883), are critical works of decided merit and interest. Lanier died of consumption, after years of suffering. Some of his best works appeared posthumously.

In this chapter we have considered:—

1. Dana, Bryant, and their Contemporaries.
2. Longfellow, Whittier, Holmes.
3. Minor American Poets.

CHAPTER VI.

NATHANIEL HAWTHORNE AND MINOR NOVELISTS.

"Mr. Hawthorne's difficulty seems to have been to find in the vast human work-shop of *America* a frame sufficiently picturesque for the reception of his richly colored pictures."—*London Times.*

"The supernatural here never becomes grossly palpable; the thrill is all the deeper for its action being indefinite and its source vague and distant."—*London Athenæum*, 1850.

"It would be difficult to deny the gift of 'poetic insight' to this mixture of admirable detail with something at once higher and deeper."—*Miss Mitford.*

NATHANIEL HAWTHORNE (1804–1864), (**296—302**). The delicate health or inherited morbid dis-position of Hawthorne will not alone explain the curious mental bias that makes all his psychological narratives turn on the pivot of conscience and its natural or perverted action. Joined with his analytical insight is a command of all that is quaint, delicate, and suggestive in the English tongue. The result is a literary talent unusually limited in its range, but wonderfully perfect in its expression.

Hawthorne was born in Salem in 1804. He was gradu-ated at Bowdoin with Longfellow, and was the intimate friend of Franklin Pierce. His life after leaving college was one of seclusion, the beginning of hermit-like habits that lasted all his days. *Fanshawe* (1828), a romance, was prob-ably the first of his published works, although Hawthorne never acknowledged its authorship. His early efforts to make literature pay were pathetic. There was little appreciation for the finished work of his pen until the republication in 1837, of some early stories under the title of *Twice Told Tales* called out the hearty praise of Longfellow in the

North American Review. While the public was deciding whether it approved of this somber playfulness of style, Bancroft, then Collector of the Port, gave the struggling author a place in the Boston custom-house. About this time he joined the group of men and women who were testing their sociological theories at Brook Farm. He seems to have been in the life, but hardly more of it than when his abiding place was in Salem or Boston. *The Blithedale Romance* (1852), **(298)**, was the comment that his genius made upon the experiment, and upon his own lack of sympathy with the principles involved. Hawthorne had been living for three years in his favorite residence, the Old Manse, at Concord, when, in 1846, *Mosses from an Old Manse* appeared, a title given to a collection of papers republished from various magazines. In the same year the return of his friends to political power secured his appointment as surveyor of the custom-house in Salem. *The Scarlet Letter* was published in 1850, and found for its author an appreciative audience. The book is a study of fiery passions outlined against a background of New England Puritanism. There is something fantastic in its realism ; nature seems to become dramatic in the over-strained emotion. Meantime Hawthorne had moved to Lenox, where he wrote (1851) *The House of the Seven Gables*, another novel of somber theme, where the gloom of ancient wrong and hereditary crime is brightened by occasional glimpses of youth, beauty, and happiness. In 1852 Hawthorne was busy with a third series of *Twice Told Tales* and with the biography of Franklin Pierce, written when the latter was nominated for President. On the election of Pierce, in 1853, Hawthorne was given the position of consul to Liverpool. The seven years which he spent in Europe were rich in enjoyment and in observation. *The Marble Faun* **(299)** was the only work of any compass that seems to have had its inspiration there. He returned to America in 1860. Hawthorne's life had never been radiant, but from this time it was under a heavy cloud. His country was plunged in civil war, and he had no heart for the desperate measures of the time. In vain he tried to interest himself in literary work; he never finished any of his undertakings after *Our Old Home* (1863), dedicated, with stubborn loyalty, to Mr. Pierce. *Septimius Felton*, *The Dolliver Romance*, *The Ancestral Footstep*, and *Dr. Grimshawe's Secret*, are more or less complete fragments or studies found among his papers after his death in 1864. Their publication has been of interest, chiefly, as showing the process by which his stories took shape in his mind.

The works of Hawthorne stand alone in American literature. Nowhere else is to be found such moral power combined with an artistic finish so perfect. His province was narrow, but within its limits he was master.

Although Hawthorne stands without a peer in his own line, a host of contemporary or nearly contemporary writers published novels which won popular favor.

First among these is **George William Curtis** (1824–1892), the author of *Nile Notes of an Howadji*, *The Howadji in Syria*, *Lotos Eating*, *Prue and I*, *Trumps*, *The Potiphar Papers*, and various sketches and critical essays in *Putnam's Magazine*. For more than thirty years, beginning in 1857, Curtis was an editorial contributor to *Harper's Weekly* and *Harper's Magazine*, and during the same period he had universal recognition as an eloquent orator. His reputation was first won through the grace and original charm of his sketches of travel. These disclosed a vein of æsthetic sympathy with foreign life and historic scenes. The critical reader now finds them somewhat overloaded with the ornaments of style, although containing many a promise of the virile mental qualities and the stanch moral earnestness which characterize his later productions. It was, however, the grave crisis of the Civil War that developed the best powers of Curtis's pen. As the political editor of *Harper's Weekly*, he made that paper a potent ally of the Union cause, and a dominating patriotic force in the field of journalism. In the " Easy Chair " of *Harper's Magazine*, he displayed the highest qualities as an essayist. His province and his influence resembled those of Addison and Steele in the best issues of the *Spectator*. Comment on art, music, literature, current events, politics, society, was here set forth, month by month, in graceful and flexible style, animated by genial humor, often by keen satire, but always regulated by the purest taste. So nice was his sense of literary proportion, that local and ephemeral circumstances, preserved in these monthly records, have keen interest for the reader of to-day.

Many published addresses attest Mr. Curtis's eloquence and his discriminating judgments of men and measures. Notable among them are memorial orations on Burns, Bryant, Sumner, Phillips, Irving, Lowell, and the addresses which he delivered as President of the National Civil Service Reform League. The charm of his speech was made well-nigh irresistible by his graces of manner, and by the self-sacrificing nobility of his private life. His style lacked the epigrammatic conciseness which provokes frequent quotation, and the fact that his best writing concerned themes of passing interest, must render his literary fame less universal than his contemporary influence. But patriotic Americans will cherish his work as a noble example of high morality rendered effective through the best literary form.

Donald Grant Mitchell was born in Norwich, Conn. (1822). After his graduation at Yale he went to Europe, where he rambled about on foot and wrote letters for the *Albany Cultivator*. He has written *The Reveries of a Bachelor, Dream Life,* and *Dr. Johns,* besides essays on rural and literary subjects (**239**).

Mrs. Lydia Maria Child (1802–1881), a woman of earnest and beautiful character, while she was still Miss Francis, published her first story, *Hobomok* (1824). *The Rivals* next appeared. In 1826 she was married, and for some time confined her attention to juvenile and dramatic literature. Her *Appeal in Behalf of that Class of Americans called Africans* was one of the earliest anti-slavery books. In 1836 she published *Philothea,* a Grecian romance of the time of Pericles. She was editor of the *National Anti-Slavery Standard* for two years. In 1855 she published the *Progress of Religious Ideas.* (**294**).

William Ware wrote historical novels *Aurelian* (**293**), *Julian, Zenobia.* W. G. Simms (**303, 304**), J. E. Cooke (**311**), and J. P. Kennedy (**290–292**), have treated various phases of American life. The series of novels written by the Warner sisters is still read and cried over by the sentimental. Sara J. Lippincott (Grace Greenwood) (**245**), Mrs. James Parton (Fanny Fern), and Miss C. M. Sedgwick, well known to the readers of thirty years ago, have written novels and prose sketches of the lighter order.

In this Chapter we have considered:—

1. *Nathaniel Hawthorne.*
2. *George William Curtis.*
3. *Donald G. Mitchell.*
4. *Mrs. Lydia Maria Child.*
5. *Minor Novelists.*

CHAPTER VII.

JAMES RUSSELL LOWELL AND THE HISTORIANS.

"Lowell's genius everywhere appears in contrast to Bryant's. Far from shrink-
ing into solitary places, he loves great cities and their cries, and sets them to rhyme
with hearty good-will."—*North British Review*, 1867.

"Lowell, in whom the youthful fun and freshness of the nation seems typified."—
Westminster Review, 1870.

"There is Lowell, who's striving Parnassus to climb
With a whole bale of *isms* tied together with rhyme."
Fable for Critics.

JAMES RUSSELL LOWELL (1819–1891), (217–
220, 380—382). It is difficult to characterize this
poet, or to do justice to his work in its various departments. His prose lacks the charm of Hawthorne and
the neatness of Holmes; in poetry he is not a Druid
like Bryant, nor a preacher like Whittier. The apparent ease of his verse did not make him profuse. He
seemed to take life in a leisurely way, and yet neither
indolence nor lack of purpose may be charged against
him, for through the whirling half-century of his public
career, he was eminent as critic, as poet, as teacher, as
editor, as diplomat, and as man of affairs. He might
have won pre-eminence by devoting his great powers to
some one pursuit; but his versatility, always guided by
high moral purpose, enriched the lives of many classes
of people, while consummate skill in one line would
have gratified critics only. In short, where other men
of letters have represented this or that theory or
sentiment or "section," Mr. Lowell has been broadly
American, and as long as we are interesting to ourselves or to other nations, his works will have readers.

The pathos, the fun, the mimicry, the sensitiveness, the boastfulness, the stern justice, the many-sided facility of our national character, find alternate sympathy or criticism, but always a mirror, in Mr. Lowell's pages. To our shame be it said that foreigners have sometimes understood and appreciated him better than his own countrymen.

It has been urged that Mr. Lowell was born too late; that Boston, in the year 1819, was already too far advanced to give the bracing atmosphere necessary for his development. He had the misfortune, too, of being some years younger than Tennyson, and of reading his English contemporary instead of forming himself on classic models. Mr. Lowell has judged himself as severely as his critics have done, has winnowed his early poems, and written but sparingly in later years. The work of the law office opened by him in 1840, and very soon closed, was succeeded by labors equally exhausting though more congenial. In 1843, with Neal, Hawthorne, Poe, and Parsons for helpers, he began the task of editing *The Pioneer ;* but his literary standard was high, and only three numbers were published. His first collection of poems, *A Year's Life* (1841), was followed in 1844 by *The Legend of Brittany, Miscellaneous Poems and Sonnets.* Already Mr. Lowell had announced his antislavery views, and had allied himself with Wendell Phillips and other agitators. A series of *Conversations on the Old Poets* was the result of an attempt to interest the public in English literature, but the criticism was very much hampered by the dialogue, and the work was never popular. *The Present Crisis,* whose verses throb with patriotism and with hatred of oppression, was printed in a volume of poems in 1848. *The Vision of Sir Launfal, A Fable for Critics,* and *The Biglow Papers,* appeared in the same year. The first of these is the most sustained of the author's works, and contains exquisite descriptions and poetical fancies ; the *Fable for Critics* comments shrewdly on the literary characters of the day ; the *Biglow Papers* is a dramatic reproduction of thought and dialect in New England. The Mexican war and the extension of slavery are the principal themes touched by its keen satire. In 1855, Mr. Lowell was appointed to succeed Mr. Longfellow in the professorship of Polite Letters at Harvard. He accepted the position, and at once went abroad for special study. After his return he seems to have devoted himself very persistently to the duties of his chair. In 1867 the second series of the *Biglow Papers* appeared, followed, in 1869, by a collection of poems entitled *Under the Willows. The Commemoration Ode*, recited in Cambridge, in 1865, in honor of the Harvard alumni who fell during the Civil War, is full of elevated feeling, and contains a noble tribute to the memory of President Lincoln. Mr. Lowell was editor of *The Atlantic Monthly* from its foundation in 1857 till 1862. His editorial connection with the *North American Review* extended from 1863 till 1872. In these magazines were printed many of the articles that make up the volumes entitled *Among my Books* (in two series) and *My Study Windows*. From 1877 till 1884, Mr. Lowell represented our government, first at the court of Spain, and later at the court of St. James. During and after his brilliant diplomatic service, his pen was busy in writing learned and eloquent papers on themes literary and statesmanlike. The most important of these productions was his thoughtful oration on Democracy, delivered at Birmingham, in 1884.

Political and Historical Literature. The political element in American life has had definite representation in the work of nearly every writer of this period ; its more exclusive development, however, is to be found in the speeches of orators and in the work of historians, whether they have been occupied with the United States, the Western Continent, or the development of liberty in Europe.

The historical labors of American men of letters were foreshadowed by the colonial records and by the historical societies of our first half century of national existence. Much of what was done possesses little or no artistic merit, but is most helpful to the later historians. Our colonial period has been exhaustively treated by Francis Parkman (145), who has published five parts of a work on *France and England in North America.* Henry Cabot Lodge has written *A Short History of the English Colonies in America* (1881). Its last three chapters are of special interest to the student of American literature. The men and times of the Revolution have been studied by George W. Greene (108), Dr. Benson J. Lossing, and Dr. Jared Sparks (124). Dr. Sparks published (1834-40) editions of the writings of Washington and Franklin, containing careful biographies. In 1830 his *Diplomatic Correspondence of the American Revolution* appeared.

The Civil War called forth Horace Greeley's *American Conflict* (1864), an animated account of the struggle in which he, as editor of the New York Tribune and an ardent supporter of anti-slavery principles, was deeply interested (164—167). *The War between the States,* written by Alexander H. Stephens, recounts the Southern view of the same questions (100). Dr. John W. Draper (215—216), and Vice-President Wilson, have also contributed to this branch of literature.

Kirk's history of *Charles the Bold,* Eliot's *History of Liberty,* and the popular histories of Jacob and John S. C. Abbott, fairly represent our labor in foreign fields.

James Kent's *Commentaries on American Law* (76), Henry Wheaton's *International Law,* Dr. Woolsey's works on international and political science (161), and Henry C. Carey's efforts in favor of Protection (155), are the best known of a large class of books written in the interest of justice and material welfare.

Curiously enough, the group of men who have reached the highest distinction in this line of work are all from Massachusetts. The *History of New England* (1858), (149), was by **John G. Palfrey** (1796–1881), a Bostonian, a professor at Harvard, the editor of the *North American Review* (1835–1843), a leader of the Free-Soil party, and, as one of his friends has expressed it, "an example of the accomplished Christian lawyer."

Richard Hildreth (1807–1865) made his way to the authorship

of a successful *History of the United States* through practice in other
branches of literature.   Having graduated from Harvard at nineteen, he studied law, wrote newspaper articles on the annexation
of Texas, a *History of Banks* (1840), and an anti-slavery novel called
Archy Moore, which was republished in England.

His *Theory of Morals* (1844), and the *Theory of Politics* (1853),
embody an attitude similar to that of Jeremy Bentham.   The first
volume of the *History of the United States* appeared in 1849, the last,
three years later.   Mr. Hildreth was remarkable for his power of
long-continued mental application.

George Bancroft (129—133) was born with the century (1800–
1891).   He graduated from Harvard in 1817, and continued his
studies in Europe.   As a prominent member of the Democratic
party, he received the position of Collector of the Port of Boston
(1838), was made Secretary of the Navy in 1845, and Minister Plenipotentiary to England (1846–1849).   His *History of the United
States* is not only his most important work, but is the best that has
been written on the subject.   The first volume appeared in 1834, the
twelfth in 1882.   The style is clear and picturesque, all events being
treated in the light of the philosophical development of certain principles inherent in the character and conditions of the early colonists.

John Lothrop Motley (1814–1877) graduated at Harvard in
1831, studied in Göttingen and Berlin, and was admitted to the
bar in 1836.   He wrote two unsuccessful novels, *Morton's Hope* and
Merry Mount; but in 1846 he had definitely addressed himself to
the task of writing a history of Holland.   He became dissatisfied
with the materials at his command in America, and in 1851 sailed
for Europe with his family.   *The Rise of the Dutch Republic* (1856)
was the result of his studies in Berlin, Dresden, and The Hague.
It was received with enthusiasm in Europe as well as in America;
was translated into Dutch, German, French, and Russian.

The History of the United Netherlands appeared between 1861
and 1868, and the *Life of John of Barneveld* in 1874.

Motley's histories have the interest of thrilling narration.   He
was Minister to Austria from 1861 until his resignation in 1867, and
was appointed to represent America at the English Court in 1869
(139—141).

William Hickling Prescott (1796–1859) was one of the oldest, and in many respects the most remarkable, of American historians. He was a junior at Harvard in 1813, when an accident put out one of his eyes and seriously injured the other. Thenceforth he was obliged to regulate the activity of his life in accordance with the requirements of this infirmity. He determined to be an historian, undertook a vast and varied amount of study, and carried it through successfully with the help of secretaries. In 1838, after nearly ten years of labor, he had written the history of *Ferdinand and Isabella.* It was at once translated into Spanish, Italian, and German. *The Conquest of Mexico* (1843), *The Conquest of Peru* (1847), and *Philip the Second* (1855–1858), have fully sustained the interest roused by his first attempt. Mr. Prescott also published, in 1849, a volume of Critical and Historical Miscellanies (**126—128**).

In this chapter we have considered :—

1. James Russell Lowell.

2. Political and Historical Literature.

3. Henry Cabot Lodge.

4. Richard Hildreth.

5. George Bancroft.

6. John Lothrop Motley.

7. William Hickling Prescott.

CHAPTER VIII.

EMERSON AND THE CONCORD SCHOOL.

" All his earnest is good earnest ; and, unlike many critics, as well of philosoph as of literature, he shows no trace in himself of the evils he deprecates in others.' — *Westminster Review*, 1840.

" Emerson sits under the tree planted by Fichte."— *Westminster Review*, 1870.

"No sweeter soul e'er trod earth's ways."
— *William Sharp.*

" More genial and more delicate than Carlyle, he nevertheless had much in com mon with the English philosopher, and his loss will be keenly felt on both sides of the Atlantic."— *London Standard.*

" As Wordsworth's poetry is, in my judgment, the most important work done in verse in our language during the century, so Emerson's essays are the most impor tant work done in prose."— *Matthew Arnold.*

RALPH WALDO EMERSON (**199—202, 356—358**), (1803–1882). The religious controversy which arose in Boston in the early part of the nineteenth century grad ually took a more general form. Theological formulas became too narrow a limit for curious thinkers, and Theo dore Parker's example was followed by a group of young people, who abandoned sectarian debate for the sake of becoming philosophers. The master-mind among them was Ralph Waldo Emerson, whose place of residence has sup plied the name by which they are known—The Concord School.

Emerson invested the platform of the lyceum with a charm and influence which it has lost in later days. His lectures were essays collated from his voluminous common place book, and were delivered in a style of oratory com bining neighborly familiarity with oracular emphasis. The

strongly moral bent of his mind may have been an inheritance from the eight generations of clergymen among his ancestors. He graduated at Harvard, studied divinity, and was
ordained as a Unitarian minister; but he soon gave up the
charge of his congregation, and, in 1832, began a life of
meditation and literary aims. In 1833 he made a short
visit to Europe, and then began a lasting friendship with
Carlyle. He was one of the original editors of *The Dial*, a
magazine begun in 1840, devoted to literature, philosophy,
and religion. The writers were all more or less at variance
with ordinary standards of life, and they expressed their
views with more force than consistency. Among them were
Margaret Fuller, Alcott, and Thoreau. In 1841 and 1844
the two series of Emerson's essays were published; in 1847,
his poems. The year 1848 found him traveling and lecturing in England, where he renewed his old intimacy with
Carlyle. On his return to America he lectured on *English
Character and Manners*, and his lectures were published in
1856 as *English Traits*. Others of his works are *The Conduct of Life*, *Society and Solitude*, *Representative Men*,
and *Letters and Social Aims*. In 1872 he went to Europe
again, said farewell to Carlyle, traveled on the Continent
and in Egypt, returning in 1873. The last years of his life
were spent among friends and admirers, who treasured his
every saying, and made as light as possible the burdens and
privations of old age.

Emerson's somewhat contradictory traits put him in the
position of a preacher who does not try to make converts.
His philosophy was devoid of system; his poetry by turns
obscure and luminous. The peculiar quality of his mind
has been likened to German mysticism and the visions of
the Neo-Platonists, while the Hon. Anson Burlingame declared that "there are twenty thousand Ralph Waldo Em-
ersons in China."

But it is not as essayist, philosopher, or poet that Emerson will be longest remembered. There was something in the man himself that commanded admiration. His friends have declared that he was perfect in courtesy, kindliness, and practical sympathy. The man did not live secluded from his fellows, however much the philosopher counseled retirement; but came out into the world and generously paid it tribute in love and in service.

Margaret Fuller Ossoli (1810–1850) was a precocious child, and became a woman of strongly marked character, and of brilliant literary acquirements. Her sparkling conversation gave charm to a personality that was otherwise rather repellent. For a time editor of the *Dial*, she was afterwards employed as a critic for *The Tribune*. Her influence upon the thought of the time, especially upon the movement known as Transcendentalism, though now a matter of tradition, was undoubtedly considerable; but her literary remains are few and unimportant (**210**).

Henry David Thoreau (1817–1862) early withdrew from the demands and restrictions of society to develop his nature in seclusion. Living in his hut on the shores of Walden Pond, hoeing his garden, keeping his house in order, studying nature and his books, he was moved to write down the facts and fancies that came to his mind. He produced literature of the same order as Abraham Cowley's essays, and Gilbert White's *Natural History of Selborne* (**231—233**). It is significant that in the seven volumes of his published works there is not one complete contribution to any department in which he was interested. Everything is suggestive, but nothing is scientific or artistic. His biography has been written by the younger Channing.

Two other members of the so-called *Transcendental School* are **Amos Bronson Alcott,** the " teacher by conversations," and **Jones Very,** a poet-mystic, who lived, rambled, and preached in Salem (1813–1880).

The practical bent of American genius has been shown in the growth of technical literature of various sorts. Philology, etymology, natural science, mathematics, the history of literature and criticism are represented by names like Whitney, Marsh (**196**),

Noah Webster, Audubon (**258—260**), Agassiz, Bowditch, Pierce, Ticknor, Whipple (**236**), Hudson (**224**), and Richard Grant White (**240**).

In this chapter we have considered:—

1. Ralph Waldo Emerson.

2. Margaret Fuller Ossoli.

3. Henry D. Thoreau.

CHAPTER IX.

THE ETHICAL NOVELISTS AND MISCELLANEOUS WRITERS OF PROSE AND VERSE.

JOSIAH GILBERT HOLLAND (1819–1881), as editor and author, moralist and poet, will always take rank among those whose literary efforts have been of the people and for the people. He early showed evidence of the ambition and energy that enabled him to gain an education and to study medicine, in spite of the poverty that dogged his steps. From 1849 to 1866 he was connected with the *Springfield Republican* (established 1847), a paper to whose success his strong moral sense and literary judgment greatly contributed. The *History of Western Massachusetts* appeared serially in its columns, as did also the novel called *The Bay Path* (**310**), and both may be considered fair specimens of the kind of energy which he lavished on his work. "Timothy Titcomb" was the signature over which he published his *Letters to Young People, Married and Single* (1868). The industry of Dr. Holland's earlier authorship is shown by the list of his publications: *Bitter-Sweet* (1858), *Goldfoil* (1859), *Miss Gilbert's Career* (1860), *Lessons in Life* (1861), *Letters to the Joneses* (1863), *Plain Talks on Familiar Subjects* (1865), and the life of *Abraham Lincoln* (1866). In 1867 appeared *Kathrina*, which has had a larger sale than any other American poem except Hiawatha. Dr. Holland took charge of *Scribner's Magazine* from its foundation in 1870, and wrote for its pages a series of novels: *Arthur Bonnicastle, Sevenoaks*, and *Nicholas Minturn*. All treated of subjects appealing directly to public interest, and their success, together with the author's editorial skill in collecting and disposing talent, did much to establish the new magazine on a firm footing. Scribner's Magazine was in some sort the successor of "Knickerbocker" and "Putnam's," and many people predicted for it a like short life; but the energy of its management gave it quick and great success. The wandering life, the constant ills and poverty of his early youth and manhood, were a strong bond between Dr. Holland and his readers. He made of his past struggles a background for the action of his stories, and thus gave an additional force to the moral lessons he was always teaching. He was a preacher of self-respect and independence; of that religion which is founded on right feeling and not on dogma.

Dr. Holland is the type of a class of writers who have made a moral of some sort more or less evident in their work. They have written novels, essays, sketches, and children's books, differing in style and grade of merit, but similar in the prominence which they give to the didactic element.

Edward Everett Hale, born in 1822, has written extensively for the magazines. His style is clear, and his methods of conveying moral instruction or criticism ingenious. *How To Do It, His Level Best, Ten Times One is Ten,* are among his most popular volumes. *The Man Without a Country* is a remarkable example of well-sustained pathos, which has probably deceived more readers than any similar fiction of our time. Mr. Hale's views on philanthropy and other social topics present a curious parallel to those of Franklin. His style is perfectly clear, is often fervent and dashing, and is usually without ornament. Droll humor pervades all that he writes, and gives charm to his most serious pages. He is in hearty sympathy with whatever contributes to the happiness of humanity. His best strokes of invention have their impulse in his devotion to the welfare of his fellow-man.

Edward Payson Roe (1838–1888) was a voluminous and popular writer of books which are lacking in the first principles of modern realism, and yet appeal strongly to the imagination of the middle classes by their hearty support of virtue in the most trying circumstances. The ideal world which Mr. Roe represents, puts all its rewards within the reach of industry and integrity. One of the most popular of these stories is *Barriers Burned Away,* in which the climax of the plot and of the reader's interest is reached in the midst of graphic descriptions of the great fire in Chicago.

MISCELLANEOUS WRITERS OF PROSE AND VERSE.

Bayard Taylor (1825–1878), (**273—275, 414**). Three years after the publication of *Miss Gilbert's Career*, a novel occupied with the somewhat vexed question of woman's proper sphere, appeared another, called *Hannah Thurston*, in which the same theme was treated in a much broader manner. The author, Bayard Taylor, was already well known as the hero of a pedestrian tour in Europe, the author of several books of travel, a poet of sufficient merit to be only temporarily eclipsed by his success as a lecturer, and as associate editor of *The Tribune*. *John Godfrey's Fortunes* embodied sketches of the author's Bohemian experiences, and was speedily followed by *The Story of Kennett* and *Joseph and his Friend*, the last named being written for the *Atlantic*. *The Story of Kennett* describes the author's birthplace and home in Pennsylvania, and is a novel of decided power. Mr. Taylor wrote with great facility, and cultivated his poetical gifts amidst the humdrum and constant industry necessary to a man who lived by his pen. The man and his imagination were both the reverse of feeble. His nature was rich and generous, overflowing in a broad and hearty sympathy that made him a prince of good fellows. A lusty strength abounds in his pages. His intimate acquaintance with foreign lands and customs gives his work warmth and richness of coloring. Like Emerson, he had something of the Oriental in his bent of mind, but it was the art of the East that attracted him, not its mystery.

An edition of his poems was published in 1865. *The Picture of St. John, The Masque of the Gods*, and *The Prophet*, a Mormon drama, are others of his works. *Prince Deukalion* (1878) has gained admiration from literary people rather than from the rank and file of readers. A very appreciative criticism of it is to be found in Sidney Lanier's *Theory of the English Novel*. *The Echo Club* (1876), a series of clever parodies of modern poets, grew out of the practice gained in the author's friendly meetings with R. H. Stod dard and Fitz-James O'Brien. The influence of German literature, and its attraction for American scholars, have for a number of years been strongly felt in both prose and poetry, manifesting themselves in the number and high order of the translations which have appeared. C. T. Brooks (born in 1813) worked ably in this field, translating Schiller's *William Tell*, the *Titan* and *Hesperus* of Richter, and the first part of Goethe's *Faust*. In 1870–71 appeared Mr. Taylor's complete translation of the great Teutonic drama. It reproduces, as far as possible, the original meters, and offers the next best thing to those who cannot read the German. Mr. Taylor also added several essays and sketches to our voluminous Goethean literature, and translated Auerbach's *Villa on the Rhine*. He had gone to Germany as American Minister, with a view to further studies, when his death occurred in 1878.

Thomas Wentworth Higginson, born at Cambridge, Mass., in 1823, is a lineal descendant of the Rev. Francis Higginson, of early colonial fame. It was perhaps a mental bias derived from the sturdy old nonconformist himself that made Higginson so early an advocate of the despised cause of anti-slavery, and led him, in 1862, to accept the command of a regiment of negroes. His *Army Life in a Black Regiment* is the narrative of his experience. He has written polished essays on a variety of subjects, foremost among which are the *Atlantic Essays* (**241**), and *Oldport Days*. He has done much editorial work for *The Woman's Journal*, and has allied himself with those literary and social circles of Boston whose members are interested in the reform of government, of education, and of the status of woman. His *Young Folks' History of the United States* has made the subject pleasant and intelligible to thousands of boys and girls. *Malbone*, Colonel Higginson's only novel, is marked by charming qualities of style.

Richard Henry Stoddard was born in 1825 at Hingham, Mass. He presents another instance, among the many, of a poet who nursed his talent under the stress of uncongenial employment. Hard work in a New York foundry did not prevent him from writing with grace and spirit, until he had won his way to a fixed position among the literary men of this generation. Mr. Stoddard has been an independent artist, maintaining a theory and practice not always in accord with the more prosaic spirit of the times. He has been, moreover, a most industrious writer, having published several volumes of prose, edited collections of verse, and written many short poems.

Edmund Clarence Stedman, born in 1833 (**423**), the "broker-poet," has pursued the fickle muse in Wall Street. In 1873 a collected edition of his poems appeared. They are marked by lyric beauty, and by a graceful combination of satire and pathos essentially modern and artificial. The tone of a very frank sentiment is occasionally distinguishable in them, as in *The Heart of New England*. The *Victorian Poets* (1875) contains excellent, though unequal criticism of modern English poetry.

The purely satirical poetry of America is not represented by many names. The author who has written most in this department is **John Godfrey Saxe** (**392—396**). He was born in Vermont in 1816, graduated from Middlebury College at twenty-three, and studied law, which he afterward abandoned for lecturing, editorship, and general literary labors. His verse is fluent, his satire sharp and imperturbably good-natured. Mr. Saxe lashes social foibles with a steady hand. The reader of *Proud Miss McBride* and *The Money King* laughs at the moment, but nevertheless feels twinges of conscience. Saxe's cleverness, though sometimes suggestive of Hood, is purely American in its powers and its limitations.

William Allen Butler (**413**), born in Albany in 1825, and now a practising lawyer in New York City, published in 1857 a social satire called *Nothing to Wear*, quotations from which were at once in everybody's mouth. Some of its phrases have been adopted as part of the common stock of description, to be used without being accounted for. In 1871, in *Harper's Magazine*, appeared *General Average*, a spirited comment on business morality.

Celia Thaxter (born in Portsmouth, N. H., 1833) passed most of her early life upon the rocky Isles of Shoals, then a spot of primeval simplicity and loneliness. She has published a number of exquisite poems, redolent of the true spirit of the sea. Two graphic descriptive articles concerning her early home published in the *Atlantic Monthly* for 1867-8, had the double effect of making it a spot of great interest to tourists, and of setting curious observers on the track of the many quaint varieties of human life existing along our Atlantic coast.

Mary Abigail Dodge, " Gail Hamilton," (born in Massachusetts, 1838,) has been for a score of years among the most prolific and popular contributors to our periodical literature. Her numerous books exhibit in various degrees the same qualities that characterize her dashing articles on Civil Service Reform, contributed to the *New York Tribune*, and her recent vindication of Mrs. Carlyle's memory. She writes with fire, freedom, and point, is a mistress of the *argumentum ad hominem*, and often uses her ready wit with telling effect. She is by nature a partisan, however, and is neither profound nor logical. In her self-appointed role of censor of the public morals she brings more of entertainment than of conviction to her readers.

In this chapter we have considered:—

The Ethical Novelists.

1. *Josiah Gilbert Holland; 2. Edward Everett Hale; 3. Edward Payson Roe; 4. Mary Virginia Terhune (Marion Harland).*

Miscellaneous Writers of Prose and Verse.

5. *Bayard Taylor; 6. Thomas Wentworth Higginson; 7. Richard Henry Stoddard; 8. Edmund Clarence Stedman; 9. John Godfrey Saxe; 10. William Allen Butler; 11. Celia Thaxter; 12. Mary Abigail Dodge (Gail Hamilton).*

CHAPTER X.

AMERICANS and Europeans who, uniting the offices of critic and prophet, have insisted upon the development of some peculiarly national traits in our literature, have heralded several authors as the forerunners of an *American School*. These writers, however different in other respects, are all characterized by a freedom of manner or matter which is lauded or deplored in accordance with the preconceived theories of the reader. Foremost among these, both for the extreme character of his literary doctrine and for its uncompromising practice, is **Walter Whitman (401)**, who was born on Long Island in 1819. He had a public school education, followed alternately the trades of printer and carpenter, lived in the great cities of the East and West, edited newspapers, nursed the sick and wounded in the Washington hospitals during the Civil War, and seems to have gained the personal friendship of the poets and thinkers with whom he came in contact. The work which first brought him prominently before the public was a volume of poems called *Leaves of Grass*, published in 1855. A later issue, with additions and corrections, was issued in 1882. Mr. Whitman throws away rhyme and conventional meter, depending for his poetical effects upon the stress of feeling and the truth of the sentiment he expresses. That he can use rhyme is proved by occasional lyric bursts like *O Captain, my Captain;* that he does not choose to do so is shown by expositions of his literary theory which have appeared in the *North American Review*. Some critic has said that if he wished to train a boy up to be a poet, he would set him to reading Whitman. This is a fair comment on the author, for his work seems to be rather the rough material of poetry than the finished article. A dozen lyrics might often be elaborated from one of Whitman's catalogue lines. In the chaotic display of rhetorical goods which he puts before one there is many a Shakespearean phrase, many a burning thought; but their form, or lack of form, is an insuperable obstacle to recognition in many cases.

Cincinnatus Heine Miller (432), better known as Joaquin Miller, was born in Indiana in 1841. He experienced the "ups and downs" of Western life among miners and frontiersmen, studied law, was an express messenger, managed a weekly newspaper, was made judge in Grant County, Oregon, and published *Songs of the Sierras* in London in 1870. The personality indicated by these poems is a curious one—the author poses as a "child of nature," with a strong leaning to Byron and Swinburne, whose influence has certainly polished his verse. Miller has written prose sketches under the title of *The First Families of the Sierras*. Other works of his are *Songs of the Sunlands*, *The Ship in the Desert*, and *The Baroness of New York*. European critics praise his work for its freshness and poetic feeling.

Francis Bret Harte (246, 428, 429) was born in Albany in 1837. While still a child, a spirit of independence and adventure urged him towards the West, and the year 1854 found him entering on a career of gold-digging, school-teaching, and type-setting in California. In 1864 he was made secretary of the San Francisco mint. His varied experience was first turned to literary account when he assumed the editorship of the *Overland Monthly* (1868), for which he wrote *The Luck of Roaring Camp* and *The Outcasts of Poker Flat*. These were received by the public with an odd mixture of emotions; they revealed life under conditions new, startling, incomprehensible, yet of fascinating interest. In 1870 appeared *Plain Language from Truthful James*, or, as it is usually styled, *The Heathen Chinee*, which has been more widely copied and quoted than any other poem of the day. It was soon evident that Mr. Harte had founded a new school. He was floated high on the tide of popularity, and at the solicitation of his publishers, Messrs. Fields, Osgood & Co., he came to the East. Here he made his home for some time, and wrote for the *Atlantic* and other magazines. Besides a volume of poems, Mr. Harte has written many short stories and sketches; prose burlesques, under the title of *Condensed Novels*; three novels, *Gabriel Conroy*, *Thankful Blossom*, *The Story* *of a Mine.* His best work has been done under the direct influence of the life and scenery of the Pacific slope. It has a freshness born of the forests and sierras, and a subtle sympathy with the undisciplined human nature in gamblers and half-breeds. This native exhilaration and buoyancy of style are lacking in some of his later works. In their place we find a kind of literary ennui, which occasionally flashes up into an emotion that is stagy rather than spontaneous. *Flip*, and *In the Carquinez Woods*, are his latest publications.

The influence of Harte, Whitman, and their many followers has been much discussed. It has been urged that decency is not compatible with Mr. Whitman's art, nor morality with Mr. Harte's. French realism is believed to lurk under the careless exterior of one, and all the horrors of the Minerva Press in the unvarnished tales of the other. Whitman apparently leaves his readers to find their own moral, while Harte points out the wrong one. In reply to this, it can only be said that there have always been writers of whom these things were said, and who yet had readers and admirers of unquestioned taste. Emerson praised Whitman's poetry, and Thoreau admired, while he admitted that he could not understand the man.

Recent American Humorists. Closely allied to this development of what may be called Young America in our more formal literature, is the keen sense of humor which has inspired dialect poems and sketches, burlesque lectures, bad spelling, and every variety of comicality that has amused the crowd or paid the newspaper hack. In spite of our host of humorists, however, America has never had a *Punch* or a *Charivari*, though efforts have been repeatedly made to establish comic newspapers in our large cities. Among the least unsuccessful of these attempts was *Vanity Fair*, published in New York from 1859 to 1863. Its pages were brightened by the *McArone Letters* of George Arnold, the editorial work of Artemus Ward and Charles Godfrey Leland (Hans Breitmann) (242). *Puck* and *Life* are two illustrated comic papers of the present day which have prolonged their existence beyond the average term of their prototypes.

Some of the names connected with these efforts merit more than a passing mention. George Arnold (1834–1865) was a poet of brilliant promise. His lyrics throb with a passion of pathos, and his verse is very musical. His poems were reissued a short time ago under the editorship of William Winter; and one of E. C. Stedman's shorter poems expresses the sense of loss which Arnold's friends felt at his untimely death.

Charles Farrar Browne (1834–1868) became famous as Artemus Ward. He began his literary career while setting type for the *Boston Carpet-Bag*, and wrote his first jokes for its columns. He soon tired of such monotonous duties, as he did later of newspaper work in Cleveland and in New York. His humor was broad and somewhat farcical, and he brought the art of bad spelling to a point of artistic perfection. As a comic lecturer he was very successful, assisted, no doubt, by his ungainly and awkward physique.

David Ross Locke (1833–1888), "Petroleum V. Nasby," like Browne, began life with the varied but uneventful round of printer and editor. He was engaged for a time as compositor, and later as reporter, for the *Cleveland Plaindealer*, with which Artemus Ward was also associated. The second letter over the signature which made him famous was published in 1861 in the Hancock (Ohio) *Jeffersonian*. It was a mock petition against the negroes, ostensibly drawn up by an ignorant secessionist, and its satire was so telling that it was copied all over the country. Later efforts in the same line won for their author reputation and considerable influence.

Other humorists who have amused the public, with less of originality or of moral point in their satire, are **G. H. Derby** (John Phœnix), **Seba Smith** (Major Jack Downing), **B. P. Shillaber** (Mrs. Partington), **George D. Prentice** (351), and **Charles G. Halpine** (Private Miles O'Reilly). During the war, **Robert H. Newell** (Orpheus C. Kerr), wrote some excellent serious poems, as well as the prose satire which he made his chief political weapon.

More varied than the phases of his authorship, and more subject to fluctuation than the quality of his humor, has been the career of **Samuel Langhorne Clemens** (Mark Twain). He was born in Missouri in 1835. Printer's "devil," Mississippi pilot, miner,

Western editor, European tourist,—all his experiences have paid contribution to his authorship. *The Innocents Abroad* (1869), *Roughing It* (1872), numerous short magazine articles full of fun and point, and an inimitable gift as a humorous speaker, have won him reputation and much hearty good-will. He may fairly be called the favorite American humorist; and, over and above this, the *Prince and the Pauper* (1881) has lately proved him a master of simple and graceful narrative.

John Hay (431), (born 1839), President Lincoln's private secretary during the civil war, and since 1870 one of the *Tribune* staff, is a poet of careful workmanship. He has made exceedingly painstaking studies in dialect, and has not repeated the same types, as too many of his imitators have done. *Jim Bludso* is perhaps his best known poem. He has published *Pike County Ballads* and *Castilian Days*.

William M. Carleton, while still a young man from Hillsdale, Mich., attracted public attention by the four poems of the "Betsy and I" series, which were published in Mr. Locke's paper, the *Toledo Blade*. They have since been republished with others under the title of *Farm Ballads*.

In this chapter we have considered ⌐

    1. Walt Whitman.

    2. Cincinnatus Heine Miller.

    3. Francis Bret Harte.

    4. Recent American Humorists.

        a. Charles Farrar Browne.

        b. David Ross Locke.

        c. Samuel Langhorne Clemens.

        d. John Hay.

        e. William M. Carleton.

CHAPTER XI.

SCHOOLS OF CONTEMPORARY AMERICAN FICTION.

Fiction Delineating Provincial Characteristics. The mere outlines of biography given in the preceding pages must have suggested the difficulties which have beset American men of letters. These very obstacles, however, have curiously determined some forms of our literature. In the hurry of business, the confusion of manners, and the license of pioneer life, there have been keen-eyed observers who busied their pens with these special or imperfect developments of character fairly described by Ben Jonson's old term *humors.*

Foremost among these was **Sylvester Judd** (1813–1853), a Unitarian minister in Augusta, Maine. Mr. Judd's early associations had been among Calvinists, so that he brought to the work of his maturer years all the zeal and enthusiasm of a recent convert. *Margaret* (1845) was written with the avowed object of filling a gap in the religious literature of the Unitarians. Mr. Judd was hampered by the moral of his story and by his learning, so that the action of the story is halting and clumsy, but there are isolated passages of great force and beauty in the book. It was greatly admired by Emerson, Lowell, and other critics, as an original picture of some of the most salient features of American life.

Mr. Judd wrote several other works: *Philo* (1850), which the author called an "epical or heroical attempt"; *Richard Edney* (1850), *The Church* (1854), and a posthumous drama called *The White Hills.*

Some very remarkable sketches of a certain phase of New England life have been made by **Elizabeth D. B. Stoddard** (born 1823), the wife of the poet, Richard Henry Stoddard. In *The Morgesons*

(1862), *Two Men* (1863), *Temple House* (1867), she has treated with dramatic vigor the repressed yet ardent passion, the intellectual courage, the material limitations, and the curious social distinctions of New England life.

Theodore Winthrop, a descendant of Governor John Winthrop and of Jonathan Edwards, was born in New Haven in 1828. A delicate, studious child, he grew up into one of Yale's prize scholars. Continued ill-health and sensitive self-exaction made him delay undertaking any great literary work until the expectancy of his friends began to take the form of doubt. He had practised law in New York and St. Louis, had spent two years at Panama, and had been with Lieutenant Strain to Darien, when, in April, 1861, he joined the famous Seventh Regiment of New York on its march to Washington. He was promoted very soon to the rank of major, acting as secretary to General Butler, and was killed at Big Bethel while leading a charge.

His novels, all published since his death, give evidence of their author's mental health and enthusiasm. They are crude, however, and in the opinion of his friends are mere promises of what he would have done had he lived. *Cecil Dreeme* is a powerful sketch of the darker side of city life in New York; *John Brent,* a breezy story of the plains; *Edwin Brothertoft,* a romance of the Revolution. *The Canoe and the Saddle* and *Life in the Open Air* are reprints of essays and sketches from his note-books and the magazines. Winthrop was a great admirer of the Saxon type of body and mind, and endows all his heroes with pluck, persistence, and a love of horse-flesh.

William Mumford Baker (1825–1883), born in Washington City, a graduate of Princeton, and a Presbyterian minister in Texas and other parts of the United States, has worked a comparatively untilled field in his esoteric studies of "poor whites," secession and pulpit orators. His novels have a social and historical value quite apart from the incident which they detail. His first book was a life of his father, Rev. Daniel Baker, D.D.; his first story *The Virginians in Texas,* written for the amusement of his children, was submitted to their criticism and approval long before any thought of publishing it had occurred to the writer. *Inside,* an almost literal history of the Civil War as Mr. Baker saw it, appeared as a serial in Harper's Weekly. *The New Timothy, Carter Quarterman, A Year Worth Living, Col. Dunwoddie,* all received flattering testimony to the truth and power of their delineations of out-of-the-way types of character. *His Majesty Myself,* as a brilliant and satirical description of a sensational preacher, and offering sketches of some well-known characters in Princeton, caused a great deal of comment and inquiry. *Blessed Saint Certainty* presents a very spirited portrait of Governor Sam Houston.

Edward Eggleston, born in Indiana in 1837, displays a vivid and powerful art in representing the dramas of crude civilization. True, the incidents he narrates are of themselves interesting, and the views of life novel, but it takes the sympathy of an artist to find the "touch of nature" under the superstition, vulgarity, and sordid aims that make up the surface life of the backwoods. *The Hoosier Schoolmaster* and *The Circuit Rider* are generally considered his most vigorous stories, although *The End of the World* and *The Mystery of Metropolisville* have many readers. *Roxy* is in many respects the most artistic of his works.

The slavery agitation, the Civil War, and the vexed questions of reconstruction and negro suffrage, furnished themes for novels which seem to have gained a permanent place in literature. First in the list, of course, is *Uncle Tom's Cabin,* published in 1852. Over five hundred thousand copies have been sold in this country, and it has been read, and many times translated, abroad. Its author, **Mrs. Harriet Beecher Stowe (305, 306, 308)** was born in Litchfield, Conn. (1812), and had shown literary skill in her treatment of New England historical topics before *Uncle Tom* made her famous. She wrote this great story for the *National Era,* a Washington newspaper, and afterwards republished it in two volumes. *Dred, A Tale of the Great Dismal Swamp* (1856) did not equal the popularity of its predecessor. Her later stories have been studies of New England character, or of the romance of modern life. *The Minister's Wooing* (1859), *Oldtown Folks* (1869), and *My Wife and I,* best typify her literary merits.

The great charm of her novels lies in their knowledge of human nature, and in an exquisite sense of humor that stops just short of the grotesque. Sam Lawson and a score of other figures were rescued by her from oblivion. The race of shrewd New England villagers, of black cooks, of angular, energetic old maids, of illogical and warm-hearted grandmothers, of sweet, conscientious, introspective maidens, found in her an appreciative observer and a faithful limner.

Cudjo's Cave and *The Three Scouts* added greatly to the popularity of **John Townsend Trowbridge** (born 1827), (415), who was already known by his children's stories over the signature of "Paul Creyton" (1857). Since the war, Mr. Trowbridge has been a constant writer of tales, sketches, and poetry for the magazines. For some years he took the place of another Oliver Optic, writing stories full of a vigor and dash that made them fascinating to young and old alike. His poetry is moderate in quantity, but it is carefully finished and full of suggestion, often of pathos.

A Fool's Errand, in 1880, revived some of the issues that short-sighted critics had supposed laid to rest with the war, and opened to its writer, Judge **Albion W. Tourgee**, a career of popular authorship. *Bricks Without Straw*, *John Eax*, and *Hot Plowshares* followed in quick succession, but without sustaining the reputation of the first venture. These books are a kind of dramatized politics for young Americans, and they divide the reader's interest between campaign documents and fervid love-making. Judge Tourgee has established another representative of periodical literature, *Our Continent*, in which several of his stories have appeared as serials.

Critical Fiction. If the tone of the earlier English comments on American fiction be remembered, a very marked change of sentiment is evident when English magazines, in 1883, quote with approbation the following statement from the *Revue des Deux Mondes:* " It is to America, beyond all doubt, that we owe to-day the best novels written in English." One of the most finished novelists of America has given his views of the present and future of his art. He says: " The moving accident is certainly not its trade, and it prefers to avoid all manner of dire catastrophes. In one manner or other, the stories were all told long ago." So much for the present; the novel of the future will be "an analytic study rather than a story, which is apt to leave the reader arbiter of the destiny of the author's creations." It is undoubtedly true that many of the so-called stories which engage our attention have been constructed on this principle, but it is equally true that we can point to certain other authors who still display something less of skill and more of sentiment, who write, not because they wish to narrate, but because they have a story to tell. One of the principal names in the group of writers avowing the theory first described is

William Dean Howells (247). He was born in Ohio in 1837, and picked up his education while working as printer, reporter, and news-editor for the *Ohio State Journal*. Among his friends in early manhood were the sculptor, J. Q. A. Ward, and the poet, John J. Piatt. Howells is described as shy, even bashful, when in the company of strangers, but a keen observer, and given to amusing his companions by racy accounts of absurd things that had happened under their unseeing eyes. As the co-laborer of Piatt, in 1860 he published his first poems, which show the influence of Heine in their grace of touch as well as in their gloom. Mr. Howells stands next to Longfellow in his control of hexameters. The poem called *The Mowers* is a fair example of his skill. In 1861 he wrote a life of Mr. Lincoln, and soon after was appointed consul to Venice. *Venetian Life* and *Italian Journeys* record in charming fashion the impressions which he received during his four years in Europe. On his return to America he was employed on *The Nation* for a short time, and then went to Boston as assistant editor of *The Atlantic*. The entire control of the magazine became his on the retirement of James T. Fields in 1871, and he retained it for ten years, spending much time and thought in reviewing books. *Suburban Sketches* was made up of essays written for the *Atlantic*, and most of Mr. Howells's novels have appeared as serials in its pages. *Their Wedding Journey* was his first effort in the line of sustained narrative, and he has never surpassed some of its felicitous touches of humor. *A Chance Acquaintance* is used as a guide-book upon the St. Lawrence, so faithful is its description; but it is in *A Foregone Conclusion* that the author's poetic feeling has freest play. In his later works the humor has deepened into satire, and there seems to be a languid assumption of the unsatisfactoriness of life. Descriptions of scenery are not so prominent in his later work, which concerns itself with development of character and phases of American life. *Private Theatricals* is a clever analysis of the rival claims of love and friendship. In the sharp-spoken, keen-witted invalid of this story is found one of the author's most perfect portraitures. *The Lady of the Aroostook* depicts a young, beautiful, unsophisticated girl amidst circumstances which only her innocence can fail to recognize as trying. The plot turns on the curious charm which she exerts upon a party of young men thoroughly appreciative of the situation. *The Undiscovered Country*, on the whole, perhaps, the most serious of Mr. Howells's works, partially fails for that very reason. Its problem is insoluble, and the enthusiastic hero of the story appears pitiful rather than heroic or even pathetic. *A Fearful Responsibility, Dr. Breen's Practice,* and *A Modern Instance* have, in rapid succession, afforded texts for the critics and topics for the chit-chat of parlors. *A Woman's Reason* is his latest work, and considered by one critic, at least, his best. Mr. Norman says: "In *A Woman's Reason* he has given us a study of a few eventful years of a woman's life, characterized by his unequaled knowledge of the mysterious working of woman's mind and heart, and told with great power and truth to nature. The environment—so important a feature in the methods of the *école naturaliste*—is perfect." Mr. Howells has written several clever comedies, of which *The Parlor Car* and *Out of the Question* are the best.

The life of **Henry James, Jr.** (born 1843), presents marked contrasts to that of Howells. The child of an old and cultured family, he was born in New York, and carefully educated, for the most part under private tutors. He spent a few years at the Harvard Law School, and in 1869 went abroad, where he has since lived. His home has been chiefly in England and in Italy. From the appearance of *The Story of a Year* in the Atlantic for March, 1865, to *The Portrait of a Lady* (1881–82), the public has read his writings with a constant protest. Meantime, every young author strives to model his style on that of James, and James himself continues to produce the highly-finished psychological and thoroughly artificial "studies" in which he delights. *Poor Richard* (1867) and *Roderick Hudson* (1876) have more dramatic force and spontaneity, in short, are less sophisticated, than most of his longer stories. *An International Episode, The American, The European,* and *The Portrait of* *a Lady*, are Mr. James's most noteworthy contributions to our abundant "international literature." *Watch and Ward, Confidence, A Bundle of Letters, Washington Square, The Point of View*, and *The Siege of London*, are other of his fictions. James's *Life of Hawthorne*, in Morley's English Men of Letters series, pronounces an estimate of Hawthorne's genius which was considered far too low by many ardent admirers of the Concord genius. It must be said, however, that the book is charmingly written, sets forth merits in Hawthorne that had never before been put into words, and is a most suggestive comment on American character. His other writings are critical essays, which are always pointed and original, and disappointing sketches of travel. Description of scenery and pictures does not offer scope for James's greatest talent—analysis of motive. Mr. James is an accomplished student of French literature, and owns himself the admiring pupil of Alphonse Daudet.

Howells and James are in some sense rivals, though friendly ones. Mr. James is perhaps the more finished artist, but Mr. Howells is the more entertaining writer. Mr. Howells shows us the most common actions of the people whom we meet every day, Mr. James lays bare the souls of two or three remarkable people. If we follow Mr. Howells we have the completest satisfaction at every step ; if Mr. James is our guide, we have the interest of eternal query. In writing of this quality of Mr. James's work, the critic who has been already quoted says : " The reader feels that when the author unseals the vase of his cultivated fancy, and the *dramatis personæ* issue and begin their maneuvers, their liberator does not care much what they do or what finally becomes of them, and the idea involved in their existence, so long as their conversation keeps up to the proper standard of ingenious and cultured ambiguity."

George Parsons Lathrop was born in Honolulu, Sandwich Islands, 1851. His marriage with Rose Hawthorne, the daughter of the novelist, naturally brought him into personal contact with the literary people of Concord and Boston. He is himself a poet, critic, and novelist of marked ability. His work in all departments shows subtlety of thought and elaboration of detail. *Rose and Roof-Tree, An Echo of Passion*, and *Newport*, are some of his more elaborate and later works.

William Henry Bishop (born 1847) was the author of a short story called *One of the Thirty Pieces*, published in the Atlantic in 1876. Its analysis of motive and somewhat tragic pathos attracted attention. In 1877-8, *Detmold*, a continued story, appeared in the *Atlantic*, and *The House of a Merchant Prince* in 1882. The last is his most sustained work, and gives evidence of great power of observation and satire. Mr. Bishop has written entertaining accounts of travel in Mexico and the West.

Readers of *Scribner's Magazine* are familiar with the stories of *Rudder Grange*, which narrate all the absurdities of an unconventional mode of life in New York. **Frank R. Stockton,** their author, (born 1834), is a well-known contributor to magazine literature. His children's tales long ago gave him a place in their hearts, and older people have not failed to appreciate the quaint turns of fancy that adorn his simplest stories. Mr. Stockton writes apparently with the single purpose of amusing, but his neatness and finish of touch are those of a worker in the school of Howells and James. *The Floating Prince and other Fairy Tales* was published in 1881. Most of the Rudder Grange sketches have also been collected in a volume.

Miscellaneous Fiction. Charles Dudley Warner (born 1829), a native of Massachusetts, has written for the *Atlantic* many essays and sketches marked by a most exquisite sense of humor, kept always on the sober side of frolic, and by a style whose art consists in an exquisite appearance of naturalness. Mr. Warner is master of a certain kind of pathos, as those can testify who have tried to read aloud his *Hunting of the Deer. My Summer in a Garden, Backlog Studies, Baddeck and That Sort of Thing, In the Wilderness, In the Levant, Saunterings,* and *Mummies and Moslems,* are titles of his collected essays. *Being a Boy* (1877) ranks among the classics of juvenile literature.

Thomas Bailey Aldrich (born 1836), **(427).** a native of New Hampshire, displays in his literary work certain qualities not often found in unison. He writes at once with dash and care, has a wonderfully pure taste in poetry, and produces novels displaying analytic skill and considerable interest of plot. There is more of the spirit of genuine mischief in his literary jokes than in those of any other writer of the present day. But for his pathetic lyrics and his polished sonnets, one would think that he had never outgrown the boy in his own character.

Babie Bell, Majorie Daw, and *The Story of a Bad Boy* are among his most widely known efforts; *Prudence Palfrey, The Queen of Sheba,* and *The Stillwater Tragedy* are his most elaborate novels. A complete edition of his poems was issued in 1865, *Cloth of Gold* appeared in 1875, and *Flower and Thorn* in 1876.

From time to time novels of secondary merit have appeared, which have attracted attention for their promise or their local coloring. Such are **Miss Sprague's** *An Earnest Trifler,* and *Guerndale,* by **J. S. of Dale.**

The literary characteristics which have been described do not prevail in all American fiction. Here and there a warmth of coloring, an energy of sentiment, marks an author as belonging to a different literary guild. The character of his workmanship is not necessarily less excellent. Such an exceptional writer is **George W. Cable.** He is a native of New Orleans, and is still under forty years of age. His life in the Sunny South has not been an easy one, for he left school at fourteen to be the only support of his family, and served as a clerk until he was nineteen. He was a member of the Confederate army, where he is remembered as a good soldier, a constant student of the Bible, of mathematics, and of the Latin grammar. He was seriously wounded in one of the engagements of his brigade, and returned to New Orleans after the war to begin life over again as an errand-boy. His first literary efforts appeared in a special column of the New Orleans *Picayune,* and were signed "Drop-Shot." For a short time he was connected with the editorial staff of this paper, but was discharged because his religious scruples made him refuse to report theatrical news. He returned to mercantile pursuits, writing only in the intervals of business, until the success of the sketches collected under the name of *Old Creole Days* justified him in adopting literature as a profession. *The Grandissimes* and *Madame Delphine* are stories of Creole life and character which are without rivals, as they were without precedent. Mr. Cable has also written a history of New Orleans, displaying in it the same powers of patient investigation which mark his reproductions of curious customs and difficult patois. The fact that Mr. Cable is a man of simple and even stern views of life does not surprise those who have felt the undercurrent of serious purpose in the humor and pathos of his descriptions. There is a tenderness in his handling of many social topics that betrays a more than artistic interest. His studies are the result of long and careful investigation of records and history, as well as of personal observation.

For a number of years **Mrs. Frances Hodgson Burnett** (born in Manchester, England, 1849) had written stories for various magazines without attracting much notice, until, in 1877, *That Lass o' Lowrie's* appeared. The author's wonderful control of the Lancashire dialect, and her apparently intimate knowledge of the manner of life among miners, were such as to compel admiration, even from the critics who thought her plot improbable and the treatment sensational. *Haworth's* was a novel of equal power, though perhaps of less general interest. It dealt with questions of social economy, treating them, for the most part, with satire rather than with pathos. *Louisiana*, and *Esmeralda*, a drama, portray phases of life in the mountainous country of the South, where there is often more genuine affection than culture among the fathers and mothers. Mrs. Burnett has treated these subjects with real feeling. In *Through One Administration*, a story of Washington life, the action is halting and the treatment more artificial than in most of her other books.

The novels of **Julian Hawthorne** (born 1846) are marked by much that he has in common with his father, Nathaniel Hawthorne. In both is the same love of psychological drama, the same attraction toward out-of-the-way themes; but here the resemblance ends, for up to the present time the clever son has not succeeded in mastering his own talent. *Bressant, Idolatry, Dust, Sebastian Strome*, and *Garth* are all titles that call up impressions of strength and vigor, of eccentricity and weakness, in almost equal proportions. *Saxon Studies* and *English Studies* are the results of Mr. Hawthorne's observation during a residence abroad which covers some years.

Harriet Prescott Spofford has written both prose and poetry in a style so unmistakable that her productions need no signature. Her descriptions of Southern life have a peculiar passion and languor that seem born of the heavy golden atmosphere and luxuriant vegetation which she so often introduces into her backgrounds. Mrs. Spofford is a most daring writer, limiting herself only by the physically impossible in her construction of plots, and carrying her description of emotion to the verge of indelicacy. *The Amber Gods, The Thief in the Night, Azarian,* and *Sir Rohan's Ghost* are her most ambitious works, while numerous shorter tales published in *Harper's Magazine* and *The Atlantic* show the same traits.

Elizabeth Stuart Phelps is the daughter of Professor Austin Phelps, and well known, on her own account, as the author of many popular magazine stories, a few poems, and several novels. Miss Phelps is an invalid, suffering intensely from chronic sleeplessness, which makes it impossible for her to maintain any regular system of work. Her prejudices are strong, her character intense, as may be gathered from her writings. The artistic perfection of her work is marred by a sentimentality in the choice of words, as is its strength by the morbidness of much of the thinking. She is, however, mistress of great pathos and vivid descriptive power. Most of her stories have been written in the interest of a broad philanthropy, and have attained great popularity and influence. *Men, Women, and Ghosts* appeared in 1869; *Hedged In,* in 1870. They were followed by *The Silent Partner, The Story of Avis, Friends,* and *Dr. Zay* (1882). *The Gates Ajar* (1868) gave the author's rather original conception of the future life at a time when there was less open speculation on such subjects than at present, and made a sensation. The change of public opinion in this regard may be inferred from the fact that the issue of a companion work, *The Gates Wide Open,* in 1883, has been attended with very little comment, although the views expressed are much more radical.

Constance Fenimore Woolson is a great-niece of James Fenimore Cooper. Her first published work was a sketch in *Harper's Monthly* called *The Happy Valley.* She has written constantly ever since, and with increasing breadth and power. *Castle Nowhere, Two Women,* a poem, *Rodman the Keeper* (1880), *Anne* (1882), and

For the Major (1883), are the titles of those sketches and stories which have appeared in book form. Miss Woolson succeeds in writing with great truth and simplicity, dealing often with rare types of character. Her pathos is not strained, but is the natural outgrowth of the circumstances, and makes its own appeal. *Rodman the Keeper* is one of the most touching stories which have grown out of the hard conditions of the Civil War.

H. H. is the modest signature over which **Mrs. William S. Jackson** wrote her early poems and more charming sketches. Mrs. Jackson is the daughter of the late Professor N. W. Fiske, of Amherst College, and was born in Amherst in 1831. Her first volume of poems was published in 1874, and received the praise of Mr. Emerson. Mrs. Jackson writes for several magazines, where her graceful style and sympathetic touch are always welcomed by their readers.

Professor Hjalmar Hjorth Boyesen, of Columbia College, though a Norwegian by birth, has written characteristic prose and poetry in English. *Norse Idyls*, and *Gunnar; a Norse Romance*, are among his most important efforts thus far.

Mrs. Rebecca Harding Davis draws with a vivid, heavy stroke pictures of the doubt and distress which grow out of " the force of circumstances." She has a singular knowledge of the brute that lies deep down underneath the surface virtues of the best of us, and shows us the injustice we do the members of the so-called lower classes in judging them harshly, without making allowance for the restraining influence of those conventional barriers which protect our own lives. *Paul Bleeker, Margaret Howth,* and *Waiting for the Verdict* are among her best known stories.

F. Marion Crawford was a name little known when *Mr. Isaacs* appeared in 1883. It was soon learned, however, that Mr. Crawford had come back from India about two years before, announcing his intention of adopting journalism as a profession; that he had forthwith written a few articles for the *World*, the *North American*, and the *Critic;* that the success of *Mr. Isaacs* surprised him and all his friends. Like the later stories of the same author, *Dr. Claudius* and *A Roman Singer*, it is marked by the intrinsic interest of the narrative and the simple, logical development of the plot. Mr. Crawford has written many books. His extended travels and his residence in many countries have given him bountiful stores from which to draw material for his fine workmanship.

The monthly magazines have afforded scope for the development of talent which can hardly be classified as belonging to any particular school. The poems and sketches and essays of **Edith Thomas, Rose Terry Cooke, Nora Perry,** and **Lucy Larcom** have all the care for detail, the genuine sentiment, and literary skill necessary for wide popularity. At the same time, one finds in them but a small modicum of that creative power requisite to a literature which endures.

Joel Chandler Harris (b. 1848) the editor of the *Atlanta Constitution*, as "Uncle Remus," has reproduced the dialect and folk-lore of the negroes with marvelous nicety. He is a careful student of all matters bearing on what, for want of a better term, may be called the social philosophy of the colored people in the South.

Louisa May Alcott (1832–1888) was a daughter of A. Bronson Alcott, the celebrated transcendentalist and teacher by conversations. With great success, she has written for the amusement and instruction of children and young people. Her style is fresh, breezy and wholesome; the principles she inculcates are always noble. *Little Women* (1867) was probably her most successful story. *Moods* is exceptional among her literary efforts, because of its somewhat morbid sentiment. It was an early work, marked by the uncertain touch of a tyro.

In this chapter we have considered:—

Fiction Delineating Provincial Characteristics.

> 1. *Sylvester Judd;* 2. *Theodore Winthrop;* 3. *W. M. Baker;* 4. *Edward Eggleston;* 5. *Harriet Beecher Stowe;* 6. *J. T. Trowbridge;* 7. *A. W. Tourgee.*

Critical Fiction.

> 8. *W. D. Howells;* 9. *Henry James, Jr.;* 10. *George P. Lathrop;* 11. *W. H. Bishop;* 12. *Frank R. Stockton.*

Miscellaneous Fiction.

> 13. *Charles Dudley Warner;* 14. *T. B. Aldrich;* 15. *G. W. Cable;* 16. *Mrs. F. H. Burdett;* 17. *Julian Hawthorne;* 18. *Harriet P. Spofford;* 19. *Elizabeth Stuart Phelps.*

The religious principles which played so prominent a part in the earlier history of literature in America have been gradually crowded out of the general field, and now form a special department. The thoughtful religious literature of the present time has been philosophical and expositional.

The first class includes the writings of President Porter, Dr. McCosh, Thomas C. Upham, James Marsh, Mark Hopkins, Laurens S. Hickok, Henry James, the father of the novelist, and Borden S. Bowne. These men have all exercised their learning and their literary skill in defending certain views of Christianity, or certain fundamental theories of religion and morality. President Porter's work on *The Human Intellect; The Laws of Discursive Thought,*

Christianity and Positivism, and *The Scottish Philosophy* of Dr. McCosh; the *Studies in Theism* and *Metaphysics* of Professor Bowne; *The Nature of Evil* and *Substance and Shadow* of Mr. James—all are works written from different points of view, but having a common purpose—to strengthen the defences of religion and morality.

The expository literature of this class covers an immense amount of technical research. Dr. Charles Hodge in his *Systematic Theology* has made the most complete showing of Calvinistic views since the days of Jonathan Edwards. Professor Tayler Lewis has published a work called *Science and the Bible.* Philip Schaff and W. G. T. Shedd have labored diligently in the department of Church history; Dr. Conant and Dr. Barnes in that of Biblical exposition. The prominent pulpit orators of the day have been influential in directing public opinion by lectures, addresses, printed sermons, and occasional books. Henry Ward Beecher has written a *Life of Christ;* John Hall, W. M. Taylor, Phillips Brooks, and Richard S. Storrs have all been active in these lines of usefulness. Dr. N. W. Taylor, President Finney, and Dr. Bushnell have written formal works on theology.

Explanation of the comparatively small number of writers in the special department of theological literature is found in the fact that the Puritan interest in such literature, once prevalent in our country, has abated. Books of religious and ethical quality are abundantly produced. Their authors, with American readiness of adaptation, put them in dress suited to popular taste. Many a writer, animated by the earnest spirit of a preacher, is publishing his doctrines of religion and morality in the chapters of a story. Such a writer was Dr. Holland, such was Rev. E. P Roe—each of them the moral teacher of vast numbers of readers.

The distinguishing excellence of literature in America is its variety. The activity of national thought touches all subjects. Our men of letters are discussing questions of the mental, the social, and the physical sciences with incisiveness, with breadth of understanding, with raciness and vigor of expression not surpassed by writers in England; but, granting a few distinguished exceptions, it must be admitted that in nicety of idiomatic usage, in freedom from the taint of provincialism, and in deliberate consideration of theme, the majority of American authors have much to learn from their transatlantic contemporaries.

INDEX.

TO THE ENGLISH LITERATURE.

498

INDEX.

TO THE AMERICAN LITERATURE.

501